Accounting Information Systems and Internal Control

Second Edition

Accounting Information Systems and Internal Control

Second Edition

Eddy Vaassen, Roger Meuwissen and Caren Schelleman

A John Wiley and Sons, Ltd, Publication

Library of Congress Cataloging-in-Publication Data

Vaassen, E. H. J. (Eddy H. J.)
  Accounting information systems and internal control / Eddy Vaassen, Roger Meuwissen and Caren Schelleman.–2nd ed.
      p. cm.
  Includes bibliographical references and index.
  ISBN 978-0-470-75395-8 (pbk.)
  1. Accounting–Data processing. 2. Information storage and retrieval systems—Accounting. I. Meuwissen, Roger. II. Schelleman, Caren. III. Title.
  HF5679.V33 2009
  657.0285—dc22   2009017247

A catalogue record for this book is available from the British Library.

Set in 9/13 Kuenstler 480 BT Roman by Thomson Digital, India
Printed in Great Britain by Bell & Bain Ltd, Glasgow

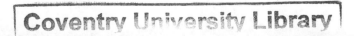

Contents

About the Authors

Eddy Vaassen

Eddy Vaassen is a professor of Accounting Information Systems (AIS) at Maastricht University and Universiteit van Amsterdam. He wrote his dissertation in 1994 at Universiteit Maastricht. He graduated from the Accountancy programme of Universiteit Maastricht in 1990 and from the Economics programme of the same university in 1988. He has Dutch and international publications – including six textbooks – within the fields of AIS, Information Management, Auditing and Management Control.

Eddy Vaassen is a member of the editorial boards of the *Journal of Information Systems*, the *International Journal of Accounting Information Systems*, *Global Perspectives on Accounting Education*, the *Journal of Emerging Technologies in Accounting*, the *International Journal of Digital Accounting Research*, *Management Control & Accounting*, *Accountant Adviseur* and *Controllersjournaal*. He is the director of the International Executive Master of Finance and Control programme (Registered Controller) and a member of various councils, including the Board of the European Accounting Association. In 2005–2007 he was the Vice-President Europe/Africa/Mid East with the SIG-ASYS of the Association for Information Systems. In 2003–2004 he was the International Member at Large of the Council of the American Accounting Association. He is the co-founder and co-chair of the annual European Conference on Accounting Information Systems. He is also the co-chair of the International Research Symposium on Accounting Information Systems.

His research interests are in the areas of the use of decision aids in auditing, professional judgement in audit decision-making and the interaction between management controls and internal controls. He supervises and has supervised doctoral dissertations on the factors explaining ERP use, decision aid use in auditing, contract auditing, professional judgement in internal control assessments and just-in-time information provision.

Roger Meuwissen

Roger Meuwissen is professor of Control and Auditing at Maastricht University. He currently serves on the Board of the Faculty of Economics & Business Administration as vice-dean and is responsible for education. He previously chaired the Department of Accounting and Information Management and was director of the Maastricht Accounting, Auditing and Information Management Research Center. Professor Meuwissen received his PhD from Maastricht University. He also finished the postgraduate programme in auditing to become a licensed auditor in the Netherlands.

His primary teaching areas are internal control and auditing. He teaches undergraduate and graduate courses on internal control and accounting information systems as well as on assurance services. His research interests lie primarily in the areas of audit markets, audit regulation and internal control. He is author of several articles in both academic and practitioner journals, and has conducted several commissioned research projects on the market for audit services and audit regulation. He has also published several Dutch textbooks on internal control and accounting information systems.

Caren Schelleman

Caren Schelleman is assistant professor at the Department of Accounting and Information Management at Maastricht University, where she also completed both her MA and PhD. She received part of her research training at the Fisher School of Accounting at the University of Florida in Gainesville, Florida, and was a visiting professor at the University of Auckland, New Zealand.

Caren's research and teaching interests focus on auditing and accounting information systems and internal control. She has presented her research at leading accounting and auditing conferences and seminars in Europe, the US, Australia and New Zealand, published in leading accounting journals and has been involved in several research projects commissioned by, amongst others, the European Commission and the Fédération des Experts Comptables Européens.

Caren has been developing, coordinating and teaching courses on accounting information systems and internal control, at both undergraduate and graduate levels, for more than 10 years.

Preface

The field of Accounting Information Systems and related Internal Controls can be studied from various perspectives. However, the bottom line will always be that organizations by using their information systems want to come from a state of being out-of-control into a state of being in-control. To enable this, the organization's information systems must meet certain quality criteria. Hence, there is a continuous interaction between information systems and control. This book focuses on a specific type of information system, namely the accounting information system. The predominant type of control that relates to the accounting information system is internal control. This explains the title of the book: accounting information systems and internal control.

In contrast to most other AIS textbooks, we focus strongly on controls and less on the technologies that are applied in accounting information systems. We introduce an approach to AIS that distinguishes various types of organizations, whereas each type of organization is a unique combination of processes. Hence, we first describe the controls of processes in organizations. We then develop our typology of organizations. Essentially this is a contingency approach to controls in organizations.

We always follow a systems-thinking approach. This means that, when describing systems, we always look for the effects of system components on any of the other system components. Applied to the theme of this text, this means that we follow an integral approach to accounting information systems and to the applicable internal controls. This integral approach aligns the business with the information and communication technology used, and it translates strategy into action by aligning the formulated strategies with the controls that are aimed at implementing these strategies. Hence, we look upon an organization's accounting information system and its internal controls as vehicles to reach operational excellence.

The book consists of three parts. Part 1 discusses the foundations of internal control. Internal control is always embedded in organizations. Hence the prime foundation is the organization, with its governance problems, its information and communication technology (IT) and its information flows. A basic discussion of the tools and frameworks that internal control uses then follows, as well as the relationship with management control and IT control. The first part of the text concludes with the communication element of internal control by discussing the documentation and evaluation of internal control systems. Part 2 discusses the internal controls that should be put in place in various processes in organizations. We use the framework of the value cycle, which is merely a didactical tool to explain how processes in organizations interact. Within this framework we provide an in-depth discussion of the following primary processes: purchasing, inventory, production and sales. We also briefly discuss the following secondary processes: human resources management, investment in fixed assets, cash management and treasury, and accounting and general ledger. Part 3 discusses the internal controls to be put in place in various types of organizations. We develop a typology of organizations that uses as its main contingency factors the flow of goods and the potential reliance (or nonreliance) on a market mechanism for control purposes. This typology consists of the following types of organization: trade, production, service (in various appearances) and governmental and other not-for-profit organizations.

The text gives a detailed overview of internal controls in organizations and their accounting information systems. Comments, questions, suggestions for improvements and the like can be addressed to the first author.

Dr. E.H.J. Vaassen
Maastricht University/University of Amsterdam
Address for correspondence:
Maastricht University
Department of Accounting and Information Management
PO Box 616
6200 MD Maastricht
The Netherlands
e.vaassen@maastrichtuniversity.nl

Dr. R.H.G. Meuwissen
Maastricht University

Dr. C.C.M. Schelleman
Maastricht University

Foundations of Internal Control

Organizations and their Systems

In this chapter:

Introduction

Organizations need information just like people need food: without it, there will not be much activity. Information can come in many forms and can be used in many different ways but it always boils down to getting an organization from a state of being out of control into a state of being in control. Obviously, organizations that have good information at their disposal will not automatically be in control. This chapter discusses the relationship between information, information systems and control. Because information is so crucial in organizations information and the systems that produce it must also be controlled. We will investigate this relationship from the following three perspectives:

1. Internal Control
2. Information Management
3. Management Control.

We will use a model, which we refer to as the integral control framework, to explain this relationship. Organizations are goal-oriented cooperative entities that bring together people and other resources. Hence, people are key elements of any organization. The following three functions play a quintessential role in information provision aimed at controlling organizations:

1. The information manager. The tasks of the information manager concern the managerial aspects of the information provision within and by an organization. The information provision relies on the available information systems, which for their part predominantly rely on the available information and communication technology (IT). The rise of the information manager took place in an era in which automation of information provision gradually obtained a regular place in management. Therefore, the information manager will be the expert *par excellence* in the field of IT.

2. The controller. The controller is a generalist whose competences concern the entire company, as he is the one pulling the financial strings. Incidentally his influence can be more or less far-reaching, dependent upon his position in the organization as either a line or a staff functionary. The controller is the intermediary between the shop floor and management and must understand both the language of the white collar workers and the language of the blue collar workers. He is also the financial conscience of the company. For example: an investment decision is made based on, among other things, market expectations and the technical state of the existing production installation. The commercial manager may insist on optimal use of market opportunities, the technical director may insist on installation renewal. However, the controller will have to indicate whether certain wishes are feasible from a financial point of view.

3. The auditor. The core task of the auditor is to audit financial statements and to provide reports on these statements based on his findings. The auditing process consists in part of judging the quality of the internal control system and in part of determining the reliability of the information as contained in the financial statements. Both assessments need to be seen as related: after all, as the quality of the internal control system improves, the auditor is more able to rely on this system and will in principle see less need for substantive tests which are controls aimed at directly establishing the reliability of the financial statements.

Although they are experts in the field of control, the auditor and the controller will be knowledgeable about IT as well. Yet this knowledge needs to be much less profound. The information manager as an expert *par excellence* in the field of IT will also be knowledgeable about control issues, but in turn this knowledge needs to be less profound. This means that the auditor, the controller and the information manager play complementary roles in organizations.

Internal Control focuses on the governance and control of organizations and therefore – in view of our definition of an organization – on managing people. However, the applicable instruments are predominantly mechanistic by nature. This means that procedures and controls are put in place and that hardly any attention is paid to problems stemming from employees not knowing what is expected from them, not being motivated to do what is expected from them and not being able to do what is expected from them. To get a grip on people's behaviour in organizations, a whole range of other control instruments may be applied that have their origins in the management literature. Following authors such as Simons (1994, 1995a and 1995b), Merchant and Van der Stede (2007) and Ouchi (1979), contemporary approaches to control explicitly consider the human factor. Thus, a completely separate category of governance and control measures is introduced, generally denoted Management Control. Typical of this collection of control concepts is that, besides formal governance and control measures, ample attention is given to formalizing informal measures; for example, motivating people by means of incentive schemes, or creating a desirable organizational culture by means of setting the right tone at the top can become formal control procedures. In management science several theories in this field have been developed; for example, creating a balance between salaries and working conditions can contribute to a situation where people develop a certain loyalty to the organization and where they will mainly perform activities that contribute to attaining the business goals. Obviously, in view of the rationalities and irrationalities of users of systems in organizations, an approach to Accounting Information Systems that does not consider the human factor is too narrow. For example, if a procedure is put in place (a typical internal control measure) then people will not automatically live up to that procedure. Management controls must provide reasonable assurance that procedures are followed by the employees in question.

Learning Goals of the Chapter

After having studied this chapter, the reader will understand:

- the meaning of information for governing and controlling organizations;
- the headlines of Management Control, Internal Control and Information Management and the interrelationships between these disciplines;
- the components of the integral control framework;
- the roles of the various functions, including information system users, the controller, the information manager and the auditor with respect to information problems.

Information in Organizations

To realize the strategic organizational goals, strategic management will perform the following activities:

- Formulating the strategic organizational goals (planning).
- Creating cross-functional collaboration between employees (structuring).
- Allocating task assignments and providing resources to these employees (execution).
- Testing the realization of the goals (evaluation).
- Undertaking corrective or preventive measures if goals are not or are insufficiently realized (adjusting).

On the tactical and operational level similar activities will be developed. However, as the specification of these activities gets more detailed differences will arise, including:

- The goals become more concrete. For example, the head of the purchasing department is responsible for keeping inventory above minimum level X.
- The number of degrees of freedom in creating cross-functional collaborations will be more limited. For example, if tactical management has developed an organizational structure that includes a separate warehouse and purchasing departments, then operational management cannot create a position in which warehousing and purchasing are combined.
- The task assignments will be more specific and will contain more detailed instructions. For example, supported by the information system, the head of the purchasing department will charge his subordinate with ordering Y units of product A from supplier B if the inventory records indicate that the minimum inventory level X has been reached.
- The norms for testing whether goals have been realized will be more specific. For example, tests will establish whether the actual inventory is larger than the minimum level X.
- The measures taken to get out of a situation where goals are not realized are of a routine nature. For example, if the actual inventory level is found to be below the minimum level X, then the necessary amount is purchased.

Thus it seems that the strategic business goals can be divided into more concrete goals that, in turn, can be further concretized as well.

Information provision is never a goal as such. Information is always provided because there are users of that information. In general users of information need it for the following three distinct purposes, or roles:

1. Information for delegation and accountability
2. Information for decision-making
3. Information for operating the business.

Information for Delegation and Accountability

If a person's job responsibilities are so extensive that in fairness he cannot perform these on his own, and if it is possible to divide the strategic business goals into subgoals, then labour can be divided. This way, power and responsibilities are delegated between hierarchical management levels to mitigate problems stemming from managers' limited spans of control. However, if power and responsibilities are delegated the need for management control arises. After all, the higher level needs to establish that the goals that were set are indeed realized. To enable management to exercise control, the lower levels must account for the power and responsibilities delegated to them. The process of delegation and accountability is effectuated by information provision.

Information for Decision-making

Besides the delegation and accountability role of information, it also plays an important role in decision-making. For example, a sales person will make the decision to purchase a certain quantity of a product from a certain vendor using information from the warehouse, the production department or the sales department.

Table 1.1 The characteristics of information for higher and lower hierarchical levels in organizations.

Criterion	Information for ...	
	higher hierarchical levels	**lower hierarchical levels**
Source	external; for example information about new products that a competitor wants to market	largely internal; for example information about the status of the inventory
Scope	very wide; for example information about the financial state of an organization	well-defined and narrow; for example information about outstanding accounts receivable
Level of aggregation	aggregate; for example information about total sales in a certain period	detailed; for example information about the sales for a specific employee, of a certain product in a certain period
Time horizon	future; for example information about expected conditions in the market for personal computers in the forthcoming five years	historical; for example information about the sales in 2007 of personal computers
Currency	quite old; for example information about market shares does not need to be continuously updated	highly current; for example information about the inventory level of a certain product
Required accuracy	low; for example information about the expected return on a substantial investment	high; for example information in the sales ledger or in the purchase ledger
Frequency of use	infrequent; for example information for deciding where to build a new factory	very frequent; for example information for deciding on the payment of outstanding debts

(*Source:* adapted from: Gorry and Scott Morton, 1971, p. 59.)

To make that decision he will also collect information about potential vendors, their prices, times of delivery and other conditions, and various subjective factors, including a vendor's reputation and reliability. On a higher level the decision will be made to put a certain product on the market. The information needed to make that kind of decision pertains to the needs of potential customers, the availability of the required production capacity and competences within the organization and the capital needed to market the product.

Information for delegation and accountability, and information for decision-making flow vertically through the organization. For example, a foreman in a production unit will assign tasks to workers, supervise them and hold them accountable for their task performance (accountability). That very same foreman will in his turn provide a progress report to the operations office (accountability), which the operations office may use for production order issuance (decision-making). Vertical information flows will differ as information is intended for lower or higher hierarchical levels. Gorry and Scott Morton (1971) position information within the following seven dimensions: source, scope, level of aggregation, time horizon, currency, required accuracy and frequency of use. Table 1.1 summarizes the characteristics of information that is intended for higher hierarchical levels and information that is intended for lower hierarchical levels.

Information for Operating the Business

The third purpose of information is not so much for accountability or decision-making but rather for making the organization function as intended. This type of information merely aims at sharing knowledge to enable the organization to realize its goals, coordinating the activities of two different organizational units (for example, of two departments), or communicating a decision made by management. Often, this information flows horizontally through the organization; for example, between the warehouse, the sales department, the financial administration, the production department and the purchasing department there is a horizontal information flow about goods to be ordered, ordered goods and received goods, received invoices, sold goods, shipments to be billed, billed shipments, payments, cash receipts and arrears. To support such information provision a coordinating function is needed to control knowledge sharing between these departments. As a result, the horizontal information flows within organizations often cannot be decoupled from the vertical information flows.

Starreveld et al. (2002, 9) give the following definition of the field of Managerial Information Provision that fully covers the aforementioned three purposes of information provision:

> The systematic gathering, recording and processing of data aimed at the provision of information for management decision making, for operating the entity and controlling it, including accountability.

Whether information is provided to internal or external stakeholders is – in our view – not a relevant question. For example, information production by placing an order or publishing an organization's financial statements, just like information that is exchanged within the organization, is aimed at delegation and accountability, decision-making and operating the business. This means that managers are also responsible for the quality of external information. Most of the scandals that we have seen in the corporate world in the last decades involved deficient information to external stakeholders. Case 1.1 illustrates this.

Information can only be provided when data is collected and recorded. To put it simply, information can only be called information if it has meaning for its user. Hence, data collection and recording is

Case 1.1

Royal Mess at Royal Ahold

Company probe shows retailer overstated earnings by nearly $900 million over a three-year period.

Marie Leone

With the help of forensic accountants from PricewaterhouseCoopers, international food retailer Royal Ahold NV confirmed that profits at the company's U.S. Foodservice subsidiary were overstated by $880 million.

The internal probe was launched on February 24 after the parent company announced the accounting problems at the U.S. affiliate.

Reportedly two U.S. Foodservice procurement executives, Mark Kaiser and Tim Lee, were implicated by the internal investigation. Kaiser and Lee were suspended in February after company executives became suspicious that the two had improperly booked supplier rebates. This according to a report from Dow Jones Newswires.

Some analysts reportedly were stunned that the PwC investigation did not implicate any other Ahold executives. The company's CEO, Cees van der Hoeven, and CFO, Michael Meurs, both resigned in February when news of the bookkeeping scandal first broke.

Ahold management originally indicated it thought the company's earnings had been inflated by about $550 million. Now that number is closer to $900 million. And the food retailer is expected to adjust its balance sheet by nearly $1 billion to account for the understated liabilities. Just last week, Ahold auditor Deloitte & Touche resumed work on the Dutch company's financial statements.

The PwC investigation had halted progress on the 2002 earnings statements, which was a major concern for Ahold management. Apparently bank loans needed to pay off maturing debt obligations hinged on meeting a June 30 filing deadline. Royal Ahold management is confident the deadline will be met, according to Dow Jones.

The Securities and Exchange Commission, as well as Dutch regulators, are also investigating the problems at U.S. Foodservice and the parent's accounting practices. Ahold owns American grocery chains Stop & Shop and Bruno's.

Source: CFO.com, May 9, 2003

crucial in the process of information provision. For example, when a data base contains the numbers 4, 1, 0 and 1, then this is data since we do not know what these numbers mean without further explanation. However, if a user of this data base knows that these numbers are the scores of a football team in the semi-final and the final of the European football championship, then he knows who became the champion; hence this data has meaning for him, and hence this is information: the Netherlands won the semi-final with 4-1 and lost the final with 0-1. Hence, a formal definition of information seen in relation to data is:

> Information is all the processed data that contributes to the recipient's understanding of applicable parts of reality.

The remainder of this text builds upon the body of knowledge that underlies the field of managerial information provision in the sense of the aforementioned definition, complemented by insights from international literature and contemporary practice. These insights include the predominance of IT when discussing issues pertaining to information provision. The field of Accounting Information Systems (AIS) distinguishes itself from Managerial Information Provision in that it focuses substantially more on IT. Consequently, AIS gives in-depth discussions of such topics as information analysis, data modelling, data bases and systems development.

Information and Communication Technology

Information and communication technology (IT) plays an important role in the recording and processing of data, and in information provision. Initially, IT was considered just another tool to support data collection and processing, and information provision. Nowadays, IT is at the heart of any contemporary organization since it is applied for internal as well as external information provision and communication. For example, vendors through the Internet may be allowed to access the inventory records of an organization to replenish its stocks when a minimum inventory level has been reached, or an organization uses scanning and optical character recognition (OCR) when an invoice is received to automatically match it with the order and the goods receipt note. The more advanced an IT application, the more it may be considered a critical success factor for organizational performance.

Information and communication technology can be defined as:

> All the electronic media used to collect, store and process data, to produce information, and to support or enable communication.

In the case of non-electronic media, then the term IT should not be used. Instead, the more abstract notion of documentary media would more accurately describe all the media, electronic as well as nonelectronic, used to transport information. In this sense a piece of paper is a documentary medium, but not an IT application. Following the same line of reasoning, email is an IT application as well as a documentary medium.

As we have already demonstrated, IT is an integral part of managing contemporary organizations. We believe a basic knowledge of IT is important to managers for several reasons, including the following:

- Managers are IT users since they send and receive information, and by doing so continuously communicate with other members of the organization and third parties.
- Decisions and evaluations are made on the basis of information and communication. IT is employed to make information and communication more efficient.
- IT is an enabler of organizational change. Within change processes, managers play a major role when collaborating with change agents and IT specialists. In order to adequately fulfil this role managers must be able to communicate with change agents and IT specialists. This implies that a common language must be spoken. In our current environment, IT is the enabler of most organizational change processes. Hence, IT terminology is most likely to serve as that common language.
- Management is responsible for internal control. Internal control is heavily influenced by IT developments (see Chapter 4). So, management is indirectly responsible for IT and especially for integrating IT with the information processes and the business processes within an organization and between organizations.

Information systems are the most overt manifestations of information and communication technology. A system can be defined as:

> An organized way of undertaking actions in order to attain certain goals.

Following this definition, an information system is an organized way of inputting data, processing data and providing information aimed at the attainment of organizational goals. The term information system did not blossom until data input and processing, and information provision became automated. So, in view of our definition of IT, discussing information systems implies discussing IT.

We now can give the following formal definition of Accounting Information Systems as a discipline:

> AIS studies the structuring and operation of planning and control processes which are aimed at:
>
> - Providing information for decision-making and accountability to internal and external stakeholders that complies with specified quality criteria.
> - Providing the right conditions for sound decision-making.
> - Ensuring that no assets illegitimately exit the organization.

Following Romney and Steinbart (2008), an accounting information system can then be defined as:

> An accounting information system processes data and transactions to provide users with information they need to plan, control, and operate their businesses.

However, Gelinas and Dull (2008) define an accounting information system in a more limited fashion:

> An accounting information system is a specialized subsystem of the management information system whose purpose is to collect, process, and report information related to financial transactions.

We believe some kind of evolution underlies this difference in viewpoints. In the fifties, accounting information systems were the first applications of computers to process transaction data. This concerned information systems that supported daily management by collecting data on financial facts. However, to meet managers' increasing information needs traditional accounting information systems did not seem sufficient anymore: information that is non-financial and not just focused on transactions (and therefore future oriented or prospective) also became important for managers to get and keep a grip on organizations. This led to the rise of management information systems (MIS). Regarded in this way a company's AIS would be part of its MIS. Nowadays this is only partly true: accounting information systems have obtained their own spot in the ABC – one can think of at least one type of information system for every letter of the alphabet – of information systems. Among accountants there seems to be consensus on the role of accounting information systems as the information systems of the future since they are expected to deliver all information needed for business management, and in the desired format. However, the driver remains the transaction. Starting with transactional information, it becomes further aggregated and combined with external data until it is useful for strategic management.

Governance and Control

Two important – strongly related – aspects of AIS are governance and control. Control entails a backward-looking component as well as a forward-looking component. The backward-looking component merely comprises comparing a realization (we refer to this as the 'what is' position) with an established criterion (we refer to this as the 'what should be' position). For example, the inventory records ('what is') are checked against the results of stocktaking ('what should be') and adjusted if there is a discrepancy. We label this component of control as checking. The forward-looking component merely involves decision-making aimed at enhancing future organizational performance. For example, hiring the right people and training them, setting targets and rewarding managers if they realize these targets, or communicating the organizational goals. Put in the simplest fashion, control can then be defined as:

> Continuously realizing legitimized goals.

If we consider control to be a deliberate activity by managers and other personnel of an organization then this definition can be refined to:

> All those organizational activities that are aimed at having organization members cooperate to reach the organization's goals.

By means of governing a business, management attempts to control it. From a rather traditional and narrow perspective, governance and control entail giving task assignments and holding workers accountable for the fulfilment of their tasks. Governance can then be defined as:

> The process of keeping an organization on track towards legitimized goals.

In the nineties, many texts were published on governance and control, more specifically on corporate governance and internal control. Chapter 2 provides an in-depth discussion of these.

An Integral Control Framework

This section develops an integral control framework that can be used to describe, analyse and solve AIS problems that may arise in contemporary organizations. The framework is adapted from Maes (1998) and the strategic alignment model as introduced by Henderson and Venkatraman (1993). It should be stressed that the framework is not solely aimed at AIS problems, but is generic in nature. The framework is two-dimensional. The first dimension is strategy formulation versus strategy implementation, or the external domain versus the internal domain. The second dimension is the business domain, the information and communication domain and the IT domain.

Within the first dimension, in the strategy formulation domain, the business is positioned toward the external world. The main managerial task is to formulate strategy in such a way that competitive advantage can be accomplished. In the strategy implementation domain, which by definition is internal, the business is structured and operated in such a manner that the intended strategy can be realized. The accounting information system is important in helping an organization to adopt a sustainable strategic position since it provides the necessary information to align business activities and to connect the business with the outside world. Hence, the accounting information system can bridge the gap between the external and the internal domain.

When information is provided there is always an underlying reality, namely the business, which is the object of information provision. Ideally, there is a one-to-one relationship between information and the business. In practice, this relationship is only seldom one-to-one because information often cannot provide a perfect representation of the underlying reality, or can only do so at unreasonably high costs. The efficiency of data collection, recording and processing and information provision is strongly influenced by the media – imagine them as transportation vehicles – used to inform and communicate. The collection of these media is generally referred to as information and communication technology or IT. Obviously, the current state of information and communication technology determines efficiency of data collection, recording and processing, and information provision to a large extent. So, there is a strong interrelationship between information (and communication), the business and IT.

There is a continuous alignment and balancing between the elements of the two integral control framework dimensions. As we indicated earlier the framework may be used for the description, analysis and solution of any business problem. We choose to apply this generic framework and tailor it for classifying AIS problems. Figure 1.1 depicts the integral control framework.

To make this framework more specific to AIS, a further refinement must be made. As we demonstrated in the previous section ('Governance and Control'), control is strongly related to AIS. A number of control concepts can be distinguished. The control concepts that are directly linked to the cells in the framework include, but are not limited to, internal control, information control, IT control, strategic control and management control. These control concepts can be overlaid onto the integral control framework (as shown in Figure 1.2).

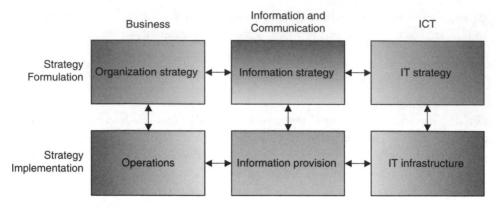

Figure 1.1   Integral control framework.

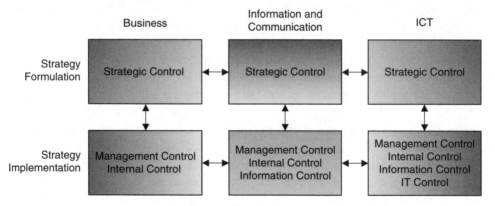

Figure 1.2   Control concepts overlaid on the integral control framework.

In the remainder of this text we will refer to the integral control framework to provide a coherent view on the sometimes seemingly remotely related topics that are discussed.

Quality and Quality Criteria

In an attempt to make an objective assessment of the quality of decision-making, some authors argue that a list can be developed containing a limited set of quality characteristics of decision-making. The line of reasoning is that the higher the quality of decision-making, the better the resulting decisions. The variables that may explain the quality of decision-making include the number of aspects involved in decision-making, the time horizon, the use of retrospective information and the system used for decision-making. In general it is assumed that using more aspects, considering a longer time horizon, effective use of ex-post information and applying fixed patterns lead to superior decisions. However, seen in the light of our remarks on the concept of quality, and indeed following a contingency approach, we believe that this assumption is rather oversimplified.

Because the quality of a decision is dependent on the quality of information, the information requirements must be determined as accurately as possible and information provision must be tailored to these requirements. Therefore some factors that play a role in the determination of information requirements must be discussed. When discussing internal controls, reliability of information provision is important, but so is reliability of the information system. Hence, the reliability of the information system must also be discussed.

Information must possess several quality characteristics. Here again, attempts have been made to provide lists of objective quality characteristics. The quality spectrum of information is an example of such a list, but so is the quality spectrum of the IT architecture.

Quality Spectrum of Information

When assessing the quality of information, the focus is on the degree to which information can be utilized in decision-making. Figure 1.3 represents the quality spectrum of information. Information is said to be reliable if it is valid, accurate and complete. Information is said to be relevant if it has the desired level of precision, is provided on time and is understandable by the user. Together, reliability and relevance contribute to the effectiveness of information. Besides effectiveness, efficiency is the other main characteristic of information quality.

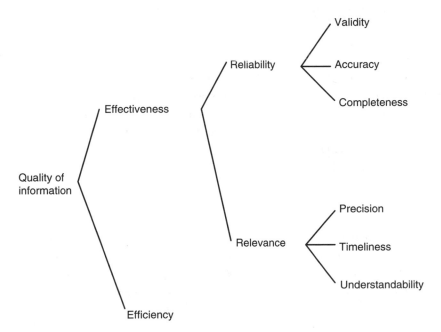

Figure 1.3   Quality spectrum of information.

Validity

Information is valid if it is in accordance with the represented part of reality, in the sense that what is reported is not too high. For example, expenses must have been made for the purpose of attaining organizational goals. The records that culminate from these transactions may contain expenses that are not attributable to the business, or to the specific cost accounts used for the postings. As a result, the recordings may be partially invalid.

Accuracy

Information is accurate if it is mathematically correct; for example, a recalculation of a footing may reveal technical errors such as calculating the sum of a column at 451 whereas it should have been 551 or reversing the order of digits (35 instead of 53).

Completeness

Information is complete if it is in accordance with the represented part of reality in the sense that what has been reported is not too low. For example, the accounts receivable listing of company A shows a balance of € 100 000, consisting of three debtors: X, Y and Z. X has a debt of € 25 000, Y has a debt of € 70 000 and Z has a debt of € 5000. There are two completeness issues that may emerge. Firstly, each of these three debtors may have a larger debt than recorded in the records of company A. Secondly, there may be a fourth debtor who is not in the accounts receivable listing of company A.

Precision

Information is more precise if it has a higher degree of detail. The higher the hierarchical level of decision-making or the longer the planning horizon, the less precise information normally needs to be. The alleged bean counter mentality of accountants is typical for providing extremely precise information in two decimals. Obviously the accounting information system can provide this accurate information. However, it is not necessary, and even dysfunctional, to do so in every decision-making situation regardless of contingent factors like the hierarchical level.

Timeliness

Information is timely if it is provided on time to affect the decision-making process. For example, suppose a client calls to place an order. The order processing clerk enters the client code (or his name), the product code and the ordered quantity into the order-processing module of the information system. Via a programmed procedure checks are made as to whether the client is creditworthy and hence is allowed to be delivered to, and whether the required goods are in stock. The decision to be taken here is whether or not to deliver the required goods to a specific client. If the credit rating system provides delayed information, this may lead to delivering to a client who may be in financial distress. If the perpetual inventory records provide delayed information, the ordered goods may be out of stock without the system informing the order processing clerk.

Understandability

Information is understandable if it is presented in a format that is useful for and intelligible to its user. Understandability concerns the unambiguous interpretability of information. In general, the more quantitative the information, the higher the understandability. For example, compare a verbal performance report with a quantitative performance report. The verbal report could read as follows: 'Business unit X performed satisfactorily. Profits increased, clients were again satisfied, the internal organization was restructured in order to meet market demand for more customized products, and some new products were developed.' The quantitative report could read as follows: 'Business unit X showed an increase in net profit of 15%. The survey-based client satisfaction index slightly dropped by 1%. The number of complaints about tardy front-office service increased by 10%, however the restructuring of the organization is expected to lead to a turnaround. Five new products were developed, two of which caused the increased profit.' Clearly, the quantitative report is much less ambiguous and hence better understandable. In the end, this report will lead to an enhanced performance judgement of business unit X.

Efficiency

Information provision is efficient if it is economically justified and hence if it is produced at the lowest possible cost. The issues that are dealt with here do not pertain to the hardware and software requirements to provide certain information, but are limited to the reports that are produced. Note that efficiency is also a component of the quality spectrum of the IT infrastructure.

Quality Spectrum of the IT Infrastructure

In assessing the quality of the IT infrastructure, the focus is on the degree to which information systems meet the requirements of the data processing department. The foremost important quality characteristic of the IT infrastructure is its ability to provide high-quality information. This is the link between the quality spectrum of the IT infrastructure and the quality spectrum of information. Figure 1.4 presents the common quality characteristics of the IT infrastructure.

Maintainability

Maintainability concerns the degree to which information systems can be tested, renewed and changed at reasonable cost. For example, a customized information system must always have thorough technical system documentation. If this documentation is omitted, system maintenance becomes heavily dependent on

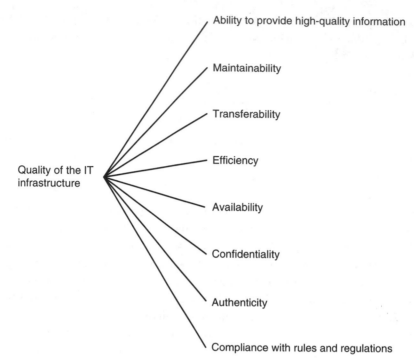

Figure 1.4   Quality spectrum of the IT infrastructure.

the availability of the system developers who originally designed the system and wrote the software. Should these system developers no longer be available, a so-called retro-fit is the only solution to regain a grip on maintainability. Such a retro-fit is a method to reconstruct the system specifications from the system as is. Retro-fitting can be compared to backward engineering.

Transferability

Transferability refers to the degree to which information systems can be transferred from one environment to another. This may imply the system can easily be adjusted to changing situational conditions like the state of the available IT, or changing user requirements. In general, transferability is a characteristic that receives more and more attention in our current dynamic environment. Transferability in general has within it aspects of adaptability to changing circumstances, preparedness to change and ability to stimulate renewal and innovation processes. Applied to information systems, transferability then refers to the dynamic interplay between the system and its environment, the dynamic interplay within the system between its components and the complete absence of rigidity. Transferability in this sense may pertain to the chosen hardware platform, the operating system and the applications, as well as to the business environment surrounding the system. For example, using a client-server architecture instead of a customized computer system increases transferability because any available application for Windows can be run regardless of the PC brand or the country of origin of the software.

Efficiency

The IT infrastructure is efficient if the costs of the IT investments are in control. For example, an IT project far exceeding its budgeted costs is an indication of the IT investments not being in control.

Availability

This means that IT must be at the intended user's disposal, on time and at the right place. Instances of threats in this category are denial of service as a result of defects, denial of service as a result of system overload and unauthorized use of hardware.

Confidentiality

This means that only authorized persons are allowed to have access to specific parts of IT. Confidential information should not become available to people who want to use it to their own advantage or to the disadvantage of the entity to which the information relates.

Authenticity

Authenticity means that the sender and receiver of a message are who they claim to be. In IT dominated environments where face-to-face contact has become rare, authenticity is a real problem.

Compliance with Rules and Regulations

The main focus here is on laws and regulations in the realm of computer crime, including accessing others' computers and making copies of software or data. Lately there has been a lot of attention to privacy law enforcement aimed at prohibiting the combination of files from different sources. Also, unauthorized reproduction of software is practised by many people without bothering too much about its illegal nature. The term generally used here is software piracy. The software or data contained on floppy disks and CD-roms, or which is downloadable from websites may or may not be free. If it is not free, then making a copy of it should always result in a payment.

An information system can be considered the combination of the information content as represented by the information and communication domain in the integral control framework and the media used to inform and communicate as represented by the IT domain in the integral control framework. Hence, if we combine the quality spectrum of information and that of the IT infrastructure the result is a quality spectrum of information systems.

Developments in Organizations, Technology and Society

There seems to be growing consensus between managers and information specialists that new organizational forms abandon traditional design prescriptions that praise top-down command and control, fixed structures, rationality and hierarchy as the guarantees for corporate success. In the past century, organizational thinking has been dominated by normative theories about task design, organizational design, profit maximization and hierarchy-based authority (for example, *Taylor*, 1911; *Fayol*, 1949; *Weber*, 1946). In this view, organizations are considered mechanisms with a single goal, dedicated to transforming well-defined inputs into well-defined outputs, not being able to attain other goals or to perform other tasks except after having consciously made adjustments to the organization. These normative theories are nowadays not completely obsolete since there are still extremely successful traditional organizations that apply such classical concepts as detailed work procedures and standardized products (including Starbucks, Disney and McDonald's). In this type of organization, knowledge resides in the organization and not in the individuals working in the organization. Typical controls are rules and directives, performance evaluation, compliance-based rewards and selection and placement. Employees are valued because of their ability to contribute to the efficient functioning of a fixed, pre-defined structure. This type of organization encourages people to obey orders and to know their part in the whole instead of being interested in the intrinsic characteristics of their duties and continuously bringing this up for discussion. This type of organization may suffice for stable tasks under stable circumstances as well as for changing tasks under predictable circumstances. However, when the circumstances become subject to change or become less predictable, employees should be able to question the rightness of their task assignments and adjust their actions in accordance with new situations. In contemporary organizations, knowledge residing in the heads of the people within the organization is a key production factor. These firms are knowledge-intensive and their core employees are knowledge workers. The contemporary organization gives its knowledge workers discretion over their own actions and hence empowers them. It is self-organizing, reflective and has an inherent ability to meaningfully revitalize itself and adjust to changing circumstances. Volberda (1998) refers to this type of organization as the flexible firm. We will adhere to this term and use it to refer to contemporary organizations in our current economy.

Flexible firms demand specific types of information system. Obviously, these must be at least as flexible as the firm itself. Specifically, they must have a broad scope, implying that they must be able to cover all organizational activity and serve a wide variety of purposes. Enterprise-wide systems like enterprise resource planning (ERP) systems, can meet these requirements. Considering the central role ascribed by managers (including information managers), accountants and controllers to accounting information systems, the continuously enhancing functionality of these systems, their ability to bridge the gap between accounting and information systems professionals and the recent developments within the discipline of AIS with respect to more flexible ways to model organizations for the purpose of data base design, we believe accounting information systems are the information systems of the future. In this view, the accounting information system will be an integrative force in supporting the information needs of the flexible firm in the contemporary economy. However, to allow accounting information systems to play that role, we must continuously search for ways to enhance their flexibility while simultaneously maintaining their function as watchdogs of information reliability within the limits of enhanced efficiency.

Over the last decades we have seen a strong tendency within organizations to bring certain functions or processes under a single management structure. The vehicle that has typically been used to accomplish this is the shared services centre. In achieving efficiencies in a shared services environment, the largest savings typically result from headcount reductions and rethinking the way the organization defines its data and its procedures. The latter especially is interesting from an accounting information system point of view since shared services centres always require standardized data and procedures. Hence, shared service centres should lead to quality improvements of the accounting system.

In addition to new approaches to process management in organizations, and presumably as a result of changes in process management, entirely new types of organization have emerged. Examples of such new organizations include Internet providers, mobile operators, information brokers and fully web-based stores. We will develop a classification of contemporary organizations and focus our attention on the control issues arising.

Alignment in a Complex Control Environment

Within the integral control framework the following three alignment problems can be recognized:

- informational alignment
- operational alignment
- organizational control.

Informational Alignment

Here the business domain and the IT domain are aligned to realize strategic advantage from IT. For example, a fully web-based retailer and his IT provider have agreed that the IT provider must be able to deliver the hardware instantaneously when business continuity requires so. This is laid down in a service level agreement (SLA) that includes the quality criteria of the IT infrastructure. The quality of operations is dependent upon the availability of the IT infrastructure. A proper alignment between the business domain and the IT domain contributes to enhanced organizational performance. Such alignment will always take place via proper information provision between an organization and its IT vendors, hence the term informational alignment. This organization gains competitive edge by continuously having its information systems including its website available for sales orders. Case 1.2 gives an example of the contribution of sound service level agreements with IT vendors to the quality of the IT infrastructure and the quality of operations.

Operational Alignment

Here the formulated strategy is implemented for operational excellence. The rationale behind this type of alignment is that by having its internal processes in order, an organization can gain competitive advantage – for example, when a hotel has its guests make preferred room reservations to provide optimum customer services (a strategic issue). When a guest that has made such a preferred room reservation arrives, the designated room must indeed be available for her. This means that on the reservation date, the guest's name and the preferred room must be recorded. On the arrival day, the cleaning personnel must have cleaned the room

Case 1.2

Twente University Computer Department on Fire

On November 20th a disgruntled employee set the computer department of Twente University (Universiteit Twente) on fire. The servers and storage systems, about 120 in total, were completely destroyed and the damage was estimated between € 40 and 50 million.

Universiteit Twente is a technical university that traditionally has been a forerunner with respect to IT applications. It has a high success rate in European IT projects. Of all the Dutch companies and institutions, UT ranks second – after Philips Corporation – in collecting European subsidies for research, technological development and cooperation within Europe. Examples include projects for mobile telecommunication within the health care industry, wireless sensors and an advanced toolset on a nanoscale. The university's network is one of the most advanced in the world and the university wants to maintain that position. Recently, ambitious plans for a wifi network were unfolded. One year earlier umts plans of the same calibre were presented. According to Lisa Gommer, Project manager of Wireless Campus, the umts and wifi plans do not interfere, since the goal has always been to create an as rich as possible experimental wireless infrastructure. Simultaneously, the university continues to invest in its glass fibre network. Gert Meijerink, Head of telecommunications and systems, summarizes the university's wireless strategy as follows: 'We want to have maximum coverage at our 140 hectare campus, employ the latest technology, and yet be as cost-efficient as possible.' The university is also a forerunner in the realm of contemporary IT curricula. In May 2000 it started the first Dutch E-commerce programme and in September 1998 it opened interactive satellite classrooms where students could cooperate with each other and communicate with professors through videoconferencing and an advanced audio system. The interactive satellite classrooms made it possible to maintain the same degree of contact between students and teachers while economizing on travel time.

Sir Bakx is the Deputy director of the Centre for Information Provision of UT. He describes his experiences during the first three days after the fire started (source: Computable 12/6/2002).

'While on my way to the university, I see dark clouds of smoke above the university campus. On arrival it appears that the computer department is on fire. From what I see, I conclude that there will be not much left of the 120 servers and storage systems. This means that the whole university computer network is down. There will be a lot of work to do over the next few days. We are prepared for the worst. An hour and a half later I call a meeting of the IT disaster recovery team. The first thing we do is is to prepare a priority list to be discussed by the university disaster recovery team. The university disaster recovery team acknowledges the importance of a quick recovery of the IT infrastructure. Our first challenge is to make Surfnet – the UT-network – and the e-mail facilities available again to students and employees. Students and employees, as well as third parties who also make use of the network will then be able to use Internet and e-mail. A second IT room set to be surrendered on 1 January 2003 appeared to be a blessing in disguise since it could serve as a cold site for the emergency computer equipment. The decision to locate our critical systems at two different sites for security reasons was already made a while ago. Now, in view of this disaster, we will use this second IT room as our central coordination unit. The very same day we contact Triple P, HP, Surfnet, Cisco, KPN, Quote and other IT vendors who assure fast delivery of the necessary servers, network devices and services, to build a new Internet connection as fast as possible. We have a gentlemen's agreement with our main vendors that they will take care of quick delivery in case of calamities. In hindsight, we found out that they would fully live up to this agreement. A side effect is that other vendors and troubleshooters try to take advantage of the situation. That's the last thing I need right now because our current vendors do a perfect job. The next day, Friday, the Facility department of UT in cooperation with BAM and GTI has arranged power supplies, glass fibre wires and connections. Shortly after this, Surfnet appears to work again and our clients are able to use the Internet and e-mail again. Essent and Eager Telecom take care of the home connections (dial-up access, cable connections and ADSL). We keep students and employees informed through an electronic newsletter. In the new computer room, five parallel teams are working day and night to make the system operational again. The next priority is the repair of the UT network. In the meantime we make arrangements for the physical security of the new IT room. In between the IT disaster recovery team meetings (three a day), I continuously maintain contact with my people in the Centre for Information Provision. The next day, Friday, the HP UX- and Proliant servers, and the Procurve switches will be delivered. These are necessary to get our 'network of the future' and its gigabit connections on the air again. Triple P and HP have collected parts from all over Europe. In the distribution centre of Triple P the servers are being assembled and tested. With the completely set up servers and boxes of tapes – the tapes were stored in a safe in the building that burned down – we can start the recovery operations. This takes more time than we expected. Finally, in the evening, the servers function properly. Fortunately, we make back-ups of the whole system every week. These back-ups are stored in another building. The most recent back-up was made three days before the fire. As a result, only a relatively small amount of information was lost. The day after, Saturday, the UT network is operational again! Our next challenges are reinstalling Teletop, the digital learning environment of the university, the accounting systems, the library system and the other production systems. On Sunday we continue to work hard. Step by step all the applications and systems start running again. We expect to have the complete system up and running again by Monday.'

Despite the miraculous recovery of the IT infrastructure, there are still some hectic weeks to go. Since not only the computer department was housed in the building that caught fire, but also

(*Continued*)

some of the university's programmes, including Communication Sciences, Applied Mathematics, Philosophy and Social Sciences, and Science of Public Administration. Also, because the second IT room is now in use as the main computer centre, another location for the second IT room must be found. The IT management is contemplating whether or not this new venue must be on campus. By finding an off-campus location, the risk will probably be reduced.

In hindsight, the IT management of UT concluded that the disaster recovery plans and protocols have proven to be extremely valuable and worth every second and Euro invested in them. However, these remain paper agreements. Substantiation will only take effect if the students, employees and vendors involved show an incredible commitment.

Source: Computable, 6 December 2002 (adapted)

on time and the reception desk must know that the guest has made a preferred room reservation. Hence, to implement the 'optimum service strategy' all kinds of processes must be properly put in place. This is done on the operational level, hence operational alignment.

Organizational Control

Here a framework is developed that serves as the standard or norm ('what should be') for the solution of problems stemming from informational and operational alignment. Control may pertain to realizing intended strategies. Intended strategy is the strategy as formulated by strategic management and which is recorded and communicated as such. This strategy will not necessarily be realized. All kinds of changes in the organization's environment may lead to adjustments in the formulated strategy. For example, if one of an organization's competitors continuously brings new products to the market then the organization's competitive position may be hampered unless the organization becomes more innovative itself, even if this deviates from its intended cost-leadership strategy. However, control may also pertain to superior performance in the realm of business operations, appropriately measuring performance and putting in place an appropriate IT infrastructure so that information provision can indeed contribute to superior performance. For example, quality criteria for IT may pertain to availability of the IT infrastructure so that information provision – including e-mail and Internet traffic – can take place without any major disturbances and the information provided will meet its reliability and relevance quality criteria. Only if these quality criteria are met, may business operations lead to superior performance.

Case 1.2 is an appealing example of organizational control as defined in the integral control framework. Twente University is leading in the area of complex technologies. Should its computer systems have been down for too long a period or should important data have been lost in the fire, the university might have been put behind for years. An interesting detail in the recovery operation is that the commitment of personnel,

students and IT vendors (mainly motivation) has played a significant role and not only formal and technological factors.

The Relationship between Information Disciplines

Accounting can be defined as:

> The process of identifying, measuring and communicating economic information to permit informed judgements and
> decisions by users of the information.

This definition suggests that accounting uses information as its main vehicle to realize its objectives. Accounting information is economic information because it relates to the financial activities of an organization, i.e. it represents financial facts, which find their source in accounting transactions. These financial
facts are generally identified and measured by way of a double-entry system of accounting. The definition
also identifies the need for accounting information to be communicated. The ways in which this communication is achieved may vary. However, there is always some kind of technology involved when information
is to be communicated. The simplest technologies are manual systems, whereas more advanced technologies are computerized systems. Information and communication technology (IT) generally is considered
advanced technology and hence – by definition – uses computerized systems. Obviously, modern accounting
information systems draw heavily upon IT.

AIS, like Accounting and the more generic discipline of Information Systems, is an information discipline. To study AIS as a separate and unique research, education and practice area, a positioning of AIS *vis-
à-vis* its adjacent disciplines is needed. Given that all adjacent disciplines have information as their object
of study, we put information at the heart of our analysis. Information can be studied from a supply side
versus a demand side (information providers versus information users) and from a behavioural versus a
mechanistic approach. Information systems (with IT as its focal point) looks at information from a supply
side perspective, i.e. the way in which information systems can provide the necessary information. It does
so from both a mechanistic and a behavioural viewpoint since every system or system development process
contains technical components (steps in system development projects) juxtaposed with the human factor
(man–machine interface design). Management Accounting and Management Control (with Accounting as
its focal point) look at information from a demand side perspective, i.e. the way in which information is
used for decision-making and accountability. Analogous to Information Systems, they do so from both a
mechanistic and a behavioural viewpoint since every accounting and control process contains technical (for
example, making calculations) as well as behavioural components (for example, influencing human behaviour through incentives). AIS (with control as its focal point) looks upon information in a narrow fashion
from a mechanistic viewpoint (for example, designing procedures, programmed controls and segregation of
duties), but considers both the supply and demand of information perspectives. Hence, it bridges the gap
between Information Systems and Management Accounting and Management Control. Figure 1.5 depicts
the interrelationships between AIS and its adjacent disciplines. Insights from this model provide us with a
sound basis for our further study of AIS.

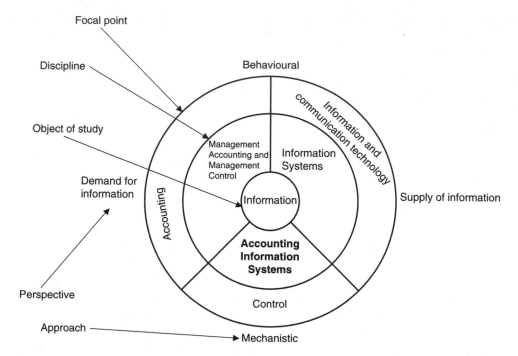

Figure 1.5   Object of study, disciplines, focal points and approaches in AIS and internal control.

Summary

This chapter provides an introduction to the field of Accounting Information Systems and Internal Control. We develop a model, the integral control framework, to present various topics that will be covered in this book, including information and communication technology, internal control, management control, governance and information provision.

Internal Control

In this chapter:

Introduction

This chapter discusses a number of core concepts and issues that form the conceptual foundations of the discipline of internal control. More particularly, we will discuss the importance and evolution of internal control, the authoritative COSO reports on internal control and enterprise risk management, the Sarbanes-Oxley Act of 2002, the scope of internal control, cornerstones of internal control and finally a number of important internal control concepts.

Learning Goals of the Chapter

After having studied this chapter, the reader will understand:

- the importance of internal control;
- important concepts and cornerstones of internal control;
- the limitations of internal control; and
- the meaning of internal control to managers.

The Importance of Internal Control

Ever since there have been organizations, there has been a need for control over these organizations. However, as we have seen in the past, organizations have not always been able to fulfil their internal control needs. The top management of Belgian speech technology company Lernaut and Hauspie was able to present large fictitious revenues and thus seriously mislead the capital market. For a number of years the top management of Robert Maxwell's Mirror Group withdrew large sums of money from two organizations and the company pension fund to save the organization. An employee of Barings Bank was able to engage in large derivatives transactions, even though he was not authorized to do so, given his position in the organization. On the so-called Walrus project of the Dutch Ministry of Defence, involving two sophisticated submarines, large budget overruns went unnoticed by the management of the Dutch Royal Navy and the Ministry of Defence. The Deutsche Metallgesellschaft engaged in forward oil transactions so large and risky that it nearly signalled the downfall of the organization. During the years before its downfall, the financial statements of Dutch shipyard RSV provided a very distorted image of the actual results and position of the organization. Over a number of years, the British and Commonwealth Bank and the Bank of Credit and Commerce International provided loans to noncreditworthy customers, and available funds were invested in nonprofitable projects. An employee of an Amsterdam diamond dealer was able to steal 20 million (at that time) guilders' worth of diamonds. Enron used various complex capital structures to hide the fact that its cash flows were very limited and its debts many times larger than reported. US Foodservice (an Ahold daughter) inflated its turnover bonuses on the profit and loss account, painting a more favourable picture of its results. Parmalat was a company in distress in every respect, but its financial statements did not reflect this. A number of Dutch contractors made secret price agreements and produced false invoices to maintain the system. Shell overstated its oil reserves on the balance sheet, showing a better picture than reality.

This random selection of cases stresses the importance of internal control. After all, had the companies above had appropriate internal control systems, then the fake invoices would have been discovered or not even made, the billions of Parmalat euros would not have disappeared without a trace, no loans would have been provided to noncreditworthy customers, the budget overruns on the Walrus project would have been discovered in time and so on.

Internationally, internal control has received a lot of attention. Also because of the high-profile cases discussed above, in the past decades research committees have been established worldwide charged with thoroughly investigating the concept of internal control. The results of these efforts are highly visible. In the United States the so-called Sarbanes-Oxley Act has been enacted and in almost every country in the world guidelines have been issued to prevent further corporate abuses.

The cases discussed above suggest that there are many reasons to assign great importance to internal control. The reasons are different depending on whether the importance for management or the importance for the auditor is considered. Management has a direct interest in securing the quality of its operations, whereas the auditor has a direct interest in securing the reliability of information. In this book we maintain a broad view of internal control and therefore do not a priori approach internal control from the point of view of either management or the auditor.

The Evolution of Internal Control

Internationally, the development of the concept of internal control shows a somewhat diffused picture. Before we consider the importance of internal control more closely, we therefore have to examine the different meanings that are associated with this concept internationally. In contrast to a continental European tradition where the theoretical foundation for internal control can mainly be found in the financial statement audit, in the 1940s a first attempt at formalizing an internal control concept was made in the US, where from the beginning this concept focused on getting organizations under control. Although this was a clear step in the direction of internal control as a tool to manage organizations, in the US too the origins of internal control can be found in the financial statement audit. This somewhat paradoxical situation can be explained by the fact that auditors – more so than the broad and therefore heterogeneous occupation of managers – are traditionally more prone to codify their body of thought. One of the first published definitions of internal control can be found in the 1949 research report of the Committee on Auditing Procedure of the American Institute of Certified Public Accountants (AICPA), followed by many adjustments and refinements. Management's role in internal control was explicitly discussed for the first in the Statement on Auditing Standards No. 1, issued by the AICPA in 1972, and in 1983 the Institute of Internal Auditors published a very broad definition of internal control. In 1985 the Treadway Commission was established to examine the causes of fraudulent financial reporting by leading organizations of which some went bankrupt entirely unexpectedly and auditors had apparently not been able to discover this in time. In 1992 the cooperation of five US regulatory institutes[1] resulted in the report of the Committee of Sponsoring Organizations of the Treadway Commission, or in short the COSO report.[2] This report was prepared based on recommendations of the Treadway Commission to have management report on the effectiveness of its internal controls, to create greater management awareness that the control environment, the audit committee, codes of conduct and the internal audit are important elements in an internal control system, and to arrive at a consensus as to the various internal control concepts and definitions that were in use until that time. The COSO report provided a broad definition of internal control that is currently still authoritative. The fact that not only audit(or) organizations were members of the Committee of Sponsoring Organizations indicates that internal control has moved beyond the realm of the audit profession and should rather be considered as a management tool.

Over time and internationally the definition of internal control as provided in the COSO report has gained wide support. This support has only increased with the recent enactment of the Sarbanes-Oxley Act since this Act primarily adopts the COSO definition of internal control. We will therefore discuss the basic premise of the report below. In addition we will also discuss a report issued by COSO in 2004 which extensively discusses risk management. Informally this report is known as the COSO II report, but we will refer to this report as the ERM COSO report to indicate that it does not deal with just internal control, but with Enterprise Risk Management (ERM), of which internal control is a part.

The COSO Reports

COSO (1992) provides the following definition of internal control:

> Internal control is a process, effected by an entity's board of directors, management and other personnel, designed to provide reasonable assurance regarding the achievement of objectives in the following categories:
>
> - Efficiency and effectiveness of operations;
> - Reliability of financial reporting;
> - Compliance with applicable laws and regulations.

In addition to the objectives of internal control according to COSO the Government Accountability Office (GAO)[3] in the US later provided a fourth objective:

> - Safeguarding of the assets of the organization.

In the remainder of this book we will also consider this internal control objective.

The COSO report distinguishes five interrelated components of internal control:

1. Control environment;
2. Risk assessment;
3. Control activities;
4. Information and communication; and
5. Monitoring.

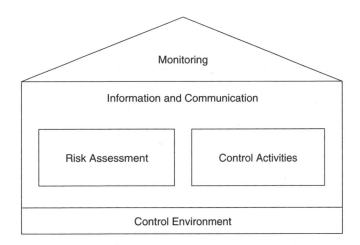

Figure 2.1   The COSO house.

Together these components form a structure and therefore the system of internal control components is presented as the COSO house (see Figure 2.1). The foundation of this house is the control environment, and monitoring is its roof, so as to make sure that the risk analysis, control activities and information and communication are functioning and keep functioning as intended.

Control Environment

The control environment is the organization's culture with respect to the importance of internal control. This forms the basis for any internal control system. The control environment encompasses a wide variety of organizational characteristics, but in essence a good control environment is one where people in the organization are aware of the importance of internal control and behave accordingly. Therefore, the control environment consists of:

- Integrity and ethical values;
- Commitment to competence, reflected in the presence of job descriptions and analyses of knowledge and skills required for these jobs;
- Interpretation of the tasks of the board of directors, the audit committee and other organizational bodies that supervise and control the management of organizations;
- Management philosophy and operating style, including its risk appetite;
- The attitude of management and other personnel towards information technology and information provision; and
- The hierarchical and lateral lines of reporting and communication as defined in the organizational structure, which have to be followed by employees to make sure that the organization, at least formally (see 'Formal and Material Checks', p. 51), functions as intended.

Risk Assessment

Risk assessment is focused on establishing such measures that the residual risk is reduced to an acceptable level (see Knechel *et al.*, 2007). Residual risk can be defined as the risk that control problems cannot be avoided, and both preventive and detective control measures are not effective and/or not taken. Risk is assessed to allocate the organization's resources in the most efficient way. Internal control measures are costly and it is important to make sure that the costs of these measures are not higher than the benefits that they generate, i.e. the achievement of internal control objectives. Figure 2.2 shows the subsequent stages of risk assessment.

In the first stage, an organization should examine whether control problems can be avoided. We will further discuss this matter in Chapter 3. If control problems cannot be avoided, two options are available: implement internal control measures or do nothing (i.e. accept the control problems). It may seem rather thoughtless to accept control problems, but if this happens after the manager has made a cost–benefit analysis his decision may be entirely justifiable. Furthermore, risk is inherent in entrepreneurship. However, if a manager decides to implement internal control measures, he will usually implement a combination of preventive and detective control measures (see 'Control Activities', p. 35).

The decision to avoid control problems, as well as the decision to implement internal control measures should be based on a cost–benefit analysis. A useful tool to make such decisions is a risk map. Using this tool risk can be assessed on two dimensions: the probability or likelihood that a certain risk will occur and the impact or effect of that risk. Figure 2.3 is an example of a risk map. Managers will have a certain risk appetite. This appetite is reflected in the diagonal line. All dots above this line represent risk that the

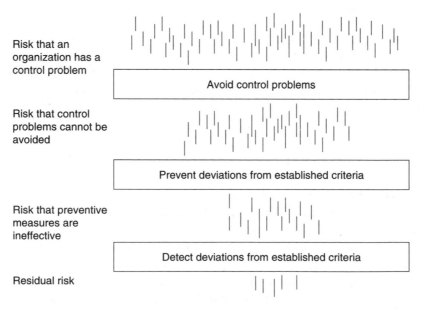

Figure 2.2   Risk assessment.

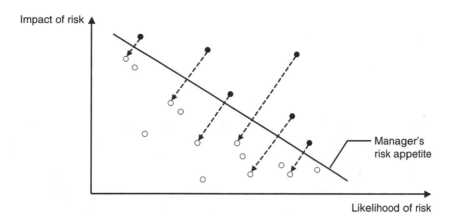

Figure 2.3   Risk map.

manager considers unacceptable. All dots below the line are risks that are considered acceptable. Each solid dot therefore represents a risk that needs to be considered. Importantly, dots above the line need to be reduced to a location below the line either by avoidance – for instance by insuring against the consequences of the risk – or by implementing internal control measures. Transparent dots are residual risks that by definition should be in line with the manager's risk appetite.

To clearly define the concept of risk management, the Committee of Sponsoring Organizations of the Treadway Commission published a second report in 2004, in which it thoroughly examines the concept of Enterprise Risk Management (ERM).

The report defines Enterprise Risk Management as follows:

> Enterprise Risk Management is a process, effected by an entity's board of directors, management and other personnel, applied in strategy setting and across the enterprise, designed to identify potential events that may affect the entity, and manage risk to be within its risk appetite, to provide reasonable assurance regarding the achievement of entity objectives.

In many respects this definition is similar to the COSO's definition of internal control. This is of course no coincidence since internal control is considered part of Enterprise Risk Management. The report also notes that everything discussed with respect to internal control in the COSO report on internal control remains in full force. COSO's ERM report therefore builds on COSO's internal control report.

ERM consists of eight components:

1.   Internal environment;
2.   Objective setting;
3.   Event identification;
4.   Risk assessment;
5.   Risk response;

6. Control activities;
7. Information and communication; and
8. Monitoring.

Internal Environment

The internal environment forms the foundation for all other ERM components. As part of the internal environment, management will develop a risk management philosophy ('How should we deal with risk?') and define its risk appetite ('Which risks are acceptable?'). Thus, the internal environment consists of a broad range of factors related to an organization's risk culture. Other elements of the internal environment are the role of the Board of Directors, the organization's integrity and ethical values, competencies of personnel, leadership style and assignment of authority and responsibility.

Objective Setting

Objectives should always be in line with the mission and vision of an organization. COSO-ERM distinguishes four categories of objectives: strategic objectives, operations objectives, reporting objectives and compliance objectives. For certain objectives these categories can overlap and different officers may be responsible for their realization.

Event Identification

Risks can be defined as the probability that a critical event occurs and negatively affects the achievement of objectives. Therefore, for appropriate risk assessment, critical events need to be identified. Such events may be caused by external (e.g. economic, political, social, or technological) factors, or by internal factors (e.g. organizational structuring, processes, personnel, or systems).

Risk Assessment

Risk assessment involves estimation of the likelihood of a critical event occurring and the impact of the occurrence of that event (see Figure 2.3).

Risk Response

An effective ERM-system requires management to reduce the likelihood and impact of events to below its risk tolerance, in line with management's risk appetite.

Control Activities

Control activities are aimed at reasonably assuring that risk responses are carried out appropriately. This encompasses all control measures discussed in the internal control and management control literatures.

COSO-ERM particularly focuses on IT-related control measures. Implicitly, therefore, it indicates that the ERM-framework applies to modern organizations that are heavily dependent on information technology.

Information and Communication

Information is the basis for such communication that individuals and groups of individuals can effectively carry out their tasks. With respect to ERM, information is necessary to identify and assess risks, and decide on the appropriate risk response.

Monitoring

The existence and operation of the ERM-components, as well as the quality of these components should be established over time. This can be accomplished by means of separate evaluations (e.g., by means of operational audits or business risk audits that are currently an integral part of the audit approach of most large audit firms), or ongoing activities. Many organizations will choose a combination of both.

Together the ERM-components should lead to achievement of the objectives of ERM. Objectives related to the reliability of reporting and compliance with laws and regulations can be reasonably assured by implementing the appropriate internal controls. This is different for objectives related to strategy and operations. ERM can only play a role in providing reasonable assurance that management and supervisory boards are informed in a timely fashion about the organization's ability to achieve its objectives. Specifically this means that early warning signals are provided, which allows the organization to deal proactively with the uncertainties that it faces.

Although the ERM-concept has already been applied for many years by managers, Boards of Directors and Supervisory Boards that take their jobs seriously, the synthesis of all related available knowledge provided in the COSO ERM report is very useful. Although the report often states the obvious, it also makes risk management and the associated jargon explicit and systematically relates important concepts. In this way related knowledge is transferable and organizations and their employees are better able to learn from their mistakes.

Control Activities

Control activities can be classified in many ways. This chapter discusses a number of these classifications ('Classifications of Internal Controls', p. 49). A useful classification, based on risk assessment, is a distinction between preventive and detective measures. Preventive measures focus on avoiding deviations from set criteria, and detective measures focus on detecting deviations from these criteria. Deviations from set criteria are budget overruns, noncompliance with a certain internal procedure, costs that are reported to be higher or lower than in reality, certain revenues that are not reported, or fictitious revenues that are reported. Examples of preventive internal controls are segregation of duties, physical protection of assets and setting procedures for executing certain activities. Examples of detective controls are reconciliations, analytical review, physical inventory counts, variance analysis and reperformance of certain calculations.

Preventive measures are often of an organizational nature and detective measures are often specific control activities. A third category of control measures is formed by corrective measures, focused on solving control problems detected by means of detective measures.

Information and Communication

Information and communication are necessary to facilitate control. This internal control component relates to recording transactions, matching internal with external documents, confirmations from/to third parties, communication of procedures and tasks, accountability and formal management reports. Information should meet certain quality criteria to facilitate proper control. Thus, information is both subject to control (how can the quality of information be improved?) and a means to control (how can information be used to better control the organization and its people?). Many management controls assume reliable information provision. For example, when an officer is awarded a performance reward based on reported results, those results should be in line with reality and therefore reliable.

Monitoring

Monitoring assesses the quality of internal control systems over time. Two forms of monitoring are distinguished:

1. Ongoing activities; and
2. Separate evaluations at a certain moment in time.

Internal control systems can change over time because the organization and its environment also change over time. Because of this controls that were once effective may no longer be effective. Monitoring should detect and correct this on a timely basis. Thus, there is a certain overlap between the internal control component 'Control activities' and the component 'Monitoring'. For instance, a periodical physical inventory count is a separate evaluation at a certain moment, but also a control activity. If results from inventory counts are compared to inventory levels reported in the general and subsidiary ledger and reported to management, then management can evaluate the effectiveness of the internal control. Recent interesting IT-related developments facilitate ongoing monitoring activities. So-called 'continuous reporting' and 'continuous assurance' methods are developed to incorporate monitoring components into information systems. For instance, as soon as a transaction is input into the information system, a programmed procedure evaluates the possibility of this transaction, taking into account certain expectations built into the monitoring systems as the norm.

The internal control objectives as defined by the COSO and the GAO show that internal control covers the business domain, the information and communication domain, as well as the IT domain. However, within these domains major changes are currently taking place, which affect the scope of internal control. Before we explore this further in 'The Scope of Internal Control' (p. 39), we will first discuss one of the most influential pieces of legislation on internal control of the last few decades: the Sarbanes-Oxley Act of 2002.

Corporate Governance ✕

The last decade has shown an overwhelming interest in internal control issues related to corporate govern-ance. In brief, corporate governance deals with:

- control;
- decision-making power;
- responsibility;
- oversight;
- integrity; and
- accountability.

Corporate governance is aimed at securing the continuity of organizations by maintaining good relations with stakeholders. Therefore, organizations are held accountable for their activities and hence they should undertake the right activities in the right way, thereby explicitly showing that they do so. So, organizations – by way of their management – enable stakeholders to form an opinion with respect to the quality of the control systems that are in place, decision-making power, responsibilities, oversight by independent parties and management's integrity.

In addition to the COSO reports a number of internal control and related frameworks have been issued over the last decades, including the Cadbury report, the CoCo report, the SAC report, the COBIT report, SAS 55/70/78 and KonTraG (Kontrole und Transparenz Gesetz). The latter is not a framework as issued by a private body but a law issued by the German government. Although these reports and laws rely heavily on one another's findings they look upon internal control from different viewpoints, on behalf of different audiences and aimed at different goals. COSO, CoCo, SAC and SAS primarily seek to provide a definition of internal control. Cadbury, KonTraG and COBIT do not explicitly mention this goal, but they use a defini-tion that closely resembles the COSO definition. All these reports give guidance to the development of more effective internal control systems within organizations. Furthermore, all these reports contribute to better corporate governance of organizations. KonTraG provides a further refinement, aimed at the implementation of recommendations of previous reports. The influence of these frameworks and laws on corporate govern-ance practices has not been tremendous. However, with the Sarbanes-Oxley Act this changed radically.

In 2002, after a series of corporate scandals involving companies such as Enron and WorldCom and the resulting demise of Arthur Andersen, the US Congress passed the Sarbanes-Oxley Act to restore investor confidence in the capital market and the audit profession '. . . by improving the accuracy and reliability of corporate disclosure . . .' (US House of Representatives, 2002). Some of the most prominent provisions of the Act are those that relate to internal control, contained in Section 302 (Corporate Responsibility for Financial Reports) and, most comprehensively, Section 404 (Management Assessment of Internal Controls).

Section 302 stipulates that CEOs and CFOs must certify in both quarterly and annual financial state-ments that they have reviewed the financial statements, that these contain no material misstatements and are not misleading and that the organization's financial position is fairly presented. More importantly, the officers also have to declare that they are responsible for internal controls, that they have evaluated the effectiveness of these internal controls and that they have reported the results of this evaluation in their report. Furthermore, they should disclose to their auditors and audit committee all material weaknesses in internal control, significant internal control deficiencies,[4] and any related fraud. Finally, they should report any significant changes in internal controls if these have occurred after their date of evaluation.

Section 404 extends these requirements by mandating the annual filing of an internal control report to the Securities and Exchange Commission (SEC), in which management states that they are responsible for establishing and maintaining an adequate internal control structure and appropriate internal control procedures for financial reporting. The report must also contain management's assessment of the company's internal controls as well as the company auditor's attestation of these internal controls. Section 404 explicitly indicates that this internal control audit should be part of the company's annual financial statement audit. Together, the internal control audit and the financial statement audit are commonly known as the integrated audit.

In a final rule promulgated in 2003, the SEC provided more explanation of and some amendments to the rules in the Sarbanes-Oxley Act. In specifying the definition of internal control in the Act, the SEC (2003) refers to COSO's internal control framework and indicates that the concept of internal control as contained in the Sarbanes-Oxley Act is broadly defined and goes beyond the accounting functions of a company. However, the rule also indicates that the Sarbanes-Oxley Act is limited to internal control *over financial reporting*, and thus effectively only refers to the second category of objectives as defined in COSO's framework. That is, the Sarbanes-Oxley Act does not consider the efficiency and effectiveness and compliance objectives (apart from laws and regulations that relate to the preparation of financial statements). The final rule provides the following definition of internal control over financial reporting:

> A process designed by, or under the supervision of, the registrant's principal executive and principal financial officers, or persons performing similar functions and effected by the registrant's board of directors, management and other personnel, to provide reasonable assurance regarding the reliability of financial reporting and the preparation of financial statements for external purposes in accordance with generally accepted accounting principles and includes those policies and procedures that:
>
> 1. Pertain to the maintenance of records that in reasonable detail accurately and fairly reflect the transactions and dispositions of the assets of the registrant;
> 2. Provide reasonable assurance that transactions are recorded as necessary to permit preparation of financial statements in accordance with generally accepted accounting principles, and that receipts and expenditures of the registrant are being made only in accordance with authorizations of management and directors of the registrant; and
> 3. Provide reasonable assurance regarding prevention or timely detection of unauthorized acquisition, use or disposition of the registrant's assets that could have a material effect on the financial statements.

The final rule also indicates that management should base its evaluation of the effectiveness of an organization's internal control over financial reporting 'on a suitable, recognizable framework that is established by a body or group that has followed due-process procedures, including the broad distribution of the framework for public comment' (SEC, 2003). The rule goes on to state that COSO can serve as such a framework, but that other frameworks, provided they meet certain requirements, can be used as well.[5] In any case, the management report should indicate which framework management has used in evaluating the effectiveness of the internal control system.

Finally, the SEC clarifies that management cannot judge its internal control system to be effective if it identifies one or more material weaknesses in its internal control system. Furthermore, management should disclose any material weakness in its internal control system in its report.

Although the Sarbanes-Oxley Act is not the first piece of legislation to regulatorily require organizations to not only design and maintain proper internal controls but also periodically evaluate the quality of those internal controls, it certainly is the most extensive, affecting more organizations than ever before.

The Scope of Internal Control

Traditionally, internal control focuses on financial information and is therefore retrospective. However, society has changed to such an extent that a modified importance is assigned to information for optimizing operational management. In this social development three periods, or waves, of economic evolution can be distinguished. The first is the agrarian age, which lasted until the mid-eighteenth century. The second is the industrial age, which continues to this day. The third is the information age. We are currently in the transitional stage between the industrial age and the information age.

The agrarian age was characterized by the power of guilds. Within the guilds, clear agreements were made and there was no real competition. The industrial age is characterized by concentration of power in production companies that were increasing in size and by increasing competition between these companies. The information age is characterized by an increase in new organizational forms that transcend branches, national borders, cultures and markets. The economy of the third wave is dominated by service organizations (including trade and the financial sector) where information and knowledge are the most important resources with which to compete. Production activities that were the key competences of production organizations are increasingly outsourced to low-wage countries, whereas new products are developed in Western economies. Furthermore, service industries increasingly determine the conditions of contracts entered into with production organizations.

Specialization is necessary due to knowledge of products, local markets and the need to combine different production, information and communication technologies. With reference to Harvard professor Michael Porter, a focus strategy will become increasingly important. This implies that more and more organizations will focus on those activities in which they excel and, to compensate, engage in cooperation with other organizations. New forms of cooperation are alliances, partnerships, joint ventures, outsourcing, but particularly economic networks built around a particular IT platform. Such forms of cooperation require adequate provision of information between the associated partners (internal information provision) and between the cooperating partners and third parties (external information provision).

The so-called virtual organization is a consequence of thinking in economic networks. The dependence on information in these types of organization is increasing, and physical flows and stocks of goods and money are of secondary importance. Much more important is the availability of information about the location of those physical stocks and the associated physical flows. For these networks of organizations to function and be maintained, the reliability of information is of vital importance. For this reason the aggregate of activities aimed at establishing and maintaining the reliability of information, i.e. information control as a specialization of internal control, has been considered with renewed interest. However, the aspect of relevance should not be neglected. Modern information and communication technology facilitates the flow of information, which might induce one to supply and ask for as much information as possible without considering the relevance for the management and control of organizations. This increases the danger of information overload. Therefore, in our modern society, reliability and relevance should be considered as complementary issues and should be pursued simultaneously. A complicating factor is that information increasingly has a nonfinancial character, which makes it harder to establish reliability and relevance using traditional internal controls.

Cornerstones of Internal Control

If a theory of internal control were to be developed then several concepts should minimally be incorporated. These concepts are considered to be the cornerstones of internal control. This section discusses these concepts:

1. The steering paradigm;
2. The management cycle;
3. The basic pattern of information provision; and
4. The value cycle.

The Steering Paradigm

Steering and control cannot be separated: by steering an object in a certain direction, control of that object is achieved. Objects of control can be an organization, a division, a business unit, a department, a process, a task force, or a specific employee. Whatever the object of control, the following four elements will always be present when dealing with management and control:

1. The controlled system;
2. The control system;
3. The information system; and
4. The environment.

These elements are related and together they form a pattern that is generally referred to as the steering paradigm (see Figure 2.4).

An organization can be considered a controlled system. This system is controlled by the organization's management. Thus, management is the control system. Management needs information to manage the organization. This information is received from either the information system or straight from the environment. Internally management will issue task assignments to employees, who will subsequently give account about the extent to which they have fulfilled their tasks. They do so by means of the information system. In addition, management will also give account to society at large (the environment).

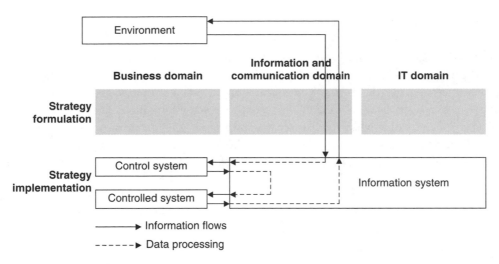

Figure 2.4 The steering paradigm.

By means of the steering paradigm, expression is given to the fact that (1) information, and more specifically the information system is key to controlling a system; (2) there is a continuous interaction between the environment and the system; (3) the subjective choice of the system boundaries determines what information is considered internal or external; and (4) there is a manager or device (control system) who attempts to control the behaviour of a subordinate or organizational unit (controlled system) on the basis of, often imperfect, information. This system is controlled by the management of the organization. Hence, management is the control system which needs information to control the business. This information is acquired from the information system, directly from the environment, or both. Management will give task assignments to workers within the business, who will account for their task fulfilment using the information system. In addition, the business will also account for its task fulfilment directly toward the environment, or more specifically toward stakeholders (see 'The Bus' below).

The Bus

Steering a business may be compared to driving a bus. The driver is seated in front of the bus, behind the steering-wheel. His task is to drive the bus to its destination. The windscreen and the rear-view mirrors provide him with the necessary information. In addition, the passengers of the bus are a source of information. It is well known that driving a bus is a relatively easy task when compared to steering a business. Hence, the comparison between a business and a bus holds only partially. The windscreen which provides the driver – in this case, the manager – with a substantial part of the

(Continued)

(Continued)

necessary information, is blinded and indeed the manager cannot look into the future. As a result, the manager has only the rear-view mirrors and his passengers as sources of information. Here, two problems emerge. Firstly, the rear-view mirror can only provide information about the past. Secondly, the passengers do not always provide the driver with reliable information. There is another complicating factor. The steering-wheel that the driver – in this case, the manager – uses to steer the bus in the right direction is not directly connected to the wheels of the bus. Instead, the passengers – in this case, the manager's subordinates – each have a steering-wheel of their own, which indeed is connected to the wheels of the bus. When the manager turns the steering-wheel, he wants his subordinates to follow his example. From this viewpoint, steering a business (driving) in order to control it (reach the destination), is merely a matter of collecting reliable and relevant information and trying to move the people within the business in the right direction.

There are two generic modes of reaction to control actions by control systems: feedforward mechanisms and feedback mechanisms. Basically, a feedforward mechanism tries to prevent undesirable events from occurring, whereas a feedback mechanism tries to transform undesirable outcomes of events into desirable outcomes. To make a well-grounded choice between feedforward and feedback mechanisms as control instruments, the consequences of each of the two must be known in advance.

The steering paradigm is based on the traditional view of organizational control, derived from cybernetics. Anthony (1965) is generally considered to be the founding father of management control. He used a cybernetic approach to control problems and used the example of the thermostat of a heating system as an illustration. A cybernetic control system consists of four components:

1. A measurement instrument that measures reality (e.g. the actual room temperature, the 'what is' position). This is part of the information system;
2. A mechanism that measures deviations from an established criterion (e.g. the pre-established desired room temperature, the 'what should be' position). This is also part of the information system;
3. An instrument that adjusts the behaviour of the controlled system (e.g. switching on the heating) if the deviation from the established criterion exceeds a certain critical threshold. This is part of the control system; and
4. The controlled system itself (e.g. the heating system, which can be either on or off).

In an organization the controlled and control system are part of the business domain. Because the information and communication domain and the IT domain together form the information system, measurement and evaluation instruments are part of both the information and IT domain.

Defining the elements of the steering paradigm determines the borders of the system. For example, when a department is the controlled system, the control system is the head of that department and the organization is the environment. Chapter 3 further explores cybernetic control mechanisms as the basis for many management control systems.

The Management Cycle

Steering and control are the most important processes for managers. The steering paradigm specifies a particular way of analysing steering and control processes, whereas the management cycle indicates in detail which steps management activities consist of. Several definitions of management are in use. However, an important common characteristic of these definitions is that people need to be managed to move them in the desired direction. Ideally, there is perfect congruence between the goals of the organization, represented by management and those of the individual members of the organization. This congruence hardly exists by itself and therefore management needs to make an effort to work towards such congruence. According to the management cycle this process consists of five stages:

1. Planning;
2. Structuring;
3. Execution;
4. Evaluation; and
5. Adjustment.

This cycle is also known as the Deming cycle, after the American statistician William Deming. After the Second World War he was involved in many quality improvement projects in organizations across the globe. He stated that every analysis of a business process should follow the sequence of four repetitive steps: Plan, Do, Check, Act. For this reason, the cycle is also known as the PDCA cycle.[6] Compared to the management cycle, the stages Structuring and Execution are put together in the 'Do' stage. In addition, the PDCA cycle focuses on change, for example quality improvement, whereas the management cycle is more generally applicable. Because this book is not specifically focused on quality improvement we will further discuss the more general management cycle instead of the PDCA cycle.

Planning

Planning involves the systematic preparation of activities to be performed at a later stage. For good planning the planner hopes to achieve insight which is as clear as possible into the future. Unfortunately there are no crystal balls to predict the future and that is why the planner has to settle for information about the present and the past. Therefore, two rules for effective planning are:

1. Planning quality improves when the object of planning is (physically) closer to the planner, because information related to the object will be more reliable. For instance, a purchaser will make better purchasing decisions than the top manager since the purchaser is closer to the suppliers and is more aware of their strengths and weaknesses; and
2. As time goes by information about a future event will be more reliable because the future event draws nearer. This will improve the quality of planning and the related decisions. For instance, it will be easier to more accurately determine necessary production capacity for tomorrow rather than for a month into the future.

Planning decisions are always related to certain objectives. For instance, an organization wants to be the market leader in five years' time. To this end, plans are made on a strategic, tactical and operational level.

Structuring

When objectives are known and plans are made, the organization needs to be structured in such a way that plans can be realized in the best way possible. For example, an organization invests in machines and buildings, hires people and chooses a particular organizational structure.

Execution

After an organization has been structured, it is ready to execute plans that are made in the planning stage. For example, an organization starts selling its products; to that end it produces the desired quantities and qualities and purchases the required resources. Ultimately, in the execution stage the organization attempts to realize the plans that are made to the best of its ability.

Evaluation

Whether a plan has been realized can be established by comparing the realization with the plan. This is the evaluation stage. For example, the organization continuously collects information on the organization's market share and increases compared to the competition. This way the organization gains an understanding of the extent to which it will realize its objective to be the market leader within five years.

Adjustment

Based on the results of the evaluation the organization may decide to make adjustments. Adjustments can be made to the realization, called single-loop learning, or by changing the norm, called double-loop learning. For instance, the organization finds that it has gained less market share than desired. It may then decide to launch an advertising campaign, improve its internal processes, improve its products and so on, to try to raise the market share to the desired level. However, the organization may also decide that the market has changed in such a way that it is better to start operating in a different market and thus adjust its goals based on the changed circumstances.

The Basic Pattern of Information Provision

Information is important to both the steering paradigm and the management cycle. The information system as reflected in the steering paradigm in Figure 2.4 can be broken down into a number of components. An information system processes data to produce information. The system does this by combining input data with existing data (usually contained within computer files) according to certain procedures (usually

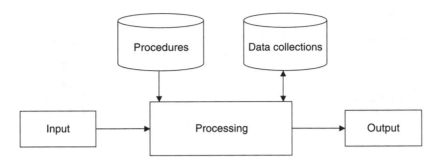

Figure 2.5   The basic pattern of information provision.

contained within computer programs) to generate the desired output. For example, when a client calls to place an order, the order department will want to know the client code, the product code and the desired number of products to be able to input the order. By means of a programmed procedure these data are processed to generate a picking ticket and an invoice. The programmed procedure will link the input data with existing data in the client file (establish name and address data based on the client code) and the inventory file (establish product description and available inventory based on the product code and the quantity ordered). In general each process of information provision has the same structure and consists of three parts:

1. Input;
2. Processing, using procedures and existing data collections; and
3. Output.

This structure is called the basic pattern of information provision (see Figure 2.5). The pattern applies to both manual and automated systems.

The pattern helps not only to gain insight into processes of information provision, but also to describe controls related to information systems. The pattern can prove to be particularly helpful for complex automated systems. For example, a well-known classification of controls for automated systems is that of programmed controls, integrity controls and user controls (see 'Classifications of Internal Controls', p. 49). This classification is fully in line with the basic pattern of information provision. Programmed controls relate to the programs that are used, integrity controls to both programs and data collections and user controls to input and output.

The Value Cycle

The value cycle is a model that enables visualization of segregation of duties and helps to describe the relationship between positions and events in organizations. Figure 2.6 shows the value cycle for a trade organization that does not engage in financial transactions other than payments to creditors and receipts from debtors. This is the most elementary form of the value cycle.

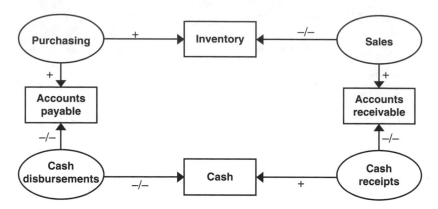

Figure 2.6   The value cycle in its most elementary form.

The value cycle unites the concepts of segregation of duties and reconciliations. By analogy with the human blood circulation, an organization can be considered as a system where flows (both increases and decreases) can lead to observable situations (positions), which can lead to other flows. These relations are generally referred to with the term BIDE formulas: opening or Beginning balance of a position + Increase in that position −/− Decrease in that position = Ending balance of that position. However, the value cycle is more than a collection of relationships that can be deducted from the various BIDE formulas. Each relationship within the value cycle has overlap with at least one other relationship within the same value cycle. For example, the relationship between the opening inventory balance, purchases, sales and ending inventory balance overlaps with the relationship between the opening accounts receivable balance, sales, cash receipts and the ending accounts receivable balance, because both relationships include the event 'sales'.

As indicated the value cycle also helps us to visualize segregation of duties. Ideally, there should be segregation between each part of the value cycle. For instance, the employee or department that purchases raw materials should be different from the employee or department that receives the raw materials in the warehouse.

Segregation of Duties

We can distinguish several types of labour divisions within organizations. Vertical division of labour exists between various hierarchical levels in the organization and is based on the premise that managers have a limited span of control and need to delegate authority to their subordinates to arrive at an effective division. Horizontal labour division is based on required common knowledge and skills and is focused on achieving the organizational goals. This division of labour focuses on efficiency and is usually organized along the lines of the functional processes of the organization, such as purchasing, sales, human resources, cash collection, payment authorization, accounts receivable, accounts payable, inventory, or production. A very different form of division of labour is one which does not focus on the functional processes themselves, but on the control of those processes. This is segregation of duties, which considers labour division from an internal control perspective.

Segregation of duties is based on the creation of opposed interests between employees and/or departments. This may be contrary to the basic principle of cooperation within an organization to achieve organizational goals. This paradox can be solved by means of a cost–benefit analysis that should be applied to any internal control measure that is considered. The costs of implementing segregation of duties for instance include increased personnel costs due to the creation of a function with such limited responsibilities that there is no direct added value. Indirectly, however, this segregation may provide added value because the related opportunity costs can be reduced to a minimum. For example, an organization combines purchasing and sales since purchasing requires a thorough knowledge of the sales market and the technical specifications of the product. This enables the employee to start a 'shop within a shop'. The associated opportunity costs should be incorporated into the cost–benefit analysis and this may lead to segregating the purchasing and sales functions, even though the resulting job responsibilities for either function individually may be considered to be too limited.

Segregation of duties involves segregation of the following five duties:

1. Authorization;
2. Custody;
3. Recording;
4. Checking; and
5. Execution.

Authorization

An authorization function can commit the organization, or part of the organization, to third parties. This can be accomplished by means of signatures or otherwise assigning certain tasks to others. An authorization function always has the authority to make decisions independently. For instance, a purchaser has the authority to decide what, when, how much and from whom he will buy. In the value cycle all ellipses (purchasing, sales, cash receipts and cash disbursements) represent authorization functions.

Custody

The custody function is charged with safeguarding goods, money, or other values (including information). A custody function should not surrender or take delivery of these resources unless an authorization function has authorized him to do so. This authorization can be granted in the form of a mandate – for instance, the warehouse manager is authorized to receive goods delivered to the warehouse without having received a message from the purchasing department that these goods will arrive – but also in the form of a specific assignment for a particular receipt or delivery – for instance, the warehouse manager receives a list from the purchasing department specifying the goods ordered in a certain period and to be delivered to the warehouse.

Recording

The recording function records data related to purchases, sales, cash receipts and cash disbursements in data collections. These recordings lead to changes in inventory, cash, accounts receivable and accounts payable. Although data is input nearly everywhere in the organization, most of this input is not considered to be independent recording. Only recording done by a separate organizational unit that does not have any other function than recording data created elsewhere in the organization is considered as a separate recording function. Usually this function is performed by the accounting department.

Checking

The checking function checks realization of plans to norms established to that end. For instance, the controller or the head of the accounting department periodically compares the revenues recorded in a certain period to the expected recording based on a BIDE formula.

Execution

The execution function is not directly recognizable in the value cycle. This function executes tasks assigned by an authorization function. Many classifications of segregation of duties leave out this category of functions. Nevertheless we consider this category important enough to include it in our classification since it is the residual category that includes all functions that cannot be classified in any of the other four categories.

Figure 2.7 represents a value cycle for a trade organization that incorporates segregation of duties, including the recording function. This function is at the heart of every organization and is therefore also displayed at the heart of the value cycle. Ideally, there should be segregation between each of the components of the value cycle. In the figure this is reflected by means of horizontal and vertical dashed lines.

Reconciliations

Segregation of duties is a preventive control measure. Preventive measures are usually not sufficient to achieve organizational goals. In addition to preventive measures, corrective measures are necessary as well. A very powerful corrective measure is reconciling recordings made at different locations and/or by different

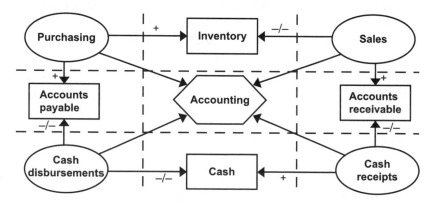

Figure 2.7   The value cycle including segregation of duties and the recording function.

Table 2.1 Network of reconciliations.

		Beginning balance accounts payable		Beginning balance accounts receivable		
		+		+		
Beginning balance inventory	+	Purchases	−/−	Sales	=	Ending balance inventory
		−/−		−/−		
Beginning balance cash	−/−	Cash disbursements	+	Cash receipts	=	Ending balance cash
		=		=		
		Ending balance accounts payable		Ending balance accounts receivable		

officers within the organization. These reconciliations are preferably performed by officers with an independent checking function. Two types of relationships are important in making these reconciliations:

- The relationship between offers and yields. For instance, to produce a certain product a particular quantity of raw materials, man hours and machine hours is required. Therefore, there is a relationship between the amounts of raw materials, man hours and machine hours used on the one hand, and the amount of products produced on the other. Another example is the relationship between the flow of money and the flow of goods: when goods are received (yields), sooner or later money needs to be paid (offers); and
- The relationship between positions and events. For instance, there is a relationship between the opening balance of inventory (B: beginning balance), purchase of goods (I: increase), sale of goods (D: decrease) and the ending balance of inventory (E: ending balance). This relationship can be generalized to all stocks (the positions: opening or beginning balance and ending balance) and all flows (the events: increases and decreases). The relationship between positions and events can be captured in a so-called network of reconciliations to reflect the interrelationships. This is actually no different from what is captured in the general ledger. After all, all general ledger accounts are related because debit and credit have to match. Table 2.1 shows a network of reconciliations for a trade organization with receipts from debtors and payments to creditors only.

Classifications of Internal Controls

This section discusses a number of classifications of internal control measures that can help to better control organizations. We will successively discuss:

- detailed checks, total checks and partial observation;
- direct and indirect checks;
- formal and material checks;

- negative and positive checks;
- policy control;
- standards control;
- expectations control;
- authority control;
- progress control;
- efficiency control;
- execution control; and
- custody control.

In automated environments the following controls also apply:

- programmed controls;
- integrity controls; and
- user controls.

These checks and controls compare an actual, realized position or event to a certain standard or norm. Borrowing from the German language, these are generally termed *Ist* (what is) and *Soll* (what should be), respectively. For example, the stock in the warehouse (*Ist*) is compared to inventory according to the general ledger (*Soll*). Every check or control discussed below compares *Ist* and *Soll*. However, they differ as to what constitutes the *Ist* and *Soll* for each particular check or control.

Detailed Checks, Total Checks and Partial Observation

Detailed checks can be performed on an integral basis or by means of partial observations. For example, the list of accounts receivable balances specifies the amounts owed to the organization by each debtor. To establish the validity of these balances the list can be checked by examining each debtor individually. This is an integral detailed check. When only a few debtors are examined this is called a detailed check by means of partial observation. If this partial observation is conducted based on statistical techniques this is called sample observation. The list of accounts receivable balances can also be checked based on totals. The reconciliation between the opening accounts receivable balance, sales, cash receipts and ending accounts receivable discussed earlier is an example of such a total check.

Direct and Indirect Checks

Direct checks are applied to processes, assigned tasks and procedures, whereas indirect checks are applied to outcomes of processes, assigned tasks and procedures. Therefore, direct checks are often also termed action control, and indirect checks are often called results control. The distinction between direct and indirect checks is a relevant one because there is a relationship between the applicability of these controls and the management level in the organization. Because direct controls are applied to processes, assigned tasks and procedures, and lower management levels are usually controlled by specifying tasks and actions that are to be taken, direct controls are usually found at the operational level. In contrast, indirect controls are usually applied at higher management levels since triggers are in general not provided in the form of specifically assigned tasks, but in the form of objectives, results and outcomes that are to be achieved. The higher the management level the more degrees of freedom in performing tasks.

Formal and Material Checks

A formal check establishes the correspondence between procedures and recordings or information. In this case *Soll* consists of procedures issued based on management directives. Material checks establish the correspondence between actual positions and events and the recording of or information on those positions and events. Here, actual positions and events represent *Soll*. For both formal and material checks *Ist* is the recording of or information on the positions and events. Establishing the presence of a warehouse manager's signature on a receiving report to reflect actual receipts of the goods is an example of a formal check. A related material check is examining the correspondence between the inventory as recorded in the general ledger and the inventory present in the warehouse (established by physical inventory counts).

Negative and Positive Checks

A negative check establishes the completeness of a recording, whereas a positive check establishes the validity of a recording. Validity has a very specific meaning in this context, namely permissibility. The terms negative and positive refer to the starting point of the check. The starting point of a positive check is the variable that is to be checked, for example a list of accounts receivable balances. The starting point of a negative check is the complement of the variable to be checked, e.g. an independently created list of cash receipts.

Because of their nature, negative checks can never be performed on a sample basis. Instead, sometimes it is possible to perform a positive check on the complement of the object to be checked because this helps to establish completeness. This is possible mainly when there is reduction of revenues due to discounts or underutilization of fixed capacity. For instance, to verify the completeness of revenues of an apartment rental company, *Soll* can be established based on the fixed capacity of apartments, subtracting apartments that are not rented out and performing a positive check on the latter (were those apartments really empty?). In performing these checks one applies both the relationship between offers and yields and the relationship between positions and events.

Policy Control

Policy controls evaluate the quality of decisions regarding the long-term strategy of the organization. This is a form of control that has traditionally received minor attention in internal control. Auditors generally never stepped into the entrepreneur's shoes to decide how good an entrepreneur he was. Therefore, not many measures have been developed to perform this type of control. Because both the auditor and controller are required to increase their knowledge of the business domain to adequately perform their duties this control has increased in importance in the past few years. In addition, the broad definition of internal control pro-moted by the COSO report suggests policy control should receive more attention.

Standards Control

Considering the meaning of checking, i.e. comparing with standards or norms, the necessity of assessing the acceptability of standards seems self-evident. If standards are insufficiently reliable then controls or checks based on those standards are meaningless. In many cases establishing the absolute validity of stand-ards will not be possible and the best that can be done is establishing the acceptability of those standards. However, sometimes the validity of standards can be verified. For example, actual results cannot be com-pared to budgets until it has been established that the cost and revenue categories have been included in the budget and the arithmetical validity of the budget has been evaluated.

Expectations Control

Expectations controls verify the realism of expectations and prognoses that underlie policies. In this respect the necessity of expectations control is just as self-evident as is the necessity of standards control. As with policy control, expectations control has not received wide attention in the past and, similarly, not many control measures have been developed to perform this control.

Authority Control

Competency control is applied to prevent unauthorized officers from gaining access to certain areas and/or certain organizational assets (including computer hardware), using software and reading and changing computer files. Competency control is a formal control since it verifies whether organizational activities are conducted in conformity with applicable procedures and requirements.

Progress Control

Progress controls relate to the continuity of operational processes, in particular to the timeliness and valid-ity of the execution of these processes in conformity with applicable standards. Progress control is based on feedforward and feedback principles: feedforward relates to managing (processes in) an organization, whereas feedback relates to adjusting (processes in) an organization. This can be clarified by means of the steering paradigm and the basic pattern of information provision discussed in 'The Steering Paradigm' (p. 40) and 'The Basic Pattern of Information Provision' (p. 44), respectively. In terms of the steering para-digm the control system is the controlling entity and the controlled system is an operational process. The information system is the nerve centre of progress control, since it records progress-related information and compares this information to established norms and standards. In terms of feedback, progress-related data is input into the system. By means of a programmed procedure in the programme module 'progress control' the associated standard is retrieved from the data file 'standards' and realization is compared to this standard. If there are deviations then the control system adjusts either process execution or the standards.

Feedforward activities are of a more proactive nature. Data are sent to the information system concurrent with controlling the operational process. Based on a comparison of these data with applicable standards (and based on expected outcomes), the information system will send signals to the controlling entity, which adjusts the control activities.

Efficiency Control

Efficiency control evaluates the optimization of operations in terms of adequate cost control versus adequate realization of objectives. Standards to be applied in efficiency control strongly depend on the strategic choices of management. For example, a lower cost level is a more appropriate goal for a cost leadership strategy than for a focus strategy.

Execution Control

The purpose of execution control is to verify whether delegated tasks are performed in accordance with the related task assignment(s). Execution control can be performed directly or indirectly, and at different hierarchical levels. Two examples of execution control are controlling the progress in a production process by applying measurement points in a production line and implementing corrective control measures based on feedforward or feedback information; and establishing that during the weekly meetings of the executive board attention is paid to solving structural customer complaints.

Custody Control

In line with the internal control objective of the safeguarding of assets, custody control aims to prevent unauthorized physical access to the organization's assets. In this respect the distinction between material and immaterial becomes increasingly important since more and more Western organizations are moving their production activities to low-wage countries. For this reason material assets are losing importance in Western economies. Immaterial assets, however, have gained importance, requiring a related change of focus in custody control. Physical controls become less important, in favour of logical custody control (e.g. passwords). Note: physical controls remain important since the dominance of computers requires physical protection of hardware against unauthorized use as well as catastrophes to assure continuity.

Programmed Controls

By means of programmed procedures, programmed controls establish deviations from standards and norms. Programmed controls are always part of application software. This includes edit checks that help determine whether computer input meets certain requirements, (reconciliation of) batch and hash totals and exception reports. An example of an edit check is a procedure that forces users to completely fill out all fields in a menu before users can access the next menu. A simpler example is checking whether a client number consists of x numbers. An example of a reconciliation of a batch total is a manual computation of the total monetary amount of a batch of sales invoices, manual input of this total together with all individual invoices, automated computation of a similar batch total based on the input invoices and comparison of this total to the manually computed computer total. This control helps to establish completeness and validity of input. An equivalent control based on a hash total would incorporate not just the invoiced amounts, but all numbers on the invoice (including date, client number, order number and so on). In short, this amounts to adding apples and oranges. As an example of automated exception reports, a management report could include all budget variances that exceed a certain range, or a list of all accounts receivable for which credit entries other than those related to cash receipts have been made.

Programmed controls can already be built into the system software or hardware. These are called system controls rather than programmed controls. For example, when a data file is read, a relevant system control is to read the file twice and compare the two versions before the file is released for further processing.

Integrity Controls

Integrity controls are comparable to controls for reliability. Where the term reliability is usually reserved for information, the term integrity is usually employed in relation to information *systems*. Integrity controls are particularly applied to programs and data collections. In general integrity controls are a combination of manual controls and programmed controls. Integrity controls are always applied in the computer department (computing centre, automation department, etc.). Three main categories of integrity controls are usually distinguished:

- Integrity controls related to the design of information systems. These controls should make sure that the appropriate programs are incorporated into the information system in an effective way (both at the time of completion of the system and later, after changes to the system have been made). These implementation controls include controls related to the design, testing and introduction of new information systems and adjustments, including accompanying documentations.
- Integrity controls related to the security of information systems. These computer security controls should make sure that no unauthorized changes can be made in programmes and data collections. This includes both physical and logical security controls.
- Integrity controls related to the functioning of information systems. These controls relate to consistent use of the appropriate programs. This includes formal controls on compliance with procedure regulations, as well as controls related to the correct installation of programs and data storage.

User Controls

User controls are controls executed by the users of information systems. Therefore, these controls are not applied *through* the system, but *around* the system, by critically evaluating the input and output. By their nature, these controls are mainly automated, although they can relate to automated data processing. There are three main categories of user controls:

- User controls not related to automated data processing. For example, checking that everything has been input into the information system;

- User controls that rely on effective programmed controls. For example, when supply shortages are examined based on an automated list of missing inventory, it should be reasonably sure that this list is valid and complete; and
- User controls related to the appropriate functioning of programmed controls. For example, checking the validity and completeness of a printed invoice.

Conclusion

The concepts introduced in the current chapter can be helpful to the user in building an internal control system. Setting up such a system requires risk assessment, including identification of risks, assessing the consequences of these risks and implementing internal control measures.

There are two basic approaches to setting up an internal control system. One approach is based on the typology of organizations, a framework that distinguishes different types of organizations from an internal control perspective. For example, we can distinguish trade organizations, production organizations and service organizations. Each type of organization has a number of idiosyncratic risks that need to be addressed by means of certain internal controls. Another approach is based on transaction processes, that occur within organizations, such as a purchasing process, a sales process, a production process, an accounting process, or a human resources process. We will refer to this approach as the process approach. Using the process approach, risks are identified (and controls are implemented) per process. These two approaches may seem different, but obviously every organization can be characterized by a number of processes, thus resulting in a matrix of types of organizations and processes. Simple reasoning would suggest that there are no differences between both approaches because the sum of separate analyses of risks per process within one organization should be equal to the integral analysis of risks of that one organization. Since both approaches are used in practice we cover both approaches in this textbook. Chapters 6 to 11 discuss the process approach, including the purchasing process, the inventory process, the production process, the sales process and various other processes. Chapters 12 to 18 discuss the typology approach, including trade organizations, production organizations, service organizations and governmental and other not-for profit organizations.

Summary

This chapter provides an overview of the most important concepts in internal control. It should be emphasized that the goal of this chapter is not to provide ready-made solutions for internal control problems. Instead, we provide the building blocks to be used at a later stage to design such solutions. Internal control terminology includes such terms as internal control according to the COSO report, control environment, risk assessment, risk map, control activities, information and communication and monitoring. Cornerstones of internal control that are discussed include the steering paradigm, the management cycle, the basic pattern of information provision and the value cycle. In subsequent chapters we will frequently refer to these cornerstones.

Endnotes

1. The five participating institutes were: the American Accounting Association, the Financial Executives Institute, the Institute of Internal Auditors, the American Institute of Certified Public Accountants and the Institute of Management Accountants.
2. Note that an updated version of the COSO report was published in 1994, which included the original report (consisting of the three volumes: *Executive Summary*, the *Framework* and *Evaluation Tools*) as well as an addendum, *Reporting to External Parties*, issued in May 1994.
3. The GAO is an independent institution that supervises the correct spending of United States taxpayers' money. It is the audit, evaluation and investigative arm of the United States Congress. From the organization's founding in June 1921, when it was designated as a government establishment independent of the executive branch, until July 2004, GAO was an abbreviation for General Accounting Office. The current name was established as part of the GAO Human Capital Reform Act.
4. According to *Auditing Standard No. 5: An Audit of Internal Control that Is Integrated with an Audit of Financial Statements*, issued by the Public Company Accounting Oversight Board (PCAOB) in 2007, a material weakness in internal control '. . . is a deficiency, or a combination of deficiencies, in internal control over financial reporting, such that there is a reasonable possibility that a material misstatement of the company's annual or interim financial statements will not be prevented or detected on a timely basis . . .'. A significant deficiency in internal control is '. . . a deficiency, or a combination of deficiencies, in internal control over financial reporting that is less severe than a material weakness, yet important enough to merit attention by those responsible for oversight of the company's financial reporting . . .' (PCAOB, 2007, 433).
5. For instance, the *Guidance on Assessing Control* by the Canadian Institute of Chartered Accountants and *Internal Control – Guidance for Directors on the Combined Code* (also called the Turnbull report after its chairman Nigel Turnbull) by the Institute of Chartered Accountants in England and Wales are also considered proper frameworks.
6. Although Deming made the PDCA cycle popular, Walter Shewart of Bell Laboratories should be considered the actual inventor of this concept.

Bridging the Gap between Internal Control and Management Control

Introduction

The term control has many different meanings. The term is usually accompanied by an adjective. Management control and internal control are arguably the most visible manifestations of control concepts. Management control and internal control have many characteristics in common, yet there are some significant differences. Historically, management control and internal control have evolved independently from one another. However, the last few decades have shown a convergence which has led to much confusion among academics, standard setters, practitioners and students. Hence it is important to investigate where these concepts meet and how remaining differences can be resolved. This chapter explores the boundaries of management control and internal control. To do so, an overview of management control systems is given.

Learning Goals of the Chapter

After having studied this chapter, the reader will understand:

- the difference between hard and soft controls;
- the relationship between internal controls and management controls;
- the differences and similarities between control classifications that have been developed in the field of management control in the last few decades;
- the trade-off between control and innovation.

A Management Control Framework

Along with the hierarchical levels within organizations, we can also identify management control levels. Anthony (1965), who can be considered the godfather of management control, developed a control framework that consists of three layers: strategic planning, management control and operational control. In his view operational (or task) control is the process of ensuring that specific tasks are carried out effectively and efficiently. Strategic planning is the process of deciding on objectives of the organization, on changes in these objectives, on the resources used to attain these objectives and on the policies for governing the acquisition, use and disposition of these resources. Within this framework, management control bridges the gap between strategic planning and task control. By applying management controls, managers ensure that resources are obtained and used effectively and efficiently in the accomplishment of the organization's objectives. This framework has stood the test of time. However, in contemporary texts more attention is paid to the human factor in controlling organizations. Management control, in a contemporary view, focuses on influencing employees' organizational behaviour. To influence employees' organizational behaviour managers can choose among various types of management control. Figure 3.1 shows the framework this chapter draws upon to explain the essence of management control and its interrelationship with internal control.

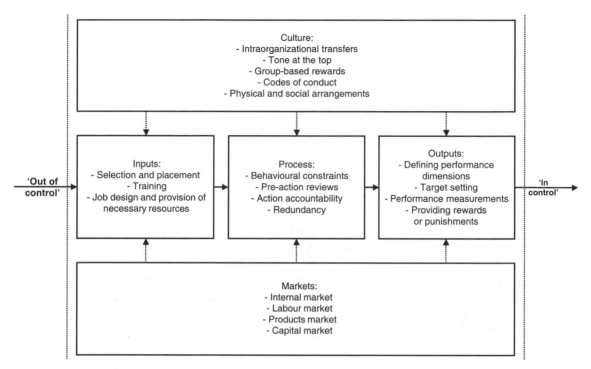

Figure 3.1   A management control framework.

Avoiding Management Control Problems

The classification as developed by Merchant (1982; see also Merchant and Van der Stede, 2007) makes a distinction between action controls, results controls, cultural and personnel controls. We will refer to these as objects of control. The goal of this classification is to demarcate a set of controls for each object of control. This classification may then serve as a sort of checklist that can be applied in the design of control systems on the operational level. Hence, this framework can easily be used for developing control systems that are aimed at the effective and economical execution of specific tasks.

The framework is based on the presumption that control is a critical function of management. Management control problems may lead to losses and even bankruptcy. Management control systems may be ineffective. The causes of deficient management control systems may be lack of direction, motivational problems and personal limitations. The first step towards mitigating risks is to try to avoid control problems. By avoidance organizations reduce their exposure to management control problems. There are four ways of doing so:

- activity elimination
- automation
- centralization
- risk sharing.

Activity elimination means that management turns over the potential profits and risks of a certain activity to a third party. The reasons for doing so may be that management feels they do not have the required knowledge or skills to perform this activity efficiently, that they expect legal problems or that the organization does not have the necessary resources. For example, information system operation is increasingly outsourced because management believes that certain third party specialists have superior task-specific knowledge and are able to employ it more efficiently. Automation is accomplished by deploying computerized systems. Unlike humans, computers are absolutely consistent in their behaviour, never have dishonest or disloyal motivations and are always accurate. Computers can enforce a certain sequence of activities and hence make systems foolproof. For example, in order to be able to input data into the second screen of a program module, the first screen must have been completed. The term foolproof can be taken literally when considering the impossibility of putting one's hand into a microwave oven and then switching it on. The person who is trying to do this will soon find out that this is impossible because the door must first be closed to start the microwave oven. Centralization means that decisions are made at a central point within the organization. Usually this is top management. The problem of trying to influence the behaviour of others is mitigated by simply not assigning authority to others. One can argue whether the exposure to control problems can really be reduced by centralization since allocating all decision-making authority to top management may result in too large a scope of control. A scope of control that is too large may lead to information overload and suboptimal decision-making. As a result managers may fail to effectively manage their subordinates. The solution to this paradox lies in the centralization of key decisions only. Thus, not all decision-making authority should be centralized. Of course, the main problem is to find a right balance between centralization and decentralization. We will elaborate further on this topic in our discussion of Simons' levers of control at the end of this chapter (Simons, 1994). In a way, risk sharing is comparable to activity elimination. However, when sharing risks activities are only partially eliminated. As in activity elimination there is usually a contract that exactly specifies the rights and obligations of the risk sharing parties. For example, insuring against business loss in case of fire or other events that lead to a temporary discontinuance of the business; or entering into a joint venture.

For those management control problems that cannot be avoided economically, preventive or detective controls must be designed. In our management control framework, market controls, cultural controls, input controls, process controls and output controls can be put in place to mitigate the risks that employees engage in undesirable behaviour.

Market Control

A central problem of organizations is that individuals or organizational units who have only partial congruent goals must cooperate. As a matter of fact, the main managerial activity is to have people cooperate to attain the organizational goals. When a team of individuals cooperates to fulfil a specific task assignment, such as the manufacturing of a certain product, then it is important for the welfare of the organization that every member of the team is rewarded in a manner that he perceives as being fair. When at least one member of a team is dissatisfied with his rewards, then he will adjust his efforts to work as a good team member in a downward direction, such that the reward is more in agreement with his efforts. As a result the organization as a whole will be worse off. If we consider our definition of control as all those organizational activities aimed at having organization members cooperate to reach the organization's goals, then it can easily be understood that the real problem of organizations is the management control problem. This notion of control includes problems arising from performance evaluation and appraisal, which is at the heart of contemporary management control systems.

The conceptual framework for the design of organizational control systems as developed by Ouchi (1979) makes a distinction between market control, clan control and bureaucratic control. The goal of this classification is to identify the factors that are germane to prototypes of control mechanisms within an organization. The classification relies heavily on the control of people, trying to provide the instruments for balancing the hiring of qualified people, and the managerial system to instruct, monitor and evaluate the (initially) nonqualified people. The framework, albeit conceptual, is efficient when designing control systems. However, the design parameters are not specific enough to serve as a checklist for developing a mature control system. Hence, it indeed serves as a *conceptual framework* that may form the basis for another, more directly applicable framework, like the objects-of-control classification scheme.

The inclusion of market control is unique in comparison with the other frameworks that are discussed in this chapter because market control is an informal control whereas the other frameworks only contain formal controls. In order to understand the functioning of the market as an enabler of control, a basic understanding of the theory of the firm is necessary.

The fundamental problem in designing an organization from an accounting point of view is how to communicate the information that its members use for planning, given that such information does not exist in a concentrated form, but merely as a highly dispersed set of incomplete and often contradictory bits and pieces that stem from the separate individuals' knowledge bases. Planning involves the complex of interrelated decisions about the allocation of available resources. The communication of information for planning purposes may be economized on by means of a market mechanism. This implies that participants only need to know the price to make the right decisions. However, to make a market mechanism work, there is a need for short-term contracting, of which the prices are the outcomes. The question then arises whether this is an efficient mechanism. In 1937, Ronald Coase suggested that there is an alternative mechanism for the market that may be more efficient under certain circumstances. This mechanism, the firm, coordinates the allocation of resources by means of the involvement of an entrepreneur who hires people, making use of long-term contracting, to bring forth products and services. These long-term contracts are of a general nature, only specifying the boundaries of the behaviour of the people hired. By introducing the concept of transaction costs, the theory of the firm argues that the hierarchical relationships between the entrepreneur and his employees may be better coordination mechanisms than markets.

There have been several attempts to extend the economic theory of the firm by integrating it with the behavioural theory of the firm (Cyert and March, 1963). As will be demonstrated later, most soft control mechanisms like clan controls (Ouchi), boundary systems, interactive control systems, beliefs systems (Simons) and cultural controls (Merchant) are much more rooted in the behavioural theory of the firm than in its economic counterpart. After these integrative attempts, various efforts were undertaken to develop a more specific theory of the firm. The resource-based view attempts to explain firm value from managerial involvement in combining resources and capabilities. On this view, the firm is a unique bundle of idiosyncratic resources. Later on in this chapter we will discuss the meaning of knowledge as the most important resource in contemporary organizations, which paves the path toward a knowledge-based theory of the firm.

The neo-classical price theory looks at organizations as black boxes. This implies that questions about how the internal organization is set up, or why a certain internal organization is chosen, are not asked, let alone answered. Relationships between an organization and the outside world only consist of purchase contracts for the acquisition of resources and sales contracts for revenue generation. On this view the organization is merely a production function. Prices to be paid for resources and to be charged for products and services sold are determined in the market by means of the market mechanism. In a perfect market this mechanism ensures that prices contain all the information necessary for efficient decision-making. A perfect market is frictionless. In such a market:

- there are many sellers and buyers;
- products and services are homogeneous;
- there are no entry barriers;
- all organizational goals can be reduced to the simple objective of profit maximization;
- there is no governmental interference; and
- production factors are completely mobile.

Prices then exactly represent the value of a product or service. As a result of this perfect information, decision-makers need no information other than these prices. Consequently, in a frictionless market there is no need for formal organizations to exist because entrepreneurs will continuously enter into ad hoc contracts with the owners of production factors. This is exactly what was suggested in the 1930s and 1940s by theorists like Coase (1937) and Hayek (1945). However, markets generally are not perfect. The frictions that cause market imperfections can be classified into four categories: transaction costs, social–psychological factors, taxes and endowments and institutional impediments.

Transaction Costs

Transaction costs are those costs involved in preparing, concluding and realizing contracts, and enforcing the obligations as agreed upon in those contracts. For example, costs of collecting information on potential vendors, prices and other terms of delivery, costs of consulting advisers, costs of a public notary, costs of internal control systems for checking compliance with contractual arrangements and costs of lawsuits.

Social–psychological Factors

Social–psychological factors are noneconomic by nature. People may have certain preferences or aversions that cannot be justified on economic grounds. Yet these preferences or aversions may have a severe impact on the functioning of the price mechanism. For example, there may be vendors or buyers that have connections with disgraced political regimes, criminal organizations or ideological organizations; there may also be vendors' or buyers' representatives that are considered sympathetic or unpleasant.

Taxes and Endowments

Taxes and endowments lead to product and service heterogeneity because they create price differences that are not in accordance with the underlying characteristics of the products and services. For example, because of differences in tax systems one country may gain competitive advantage at the cost of the other country; or protectionist government subsidies are aimed at providing greater competitive power to the recipients of endowments.

Institutional Impediments

Institutional impediments may take the form of governmental regulations or private contracts that limit individual market parties' discretionary actions. For example, during World War II, in some European countries food was only available to those who had so-called food tickets; or in modern business, insider trading regulations, limited permission to buy and sell shares of limited liability companies; and European Union milk quotas.

When controlling organizations, market control is certainly not the only system managers can rely upon. Bureaucratic control and clan control may be far more efficient or even the only feasible control systems to employ. There are two mechanisms that underlie the classification of market control, bureaucratic control and clan control: social mechanisms and informational mechanisms.

Social Mechanisms

The social mechanism in market control is limited to norms of reciprocity. A norm of reciprocity should assure that, if one party in a market transaction tries to cheat another, the cheater is punished by all members of the community in which that market transaction is completed. The severity of the punishment will typically far exceed the crime. For example, if you steal something, your hand will be chopped off. The social mechanisms in bureaucratic control are norms of reciprocity and legitimate authority. Legitimate authority in combination with norms of reciprocity imply that people hand over autonomy to their superiors in exchange for pay without risk and accept the idea that superiors have the right to take over that autonomy and engage in command and control activities. The social mechanisms in clan control are not limited to norms of reciprocity and legitimate authority, but also include a shared set of values and beliefs. Clan control relies a great deal upon agreement on what constitutes proper behaviour. For example, within the Scottish clans there used to be widespread consensus about how to behave towards the other clan members, and also about how to behave towards members of other clans. In modern organizations, there is a tendency to rely on clan control as the primary control system. However, since the social requirements to enable this are extremely demanding, the bureaucracy is often the only possible system, especially when there is a high personnel turnover.

Informational Mechanisms

Informational mechanisms, like social mechanisms, vary greatly between control systems. Market control requires valid and complete information on prices in order to make the price mechanism function properly. For example, if a person wants to buy a specific type of computer at the lowest possible price, he will want to search the Internet for all the potential vendors of this type of computer and maybe start negotiating with each of them to get the lowest possible price. However, there may be vendors that he could not find on the Internet but that offer even lower prices than those he received. Here price information may be incomplete and hence the price mechanism of vendors adjusting their prices or exiting the market may not work properly. As we have already indicated there are not many, if any, true markets. However, the preceding example of an Internet search for the lowest prices is not a random choice. The Internet makes markets much more transparent and may pave the path for enhanced market functioning in the near future. Yet, we still face the situation where most markets are imperfect and price mechanisms do not work. In that case the bureaucracy will take over the coordinating role. The informational mechanism for the bureaucracy is a set of explicit rules for members of the bureaucracy (the employees) about what actions to take under specific circumstances. In internal control jargon we refer to these rules as procedures and when these procedures are authorized by management, we refer to them as management guidelines. However, rules may be difficult or impossible to specify in advance. In that case, the social mechanism of legitimate authority will allow the internal control system to incompletely specify the duties of an employee, and instead have management specify the duties as the need arises. In internal control jargon such terms as supervision, command and control, delegation, accountability and monitoring are used to refer to the set of managerial activities involved with ad hoc duty specification. The control system that requires the least advanced informational mechanism is clan control. Here, all the information is contained in the traditions of the organization. In a clan, an outsider cannot, or can only at very high cost, gain access to information regarding the decision rules used. Because information is predominantly implicit in clans, the roles of the accountant and information manager are marginal.

If some people have more or better information than others, then this is called information asymmetry. In agency relationships, a principal (e.g. a manager) and an agent (e.g. a subordinate) communicate in order to close transactions or, in general, to fulfil specific goals. Because agents are closer to the operations and the market there is a great chance that they have more and superior information at their disposal than their principals. For example, a warehouse clerk steals goods from the warehouse and reports these goods as being obsolete. The manager who receives this report must put a control system in place to ensure that the warehouse clerk is not lying. In general, there are two threats evolving from information asymmetry:

- adverse selection; and
- moral hazard.

Adverse Selection

In new principal–agent relationships, agents that are in bad faith will be inclined to engage in that relationship under less favourable conditions than those agents that are in good faith. They will do so because they know that their information advantage allows them to gain a profit at the cost of the principal. Adverse selection takes place at the closing of a contract. For example, people that are inclined to lodge a fake claim with their insurance company will accept paying higher premiums than people who will only lodge valid claims.

Moral Hazard

Every person bears within him the risk that he will behave unethically if the opportunity is there. Moral hazard may then take place on execution of a contract. For example, a person knows that insurance companies have great difficulties checking the validity of a claim, and exploits this knowledge by lodging fake claims.

The threats evolving from information asymmetry are behavioural in nature. Since behavioural threats can be mitigated by means of typical management controls as well as typical internal controls, the following controls are applicable:

* Monitoring and reporting systems including analytical review of agents' performances. Such a system may include comparisons with other agents, other years and budgets.
* Performance-based rewards like the bonus/malus system applied by insurance companies.
* Limiting the freedom of action of agents by means of boundary systems and making effective use of programmed procedures.
* Maintaining a contract register by an independent role. This register will provide the 'Soll' position for a check on the realization of the contracts.
* Systematic selection and placement of agents by means of personality tests and screening.
* Establishing clear procedures on who is authorized under what circumstances and in what situation.

The following section elaborates on various types of management control and hence with the means of handling problems stemming from information asymmetry.

Cultural Control

Cultural controls can be effectuated by creating a coherent culture within an organization. This can be accomplished by exploiting shared traditions, norms, beliefs, values, ideologies, attitudes and behaviours. There are five complementary instruments that enable a coherent organizational culture:

* codes of conduct
* group-based rewards
* intraorganizational transfers
* physical and social arrangements
* tone at the top.

Codes of conduct: these may appear in various formats. In a broad sense codes of conduct take the form of codes of ethics, corporate principles, credos, mission statements, vision statements or communications of management's philosophy. These statements have in common that they are codified and intended to shape organizational culture. For example, a code of conduct of a commercial bank contains a section on insider trading stating that it is forbidden to own shares or any other interest in one of the bank's clients. However, codes of conduct need not be formulated so negatively. For example, the mission of DuPont is briefly formulated as: 'The DuPont Company will conduct its business affairs with the highest ethical standards and work diligently to be a respected corporate citizen worldwide'.

Group-based rewards: these should contribute to employees cooperating to attain shared goals. Group-based rewards, as opposed to individual performance-based rewards, imply that a group of employees will receive exactly the same reward if a certain task is successfully completed. Any individual trying to gain a personal advantage at the expense of his team members will be rebuked by means of some kind of social mechanism. Hence, it can be reasonably expected that group-based rewards promote goal congruence and consensus on how to accomplish these goals.

Intraorganizational transfers: these tend to improve socialization processes of individuals throughout the organization. This is done by regularly transferring employees from one department, job assignment, business unit or geographical location to another. By following this policy, employees develop a helicopter view of the organization as a result of which they will think more holistically and act more in accordance with organizational goals instead of subunit goals. For example, a major commercial bank hires management trainees with a master's degree, has them participate in a long-term traineeship programme and transfers them every three years to another part of the organization and (most of the time) another type of function. By doing so, these management trainees develop an overview of the entire organization and learn to break down the despised box mentality.

Physical and social arrangements: these help shape a desirable corporate culture in that they contain hidden messages about how people communicate and dress, how offices are furnished, how the organization's buildings are set up, what cars are driven, how technology is employed and most importantly what gives the organization its *droit à l'existence*. For example, a public accounting firm wants to convey the message that it is able to take good care of its clients because it also is able to take good care of itself. For that reason they have an extremely luxurious office building, with art all around, and their people drive classy cars.

Tone at the top: this is often considered one of the most abused and misunderstood concepts in management control. It is about management giving the right example to their subordinates. By setting the proper tone at the top, management provides the most important contribution to shaping the organizational culture. Tone at the top can be defined as:

> The consistency between managers' behaviour and their statements.

The more consistency there is between managers' behaviour and their statements, the stronger the organizational culture.

An organization can gain from a strong culture by employing it for control purposes. Hence a relationship exists between the five cultural control instruments and the degree of control. For example, the stronger the tone at the top becomes, the higher the degree of control will be.

Input Control

Input controls can be effectuated by combining the following three types of management controls:

* selection and placement
* training
* job design and provision of necessary resources.

From a management control viewpoint, these controls can be considered personnel controls.

Selection and placement: this means that the right people must be selected for a certain job position. For example, if an accounting clerk is needed, then the selection process may encompass verifying that he has mastered the technique of double entry bookkeeping. In the selection process three categories of judgement criteria can be distinguished: education, experience and personality. Personality in particular is difficult to measure. Yet organizations spend a lot of their time trying to find out if a person has such a personality structure that she will probably fit into the organization and her job assignment. Experience is a somewhat ambiguous concept. It may be task-specific or general, it may or may not have led to expertise and its interaction with personality and education is not very well understood despite massive research efforts in both accounting and cognitive psychology.

Training: ideally this should lead to employees thinking and acting in the same way as management would do under similar circumstances. This would save scarce managerial resources for strategy formulation instead of serving as an organization's watchdog. Many organizations use formal as well as informal training in order to improve the performance of their personnel. Formal training takes place in the classroom and may be in-company or outsourced. Informal training is training-on-the-job whereby peers and supervisors, as well as subordinates, provide feedback to newly hired personnel to make them learn as efficiently as possible.

Job design: this is a necessary condition to help individual employees act appropriately so that they will have a high probability of success in their job performance. Part of job design is the *provision of necessary material resources* to the employees assigned to do the job. For example, if management expects a sales person to visit customers on a regular basis, he should have a car at his disposal.

Personnel controls will contribute to organization members feeling some kind of commitment towards the organization and as a result needing no external motivators to strive for organizational goal attainment. In order to be able to assess the right approach to control tightness, the form of commitment that goes with each of the three control systems within the conceptual framework for the design of organizational control systems as developed by Ouchi is a helpful framework for analysis. If people are hired without any form of selection, then the applicable control system is market control. Here, the assumption is that the level of the price the organization pays for a newly hired worker – i.e. her salary or fee – will induce her to internalize the organization's objectives. Because of the existing norms of reciprocity there will be some kind of self-selection among potential workers. As a result they will not need to be monitored in order to have them work towards optimizing the organization's performance. However, if this self-selection mechanism does not work, and adverse selection or moral hazard occur, then training and monitoring – often even to a high degree – will be the only effective people treatments. So, if there is a selection process, but only a limited one, then the newly hired people must be trained and subsequently monitored, depending on the degree to which selection has taken place. Monitoring involves instructing workers and holding them accountable for their actions taken in following up on these instructions. Training, on the other hand, involves making workers aware of the organizational values and educating them in order that they acquire the needed skills to perform their job appropriately. The applicable control systems are bureaucratic control and clan control if the training involves identification with organizational values and beliefs. If people are thoroughly selected at the gate, then the applicable control system is clan control. By putting a lot of effort into selecting the right people for the right position, referred to as person–task alignment, there is a great chance that people will be committed and hence need less monitoring. Applying tight controls may in that case lead to employees becoming alienated from the organization and hence requiring even tighter controls. Exploiting shared values and beliefs and communicating implicit customs will be the most effective control instruments in that case. So, internalization and identification with organizational values and beliefs are the required forms of commitment when there is a thorough selection at the gate.

Process Control

Process controls are built into an organization's processes. They can be effectuated by combining the following four types of measures:

- behavioural constraints
- pre-action reviews
- action accountability
- redundancy.

From a management control viewpoint, these controls can be considered action controls.

Behavioural constraints: these should make it difficult for people to behave inappropriately. For example, locks on desks, user-IDs and passwords, but also limiting the decision-making authority of a procurement officer to a certain currency amount, and segregation of duties.

Pre-action reviews: these involve discussing and scrutinizing the plans of the inviduals being controlled. The reviewer can then suggest modifications, give tips on how to execute the plans or ask for a more detailed plan before final approval is given. For example, an audit partner scrutinizes the audit plan together with the audit team. Pre-action reviews may be formal, but also very informal. For example, a hallway chat on the progress of a certain activity may provide just the feedback needed for controlling these activities.

Action accountability: this aims to hold people accountable for the actions they have undertaken and the decisions they have made. Action accountability controls are most effective if the desired actions are well communicated, the employees understand what is expected of them and they feel confident that their actions will lead to rewards if well executed or punishment if badly executed. For example, a fast food chain has detailed formalized procedures for almost everything that must be done. Newly hired employees get acquainted with these procedures through training programmes and the store manager is rewarded or punished if his people do or do not comply with these directives.

Redundancy: this involves putting more than one person to a certain task, performing certain activities more than once or in general assigning multiple resources to a certain task. For example, a person makes a calculation and re-calculates for checking purposes. In internal control this would be called a self-check. A certain activity may also be performed twice by two different people. For example, in the pre-automation era, insurance companies used to have so-called parallel administrations. At the end of a process the outputs of these parallel administrations were compared with one another and reconciled by an internal control function. Nowadays insurance companies still make use of redundancy controls, having a primary information system and a back-up information system called a data-processing hot site. The back-up system can be reverted to immediately if the primary system has gone down. In general, this form of redundancy is frequently applied in organizations with massive data-processing activities such as banks, insurance companies, pension funds, and also large telephone providers, Internet providers and Internet stores who rely heavily on electronic data processing.

Output Control

Output controls can be effectuated by the following four steps:

- defining performance dimensions and performance measures
- setting targets for the performance measures
- measuring performance
- providing rewards or punishments.

From a management control viewpoint, these controls can be considered results controls.

Results controls are indirect controls, meaning that they are not applicable to activities or processes, but rather to outcomes of activities and processes. For results controls to be effective, the people that are controlled must know what is expected of them and must be able to influence the results by behaving appropriately. In addition, the results must be accurately and objectively measurable, must be provided on time and be understandable. The higher the hierarchical level, the more applicable results controls will be as compared with action controls. For example, the foreman (operational management) of a cleaning company may try to control his workers by supervising them on the job, watching them execute their assigned tasks and giving additional instructions if task execution is not in accordance with an implicit or explicit plan (action accountability). The top manager of that very same cleaning company will not want to scrutinize the activities of his people but will mainly be interested in the results of the cleaning activities, asking himself the question: will the customer be satisfied with the service quality in relation to the price offered? This result of the cleaning activities may be measured by means of client satisfaction surveys, or sample-based checking as to whether the cleaned spaces are as clean as agreed. In both instances the top manager will only be interested in exception reports. On an even more aggregate level, the top manager may want to know if the company is gaining or losing market share, or how shareholder value is developing.

The Relationship between Management Control and Internal Control

There are some significant differences between management control and internal control. However, these differences have been subject to change during the evolution of both disciplines. Internal control has a long history in some continental European countries. In the US, the internal control notion did not come into play until the late 1940s. Management control, on the other hand, seems to have a more Anglo-Saxon tradition. However, it is hard to deny that disciplines like internal control and management control must have originated when the first businesses were founded. It was not until certain critical complexity levels were reached (e.g. separation between ownership and leadership, strict separation between white collar and blue collar workers, multi-product businesses, vertical integration, diversification and third party finance constructions) that the disciplines became codified in textbooks and journals, taught in schools and considered to discuss themes relevant for practice and theory.

In brief we believe that the main differences between management control and internal control are as follows:

- Management control is driven by strategy, whereas internal control is driven by transactions.
- Management control focuses on influencing decision-making whereas internal control focuses on supporting decision-making.
- Management control has a predominant behavioural orientation whereas internal control has a more mechanistic orientation.

The integral control framework as introduced in Chapter 1 provides guidance for a positioning of management control and internal control. When we try to make a synthesis of these fields, management control seems to have evolved from strategy implementation problems. Hence the driver of management control is strategy. Internal control, on the other hand, seems to have evolved from the need to organize transactions within and between firms. Hence the driver of internal control is the transaction. Management control thus starts from the upper layer in the integral control framework and proceeds top-down towards strategy implementation. Internal control, on the other hand, starts from the lower layer in the framework and proceeds bottom-up to meet with management control. A second difference between the disciplines is that management control tries to influence employees' organizational decision-making, whereas internal control tries to support people's organizational decision-making by helping to provide reliable information. A third difference is that management control seeks to realize its goals by means of behavioural measures, whereas internal control seeks to do this by means of mechanistic measures, including procedures, checks and balances and segregations of duties, disregarding the human factor.

The last few decades have shown a convergence between management control and internal control. The definition and internal control components as discerned by the COSO report are illustrative of this observation. For example, the control environment in the COSO report '. . . sets the tone of an organization, influencing the control consciousness of its people . . .' (COSO, 1992). Figure 3.2

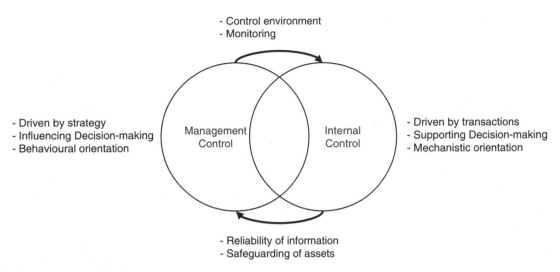

- Control environment
- Monitoring

- Driven by strategy
- Influencing Decision-making
- Behavioural orientation

Management Control

Internal Control

- Driven by transactions
- Supporting Decision-making
- Mechanistic orientation

- Reliability of information
- Safeguarding of assets

Figure 3.2   The relationship between management control and internal control.

summarizes the differences, similarities and complementarities of management control and internal control.

Control and Innovation

As we demonstrated in the section entitled 'Market Control' (p. 60), knowledge creation and knowledge integration are key to successful organizations. Should we want to develop a knowledge-based theory of the firm, it is important to assume that we do not want to explain the existence of organizations as mechanisms that deal with the shortcomings of markets. Although this view is common for the theory of the firm, we prefer to distinguish factors that explain why some organizations are more successful than others. Yet there are some fundamental concerns of the general theory of the firm that are highly relevant for a knowledge-based theory of the firm. The general theory of the firm – which is also termed the contractual theory – provides a basis for the development of a knowledge-based theory of the firm. Issues to be dealt with are the nature of coordination within the firm, the organizational structure, the role of management, the allocation of decision-making authority, the determinants of firm boundaries and the way in which competitive advantage is sought by means of innovation. It is within this arena the relationship between control and innovation must be further investigated.

The relationship between control and innovation is tense. If a manager wants his people to be creative, and hence engage in innovative actions, he must be prepared to give up control, empower his people and cease monitoring their activities. Only then can creativity flourish. On the other hand, that manager wants positive events to occur and negative events to be avoided, i.e. he wants his organization to be in control. In order to deal with this managerial problem of balancing innovation and control, Harvard professor Robert

Simons developed a classification – the levers of control – that distinguishes interactive control systems, boundary systems, diagnostic control systems and beliefs systems. The explicit goal of this classification is to balance innovation and control. Before entering into a detailed discussion of this framework it must be reckoned that it is only applicable for the development of a raw sketch of a control system because the concrete design parameters that may result are highly anecdotal and global. Also, there is still no empirical evidence of the efficiency of this framework. Moreover, the framework does not put forward any theory. It is about how to design and employ controls in a practical contemporary setting.

In balancing control and innovation IT plays a special role. IT deployment can contribute to the codification and diffusion of information as a result of which the functioning of the levers of control may be improved, and hence control problems may be mitigated when innovation is at stake. Codification refers to the formalization of information into fixed structures and patterns. For example, data about a sales transaction can easily be captured in a ledger. Since a ledger is based on fixed structures, the information on this transaction can be codified. On the other hand, gossip about a manager being fired is difficult to codify within a pre-formatted structure. Diffusion refers to the proliferation of information throughout an organization or an organization's environment and hence to the degree to which information sharing is possible. For example, the P&L (Profit and Loss) statement can easily be transmitted via the intranet of an organization and hence has a high diffusion potential. On the other hand, classified information on new market opportunities which should be discussed by the board of directors has a low diffusion potential because it is aimed only at a small subset of the organization.

Beliefs systems define the core values of an organization. These beliefs deal with how the organization creates value, the desired performance levels and human relations. These systems give guidance to opportunity-seeking behaviour. For example, mission statements, vision statements and credos. In beliefs systems, uncodified information plays an important role. This information must be distributed via personal channels. IT applications like groupware or e-mail enable such personal communication. Beliefs systems are initiated by an organization's top management, so it is top management which should make effective use of the IT applications to personally communicate their, and hence the organization's, beliefs.

Boundary systems define the risks that must be avoided. They contain formal rules that must be complied with in order to avoid sanctions. A typical feature of boundary systems is that they are always defined negatively, i.e. they state what is forbidden, not what should be done. Boundary systems are aimed at enhancing individual creativity without invoking undesirable behaviour. For example, negatively formulated ('you should not . . . . ') codes of conduct. The information as communicated via boundary systems is unambiguous and usually rule-based. This information need not be personal, but it is of great importance that organization members are well aware of the fact that top management supports these rules, and that they must be complied with. IT enables the continuous monitoring of people's behaviour by automating compliance testing with the applicable behavioural boundaries. However this requires a further codification and diffusion.

In diagnostic control systems the communication and measurement of critical performance variables plays an important role. Diagnostic control systems are aimed at realizing an effective allocation of scarce resources, defining targets, motivating people, determining guidelines for corrective measures and enabling performance evaluation. The ultimate goal of diagnostic control systems is that scarce managerial attention is re-allocated from management to staff who prepare budgets and business performance reports.

Information that is provided by means of diagnostic control systems in highly codified. For example, automation of early warning messages, information about multi-dimensional performance measures and the continuous scanning of critical performance indicators for progress checking. The degree of diffusion could also increase as a result of IT deployment. However, there might be some organizational conditions, such as internal control requirements or avoiding information overload, that prohibit the diffusion of certain information on a large scale. IT offers ample possibilities of enhancing diagnostic control systems, but in designing these systems, it should be borne in mind that they are intended to focus managerial attention on strategy formulation and exception handling rather than continuously monitoring subordinates' actions.

Interactive control systems are aimed at strategic uncertainties – at what keeps managers awake during the night. They are defined as the formal control systems that managers use to involve themselves regularly and personally in the decision activities of subordinates. For example, customer complaints are on the weekly agenda of the board of directors, managers visit the shop-floor, a plant abroad is visited by management on a regular basis or bulletin boards are read by executives. In these systems the content of information is more important than its form. The degree of codification is moderate in the sense that these systems provide the structures for data compression and data categorization and hence serve as catalysts for dialogue and debate about the meaning of information and applicable action plans. For that reason, interactive control systems must be simple to use, so that people throughout the entire organization can understand them. The degree of diffusion of information in such a system is higher than in a diagnostic control system because interactive control systems should stimulate dialogue and information sharing. As such they are important data sources for all managers within the organization. IT can improve the effectiveness of interactive control systems in at least three ways:

- Computers can transform complex data into graphical representations and tables that are easy to understand.
- By means of electronic communication, relevant global market information can be acquired, planning systems that are at lower hierarchical levels within the organization can be provided with the necessary input and information on the buying behaviour of customers and the effectiveness of promotion actions can be obtained.
- Modern data base technologies enable managers to make what-if analyses easily.

Internal control and, more specifically, internal accounting control or information control, constitute the basis for the levers of control. The underlying reasoning is that the information used for making the levers seek a balance between control and innovation must meet certain minimum quality requirements. In particular, the aspect of information reliability is crucial to the proper functioning of the levers of control. Imagine the relationship between internal control and the levers of control as depicted in Figure 3.3. The four levers are bottomless cylinders that can be filled with a liquid that flows into an underlying tank, the internal control system. Irrespective of the cylinder chosen to fill the tank, a cylinder will only be affected by pouring liquid into one of the others if the tank is filled to the rim. In other words, only when the intern control system meets certain minimum requirements can the levers start communicating. Now, given that the tank is filled to the rim, every drop of liquid that is poured into one of the cylinders will start a balance-seeking process that comes to a standstill when the levels of liquid in each of the four cylinders are even.

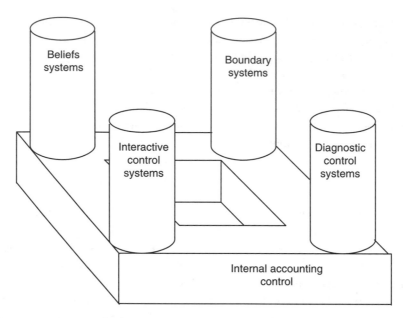

Figure 3.3 The relationship between the levers of control and internal accounting control.

Although conceptually appealing, the visualization of the relationship between the levers of control and internal controls as a system of four cylinders and a tank does not explain how the levers work in practice. To begin with, the levers of control bridge the gap between strategy formulation and strategy implementation. Strategy has several connotations, but we believe that its meaning can be straightforward in a control setting. We do not intend to define strategy nor elaborate on it, but we will mention one of its main characteristics, namely that strategy is always aimed at gaining competitive advantage. In a dynamic and increasingly competitive environment, strategy must include the concept of innovation. Innovation must nowadays be pursued on a continuous basis in order to restrain the competitive forces to which organizations are exposed. From a strategy implementation point of view, the question then arises whether control systems that spawn innovation can be put in place. The levers of control provide the answer to this question because this framework is aimed at controlling an organization's employees and simultaneously stimulating innovation. The beliefs systems and boundary systems both provide the conditions for an organization's goal achievement. The beliefs systems provide the positive signals to people to be creative, whereas the boundary systems serve as the brakes of the organization should people start to engage in so-called hyper goal-oriented behaviour with disregard for applicable laws, guidelines, codes of conduct and other implicit or explicit rules. In order to actually achieve its goals, an organization must put interactive and diagnostic control systems in place. Interactive control systems are needed for the noncybernetic information gathering on potentially harmful or beneficial events, whereas the diagnostic control systems are used for progress control on performance regarding pre-defined targets such as budgets, sales targets or productivity. From another viewpoint, beliefs systems and interactive control systems are aimed at stimulating opportunity-seeking behaviour, and boundary systems and diagnostic control systems are aimed at constraining people's behaviour in order to keep the organization in control. In addition, interactive control systems can be employed on top of any of the other levers, to make them interactive. So, the levers of control constitute a heavily intertwined framework for reconciling the seemingly irreconcilable concepts of control and innovation.

A Combination of Hard and Soft Controls

Control of outputs has become more and more important over the last few decades. The adverse effects of this trend have also become visible. The more performance-based incentives are given, the higher the pressure to perform. If performance cannot be realized as desired, personnel may engage in so-called fraudulent financial reporting. In relation to performance-based pay this means that revenues may be overstated and costs understated. In cultures that are highly individualistic – as in many developed countries, including the USA, the UK and the Netherlands – it is expected that performance-based incentives will be more effective than any other management control. Texts on modern management control systems have been increasingly paying attention to results controls that mostly consist of performance-based incentive systems (e.g. Merchant and van der Stede, 2007). Controls that are aimed at outputs instead of processes are generally more efficient. In addition, output control, being a hard management control, will have quicker effects than most soft controls such as cultural and personnel controls. However, every management control has its limitations. Therefore, in practice a combination of hard and soft controls will probably be the most effective approach. Since no single organization is the same, the required balance between hard and soft controls is situationally dependent.

Summary

Management control (MC) aims to implement strategies. Unlike internal control (IC), management control tries to influence people's behaviour within organizations directly. Hence, MC also encompasses soft controls like cultural and personnel controls, whereas internal control follows a much more mechanistic approach that considers procedures and a system of checks and balances to be the main control instruments. This chapter investigates the relationship between MC and IC. Here we arrive at a potential source of conflict between management and internal control professionals. Management wants to optimize organizational performance by developing products or services the market may want. Internal control professionals want to make recordings of all transactions the company engages in and to provide information that is as reliable as possible and that can be used for controlling the organization. However, this conflict may not be as difficult to resolve as it seems. Finding a balance between innovation and control seems to be the ultimate goal in contemporary organizations. There are several classifications of controls. This chapter discusses the main developments in this field and relates these to the balancing act between control and innovation.

The Dynamics of Control and IT

Introduction

This chapter first introduces different examples of information and communication technology (IT). It does not aspire to be an exhaustive treatment but some important IT issues are put forward. Firstly, IT is defined. The starting point is the functioning of computers and their constituent elements. Here, input and output devices, processing devices, storage devices as well as communication devices are discussed. Information systems are the most overt manifestations of IT, which justifies a brief discussion of information system development as well as a somewhat more elaborate discussion of the components of information systems. Further, some specific examples of contemporary IT applications are discussed because of their impact on modern organizations, including: Enterprise Resource Planning, Data Bases and Data Warehouses, Decision Support Systems, Expert Systems and Neural Networks, Groupware, and Executive Information Systems. Finally, some IT-enabled innovations are discussed including e-business, Business Process Re-engineering, Customer Relationship Management, Business Intelligence and Strategic Enterprise Management, Business Process Management, and Shared Service Centres and outsourcing.

The chapter further discusses the dynamic relationship between IT and internal control. The relationship is dynamic because there is a continuous interaction between internal control systems and IT. Internal controls being influenced by the application of IT can for example be observed when controls migrate from the execution stage to the system development stage when information provision becomes automated, when programmed procedures are employed instead of manual controls or when information security measures are taken to mitigate threats evolving from electronic communication. Here, a distinction can be made between positive and negative effects of IT proliferation on internal control. A positive influence may be anticipated when control problems are avoided by having a programmed procedure in place that forces information system users to follow a fixed sequence of steps in order to fulfil a specific task assignment. A negative influence may be anticipated when measurement points such as the transfer of documents, physical goods or cash from one person to another are integrated in the information system and hence are no longer visible. As a result of these intertwined relationships, any existing balance between internal control and IT is subject to continuous change and hence is dynamic by nature.

Learning Goals of the Chapter

After having studied this chapter, the reader will understand:

* the relationship between IT and information systems;
* the components of information systems;
* the distinctions between the main approaches to information system development;
* the features of some widely used information systems;
* the need for IT professionals and managers to develop a common language;
* the main characteristics of some IT-enabled innovations such as e-business, Business Process Re-engineering, Customer Relationship Management, Business Intelligence and Strategic Enterprise Management, Shared Service Centres and Business Process Management;

- the relationship between Enterprise Resource Planning, Business Process Re-engineering, Shared Service Centres and internal control;
- the role of IT in controlling organizations;
- the strategic importance of information and IT;
- the essence of codes on information security;
- the threats that stem from electronic communication;
- the appropriate measures of information security in relation to the distinguished threats;
- the threats that stem from various IT applications and IT management innovations;
- the appropriate organizational measures of internal control in relation to the distinguished threats.

Information and IT

Information can be defined as all the processed data that contributes to the recipient's understanding of applicable parts of reality whereas communication is the process of sending and receiving data or information (see also Chapter 1). Information and communication technology (IT) is all the electronic media used to collect, store and process data, to produce information and to support or enable communication. When non-electronic media are referred to, then the term IT should not be used. Instead, the more abstract notion of documentary media would more accurately reflect all the media, electronic as well as non-electronic, used to collect, store and process data, to produce information and to support or enable communication. In this sense a piece of paper is a documentary medium, but not an IT application. Following the same line of reasoning, e-mail is an IT application as well as a documentary medium.

IT is an integral part of managing contemporary organizations. A basic IT knowledge is important to managers for several reasons:

- Managers are IT users since they send and receive information, and by doing so continuously communicate with other members of the organization and third parties.
- Decisions and evaluations are made on the basis of information and communication. IT is employed to make information and communication more efficient.
- IT is an enabler of organizational change. Within change processes, managers play a major role in collaboration with change agents and IT specialists. In order to adequately fulfil this role, managers must be able to communicate with the change agents and the IT specialists. This implies that a common language must be spoken. In our current environment, IT is the enabler of most organizational change processes. Hence, IT terminology is most likely to be an important component of such a common language.
- Management is responsible for internal control. Internal control is heavily influenced by IT developments. So management is indirectly responsible for IT and especially for integrating IT with the information processes and the business processes within an organization and between organizations.

Information systems are the most overt manifestations of IT. If we define a system as an organized way of undertaking actions in order to attain certain goals, then an information system is an organized way of collecting, storing and processing data, producing information and supporting or enabling communication aimed at the attainment of organizational goals. The term information system did not blossom until data input and processing and information provision became automated. So, in view of our definition of IT, talking about information systems implies talking about IT.

Components of Information Systems

The heart of any information system is the computer. An information system consists of the following five main components:

- input devices
- storage devices
- processing devices
- output devices
- communication devices.

To efficiently discuss these components we will follow the framework as depicted in Figure 4.1.

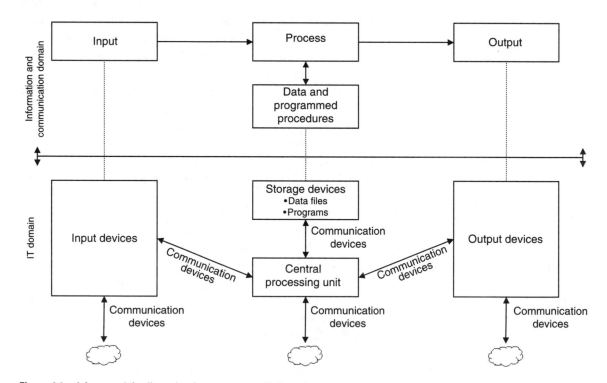

Figure 4.1   A framework for discussing the components of information systems.

The integral control framework as developed in Chapter 1 distinguishes information and communication from IT. Figure 4.1 follows the same distinction. Input, processing, data and programmed procedures, and output pertain to data and information content as referred to in the information and communication domain. Note that this part of the framework is in accordance with the uniform basic pattern of information provision as discussed in Chapter 2. Input devices, storage devices, central processing unit (CPU), output devices and communication devices pertain to IT.

Input Devices

Input devices, like output devices, impose speed constraints on information systems since they are the slowest components of any information system. Input can be done by people – we will refer to this as manual input – but it can also be done by means of computer applications, which we will refer to as automated input. In general, automated input increases data processing speed.

Data may be input on-line or by batch. In both cases data may or may not first be captured on paper as a separate recording before keying it into the computer. However, considering the speed increase that can be accomplished by inputting data on-line when compared to batch input, it seems highly inefficient to first capture data on paper in an on-line system. Conversely, in batch-oriented systems data must be captured somehow – on paper as a separate recording, or otherwise, like a pile of bills, sales orders or cash receipts – before keying it into the computer. The recordings used to capture data are generally denoted source documents. The most commonly used manual input device is the keyboard. In their quest for more user-friendly computers, computer and software builders have invented devices such as the mouse (or derived devices such as pointing pens, touch pads and trackballs), touch screen technology and voice recognition software which indeed caused a revolution in user interface development. All of these devices have in common the aim of making the action to input data more user-friendly by means of technological solutions. An alternative approach is to aim for higher quality of source documents. A typical example of this approach is the turnaround document. A turnaround document is produced by the information system of the organization that wants to initiate a certain transaction. For example, a utility company produces bills with a payment slip attached. This payment slip contains all the data needed by the accounts receivable department to process the cash receipt, whereas this information would not always have been available when a customer-made form had been used as the source document. Turnaround documents can even be designed so that they can be processed automatically.

When use is being made of automated input devices, this is generally referred to as source data automation. Examples are machine readable turnaround documents, and any other document that makes use of some kind of standard format to represent data in a machine readable form. The technology used here may be magnetic ink character recognition or optical character recognition. The old-fashioned punch card made use of a coding system that translated characters into holes in a card that could only be inserted into the punch card reader if each card in a pile was properly stacked in accordance with the stacking system. For example, the upper right corner of the punch card is cut away so that any improperly stacked card will be identified immediately. Another traditional – but unlike the punch card still viable – approach to source data automation is the bar code, which consists of a number of lines that together form a unique code which can be scanned with infrared scanning equipment. The coding systems used here may vary, but for product identification there is the Universal Product Code (UPC) standard that has been adopted worldwide.

An important application of the UPC can be found in point-of-sale (POS) systems. POS systems make use of an optical scanner for reading the barcode that contains product data which refers to a certain inventory item, and triggers further processing in the inventory files, and the cash or accounts receivable files. Nowadays frequent use is made of coding systems which make use of magnetic stripes or chips for Near Field Communication (NFC). Most debit or credit cards have a magnetic stripe or chip which may contain a wide variety of information about the cardholder, but which also may contain only a unique reference to the cardholder's files. ATM cards, bank cards or PIN cards also make use of magnetic stripes for user identification. The cardholder uses it for making payments via countertop terminals and for withdrawing cash from her bank account. By having the magnetic stripe read by the terminal the owner identifies herself, and by inputting her personal identification number (PIN) the owner proves that she is the person she claims to be, i.e. she authorizes her transaction request. The smartcard makes use of chip technology. It contains a chip, which is a microprocessor combined with a memory chip. The electronic wallet concept makes use of smartcard technology. Such an electronic wallet can be charged by the cardholder by going to a charging device comparable to an automated teller machine (ATM), using the card as an identifier, authorizing by means of a personal identification number and inputting the amount to charge to the card. From that moment on, the card contains the amount of money that was charged to it. Payments can be made by having it read by a countertop terminal operated by the vendor and connected to the bank of the cardholder or a clearing institute. When making payments like this, no authorization is needed after the identification is successful. It can easily be understood why such a card closely resembles a nonelectronic wallet. Once it is stolen, the proprietor can use it without needing any authorization. A modern approach to source data automation is the use of Radio Frequency Identification (RFID) tags. Such a tag contains a chip and is attached to a product or any other object that must be followed in one way or another. The chip sends and receives radio signals that are used to identify the object it is attached to. RFID tags are used for Near Field Communication.

Storage Devices

There are two types of storage devices: primary and secondary memory. Primary memory is used for internally storing and retrieving data and program instructions. It may be read-only. Read-only memory (ROM) is usually used for storing part or all of the operating system. For temporarily writable memory capacity, random access memory (RAM) is used. RAM loses its contents as soon as the power is shut off. A modern primary memory device is the flash memory which may easily be rewritten several times. Once it is written, it does not lose its contents even if the power is shut off. Secondary memory is used for permanently or semi-permanently storing data and program instructions on external devices like hard disks, floppy disks, magnetic tape or optical disks (CD or DVD).

In order to store data, some kind of file storage system must be used. For a clear understanding of the way data are recorded we will describe the logical – as opposed to physical – file organization. This implies that the decision whether or not to use a data base is not as yet taken into consideration. A file consists of records about a certain entity. A record is a collection of data values that describe specific attributes of an entity. A file description typically contains a primary key and the other attributes belonging to that primary key. Among the attributes there may also be references to primary keys of other files.

These references are called foreign keys. A primary key is a unique identifier of a record. A secondary key need not be unique because it may refer to a group of records. For example, an article code may be the primary key in an inventory file whereas the physical location code of the inventory item as recorded in that very same file may be the secondary key that can be used for sorting the inventory items for picking purposes.

A distinction can be made into master files and transaction files. A master file contains data that do not change frequently or that may only change as a result of transactions recorded in a transaction file that has a reference to the primary key in the master file. For example, the inventory master file has the following record layout (note the underlining to indicate that this is the primary key to this file):

article code, article description, quantity in hand, sales price, location in warehouse.

This master file will only be updated when:

- either the article description, the location in the warehouse or the sales price changes, or
- the sales or purchases transaction file indicates that during a specific time period inventory items have been dispatched or received.

The sales transaction file may have the following record layout:

sales transaction code, customer code, article code, quantity dispatched.

The purchases transaction file may have the following record layout:

purchase transaction code, vendor code, article code, quantity received.

An analogy can be made between master files and ledgers which both contain the results of transactions, and between transaction files and journal vouchers which both contain transactional data.

Central Processing Unit

The term central processing unit (CPU) stems from the time when mainframes and minicomputers were the most common computer systems used. With the emergence of the PC the term CPU seems somewhat overdone, because what is referred to here is simply the microprocessor that is the heart of every PC. The microprocessor is a silicon chip as small as a thumbnail which does all the computations the computer is supposed to do.

Output Devices

Output of an information system may well serve as input of another information system. Hence, like input devices, output devices may be paper-based or electronic. The main output devices are printers. A wide range of types of printers can be distinguished, but the most frequently used ones are – at increasing level of output quality – the matrix printer, the inkjet printer and the laser printer. Electronic output may be presented on a computer screen or a video projector, but also in a less directly readable form such as on floppy disk, hard disk, CD-rom or by using data transmission lines such as telephone lines, television cables or specialized network infrastructures such as value-added networks (VANs).

Communication Devices

Communication devices are used throughout every part of any information system. As can be observed in Figure 4.1, there may be communication between input devices and the outside world like other information systems within or outside the organization, between the CPU and storage devices, input devices, output devices and the outside world, and between output devices and the outside world.

Electronic communication generally takes place via a network. There are several types of network. A network that does not go beyond a certain geographical location is called a local area network (LAN). If a LAN is transferred to a wider area, geographically crossing organization boundaries, then it is called a wide area network (WAN). Hence, WANs are used within organizations that have more than one office, branch, outlet, or production facility and that need to be able to efficiently communicate via electronic channels with each other. Whereas communication via a LAN usually makes use of company-owned equipment to operate the network, communication via a WAN usually makes use of hired long-distance data communication channels like the Internet or a value-added network (VAN) which is operated by an independent company providing all the hardware, software and service to make the communication channel work. A WAN may be configured in either of two ways, decentralized or centralized. In a decentralized system each entity (business unit, department or any other departmental unit) connected to the WAN has its own computer and possibly its own LAN. A decentralized system is usually better equipped to meet individual entity needs than a centralized system. In a centralized system, all devices are connected to a central computer which on the one hand makes it easier to control but on the other hand makes it less sensitive to changes in individual entity needs.

Decentralization and Centralization in an Organizational Context

In view of the meaning generally given to the terms decentralization and centralization – referring to decision-making power and not to some kind of physical allocation – an analogy can be made between the role of the computer in a WAN and organizational decision-making. Managers may centralize decision-making power. When doing so they want to avoid control problems by making all the important decisions themselves instead of having them made by their subordinates (see Chapter 3). However, they may also decentralize decision-making by handing over the authority to make decisions to their subordinates. Thus they want to render responses to market changes more direct and appropriate. In analogy, in a centralized WAN, the central computer does all the processing, whereas in a decentralized WAN, processing is done on local computers.

Big automation departments usually have heavily centralized systems. The users are responsible for inputting the right data, and the automation department is responsible for appropriately processing and storing these data. Output may be generated locally or centrally. With the emergence of the so-called client/server configurations, in the eighties, a new dimension was added to the decentralization/centralization debate. As a result of the increased potential of IT for decentralized processing, the role of the automation department, with big mainframes doing all the computing jobs, has become more and more superfluous in most small and medium-sized companies, and even in many big companies. The technology applied here is to use desktop computers – or, in more general terms, intelligent terminals – as clients of a server system. The client sends requests for data processing to the server which performs some preparatory processing of the data and sends only the requested subset of a larger data base to the client for local processing. Client/server configurations are now very common in LAN and WAN applications. Clients may be fat or thin. A fat client has enough memory and processing capacity to run applications locally. A thin client does not have enough memory and processing capacity to do this. Instead, applications run on a specific server and make use of fast communication lines to enable this. The net PC is an example of such a thin client. In the early days of mainframe computing this type of computer would have been called a dumb terminal. The major advantage of the net PC over traditional client/server configurations is that data processing is concentrated at one physical location which greatly enhances controllability.

Communication by means of a WAN came within reach of even the smallest companies through the emergence of the Internet. The Internet makes use of the Internet protocol (IP) for transferring messages between senders and receivers. In order to be able to make use of the Internet, a user closes a contract with an Internet service provider (ISP) who has an infrastructure in place to provide individuals and organizations with a connection to the Internet. The Internet is intended for communication between organizations or persons that do not form legal entities. New developments regarding the Internet include intranets, where the Internet protocol is used for communication within organizations via a LAN or a WAN, and extranets for applications where limited access to internal data and information is allowed to third parties. Virtual private networks (VPN) are examples of relatively secure communication infrastructures within an extranet. In the early days (seventies) of electronically transferring data between organizations, a more rigid format was used for the lay-out of electronic messages. This format was usually industry dependent and could only be used when two parties agreed upon using that specific format. Additionally, the technical infrastructure for this type of communication required joining an existing proprietary third party network. The overall term for this concept was electronic data interchange (EDI). Because EDI basically performs the same functions as the Internet, the term could be used for all types of electronic data communication, including the Internet. However from a semantic viewpoint this might be confusing. We therefore reserve the term EDI for the standardized business-to-business transfer of electronic messages.

Web pages may or may not be connected to a data base. The simplest form of web page may only consist of data in word processor format (for example, in MS Word). However, there are languages specifically designed to create web pages and links between web pages and that eliminate the need for software that translates documents in different formats into one uniform format. In essence, a markup language consists of codes – also denoted tags – that can be attached to data elements. For example, the data element 'net income' receives the tag 'NI'. Hypertext markup language (HTML) is the simplest example of such a language. Whereas HTML gets less efficient when data structures become more complex and more flexibility is needed with respect to expandability and platform choice, extended markup language (XML) comes into play. XML is platform independent (for example, Windows, UNIX, mainframe or Linux), expandable (for example, it lets you create your own tags) and self-describing, meaning that it describes data elements in terms of their name as well as their content (for example, <date>September 11, 2001</date>). Also, compared to EDI, XML is much more flexible. Advantages of XML include: it is in a readable data format, it is vendor neutral, all major software products are becoming XML-enabled and XML will be the de facto standard for electronic communication. At the moment there are over 400 XML-based specifications and protocols, some of which already have well-developed taxonomies containing the used tags and their meaning. Extended business reporting language (XBRL) is an example of such a protocol. It is XML-based and aimed at financial accounting in a standardized format. XBRL is especially relevant for accountants because it promises to standardize financial reporting via the Internet so that companies' financial statements become more comparable.

With the increasing speed of computers and communication lines, a new type of service firm is emerging: the application service provider (ASP). An ASP is a company that offers a website containing software which can be used from a distant location and need not be downloaded in order to be able to use it. For example, SAP (in collaboration with Hewlett-Packard and Qwest) makes its ERP package available for smaller companies that do not have the budget to install it on their own computer. Making use of ASPs is a form of outsourcing.

Related to EDI is the making of electronic payments, denoted electronic funds transfer (EFT). EFT is commonplace is countries that only seldom use cheques. Most European countries nowadays have abandoned the traditional cheques and instead put great effort into improving international standardization in making electronic payments. When EFT is applied, a so-called clearing house which collects and processes all payments between banks must be in place. As an alternative to EFT, credit card payments may be used. In that case the buyer authorizes the vendor to withdraw a certain amount of money from his credit card.

Information System Development

Information system development traditionally takes place following a stepwise approach, the systems development life cycle (SDLC). This approach is strictly linear which means that a number of stages must be gone through in a prescribed sequence. However, it must be noted that returning to a prior phase in the SDLC is always possible. The stages may vary per SDLC, but in many instances the management cycle can be recognized with a lot of attention being paid to the planning phase. For example, systems analysis (planning), conceptual design (planning), physical design (planning), implementation and conversion (structuring), operations (execution) and maintenance (evaluation and adjusting) are typical stages in an SDLC. Because this approach resembles the flow of water coming down from a waterfall, it is expressively called the waterfall approach. There are several reasons for following such a stepwise approach, including:

- It leads to a systematic development of the application.
- It provides several measurement points or milestones which enable measurement of project progress.
- It facilitates communication between IT experts and users.
- It leads to a check on the inclusion of all the defined hardware, data and software requirements.

- It causes each application to be developed in accordance with agreed upon basic principles.
- It may lead to efficiency improvements.

In contemporary information system development projects, linear approaches are seldom effective. The main cause of this is that many modern information systems must be organization-wide and fully integrated as a result of which these systems become extremely complex. Often, specifications that were made at the start of the project may as well be completely discarded because they have become obsolete with the end of the project in sight. As a result of the strictly plan-wise, phased and linear approach as in the SDLC, the system is often found not to meet the newly defined specifications. In order to avoid this, system development may take place, making use of a so-called incremental method. In such a method the strictly stepwise approach is abandoned in favour of a heuristic approach that makes small steps one at a time, and that favours trial and error. An example of an incremental approach is prototyping.

Prototyping

Prototyping is an approach to systems development that develops a simplified working model of an information system or a part of an information system in order to enable user testing. Typically, prototyping involves the following activities:

- Identification of basic system requirements by meeting with the user to agree on the size and scope of the system and to decide what the system should include and exclude.
- Development of an initial prototype that meets the requirements agreed on.
- Identification of necessary changes by users, making adjustments by developers, evaluation or experimentation by users, and getting back to the users until their satisfaction meets the desired level.
- Building the production system.

Prototyping is especially useful when it is difficult to identify a usable set of requirements. For example, if users are unable to verbalize their information needs, a prototype may consist of a number of menus and screens that trigger the users to specify what part of the prototype they approve and what other specifications they would like to be included in the system. The system developer will continue to respond to the users until they agree on the system specifications and are satisfied with the system. When applying a prototyping approach it is important to recognize that users have a central role in systems development. As a matter of fact, the emergence of prototyping was fuelled by the rise of end-user computing where data processing was heavily decentralized and managers were able to extract the information they needed by using powerful, high-level end-user computing languages. Moreover, managers were highly dissatisfied with the unresponsiveness of IT specialists and were looking for ways to improve data processing and simultaneously avoid control problems within the organization's information and communication processes.

IT Applications

This section discusses some specific examples of IT applications including: Enterprise Resource Planning, Data Bases and Data Warehouses, Decision Support Systems, Expert Systems and Neural Networks, Groupware, and Executive Information Systems.

Enterprise Resource Planning

Enterprise Resource Planning (ERP) is a concept that originates in logistical concepts such as Materials Requirements Planning (MRP) and Manufacturing Resource Planning (MRP II). Instead of using several systems to manage a company's business, ERP is a means for a company to streamline traditionally separate operations into one system. Information, shared through a common ERP system, flows from operation to operation. It thereby creates more efficient processes, higher quality reporting and simpler company-wide communication. Hence, ERP is an integrated, process-oriented, organization-wide IT solution designed to facilitate the achievement of an organization's goals and objectives. So, ERP is aimed at integrating a company's operational information systems in such a way that work processes are supported. ERP systems encompass numerous business applications, such as general ledger, payroll, supply chain management, manufacturing and business intelligence. Although very costly to implement, ERP systems have been adopted by many companies in recent years due to the potential for lower operating costs, shorter cycle times and higher customer satisfaction. Successful adoptions of ERP systems have also been linked to business process re-engineering efforts and implementation of best practices such as benchmarking.

Advantages and Disadvantages of ERP Systems

Advantages:

- Implementations force the firm to critically examine existing business processes.
- ERP systems rely on open scaleable software and hardware architectures which can make the organization more flexible.
- Within a given range, ERP applications are configurable to fit the firm's business processes.
- Users are empowered due to increased information sharing across the enterprise.
- Information for decision-making gains relevance because it can combine internal with external data and information.

Disadvantages:

- High costs associated with software licence, computer hardware, implementation and ongoing maintenance.

- While ERPs are somewhat flexible when first purchased, they ultimately become relatively inflexible as the business rules are defined in the system.
- In the long run, inflexibility of ERP applications can inhibit a firm's adaptability and responsiveness to changing customer demands and competitive pressures.
- Due to the complexity of implementations, most firms end up changing their business processes to fit the ERP software.
- ERP systems are internally focused, which can be a handicap given the rapidly evolving e-business model.

Organizations which implement an ERP system will find out that its impact on the way they conduct business is tremendous. We believe that in the near future, three major extensions of ERP systems may be anticipated. The first is the extension of ERP systems from information systems to knowledge systems. The accompanying IT on top of the ERP system includes groupware, data warehouses and intranets to facilitate knowledge creation and integration. Here the information system must enable the organization to get a sound grasp of its own true abilities and how it can improve them. The second is the application of ERP systems as interorganizational information systems. The accompanying IT includes EDI, Internet and point-of-sale applications. Here the information system must enable the organization to understand the needs of its suppliers and customers. The underlying assumption is that if an organization achieves a better understanding of the needs of its suppliers and customers it will be more successful. The third extension is the use of an organization's ERP system for learning about the true abilities of its suppliers and vendors and what they need to know in order to be successful. The underlying assumption is that trading with successful suppliers and customers will make an organization itself successful as well. The accompanying IT applications are extranets and supplier and customer self-service applications whereby suppliers and customers are allowed to retrieve information from an organization's information system. For example, a vendor is allowed to check an organization's inventory files in order to be able to determine whether that organization needs a stock replenishment.

Data Bases and Data Warehouses

A data base is a set of interrelated data that has two important features. First, it is aimed at avoiding data redundancy. This implies that every data element is only recorded once. Second, it is application-independent. This implies that a multiple logical view of data is aimed for. Multiple means that more than one viewpoint to access the data can be chosen. Logical means that we are not talking about the physical appearance of the data base, but about how it appears toward the users, i.e. as one big bag of data. Data in this big bag can be retrieved or updated within the limitations of the assigned authorities. There are several types of data bases. However the type most commonly used in modern data base environments is the relational data base. The relational data base model represents each data element in the data base in the form of tables that contain cross-references – via primary and foreign keys – to other tables. In order to operate a data base – as is the case in almost every IT solution – a combination of hardware, software and people is needed. Since data bases are intended to cover the data storage needs of complete organizations, ample physical storage and processing capacity is needed. Software requirements include a number of modules that together must take care of efficient operation of the data base. The data base management system (DBMS) is the main software used to operate a data base. It is a specialized computer program that handles all the data traffic to and from the data base. In daily speech the terms data base, data base management system and data base system are often incorrectly used interchangeably. The data base system is the combination of the data base and the software used to operate the data base, including the application programs. For example, the module accounts receivable that retrieves customer payment data from the data base to construct an accounts receivable ageing report is part of the data base system although it does not belong to the DBMS nor the data base itself. The DBMS consists of several submodules. The data dictionary involves all the information about the data elements contained in the data base. It is a meta representation of the data base, meaning that it provides the semantics needed to understand what is meant by every data element in the data base. For example, the data dictionary contains the following meta data about the inventory item name in the inventory records:

- Description; complete verbal description of the inventory item.
- Record(s) in which contained; inventory record.
- Source(s); initial purchase order, warehouse keeper.
- Field length; 25 characters.
- Field type; alphanumeric.
- Module(s) in which used; inventory module, sales module, purchase module.
- Output(s) in which contained; inventory status report, picking ticket, packing ticket, purchase orders, sales orders.
- Authorized users; no restrictions.

Another element of the DBMS is the data directory which can best be compared to the contents or index of a book. It contains all the meta data needed to locate a certain data element in the data base. Usually the data dictionary and data directory are mentioned in the same breath: data dictionary and directory system (DDDS). A third module in the DBMS is the teleprocessing monitor (TPM). Since a data base is shared by multiple users at various geographical locations, there may be access conflicts and violation attempts. In order to control access, the TPM makes use of assigned priorities to users, and allows access to a certain data record only if the user-module-data combination is contained in the access control matrix. In Chapter 7 we will elaborate on the information security issues involved here. The languages used to manipulate the data base are also part of the data base system. Here, a distinction can be made between data-oriented languages and information-oriented languages. The class of data-oriented languages is generally referred to as data manipulation languages (DMLs). A DML is used for maintaining the data base, which includes such operations as altering, adding and deleting portions of the data base. The class of information-oriented languages is generally referred to as data query languages (DQLs). A DQL is used to retrieve data from the data base for further processing such as sorting, categorizing, summarizing, calculating and presenting that information in a format that is understandable to the end-user.

There are two important organizational roles that support the functioning of data bases: the data base administrator (DBA) and the data administrator (DA). The DBA must have technical skills to handle the detailed data base design work and to tune it for efficient use. The DA on the other hand must have administrative skills to handle managerial and policy issues, and to interact efficiently with data base users. Theoretically these roles could be combined in one function, but few people have both sets of skills. Moreover, the need for a specialized technical data base role has increased dramatically with the emergence of electronic communication. As a result the workload of the DBA has increased as well, necessitating a split between the DBA and the DA.

When data bases came into development the highly idealistic goal was to capture all the organizational data – and even beyond – in one large collection of records. Because IT did not allow this goal to be realized efficiently, smaller data bases came into development which were still substantial improvements of the old situation when there were many different master files, containing redundant and often inconsistent data, that did not allow access to applications other than those for which they were developed. Nowadays IT has reached such a level that these large data bases can be successfully realized. The generic term used for the concept of having large data bases covering all the data needed for decision-making and accountability is data warehousing. However, a data warehouse is more than just a big data base. Bill Inmon, one of the first advocates of data warehousing, identifies the following features of a data warehouse:

- It is subject-oriented. Data recorded in data warehouses centres around subjects such as products, markets, customers, locations etc. Since processes also centre around subjects, a data warehouse fits well into process orientations to organizations. The main issue is that every informational activity must add value to the organization. This is best accomplished by making the value driver the subject of information provision.
- It is integrated. Data is only recorded once for the whole organization. Many company-wide information systems, like ERP systems, now provide a data warehousing module.
- It is time-variant. The moment in time at which, or the time span over which, information is needed is completely irrelevant. Information can be retrieved at any moment in time, over any period. The traditional annual or quarterly closings in accounting information systems are no longer necessary if this feature of a data warehouse is met.
- It is nonvolatile. A data warehouse keeper is responsible for ensuring the integrity of all the data in the data warehouse. Modification may only be made via him. This implies that the operational systems like accounts receivable, accounts payable, inventory, logistics, marketing, human resources management etc. are not allowed to make modifications to data in the data warehouse.

Reasons for developing data warehouses may be diverse. First, it is necessary to focus on information provision in relation to clients and potential clients in a highly competitive environment. Second, because of shorter life cycles and time to market, information must be available as fast and flexibly as possible. Third, in order to ensure data integrity there must be segregation of duties between the warehouse keeper and the provider of the data. Data warehouses have the characteristics to meet the resulting requirements.

Decision Support Systems, Expert Systems and Neural Networks

Decision support systems (DSSs) are computerized information systems aimed at the improvement of human decision-making. As the term indicates, these systems support decision-making, they do not replace it. Also, DSSs contain facts and not subjective human knowledge. The basic form of a DSS is a spreadsheet used for what-if analyses, goal-seeking (for example, determining the necessary gross salary to arrive at a certain net salary, or determining the internal rate of return of an investment project), or what-is analyses (for example, constructing a business performance report comparing this year's figures to budgeted figures and reporting exceptions). Specialized DSS software may be used for computer simulation in cases where analytical tools are not appropriate because of incomplete information or when too many variables are involved. For example, a production facility has problems in determining the minimum required inventory level because vendor delivery times and sales follow an unpredictable pattern, inventory costs are only known within a certain bandwidth and out-of-stock opportunity costs are completely unknown. Obviously, in order not to waste valuable company resources, inventory should be minimized. This problem can be solved by simulating the buying, inventory keeping and sales processes, making use of probability theory. The outcome of such a simulation could then be that there is an x% probability that the company loses a certain amount of money because of too high or too low inventory levels. The decision-maker can use this information to motivate his actual decision about what, when and where to purchase.

Expert systems on the other hand, do replace human decision-making by presenting proposed decisions to their users. For that purpose, subjective expert knowledge is recorded in the knowledge bases of these sytems and this is used to simulate the experts' decision-making. When using the term expert system, it usually implies that it consists of so-called production rules, or in other words, if-then-else statements. Expert systems do not have learning abilities. So every piece of knowledge has to be put in by the developer on the basis of knowledge acquisition among one or more experts. Neural networks go one step further in that they contain learning mechanisms that enable them to fine-tune their embedded knowledge just like humans do when encountering new cases. The overall category of software that covers neural networks and expert systems is called artificial intelligence (AI).

A Car Diagnosis Expert System

A car mechanic encounters the problem of a car whose engine stops running when it takes a turn to the right. He may make the diagnosis that there must be a short circuit in the car's electronics caused by a bad wire touching the car's bodywork. If this decision were to be modelled in an expert system, some applicable production systems could be:

If: Engine malfunctions AND The car makes a turn AND The car drives faster than 50 miles an hour

Then: There is a loose contact – probability = 50% OR There is a malfunctioning gas pump – probability 20% OR There is a problem with the ignition – probability = 35% OR there is a problem with the brakes – probability = 10%

If: There is a problem when the car makes a turn into one specific direction
Then: There is a loose contact – probability = 80%

From this example it can easily be observed that only probabilities are given as outcomes of the expert system, and that inferences cannot be made with absolute certainty. Of course this is similar to how the real expert would work. Dependent on his number of years of task-specific experience, his education as a mechanic and his talent for diagnosing car trouble, the expert will be able to increase the probability of a certain diagnosis being correct. Note that in other decision-making tasks, probabilities may take a binary form, thus only having values at the scale ends of 0% or 100%.

Groupware

Groupware is the generic name of software that enables more efficient communication within organizations, and between organizations, or more specifically within any group that works towards a certain deliverable. The type of communication that is enabled by groupware is often not tied to any fixed format. Typical applications of groupware are Lotus Notes, MS Mcssenger, Yahoo Messenger, Skype but also the sharing of documents and messages via e-mail or other electronic data communication channels. Basically, groupware combines the power of computer networks with the directness and personal touch of face-to-face contact. It can be used for brainstorming sessions but also for fast information exchange for the support of business processes. In addition, it lets users hold computer conferences, schedule meetings, maintain a personal or departmental calendar, manage projects or jointly design complex products. An example of groupware aimed at the support of decision-making in groups of people is the group decision support system (GDSS). Like DSSs, GDSSs support decision-making without substituting the human decision-maker involved.

Executive Information Systems

An Executive Information System (EIS) allows end-users at the tactical and strategic managerial level to produce the information they themselves find necessary. This category of information systems is highly diverse as to its appearance. At one end of the scale an EIS may necessitate a query language to extract data from a data base; at the other end of the scale the EIS may be completely pre-programmed to provide the information the executive specified during the early stages of system development. Data warehouses enable EISs to provide superior information for executive decision-making. Especially when these data warehouses are built on top of a company's ERP system, they may be able to combine internal company data, financial as well as nonfinancial, and quantitative as well as nonquantitative, with external data about vendors, competitors and customers, and within the product markets, the labour markets as well as the capital markets.

Executives need quick access to all the information available at the moment of decision-making. Imagine a board of directors trying to formulate a company's strategy. A so-called management cockpit room would then benefit the strategy formulation process tremendously because all the information in whatever format (narratives, graphs or in figures) can be presented on surrounding electronic panels in the board meeting room. Such a room is not fiction. One of the major advantages of such an advanced IT application is that information overload can be regulated. Of course this might also be a major disadvantage since management must be skilled in operating this high-tech EIS. If they fail to achieve the right skills, the information appearing on the surrounding screens will become useless because it loses its meaning and causes information overload. A less profound, but highly pragmatic IT solution to the information relevance problem is to use software that makes nonfinancial information more understandable by having executives choose their preferred formats. Software that supports multidimensional performance evaluation, like the balanced scorecard, plays this role.

IT-enabled Innovations

IT-enabled innovations constitute a rather heterogeneous group of products, philosophies and concepts. We will briefly discuss the following examples of IT-enabled innovations:

- e-business (including Internet portals)
- business process re-engineering;
- customer relationship management;
- business intelligence and strategic enterprise management;
- business process management;
- shared service centres and outsourcing.

E-business

Electronic commerce was among the first e-business applications. It refers to all the sales-related activities that make use of electronic communication by means of the Internet. The principle is as follows: the customer determines what he wants to order via the website of the vendor or a portal that compares different vendors and, after having chosen the product and – if applicable – the vendor, he places an order via the website of the vendor, via a portal or via a traditional method such as telephone, fax, written order or just by visiting the store. So, e-commerce may be as simple as having a website for displaying the products that are for sale, which is a noninteractive application. However, it may also be more complex, such as offering customers the possibility of ordering products via the website, which is an interactive application. Interactive applications enable a full-fledged use of the potentials of the Internet for e-commerce activities. A more advanced application is the integration of an organization's website with the information systems – usually ERP systems – of that organization. When e-activities go beyond a website for marketing and sales applications, then the term e-business is most commonly used to indicate that all business processes are in one way or another influenced by the chosen electronic communication philosophy.

Internet Portals

E-business activities often make use of so-called Internet portals. An Internet portal is a website that is a major starting point for users when they want to find information or conclude a transaction on the Internet. An Internet portal can be compared to a physical portal that you can enter in order to make a choice among the several doors that can be opened from that portal. A distinction can be made between general Internet portals and specialized Internet portals. Some major general portals are Startpagina.nl, Excite.com, Altavista.com, Netscape.com, Lycos.com, CNET.com, MSN.com and AOL.com. Examples of specialized portals include whatis.techtarget.com (for IT professionals), Happytravel.nl (for travellers), Accountingweb.nl (for accountants) and Fool.com (for investors). Companies with Internet portals have attracted much investor interest because portals are looked upon as being able to command large audiences and hence large numbers of advertising viewers. Typical services offered by portals are a directory of Internet sites, facilities to search for other sites, news and weather sites, stock quotes, address information, discussion forums and product comparison sites.

In an e-business environment, a process orientation as opposed to a functional orientation seems more appropriate because it enables the organization to be in closer and more direct contact with the market, to increase operational efficiency and to achieve internal as well as external integration goals more effectively. As a result any organization can only reap the full benefits of e-business when a horizontal structure is chosen, as is the case in a process orientation. Business process re-engineering is the vehicle to arrive at such a process orientation.

Business Process Re-engineering

A modern flow in the literature at the crossroad of management, accounting and IT is business process re-engineering (BPR). BPR is aimed at designing business processes in such a way that optimal use is made of the opportunities offered by IT. It is the thorough analysis and complete redesign of business processes and information systems to achieve dramatic performance improvements. Management will focus more on the processes than on existing departments and hierarchies. This means that the organization is rotated from vertical (command and control) to horizontal where certain customer(group)s, product(group)s or markets are central. For example, the process of settling a claim by an insurer can be performed more efficiently – and in a more customer-friendly fashion – when minimal data traffic takes place between the various departments and the joint responsibility is put in the hands of the various employees involved in the relevant process.

The following seven basic principles underlie BPR:

1. Organize around outcomes, not tasks. This implies that one person is held responsible for the entire process and that the work of each person in the process is aimed at the final product or outcome of that process.

2. Have output users perform the process. This implies that the workers have more autonomy than they used to have in the functionally-oriented organization. For example, those who need a certain product must also do the ordering directly with the vendor. This usually is feasible with insignificant stocks.

3. Have those who produce information process it. For example, orders are input into the information system for processing by the same person who places them and hence produces information.

4. Centralize and disperse data by means of IT. To achieve economies of scale, businesses will centralize operations, but to be more responsive to changing circumstances and customer needs, businesses will decentralize operations. Corporate-wide data bases combine the advantages of both centralization and decentralization.

5. Integrate parallel activities. Parallel activities that contribute to the same product or service must be aligned in an early stage of the process in order to reduce additional work after the activities have been completed. For example, with building a house, the holes and the channels for the power outlets and the electric wires are already made by the bricklayers by omitting bricks at the designated places.

6. Empower workers, use built-in controls and flatten the organizational chart. Those who do the job have decision-making power for that job. As a result, managers can shift their attention from supervision and control to support and facilitation. IT plays an important role here. For example, workers are supported by expert systems, DSSs or groupware to enable sound decision-making.

7. Capture data only once, at its source. The keystone of integrated systems is to have single input combined with multiple uses.

BPR and enterprise resource planning are often undertaken for the same reasons. Organizations that implement an ERP system will have to transform from a functional to a process orientation. BPR actually performs such a transformation. So, ERP is a catalyst of process change. In addition, a good aid in determining the norms that should be strived for in re-engineering business processes is benchmarking. Benchmarking is the process of identification, familiarizing and adopting superior practices as observed in one's own or other organizations, aimed at improving one's own performance. ERP systems may play an important part in providing the necessary information for benchmarking purposes. Table 4.1 relates the basic principles of BPR to ERP.
In the last few decades BPR has gained popularity as a concept that could lead to enhanced efficiency and effectiveness of organizations. However, due to numerous BPR projects that failed or did not live up to their full potential, we believe it is 'over the hill'. In more recent literature a tendency to more flexible firms from the outset can be observed. The postmodern organization or simply the flexible firm is the new hype in this area. This concept is especially aimed at the creation and integration of knowledge in organizations in order to continuously innovate and gain competitive advantage as a result.

Customer Relationship Management

Organizations need to attempt to meet their clients' wishes in the best way they can. Customer-oriented trading demands account management or customer relationship management (CRM). Besides the general organizational information recorded in a regular accounts receivable administration, an account

Table 4.1 The relationship between the seven basic principles of BPR and ERP.

BPR	ERP
Organize around outcomes, not tasks.	ERP follows a process orientation of organizations.
Have output users perform the process.	ERP accomplishes the inputting of data from within the work processes in order to initiate those work processes.
Have those who produce information process it.	ERP accomplishes the inputting of data from within the work processes in order to track the progress of those work processes.
Centralize and disperse data by means of IT.	ERP plays an important part in work-flow management, and hence in distributing data and information.
Integrate parallel activities.	ERP follows a process orientation where multidisciplinary teams are the most important entities.
Empower workers, use built-in controls and flatten the organizational chart.	ERP enables the enforced use of specific programme modules by means of soft parameter settings.
Capture data only once, at its source.	The explicit goal of ERP is to record data only once for all applications.

management system also needs to contain information on, for example, the relevant employees and key decision-makers of the various organizations. This concept can best be illustrated by means of an example. Take a small grocery store that provides the people in the neighbourhood with the necessary food and other products needed to keep their households running. The storekeeper runs the store with his wife. They have had a long-term relationship with each customer and as a result know exactly what special treats are needed to make each individual customer happy with the service and products of the grocery store. This knowledge is not codified; rather it is in the heads of the storekeeper and his wife. When the small grocery store grows bigger, partly as a result of the extremely satisfied customers, the storekeeper will find out that he is no longer able to collect all the necessary customer information, to memorize it and to use it when a customer arrives. The workers that now do the sales may have some specific knowledge about certain customers, but this is highly dispersed, anecdotal and hence difficult to apply. IT may provide the tools to collect, store and retrieve the necessary customer information when a specific customer arrives. The process of collecting, recording and retrieving customer-specific knowledge is referred to as customer relationship management. The small grocery store that grew and started employing IT is an example of sales force automation (SFA). SFA was among the earliest CRM applications starting in the last decade of the twentieth century. A more recent development is the emergence of analytical CRM products which evolved from data warehousing and on-line analytical processing (OLAP) which enables a user to easily and selectively extract and view data from different points of view. For example, an OLAP tool enables the user to create a report that contains the sales of product X during the last month, the sales of product X in the same month last year and the sales of other products during the same time periods. An OLAP data base is generally much smaller than a data warehouse because it only contains the data needed for the required analysis. A typical representation of potential data that may be used for OLAP is a data cube (thus a three-dimensional viewpoint). OLAP is an efficient approach to get an insight into available data when the decision problem is known. A concept related to OLAP is data mining which is an efficient approach when the decision problem is not known, but there is a large data set that might be of interest. Data mining may be helpful in arriving at a manageable data base for OLAP purposes.

Business Intelligence and Strategic Enterprise Management

Whereas ERP originates from the need to control flows of goods and money at the operational level, business intelligence (BI) is primarily aimed at opening up the information contained in ERP data bases for managerial information provision. BI consists of a broad category of applications for collecting, storing, analysing and providing access to data to facilitate decision-making by managers. BI applications include DSS, OLAP and data mining. Strategic enterprise management (SEM) promises to enable managers to link strategy formulation to strategy implementation, drive product and customer profitability and increase shareholder value. Whereas BI is aimed at supporting decision-making at the tactical level in organizations, SEM aims to facilitate information provision for strategic decision-making. Typical applications of SEM are executive information systems. For example, Oracle SEM is a package that provides an organization with the ability to carry out strategic planning, taking into account that organizations' environments are subject to constant change. It operates via the Oracle Enterprise Data Warehouse which can store and retrieve data from multiple sources, Oracle as well as non-Oracle applications. The package can be built on top – as an add-on – of any ERP system.

Business Process Management

Business process management (BPM) is a field of knowledge at the intersection between management and IT, encompassing methods, techniques and tools to design, enact, control and analyse operational business processes involving people, organizations, applications, documents and other sources of information. BPM is possible without IT, but the organization will have to draw heavily on its internal controls and management controls to fully reap its benefits, making it virtually impossible to apply BPM without IT. Through BPM, processes are aligned with one another and the progress towards the objectives of these processes can be monitored. Because of these features, a generic BPM architecture consists of:

- a BPM dashboard for process monitoring: such a dashboard provides information about the progress of processes (for example, the time needed to send a confirmation e-mail to a customer who has just placed an order); this also requires just-in-time information provision for providing the necessary process monitoring information;
- supply chain management for aligning subsequent processes in the supply chain;
- customer relationship management (CRM) for enhancing customer service and gaining competitive advantage through better information about customers;

- the ERP system for integrating all the separate components of BPM: usually the ERP system is the basis for BPM; to make ERP more suited for BPM, add-ons are often needed; examples of these add-ons include CRM software, a balanced-scorecard-alike dashboard or a data warehouse.

Shared Service Centres and Outsourcing

One means of avoiding management control problems is to eliminate the activities that cause control problems (see Chapter 3). If, for example, an organization does not have the expertise to control its IT, it may outsource it to an external party and write a service level agreement (SLA) with that external party. If an organization believes it has the required expertise, but it wants to realize some economies of scale, then it may create a shared service centre (SSC). A shared service centre is one single organizational unit which provides a designated service that has previously been provided by more than one part of the organization. Thus the funding and sourcing of the service are shared simultaneously turning the providing unit into an internal service provider. Shared service centres involve more than just concentrating related activities in one location; they are usually managed like businesses. Hence the services are delivered to internal customers at a specified cost, with a specified quality and within a specified timeframe. The SSC may compete with external parties to deliver the services. Eventually, the SSC's personnel may be transferred to an external party thereby simultaneously buying the same services from that external party, but with much more flexibility. The Ericsson–Vodafone Contract is a typical example of this development. Other examples of shared service centres or outsourced activities are call centres and accounting houses.

Ericsson and Vodafone Netherlands Sign Managed Services Contract

29th March, 2006

Europe: Vodafone Netherlands and Ericsson announced they have entered into an exclusive managed services partnership. Under the contract, Ericsson will be responsible for the management of the access part of Vodafone Netherlands' GSM, GPRS and UMTS radio networks.

Under the contract, Ericsson will be responsible for engineering, implementation and operation of the access part of Vodafone Netherlands' GSM, GPRS and UMTS radio networks in the Netherlands. Vodafone Netherlands will retain ownership of the network and IT assets, as well as responsibility for the strategic direction of the network and IT infrastructure.

The five-year contract ensures Ericsson will operate radio access to the network to the highest standards, while enabling Vodafone Netherlands to manage and control its cost base, thereby enhancing the company's platform for growth.

John Samarron, CTO, Vodafone Netherlands, says: 'By transferring responsibility and the existing resources for the access part of our network, we are convinced that we will be able to capture

(Continued)

synergies with Ericsson and that the quality of our access network will be further improved. Moreover, the shift to a partnering model allows us to focus on additional elements of the value chain that will enable growth and new product introduction. It also brings yet another growth business to the region of South Limburg.'

Hans Vestberg, Executive Vice President at Ericsson and Head of Business Unit Global Services, says: 'We are very proud to be entrusted with operating the access part of Vodafone Netherlands' network and to be able to extend further our long-term relationship with this operator in one of our strategic growth areas.'

About 160 Vodafone Netherlands employees will be transferred to Ericsson under the scope of the managed services agreement.

Source: http://www.3g.co.uk/PR/March2006/2846.htm

Application service providing (ASP) is in a way related to shared service centres and outsourcing because, by means of ASP, software is not installed on the organization's systems, but remotely at the application service provider's systems. The buying organization then outsources its software and data management to the application service provider who is responsible for the proper processing of the organization's data.

The Importance of IT

There are three ages of economic evolution that can be distinguished in developed countries (see, for example, Toffler, 1990):

- the agrarian age
- the industrial age
- the information age.

These ages partially overlap and cannot be exactly positioned on a time scale because there are differences between the pace of development in different countries. To give a general indication, the agrarian age lasted until the second half of the eighteenth century, the industrial age started during the second half of the eighteenth century and has not yet come to an end and the information age started a few decades ago. Currently, we are in some kind of transitional stage between the industrial and the information age. The agrarian age could be characterized by the power of the guilds that were governed on the basis of unambiguous agreements between the members. As a result, competition was virtually nonexistent. The industrial era could be characterized by the severe concentration of power in increasingly large corporations that were mainly involved in production activities, and the important role of competition. The information era, or the third wave, can be characterized by the emergence of new organizational forms that go beyond industry boundaries, national borders and markets. The third wave economy is dominated by service organizations (including trade and the financial sector) where information and knowledge are the most important competitive instruments. Production activities that used to be core competences of many organizations are frequently outsourced to countries which are often underdeveloped, with low wage levels, whereas the development of new products takes place in the developed economies. Moreover, the service industry increasingly dictates the conditions under which contracts are settled between product developers and manufacturers.

Specialist knowledge of products, local markets and the necessity to combine a variety of production technologies and IT have led to organizations forming alliances, partnerships and joint ventures. In this setting, outsourcing and the so-called economical networks will be the new forms of cooperation. Economical networks require high-quality information provision between the affiliated partners, and between the economical network and third parties. The information provision within an economical network should be denoted internal information provision, and the information provision between economical networks should be denoted external information provision. The so-called virtual organization is an example of the economical network. In a virtual organization the activity range is dominated by electronic transactions, denoted e-activities (for example, e-business, e-commerce, e-procurement). This type of organization is highly dependent on high-quality information because the flows of physical goods and money are of secondary importance as compared to the information about the location and the state of the physical goods and money. For example, an organization that engages in e-business may not have its own inventories. Instead it knows which vendors can supply the goods its clients have ordered, or which warehouses have stored these goods. Hence, this type of organization requires information that meets the highest possible standards in order to function properly. In this arena, information control – as a subset of internal control – has received considerable attention in practice, education and theory. However, we believe that a broadening of this discipline towards the field of information security is necessary. Moreover, we believe that AIS must be the discipline that conveys this broadening because of its strong relationship with internal control, and the central role of the accounting information system in any organization.

E-activities play an unequivocal part in our current economic environment. Trade via the World Wide Web (WWW) is common and there was even a period when a so-called new economy seemed to emerge. This new economy allegedly had other rules of the game. However, the new economy's *raison d'être* was never proved. On the contrary, we encounter more and more evidence that the new rules lead to the bankruptcy of typical new economy organizations. It is a fact that from the numerous Internet businesses that were founded in the last 10 years, only a small proportion are still in the market. The estimated value of these companies appeared to be far too optimistic as a result of which the lack of a positive cash flow could no longer be offset by positive future expectations. On a macro level the new economy, as opposed to the old economy, can be used in the same fashion as the economical network, as opposed to the traditional organizational form, on a micro level. Organizations from the old economy that make the switch to e-activities often do not realize that creating a website is just the beginning of an extensive change process. In particular the adjustments or complete redesign to be made in the internal organization are often underestimated. For example, many traditional user controls can no longer be applied, and are replaced by IT controls that are often difficult to grasp. In addition, the entire control environment of organizations changes during the transition process.

Information Security

IT nowadays is pervasive throughout the operation of organizations. However, there are many threats that evolve from IT proliferation and particularly electronic communication. This section discusses some potential IT controls to be employed to mitigate these threats. There are four categories of threats in the realm of information security evolving from IT proliferation:

* confidentiality
* integrity
* availability
* authenticity.

This section elaborates on these threats. Note that each of these threats involves people that are purposely trying to make this threat become a reality. The activity of purposely trying to make one or more of these threats become a reality is generally called hacking, and the perpetrators are called hackers. Although hacking is mostly considered illegal, there are differences in individual countries' legislation. In addition, as a result of the speed of IT proliferation, legislation has problems keeping up with modern developments in this area.

Confidentiality means that only authorized persons are allowed to have access to specific parts of information. Confidential information should not be put at the disposal of people who want to use it to their own advantage or to the disadvantage of the entity to which the information relates. Instances of threats in this category are unauthorized logical or physical data access, traffic analysis, deduction and aggregation of information and unauthorized reproduction of software. Unauthorized data access may take place by physically gaining access to the system, or gaining logical access via the lines used for data communication. Less sophisticated techniques are also used such as searching waste bins for hard copies of confidential information. For example, a hospital was accused of having compromised their patients' privacy because it had thrown away, without shredding, misprinted patient files, parts of which were readily readable. The files were found in the hospital's waste container, just outside the building. Traffic analysis means that messages are intercepted by others than the intended receivers and further analysed. This usually takes place by making use of electronic eavesdropping which is the interception of radio signals transmitted by electronic communication devices or output devices like computer monitors. Deduction and aggregation of information means that different data sources, which individually do not have meaning to a noninformed person, are combined such that the result is meaningful data, hence information. For example, a student code and a grade behind that code is meaningless except for those who know what name is behind each student code. Lately there has been a lot of attention to privacy law enforcement aimed at prohibiting the combination of files from different sources. Finally, unauthorized reproduction of software is practised by many people without thinking about its illegal nature. The term generally used here is software piracy. The software contained on CDs or DVDs, or that is downloadable from websites, may or may not be free. If it is not free, then making a copy of it obviously should always result in a payment.

Integrity is often used interchangeably with reliability. Often the term integrity is used to specifically refer to information in automated systems, whereas the term reliability is of a more generic nature. We will use the terms in this fashion. Information is said to be reliable if it is valid, accurate and complete (see Chapter 8) and hence integrity means that information that is electronically communicated is valid, accurate and complete. Instances of threats in this category are unauthorized destruction or modification of data, unauthorized modification of programs, replay and invalid message sequencing. Unauthorized destruction or modification of data means that people who are not allowed to delete or modify data as stored in the system, transported over communication lines or in progress within the system, find a way to do so. Unauthorized modification of programs means that people who are not allowed to modify programs find a way to do so. Replay means that a message is eavesdropped on, recorded and sent again at the discretion of the perpetrator. For example, when an authorized person types his password to gain access to the system, this is recorded by a hacker who can use it later to gain access to the system himself. Finally, invalid message sequencing means that a series of messages is eavesdropped on, recorded and sent again at the discretion of the perpetrator, but in a different sequence. For example, different versions of a contract to be agreed upon are presented in reverse order as a result of a hacker trying to obstruct the negotiations.

Availability means that information must be at the intended user's disposal, on time and at the right place. Instances of threats in this category are denial of service as a result of defects, denial of service as a result of system overload, and unauthorized use of hardware. Denial of service as a result of defects means that a system breaks down because there are technical problems. Denial of service as a result of system overload means that a system may break down when its required capacity is not sufficient to fulfil the data-processing needs of its users. On system development the needed capacity can be calculated. However, there may be unforeseen circumstances such as a sudden increase in the activities of the organization, or hackers trying to attack the system in order to make it break down. For example, a well-coordinated attack by means of so-called e-mail bombs where hackers worldwide cooperate to send e-mails to the same server address at the same time, may overload the receiver's system. Finally, use of hardware by unauthorized persons may lead to the system being unavailable for the intended users.

Authenticity means that the sender and receiver of a message are who they claim to be. In electronic communication, where face-to-face contact is absent, this aspect of information control becomes more and more important. Instances of threats in this category are masquerading and repudiation. Masquerading means that a person appears in an electronic communication session and identifies himself as someone other than who he actually is. If that someone other is an authorized person, then the sender may send messages to the wrong person, or the receiver may receive messages from the wrong person. Repudiation means that the sender denies that he has sent a message, or that the receiver denies that he has received a message.

The examples of threats as mentioned here may pertain to more than one category of threat. For example, unauthorized modification of data (integrity) may lead to a system breakdown and resulting denial of service (availability) or a log file containing incorrect information about the sender of specific messages (authenticity).

In order to mitigate these threats, several methods for information security are available. Table 4.2 combines the aforementioned threats with the applicable methods for information security.

Table 4.2 Threats evolving from electronic communication and applicable methods for information security.

Threats evolving from electronic communication

Method for information security	Confidentiality				Integrity					Availability			Authenticity	
	unauthorized logical access to data	unauthorized physical access to data	traffic analysis	deduction and aggregation of information	unauthorized reproduction of software	destruction or unauthorized modification of data	destruction or unauthorized modification of programs	replay	invalid message sequencing	denial of service as a result of defects	denial of service as a result of system overload	unauthorized use of hardware	masquerading	repudiation
encryption	X		X	X	X	X	X						X	X
event logging	X		X	X	X	X	X		X			X		X
access control	X		X	X	X	X	X		X			X		
routeing control	X		X	X	X									
physical security		X				X	X			X		X		
fallback systems						X	X			X	X			
data recovery						X	X			X				
date and time stamps								X	X					
confirmations								X					X	X
priority and preemption											X			
authentication													X	
digital signatures													X	X
message authentication codes													X	X

Encryption

Encryption is the transformation of information by means of a specific algorithm into a format that is not understandable by those who receive it and do not know the algorithm to transform it back to the original format. There are several encryption methods. A public key infrastructure (PKI) enables users to securely and privately exchange data through the use of a public and a private key pair obtained and shared through a trusted third party. Whereas a PKI makes use of a private as well as a public key, a private key infrastructure only makes use of one key: a private key that is only known to the sender and receiver of an encrypted message. Applying a PKI should make breaking the code more difficult. Pretty good privacy (PGP) is software for encrypting and decrypting e-mails, files and digital signatures that are sent over the Internet. PGP makes use of a PKI. If PGP is used for the encryption of a digital signature then the receiver can verify the sender's identity and know that the message was not changed during transmission. PGP is the most widely used encryption software by individuals and many corporations. It has become the standard for e-mail security. A secure variant of the Internet protocol (IP) is Internet protocol secure (IPsec). IPsec is employed to make Internet connections as secure as private networks and hence IPsec is frequently used to create virtual private networks (VPNs). Secure electronic transaction (SET) is a system for ensuring the security of payment information on the Internet. It was supported initially by credit card companies and Internet software companies. With SET, a user receives a digital certificate which can best be compared with an electronic creditcard containing information that should uniquely identify and authenticate its possessor. SET makes use of Secure Sockets Layer (SSL), Secure Transaction Technology (STT by Microsoft), and Systems Secure Hypertext Transfer Protocol (S-HTTP). Just like PGP, SET uses a PKI. SET is in particular applicable in transmitting payment information over the Internet. For Voice over Internet Protocol (VoIP; making phone calls over the Internet) Zimmerman Real-Time Transport Protocol (ZRTP) encryption has been developed. For e-mail messages S/MIME (Secure Multi-Purpose Internet Mail Extensions) is a secure method. It uses the so-called Rivest-Shamir-Adleman (RSA) encryption system. S/MIME is included in the latest versions of Microsoft's Web browser and has also been endorsed by other vendors that make messaging products. MIME spells out how an electronic message must be organized. S/MIME describes how encryption information and a digital certificate can be included as part of the message body thereby using a PKI.

Event Logging

Event logging means that a log file is kept in order to record critical security incidents. After finding out that security has been broken, the log file can be scrutinized and the data contained be combined so as to take corrective measures. A special occurrence of event logging is intrusion detection. Intrusion detection uses specialized software to trace hackers by detecting atypical patterns in the usage of an infrastructure.

Access Control

The term access control refers to measures aimed at preventing logical access to the system. An access control matrix should be in place to prevent unauthorized persons from gaining access to the system.

Routeing Control

By means of routeing control, a message can be transported over a route the sender and the receiver prefer. Since Internet traffic cannot be controlled like this, additional routeing control measures must be taken to avoid messages following unsafe or overcrowded routes. An important device for routeing control is the firewall. It is aimed at concentrating all the electronic communication between an internal network (usually within one organization) and the outside world (the networks of other organizations) at one point. All the communication with the outside world then runs via the firewall which serves as the gatekeeper for the incoming and outgoing electronic communication. By concentrating the traffic at one point, security measures can be focused at this one point, as a result of which they will be easier to apply and more effective. This technique can be compared with a building having only one entrance. Everybody who wants to enter the building has to go through this entrance. By guarding this entrance, undesirable persons can be locked out, and people leaving the building can be monitored for not having stolen any of the organization's assets. A firewall consists of a combination of hardware and software. The stronger the preventive nature of a firewall, the more severe the built-in controls will be, and consequently the speed of electronic communication with the outside world. This is a trade-off that always has to be made when putting a firewall in place. Firewalls can be bypassed if the surrounding organizational measures are not adequate. For example, if a firewall is in use to protect a LAN from unwanted incoming and outgoing messages, but a user installs a modem and hooks his computer up to a regular telephone line, then the firewall is no longer effective. There are two basic configurations for installing a firewall when there are separate servers for communication via the Internet and the organization's information systems. The first option is to put the firewall between the outside world and the web server. The advantage is that penetrating the website will be frustrated; the disadvantage is that when someone succeeds in penetrating the website, then the whole information system of the organization lies open for potential hostile and harmful attacks. The second option is to put the firewall between the web server and the organization's information systems. The main advantage of this setup is that electronic communication with the outside world is not slowed down by the firewall. However, the disadvantage is that the website may come under attack and be modified by unauthorized persons. For example, a mail-order company in the Netherlands that engages in e-commerce activities via a website exhibiting a selection of its product ranges, discovered that hackers had found an easy way to modify the texts and photos on the website. Fortunately, the hackers did not find a way to get through the firewall behind the web server aimed at protecting the company's underlying information systems. As a result the only damage done was that the website looked messy. No underlying files where damaged. Usually, a combination is made of a firewall between the outside world and the website, and a firewall between the website and the organization's information systems. The zone in between the two firewalls is sometimes – and with a slight sense of drama – called a demilitarized zone (DMZ) to indicate that it is an area where there are no weapons and hence no battles between aggressors and defenders.

Physical Security

Physical security is aimed at prohibiting access to hardware, data and programs for unauthorized persons by means of physical measures. This category of measures includes, for example, putting locks on the doors to the computer rooms, safe storage of back-up files, using fire-resistant walls and doors for the computer room and employing sprinkler systems. A special physical security measure is to place computer screens only in so-called anti-tempest rooms in order to avoid unwanted electronic eavesdropping on the electromagnetic radiation normally transmitted by computer screens. Tempest is a term that originates from military jargon. It is an acronym for telecommunications electronics material protected from emanating spurious transmissions.

Fallback Systems

Fallback systems include the employment of data-processinghot sites and data-processing cold sites. These sites can be used if the primary systems break down. A data-processing hot site is a completely identical system to the primary system, and hence can also be referred to as a redundant system. It can usually be made available for operation at very short notice varying from a few minutes to a few hours. Organizations that are heavily dependent on their information systems usually have a data-processing hot site at their disposal. Examples of these types of organizations are banks, insurance companies, pension funds and investment funds. In order to make efficient use of data-processing hot sites, these systems are often used for educational purposes and off-line software development. A data-processing cold site is not readily available for operation but contains the necessary infrastructure that enables the building of a copy of the primary system within a relatively short period of time. Since the hardware still has to be installed it may take a few days or even a few weeks to make the system fully operational. Often, fallback systems are not owned by the organization itself but outsourced. Here, a commercial service organization provides the hardware required for data processing should the system of a client break down.

Data Recovery

Data recovery is the activity of restoring data that was erroneously destroyed or modified. In particular the recovery of data that has been lost during electronic communication sessions is an important issue. If such a data set is completely lost at the receiver's site then recovery can only take place by re-sending it. However, a receiver of data may not know whether or not data has been lost. For that purpose, confirmations of receipt have to be used. If data has only partially been lost, then recovery may take place by putting the message in its context and deriving the missing data elements from that context. Computerized systems are generally well equipped to apply programmed procedures for automatically filling the missing data elements. The principle behind these techniques is that every electronically communicated message contains redundant data that is used to determine whether the message has been received properly and to repair occurring errors. Data recovery is often mentioned in the same breath as back-up files. Back-up files are periodic carbon copies of the original files. These back-ups are used for data recovery purposes if data in the original files has been lost. The general procedure followed here is based on the grandfather-father-son principle. The copy then is called the son, whereas the original is called the father. When a copy is made of the son, a new son is being born and the original father becomes the grandfather. By following this procedure there is always a back-up file of the back-up file which creates additional security that data can be recovered at reasonable expense. It is important to have a plan in place that contains the procedures to be followed and the individual responsibilities of the persons involved. One such plan is a disaster recovery plan which aims to have the information system working properly as soon as possible after a disaster has taken place. Disasters may be of a general nature such as fires, earthquakes, floods, high winds, wars and terrorist attacks, but also of a very specific nature such as virus attacks, e-mail bombs, hackers gaining unauthorized access to a company's information system, software bugs, human error in inputting data or handling files and computer fraud. A disaster recovery plan should include, among other things, written instructions on how to act in case of an emergency, a training scheme for those involved, assigned authorities to champions of the plan and periodical and unannounced practice sessions.

Date and Time Stamps

By adding a date and a time stamp to a message, the receiver acquires a certain level of assurance that the message has not been delayed, that it is not a message that has been sent earlier (mitigating the replay threat) and that it has been sent in the right order relative to other received messages (mitigating the invalid message sequencing threat). Instead of or in addition to date or time stamps, messages may be sequentially pre-numbered so that each message is uniquely identifiable.

Confirmations

By using receipt confirmations, the sender acquires additional assurance that the intended receiver of a message has indeed received the message. By using delivery confirmations, the receiver acquires additional assurance that the sender indeed has sent the message. These confirmations are often automatically produced by the electronic communication system and sent to the sender or the receiver.

Priority and Preemption

Priority refers to processing the prioritized messages first when the electronic communication network gets overloaded. Preemption goes one step further by not just postponing the nonprioritized messages, but by deleting them.

Authentication

On authentication, a user in a communication session assesses that another user in that communication session is the person he claims to be. There are several authentication methods. Examples are passwords (also PIN-codes), physical possession of specific objects (for example, chipcards) and biometric keys such as iris recognition and fingerprints. In addition, in order to be sure that the right receiver is contacted, a callback system can be put in place. In such a system the sender contacts the intended recipient of a message, disconnects, and has the intended recipient call back to a pre-specified telephone number, e-mail or IP number.

Digital Signature

A digital signature may be compared to a real signature. By putting his signature under a document a person establishes accountability for the receipt of cash, goods, services or information, or he declares that he is the sender. A digital signature specifically refers to the sending or receipt of information. A digital signature is employed to prevent unauthorized modification of data, and to substantiate the identity of the person placing the signature.

Message Authentication Codes

A message authentication code (MAC) is an extra data element that is attached to a message as a check on the correct transfer of that message. For example, a control total is calculated on the basis of the number of characters in a message and added as an additional character to that message. On receipt of this message, the recipient's software uses the same algorithm for the calculation of the control total and compares this control total with the control total as added to the original message. If both control totals are equal then the recipient has acquired additional assurance that the message has been transferred correctly. A MAC used in this way is essentially a message integrity code.

Codes on Information Security

Codes on information security are aimed at the development of a system of generally accepted practices for dealing with information security issues from both an organizational and a technical point of view. These codes serve as management standards that should operationalize abstract terms such as confidentiality, integrity, availability and authenticity in order to make them understandable for consumers and business partners and hence increase their trust in electronic communication as applied in, for example, Internet commerce. The formal ratification of the structuring of a system of generally accepted practices within a specific organization is an example of certification. As with preparing for an ISO-certificate (see Chapter 9), organizations can prepare for certification against a code on information security. Among the organizations that are currently preparing for such a certificate are representatives of the old economy (traditional production and trade firms) as well as the new economy (application service providers, Internet service providers, information intermediaries and other Internet startups). Paradoxically, codes on information security, which are typical products of the old economy, are expected to play a major part in the further establishment of the new economy.

The initial attempt to develop a code on information security was made in the United Kingdom and took the form of a bundle of best practices in the field. This code was the result of the cooperative efforts of a great number of corporations and hence was broadly based. The next stage in the developmental process was a further internationalization where professionals from different European countries (including the UK, Germany, Norway and the Netherlands) started to cooperate. Each participating country chose its own means of creating a broad basis for the code. For example, in the Netherlands, the Dutch Normalization Institute (Nederlands Normalisatie Intstituut) supervised the realization of the code, and the Ministry of Economic Affairs, the Ministry of Transport and Communications, the Dutch Banking Institute (Nederlandse Vereniging van Banken), the Electronic Commerce Platform, FENIT and the major employers' associations expressed their explicit desire to stimulate the application of the code. Currently the code is more and more used by private and public organizations as a basis for their information security activities.

The code embraces more than a hundred security measures, divided over ten categories. Table 4.3 summarizes these measures.

Table 4.3 Information security measures contained in the code on information security.

Security categories	Key measures
Security policy	• Policy statement with the goals of information security. • Description of the organization's interests in having adequate information security. • Approval of the information security policy by the organization's management and setting the right tone at the top.
Organization of security	• Designing information security functions (assigning tasks and responsibilities), co-ordinating information security efforts, and holding people accountable for their actions regarding information and IT. • Explicit agreements with third parties on cooperation in the field of information exchange and the information security measures to be taken.
Classification and management of companies' assets	• Gaining insight into the company's assets and their owners. • Using classification schemes for information and information systems that enable an integrative view on business issues, information issues and IT issues in relation to information security.
Personnel	• Education and training aimed at enhanced security awareness. • Selection and placement of personnel. • Paying attention to information security issues in formal personnel evaluations.
Physical security and environment	• Putting physical access controls in place to the user environment and the automation department. • Establishing a clear desk policy. • Having wiring and computer equipment well organized. • Issuing guidelines for the use of peripherals like organizers, mobile telephones, personal modems, floppy disks, zip drives and tapes.
Computer and network management	• Organizing IT management. • Recording authorized IT management guidelines. • Exploiting technical security measures. • Providing follow-up to security incidents. • Putting information security controls in place.
Access control	• Designing a formal authorization procedure for the access to information and IT resources (password management, user registration and individual traceability). • Managing the resources for authentication and authorization.
Development and maintenance of systems	• Paying attention to security issues during system development. • Implementing sound change management practices.
Continuity management	• Having contingency plans and controls in place (disaster recovery planning, back-up procedures, fallback procedures and systems and periodical training sessions for disaster management).
Monitoring and oversight	• Periodically performing audits and other oversight activities aimed at information security policy compliance and compliance with legal and contractual obligations in the area of information security. • Performing IT audits with a focus on information security.

Codes on information security are aimed at bringing information security within organizations to a minimum acceptable level in order to increase the mutual trust between organizations or parts of organizations. These codes are baselines, implying that the elements contained are looked upon by their developers as being minimally required to meet due-diligence principles. For environments where increased information security risks are anticipated, a risk analysis may give cause for additional security measures.

Codes for information security are increasingly used as bases for the certification of information security within organizations. Certification is based on an accredited scheme and has two cornerstones: a compliance statement from the organization's management, and the results of an IT audit as performed by an independent auditor. The desired certificate can be issued by an accredited organization. The main advantage of having acquired an information security certificate is that trade partners have evidence that the information security measures of the certified organization meet certain quality requirements. In addition, the certificate can be used as an internal motivator to strive for adequate information security measures, and to visualize the results of the information security efforts. With the formulation of a code and certification on the basis of such a code, only part of the control problems that arise from IT employment are covered. In addition, there is a need for controls of a technological nature related to IT, and more specifically electronic communication.

IT-enabled Innovations and Internal Control

Many IT-enabled innovations have an effect on internal control. We will discuss the following innovations and their effects on internal control:

*   e-business;
*   business process re-engineering and business process management;
*   enterprise resource planning;
*   shared service centres.

E-business and Internal Control

Old economy organizations may make use of the traditional internal control concepts as discussed in our chapter on cornerstones of accounting information systems (see Chapter 2). When engagement in e-activities increases and organizations migrate towards forms that enable them to compete in the new economy, these cornerstones gradually become less important. One of the main problems is that flows of goods and money as well as tangible data and information carriers cease to exist as visible objects that are within reach of the organization. All the data and information enter and leave the organization electronically and flows of goods and money often by-pass the organization that buys or sells them via electronic communication. In the case of bitable goods such as music, software and texts that are electronically transmitted, there is indeed no physical flow of goods at all. This eliminates an important stepping stone for the internal control system. A related problem is that the invisibility of flows of goods, information and money is perceived by vendors and customers as an additional risk. As we will see throughout this chapter, this is completely justified. However, e-activities have many advantages. To mention but a few: work processes are upgraded and labour satisfaction increases, physical stores are no longer necessary which reduces costs, congestion of roads is reduced because the number of people travelling back and forth to work decreases, trade is done on the world market which is likely to lead to a better relation between prices and quality and customers can be approached more directly which, in particular, enables service characteristics to be tuned to the individual customer's desires. To make full use of these advantages of e-activities, vendors and customers must be convinced that engaging in e-activities is safe in many respects. A sound internal control system that has kept up with the latest developments in the new economy should contribute to enhanced trust in e-activities.

The main threat to e-activities being mitigated by means of control of an organizational nature is insider misuse. Note that insider misuse may be intentional or not, and that intentional misuse is much more difficult to trace than unintentional misuse. Fortunately unintentional misuse occurs much more frequently than intentional misuse. Because of the absence of physical and therefore visible measurement points, misuse will in general be more difficult to prevent or detect in electronic environments. When engaging in e-activities, the value cycle as introduced in Chapter 2 can no longer satisfactorily provide measurement points. Value cycle-based control totals and reconciliations as well as segregation of duties, which are traditionally considered powerful control tools, then become inapplicable. Importantly, the data base manager who plays a major part in maintaining the integrity of the data base that underlies e-activities will be able to manipulate all organizational data and hence preeminently embodies unsatisfactory pairing of duties. In order to mitigate the threats evolving from e-activities, additional preventive and detective controls have to be put in place.

Let us take the value cycle of a trade company as the starting point of our analysis. As we demonstrated in Chapter 2 there is an independent recording function that captures all the events pertaining to procurement and cash disbursements, and revenues and cash receipts. In general, the recording function is embodied by a data base. Making a transformation to e-activities leads to the following adjustments in the value cycle:

- The inventory is not under the authority of the organization. As a result there is a direct link between procurement and revenues. Since the inventory role is by-passed there may be flows of goods that are completely invisible for the organization.
- In addition to the recording – primary – data base, there is a second data base for checking purposes, denoted the checking data base.

The value cycle for a trade firm engaging in e-activities is depicted in Figure 4.2.

By employing web-based technology, an organization may realize a simplification of many processes. For example, vendor selection on the basis of inviting offers will become much easier, making use of the search engines and portals available on the Internet for product and vendor comparisons, receipt of offers from potential vendors may take place via e-mail, orders can be placed on-line at the vendor's website, receipt of customer orders may take place via the website, billing may take place via the Internet and delivery may take place directly from the vendor to the customer, by-passing the organization. However, in spite of the simplification of these primary processes, internal control measures will need some adjustments or even complete redesign when an organization engages in electronic communication.

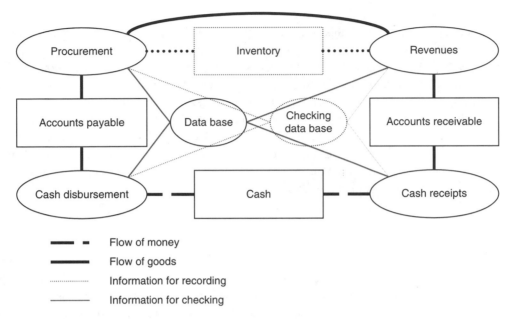

- - - Flow of money
——— Flow of goods
·········· Information for recording
——— Information for checking

Figure 4.2   Value cycle for a trade firm engaging in e-activities.

Internal Control Adjustments Induced by Engaging in Electronic Communication – Some Examples

- Parties must agree on the conditions that support electronic transactions. Of course this is no different from nonelectronic transactions, but there may be some specific caveats. For example, nonelectronic transactions are commonplace and are often supported by standard industry-wide terms of delivery whereas electronic transactions may require additional arrangements, such as privacy protection and validity of electronic signatures.
- When EDI orders are being placed there must be programmed procedures in place to check whether the order specifications are within pre-defined bandwidths. Should an upper or lower boundary be exceeded, then a further investigation is required by an authorized role within the organization. For example, if an order is placed for 100 pieces of article A, and the pre-defined bandwidth for acceptance is plus or minus 10%, then a shipment containing 89 pieces is not accepted automatically but left to the discretion of the head of the buying department. These kinds of requirements are built into the system by means of programmed procedures.
- On receipt of an electronic invoice a programmed procedure matches the invoice data with the order data, automatically produces a customer bill and makes a posting to the accounts payable

(Continued)

ledger and the accounts receivable ledger. Note that the flow of goods follows a direct path from vendor to customer as a result of which a matching of vendor invoice and a receiving report cannot be made. Instead reliance is placed on a customer complaints system which should be surrounded by clear agreements on the applicable terms. In order to receive early customer feedback, a confirmation is sent to the customer indicating that a specific shipment has been made. This confirmation may be accompanied by the bill. If a customer did not receive that specific shipment, he will notify the vendor where the head of the sales department will investigate what went wrong. If there is no customer reaction within a specified term, then the vendor invoice is approved by the head of the buying department by means of an electronic signature. Subsequently a programmed procedure initiates an electronic payment by means of EFT.

Automation as a source of threat to the achievement of internal control goals becomes even more important than it was already. However, a change in the nature of automation-related controls may also be anticipated. Segregation of duties is no longer based on a division of tasks between authorization, custody, recording, controlling and execution, but between humans and machines employing the feature that computers can force their users to go through a fixed sequence of activities. This type of segregation of duties can be denoted 'new age' segregation of duties. In the electronic environments as sketched, reconciliations and control totals are substituted by analytical review procedures, which provide less hard evidence. In this setting, the so-called soft controls will also gain importance. Importantly, soft controls are predominantly discussed in the management control literature. Finally, procedures will be put in place that apply more to the alignment between processes than to the alignment between departments. This is in accordance with the basic principles that underlie business process re-engineering.

As a result of the absence of physical inventories, flows of goods and flows of money, some control totals and reconciliations as embedded in the value cycle can no longer be employed effectively. For example, the relationship between the inventory at the beginning, purchases, sales and the inventory at the end is reduced to the relationship between purchases and sales, where there is no stocktaking possible, and the risk of bypassing the organization by means of direct sales from vendor to customer is substantial. However, controllability may also improve in an electronic environment since all information flows can be automatically reconciled by means of programmed procedures. For example, purchases according to journal voucher = sales according to journal voucher = batch total from vendor orders = batch total from customer orders = cash payments according to bank statements = cash receipts according to bank statements = picking ticket for vendor = confirmation of shipment by vendor = confirmation of receipt by customer. Additionally, in order to increase controllability a separate checking data base can be put in place. A checking data base aims to record the details of all the incoming and outgoing electronic transactions in such a way that once transactions are recorded in it, it can no longer be manipulated. This approach shows much similarity with the use of control registers in traditional internal control environments, in that they also contain redundant recordings that are also recorded in the primary data base. For example, a company records the following data on a sales transaction in its data base: customer code, product code and quantity. The same data is recorded in a checking data base. After having done this, some electronic data processing takes place where, inter alia, a vendor order and a customer bill are electronically transmitted. During this transmission the data on this transaction in the primary data base are erroneously changed and the data base becomes corrupted as a result. By having a programmed procedure in place that compares the primary data base with the checking data base, which has not been changed, the primary data base can be restored.

If the goods an organization trades are not tangible but bitable such as books in PDF format, movies in MPEG format and CDs in WAV or MP3 format then this causes some additional internal control threats as compared to physical goods that are not in an organization's own warehouses. Here again a checking data base can be employed to make a recording of all the website-related events. On the basis of the acquired records a detailed reconciliation on the article level can be made between the reported revenues and the recorded transactions.

BPR, BPM and Internal Control

Of the seven basic principles of BPR three have straightforward implications for internal control, and more specifically segregation of duties:

- Have output users perform the process. This implies pairing of duties between authorization and custody.
- Have those who produce information process it. This implies pairing of duties between authorization and recording.
- Empower workers, use built-in controls and flatten the organizational chart. This implies pairing of duties between authorization and controlling.

However, the unsatisfactory pairing of duties that may result from an ill-considered implementation is not the only threat an organization faces when embarking upon BPR. Considering the strong relationship between segregation of duties and reconciliations and control totals, the latter may lose relevance for control purposes. Consider the case of an organization consisting of the following four departments: administration, purchasing, sales and warehouse. The head of administration periodically reconciles the what-should-be position of the inventory at the end of the period with the inventory report containing information on the inventory at the beginning of the period (prepared by the warehouse keeper), the purchased goods report (prepared by the purchasing department) and the sold goods report (prepared by the sales department). This reconciliation makes sense because it may uncover any errors made by the various departments involved. When these departments are combined into processes, then the data sources are no longer separated from each other. As a result any unintended errors will be discovered in an early stage of data processing within the process itself. However, intended errors will be concealed because any what-should-be and what-is position can be reconciled by the providers of that information before handing it over to the head of administration. Hence the head of administration should put some additional controls in place. Analytical review gains importance in this setting. The head of administration will have to scrutinize the general ledger, in order to find eye-catching patterns like deviations from prior periods' sales. In addition more reliance will be placed on supervision as a control device. For example, the process owner will supervise his people and report irregularities to a designated authority. In general the control environment will have to be deliberately influenced toward more control consciousness in order to replace the reduced possibilities for traditional internal controls. Although control environment is an integral component of internal control according to the COSO report, influencing it traditionally is part of management control.

Although BPR and business process management (BPM) are two distinct concepts, there are some inter-relationships and some effects on internal control are comparable. BPR – as the name indicates – is about re-engineering; it is a way to radically change an organization from a vertical structure that is characterized by silo approaches and abundant top-down and bottom-up communication. BPM on the other hand starts after an organization is re-engineered. The horizontal structures must be managed and IT is needed not only to support, but mainly to enable the proper functioning of the created processes. This means that the effects of BPR on internal control hold as well for the effects of BPM on internal control. However, since BPM is a control tool by itself, there are more effects to be anticipated. Firstly, BPM requires complex IT infrastructures, which leads to the need for more built-in controls. For monitoring purposes, more reliance must be placed on continuous auditing tools. Hence, part of the audit (a monitoring activity) takes place within the organization's systems.

ERP and Internal Control

ERP implementation has both direct and indirect effects on internal controls (see Figure 4.3). First, as we have discussed in the previous section, BPR without additional measures will have a predominantly negative effect on internal controls. Second, ERP and BPR often go hand in hand. As a result there is an indirect effect of ERP on internal controls. Finally, ERP has positive as well as negative direct effects on internal controls, including:

- Measurement points such as the transfer of documents, physical goods or common money from one person to another are integrated in the information system and, hence, are no longer visible. As a result, controls based on manual inputs and outputs as carried out by users, often called user-controls, become less applicable. For example, establishing accountability by having someone initial for receipt of cash or goods as a preventive control measure can no longer be effectuated. This has a negative effect.
- The use of programme modules that enforce the application of programmed controls. This has a positive effect.

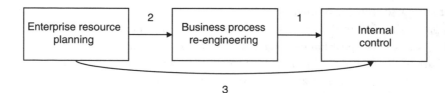

Figure 4.3   The direct and indirect effects of ERP on internal controls.

- Controls migrate from the execution stage of information system use to the implementation stage of information system development. Depending on the state of the organization's IT knowledge, this may have a positive or a negative effect. The less developed this knowledge, the more negative the effect of controls migrating to the system implementation stage and vice versa.
- Data integration, as in ERP, enables a control focus on just one object, namely the central data base. This should lead to enhanced controls and hence has a positive effect.

Shared Service Centres and Internal Control

When engaging in transactions with a shared service centre (SSC) or when outsourcing certain activities, the following controls at least must be put in place:

- Write a service level agreement (SLA) that gives a detailed specification of the rights and obligations of each of the parties involved; periodic checks must be done on compliance of realized actions and results with the SLA.
- Make a detailed specification of the terminology that will be used in the transactions between the organization and the SSC; a taxonomy must be developed that contains all the relevant terms (for example, if an amount is communicated that is labelled Gross Turnover, then both the sender and the receiver must give the same meaning to this term so that the same amount is communicated).
- Provide the necessary IT resources to the SSC; for example, if a call centre has to solve delivery problems with customers, then the call centre must have all the information about customers who may call at its disposal, which may be in the form of software for customer relationship management.
- Secure data communication so that there is reasonable assurance about confidentiality, integrity, authenticity and availability of electronically communicated data and information.

IT Governance

IT governance is the system by which IT within enterprises is directed and controlled. The IT governance structure specifies the distribution of rights and responsibilities among different participants, such as the board, business and IT managers, and spells out the rules and procedures for making decisions on IT. By doing this, it also provides the structure through which the IT objectives are set, and the means of attaining those objectives and monitoring performance. IT governance deals with the way IT is employed and controlled in organizations. It is a member of the 'enterprise governance family'. By analogy with corporate governance, IT governance consists of the following main components:

- IT control: focus on IT control goals, including cost control, information quality; compliance, availability, confidentiality, maintainability and flexibility;
- IT decision-making power: focus on who decides on IT investments;
- IT responsibility: focus on the responsibility for the realization of IT control goals;
- IT oversight: focus on who is charged with oversight on IT governance;

- IT integrity: focus on reliable systems that provide reliable information;
- IT accountability: focus on reporting on the quality of an organization's IT governance.

IT governance, by analogy with any form of governance, has the notion of 'standards' as its central tenet. So, when considering IT governance in its context we arrive at the following hierarchy of concepts:

- IT security, which looks upon IT from a technology viewpoint;
- IT control, which looks upon IT from an organizational viewpoint;
- IT risk management, which looks upon IT from a systematic approaches viewpoint;
- IT governance, which looks upon IT from a standards viewpoint.

The most widely used IT governance frameworks are ITIL, COBIT and ISO 17799. IT Infrastructure Library (ITIL) was published by the UK government to provide best practices for IT service management. Control Objectives for Information and Related Technology (COBIT) was published by the IT Governance Institute (ITGI) and is currently globally recognized as a high-level governance and control framework. ISO/IEC 17799: 2000 was published by the International Organization for Standardization (ISO) and the International Electrotechnical Commission (IEC). It provides a framework of a standard for information security management.

Before these frameworks were published, auditors, business managers and IT practitioners were talking a different language. In response to this communication gap, COBIT was developed as an IT control framework for business managers, IT managers and auditors, based on a generic set of IT processes meaningful to IT people and, increasingly, business managers.

IT governance auditing is part of the oversight component of IT governance and pertains to the process of checking whether the IT component in information systems (mainly the IT infrastructure) meets the quality criteria that have been set for these systems. IT governance attestation is the outcome of an IT governance audit and as such is also a monitoring device. Since monitoring and management control are heavily intertwined, IT governance attestation is a management control instrument. There is a 'double bind' relationship between auditing and IT governance, meaning that, whereas the IT governance attestation system, being a monitoring device, is part of the internal control system of an organization, the internal control system audit aimed at IT governance attestation is part of the monitoring system.

Summary

This chapter first introduces the concept of information and communication technology and gives various examples of IT applications and related management tools. IT is pervasive throughout virtually all contemporary organizations. Hence, the positive and negative effects of IT must be fully taken into consideration. The second part of the chapter explicitly investigates the effects of IT on internal control. The chapter concludes with some insights from IT governance to bring together all the topics as discussed in this chapter.

Documenting and Evaluating Internal Control Systems

Introduction

Internal control systems can be documented normatively or analytically. Normative documentation prescribes what internal control systems should be like, whereas analytical documentation reflects the actual state of an organization's internal control systems. Organizations prepare documentation for various purposes:

1. to improve their information system;
2. to increase the efficiency and effectiveness of operations;
3. to achieve strategic gains; and/or
4. to meet regulatory demands (e.g. the Sarbanes-Oxley Act).

By comparing normative to analytical documentation, one can identify the shortcomings of an existing internal control system. Such an analysis is often made by an external auditor, an internal (or operational) auditor, a controller or analyst, an internal control officer, or a consultant hired to design or improve the internal control system. In practice normative documentation may not always be prepared as such. However, this does not mean that there is no optimal internal control system that can serve as a benchmark for a certain organization. In such a situation the auditor or designer of the internal control system will evaluate the existing, actual internal control system and adjust the system where necessary, based on a (mental) normative framework. This may seem like a suboptimal approach, but in most cases this is the most practicable given the large variety of possible internal control solutions in identical situations. Of course the optimal approach would be to design a normative internal control system based on a thorough analysis of the characteristics of the organization and to communicate this within the organization in the most appropriate way.

In recent years pressure on organizations has increased to design and account for a high-quality internal control system. This is mainly due to the US Sarbanes-Oxley Act of 2002 (see 'Corporate Governance' in Chapter 2, p. 37). The Act requires companies listed on the US stock exchanges to report on (the quality of) their internal control system, thus regulating documentation of the internal control system.

It is useful to develop a clear approach that can serve as a guideline in preparing normative documentation of internal control systems. The knowledge that is acquired in preparing such documentation will help to develop a systematic understanding of the parts included in such documentation. It will also help to understand the vital importance of the way in which such information is communicated.

There are several methods of documenting internal control systems, including narrative descriptions and graphic documentation in the form of diagrams and flowcharts. This chapter discusses these methods, which in practice are often combined.

Learning Goals of the Chapter

After having studied this chapter, the reader will understand:

- how to prepare narrative internal control descriptions;
- methods available to graphically document internal control systems;

- how to complement graphical documentation with a checklist of applicable internal controls;
- factors that affect the documentation of internal control systems;
- the importance of proper communication of internal control systems; and
- the components of an internal control manual.

Narrative Descriptions of Internal Control Systems

Case 5.1 below contains a narrative description of an internal control system. This is an analytical description because this narrative describes the actual state of an internal control system. The narrative describes the flow of documents (how messages flow through the organization) as well as a number of internal control measures (matching the invoice with the purchase order and receiving report). The narrative is stated in English and anyone with knowledge of the English language is able to visualize this purchasing process.

For simple processes, such as this purchasing process, narratives are sufficient to achieve the three objectives of internal control documentation (improve information systems, increase efficiency and effectiveness of operations and achieve strategic gains).

Although one could conclude otherwise based on the above narrative, narrative descriptions are not necessarily unsystematic. However, a natural language generally does not provide a mechanism to force a certain structure onto the documentation, in contrast to the graphic documentation techniques discussed in the next section. To meet this objection of narrative description one could use a fixed format to present the narratives. An example is the step-by-step plan below in Table 5.1 of the purchasing process described in Case 5.1.

Case 5.1: Purchasing Process

The warehouse sends a purchase requisition to the purchasing department. Based on the information in the vendor file and the inventory file the purchasing department prepares a purchase order and sends the order to the vendor. The vendor sends an acknowledgement of the order to the purchasing department. The purchasing department sends a purchase order notification to the accounts payable department. When the goods are received in the warehouse, the warehouse clerk sends a receiving report to the accounts payable department. The vendor sends an invoice to the accounts payable department, which matches the invoice with the purchase order notification and the receiving report. If the three documents match, the accounts payable department updates the accounts payable subsidiary ledger, establishes the payable (i.e. approves invoices for payment) and thus authorizes the cash disbursements department to make the payment to the vendor.

Table 5.1   Example of a systematic narrative of an internal control system.

Process step nr	External function	Internal function	Process step	Description	Nr of next step
1		Warehouse	Purchase requisition	The warehouse sends a purchase requisition to the purchasing department	2
2	Vendor	Purchasing department	Purchase order	The purchasing department prepares a purchase order and sends it to the vendor	3
3	Vendor	Purchasing department	Order acknowledgement	The vendor sends an order acknowledgement to the purchasing department	4
4		Purchasing department	Purchase order notification	The purchasing department sends a purchase order notification to the accounts payable department	5
5	Vendor	Warehouse	Receipt of goods	The warehouse receives the goods from the vendor and sends a receiving report to the accounts payable department	6
6	Vendor	Accounts payable department	Check invoice	The accounts payable department receives the invoice from the vendor and matches the invoices with the purchase order notification and the receiving report.	7
7		Accounts payable department	Accounts payable subsidiary ledger	The accounts payable department updates the accounts payable subsidiary ledger, establishes the payable and authorizes the cash disbursements department to make the payment	8
8	Vendor	Cash disbursements department	Payment	The cash disbursements department makes the payment	and so on

The arrangement in a step-by-step plan as in Table 5.1 is arbitrary. If a process has many exceptions, and therefore many different infrequent activities, an additional column for infrequent activities will be included in the table. Obviously a table is much more systematic than the narrative that informs the table and can therefore be communicated more easily to users.

Graphic Documentation of Internal Control Systems

In complex situations graphic documentation is often more efficient than narratives because in such cases a language is used – a graphic documentation technique – that is specifically developed for preparing documentation of internal control systems, in contrast to natural languages, which are developed for many other purposes and therefore not specifically for documentation of internal control systems.

Because of this specificity, graphic documentation techniques have the following advantages over narrative descriptions:

- Higher information density. One can see a certain process at a single glance;
- Univocal representation of relationships between processes and procedures. Relationships are usually indicated by means of arrows;
- Consistency requirement. If two diagrams or flowcharts are not aligned, using a graphic documentation technique will help identify this, particularly when using software in preparing the diagrams or flowcharts; and
- Ease of maintenance. When diagrams or flowcharts are prepared at different levels of detail, systematic maintenance is simplified.

There is a large variety of available techniques for internal control documentation. We discuss the following two techniques:

1. Data flow diagrams, which can be further subdivided in context diagrams, logical data flow diagrams and physical data flow diagrams; and
2. Systems flowcharts.

We discuss these two particular techniques since they are the most applied in practice. Other, more flexible techniques are available, each using their own set of symbols. Since the symbols of these flexible techniques can differ from situation to situation we will not discuss these further and simply state that for every technique the preparer and the user of the resulting charts or diagrams have to assign the same meaning to each symbol to be useful. Just like any other language, graphic documentation techniques have a certain syntax (the symbols) and certain semantics (the meaning of the symbols).

Data Flow Diagrams

Data flow diagrams are graphical representations of information systems, consisting of the following components:

- The organizational entities or data-processing activities, e.g. the sales department, or receiving a payment;
- The data flows between those entities or activities, e.g. information about a payment or receipt of goods in the warehouse; and
- The sources, destinations and storage of data, e.g. a client, the bank, or the sales journal.

Figure 5.1 shows the symbols that are used in data flow diagrams. Data flow diagrams help us to show the data or information flows in organizational processes. We distinguish logical and physical data flow diagrams. Logical data flow diagrams visualize *what* activities are performed in the information system in a certain process, whereas physical data flow diagrams show *how*, *where* and *by whom* the activities are performed. Thus, logical data flow diagrams reflect the content of the information flows, and physical data flow diagrams concern the form (and therefore the media) that are used to process the information flows. In the integral control framework logical data flow diagrams are part of the information and communication domain and physical data flow diagrams are part of the IT domain (see Figure 5.2).

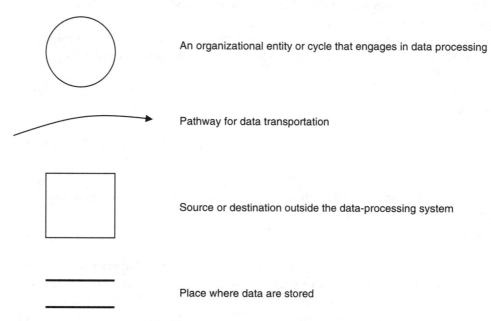

Figure 5.1   Symbols in data flow diagrams.

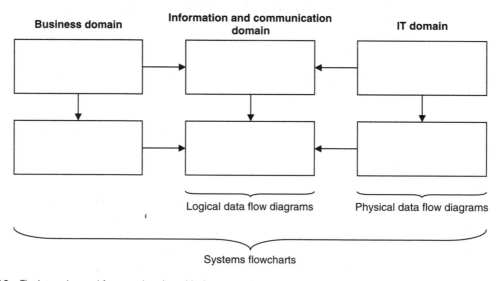

Figure 5.2   The integral control framework and graphic documentation techniques.

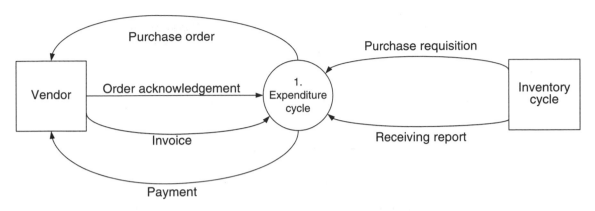

Figure 5.3   Context diagram.

Data flow diagrams can be prepared at different levels of detail. A context diagram is a diagram with the least level of detail which combines organizational units and data-processing activities into processes and positions those processes *vis-à-vis* the sources of and destinations for the data. Continuing the example of the purchasing process, the context diagram will consist of the purchasing process, the vendor and the inventory system, as shown in Figure 5.3.

We can further extend the context diagram into logical and physical data flow diagrams at different levels, blowing up each organizational unit or data-processing activity in the context diagram to such an extent that the constituent parts are visible. The context diagram in Figure 5.3 can thus be further detailed, resulting in the logical data flow diagram in Figure 5.4 and the physical data flow diagram in Figure 5.5.

The logical data flow diagram reflects the activities and content of the information flows in a certain process, and the physical data flow diagram shows the departments or employees that perform those activities and the data carriers that are used to record the data and transfer these data between two departments or employees. The logical and physical data flow diagrams therefore complement each other. Using these two diagrams in combination helps to better maintain the documentation of the internal control system. Assume that the organization that has documented its purchasing process in the aforementioned diagrams decides to switch from paper forms with signatures to an automated system where different employees communicate the various internal messages and authorizations via their computer – that is, electronically. The content of these messages does not change and therefore the logical data flow diagram does not have to change either. However, the format of the messages does change and therefore the physical data flow diagram will have to change as well.

Figure 5.6 reflects the changes in the physical data flow diagram as a consequence of the changeover to the automated system. If only one comprehensive data flow diagram had been prepared incorporating both content and form of the information flows then the switch to the automated system would have required a change to the entire diagram. The distinction between logical and physical data flow diagrams makes it easier to maintain the internal control system's documentation.

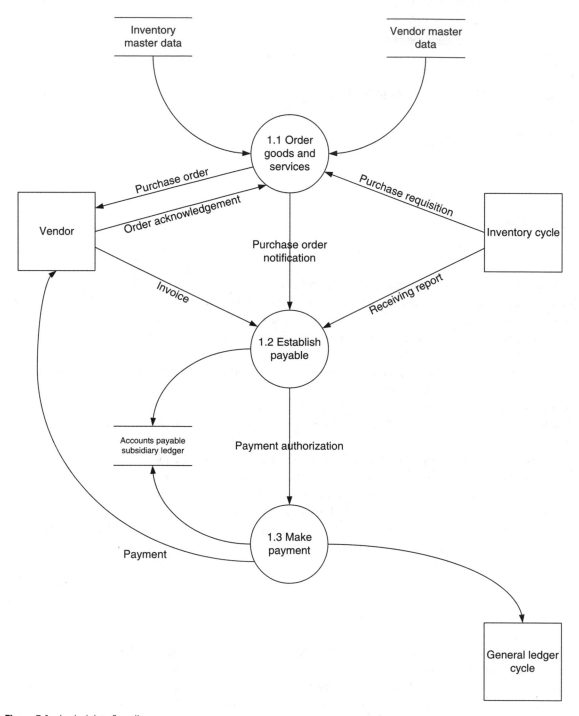

Figure 5.4 Logical data flow diagram.

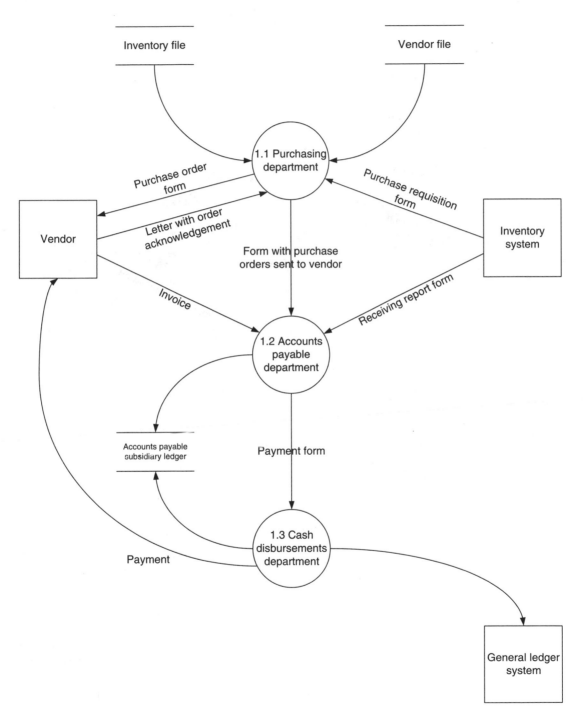

Figure 5.5 Physical data flow diagram.

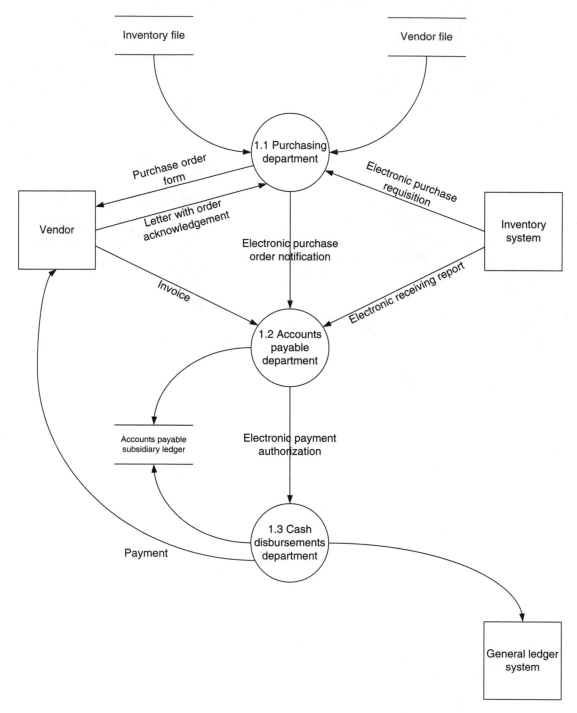

Figure 5.6 Physical data flow diagram after replacing internal paper flow with electronic communication flow.

Systems Flowcharts

A chart that can complement data flow diagrams is the systems flowchart. These flowcharts incorporate the business, information and communication and the IT domains, and thus help us to paint a comprehensive picture of a certain business process. Such a comprehensive picture will help us to understand the data flows, the IT that is used and the actual operations of that process.

Systems flowcharts use symbols that are classified according to the components of the basic pattern of information provision and the integral control framework. Figure 5.7 shows the most commonly used symbols. Figure 5.8 shows the systems flowchart of the purchasing process discussed earlier. This flowchart reflects:

- the activities in the purchasing process (including control activities);
- the departments where these activities take place;
- the documents that are exchanged;
- the data collections;
- physical flows of goods; and
- the relations between the activities, departments, documents, data collections and physical flows of goods.

Together these elements provide a systematic, comprehensive picture of the purchasing process.

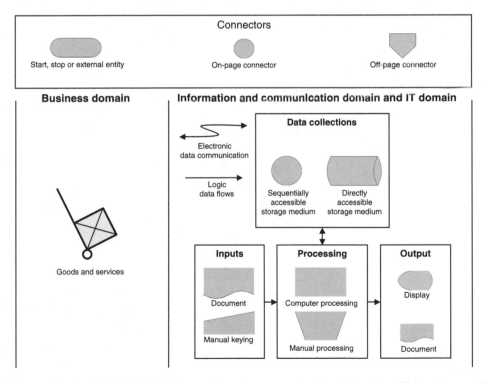

Figure 5.7 Systems flowcharting symbols classified according to the components of the basic pattern of information provision and the integral control framework, including connectors.

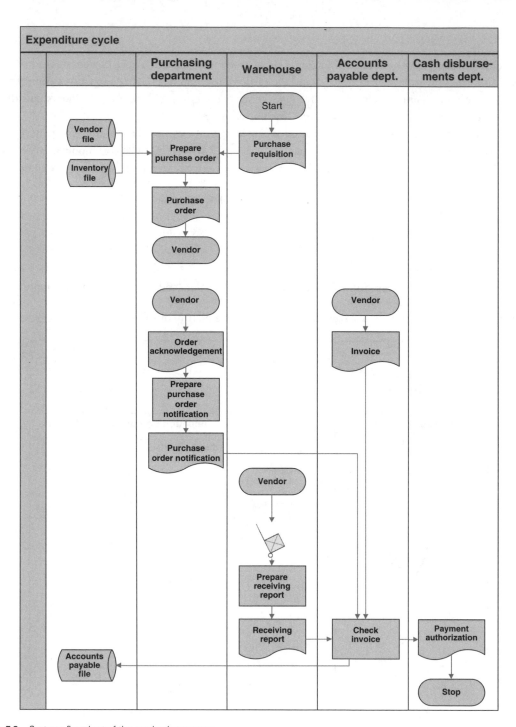

Figure 5.8   Systems flowchart of the purchasing process.

The Controls Checklist

Graphic documentation of internal control systems, in the form of the data flow diagrams and systems flowcharts discussed in the previous section, is often complemented by a listing of the internal controls that are applicable to the process being documented. This listing, which we term the controls checklist, helps us to identify the controls that can or should be present in the process at hand, as well as the controls that are currently present in this process. Together, this allows us to assess the quality of the internal control system of the process.

For convenience, the controls checklist distinguishes applicable controls in a number of categories. In order of decreasing scope these are (1) segregation of duties between the departments involved in the process; (2) independent recording of process transactions in the general ledger by the accounting department; (3) independent reconciliations by the controller or the head of the accounting department; (4) process controls and procedures; and (5) technology-related controls. Thus, we start with the category of controls that have the broadest scope and apply to the entire process, and end with categories that have a much narrower scope and only apply to parts of the process.

For each of the categories above, applicable controls need to be listed for the particular process that is documented and evaluated. Continuing our example of the purchasing process, segregation of duties is required between requisitioning, purchasing, receiving, accounts payable and cash disbursements. Similarly, process transactions in the purchasing process that need to be independently recorded in the general ledger by the accounting department include purchase requisitions, purchase orders, goods received (inventory update), increases and decreases in accounts payable (accounts payable updates) and cash disbursements. Similar listings can be prepared for the remaining three categories of controls, and examples are provided in Table 5.2 below.

To help us assess the quality of the process' internal control system as well as identify potential areas for improvement, we need to indicate for each control whether this control is present in the process that is being evaluated. Examples are also provided in Table 5.2.

Table 5.2   Example of a controls checklist for the purchasing process.

Control nr	Description of internal control	Present or absent
Segregation of duties between process departments		
1	Segregation of duties between requisitioning, purchasing, receiving, accounts payable and cash disbursements	Present
Independent recording of process transactions in the general ledger by the accounting department		
2	Independent recording of purchase requisitions	Absent
3	Independent recording of purchase orders	Present
4	Independent recording of goods received	Present
5	Independent recording of increase and decrease in accounts payable	Absent
6	Independent recording of cash disbursements	Present

(Continued)

Table 5.2   (Continued).

Control nr	Description of internal control	Present or absent
Independent reconciliations by controller or head of the accounting department		
7	Reconciliation of purchase orders and purchase requisitions	Absent
8	Reconciliation of purchase orders and goods received	Present
9	Reconciliation of goods received and invoices received from vendors	Absent
10	Reconciliation of invoices received and increase of accounts payable	Present
11	Reconciliation of decrease of accounts payable and cash disbursements	Present
12	Reconciliation of purchase requisitions, purchase orders, goods received and cash disbursements (overall reconciliation)	Absent
Process controls and procedures		
13	Approve purchase requisition	Absent
14	Purchase requisitions based on inventory levels and production and/or sales forecast	Absent
15	Requisition audit data (independent record is maintained of all requisitions at warehouse/requisitioner)	Absent
. . .		
18	Compare vendors for favourable prices, terms, quality and product availability	Present
19	Approve vendor selection	Present
. . .		
23	Confirm purchase order to requisitioning department	Absent
24	Prenumbered purchase order forms (or number automatically assigned by ERP system)	Present
. . .		
28	Count goods and compare to vendor packing slip	Present
29	Inspect goods	Absent
. . .		
36	Match invoice, purchase order and receiving report	Present
37	Vendor invoice mathematical accuracy check (by accounts payable clerk)	Absent
. . .		
39	Cash disbursement is triggered by payment due date information (tickler file of payments due)	Present
40	One-for-one checking of cash disbursements and invoice amount (by cashier)	Present
. . .		
Technology-related controls		
43	Automated data entry	Present
44	Populate inputs with master data (use of existing master data for purchase transactions)	Present
45	Independent vendor master data maintenance	Absent
46	Preformatted screens (defining mandatory data fields and acceptable format of each field)	Present
. . .		
52	Digital signatures	Present
53	Computer-generated list of invoices due	Present
. . .		

Automated Tools in Documenting Internal Control Systems

After a certain technique has been chosen to document an internal control system, one needs to select a software package from the many available packages to help prepare such documentation. Currently the most commonly used package is Microsoft Visio (see Figure 5.9). In selecting a software package the following factors need to be taken into account:

- The extent to which the package supports the purpose of documenting the internal control system.
- The user friendliness of the package. This refers to how easily the user can learn how to use the package and interpret the output.
- The presence of a help desk for user support.
- The possibility to use the package for other (quality improvement) projects, e.g. compliance with quality standards issued by ISO (International Organization for Standardization).

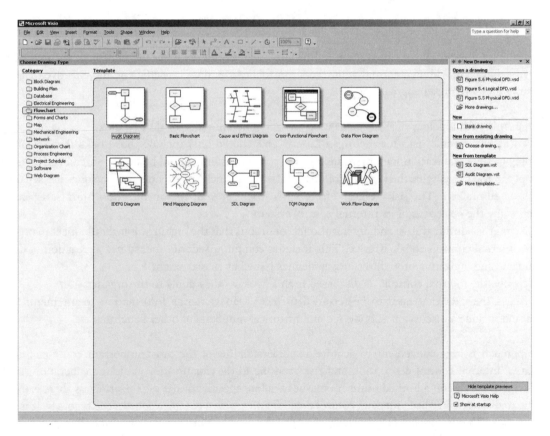

Figure 5.9 Microsoft Visio's start screen.

- The package's ability to read and modify data from other applications such as word processors and spreadsheets.
- The possibility to integrate the package with other common means of communication such as intranet, e-mail and various forms of groupware.
- The extent to which knowledge of diagrams and flowcharts that is present in the organization can be used in relation to the software package.
- The maintainability of the diagrams or flowcharts produced with the package if the organization or the organization's environment changes. This implies that the diagrams or flowcharts should be independent of roles or employees, applications, forms, or data. For instance, if a different employee is involved in a certain process, the other employee has to be changed only once (e.g. in the roles file), and not in the entire documentation of the internal control system.
- The costs of the package. These costs do not only include the purchase of the package, but in particular the hours spent on documenting and maintaining the internal control system using the package; and
- Personal preferences of the preparer and user of the documentation of the internal control system.

Normative Internal Control Descriptions

In describing the internal control system of a certain organization, as it should be from a theoretical perspective – that is, providing a normative internal control description – it is efficient and effective to apply a consistent and structured approach:

1. Determine the typology of the organization and the inherent risks for that typology.
2. Identify the specific risks for the organization. This should only include those risks that specifically apply to the organization for which the internal control system should be documented. The risks that apply to the category in the typology of organizations to which the organization belongs are separately discussed under 1. The risks relate to factors that could prevent the organization from (satisfactorily) achieving the objectives of its internal control system.
3. Discuss the administrative and organizational conditions that the organization should meet in order for the internal controls to be effective. This includes computer security measures, segregation of duties, budgets and budgeting procedures and guidelines issued by management.
4. Describe the internal controls as discussed in this book, as they apply to the organization.
5. Discuss the data that need to be recorded to meet management's information requirements. This should include a discussion of budgeted and historical numbers, or other benchmarks.

This approach is very convenient to acquire an understanding of the most important components of a normative internal control description and risks specific to the organization under consideration. It also allows concentration on a limited number of issues that are specific to that organization, as there is usually no time to discuss every little internal control detail for all types of organizations in the typology. It is obvious, therefore, that we choose breadth (different types of organizations) over depth (not all internal control aspects, but just those that are specific to the organization).

Typology

To classify an organization in the typology of organizations, for each category of revenues generated by that organization one should identify the category in the typology to which it belongs. It is entirely possible that one organization generates several categories of revenues that differ from each other to such an extent that the organization can be classified in more than one typology category. For instance, assume that a transportation company also has a petrol station and a car repair shop, both used by the company as well as by third parties. Each of these revenue categories implies different internal control measures, and therefore a typology category should be determined for each revenue category. When discussing the typology one should also discuss the risks inherent to the categories in the typology. Specific risks are not discussed until the next step.

Inherent risks are risks that apply more to one type of organization than to another. In other words, these are typical for a certain category of organizations. For instance, if an organization can be classified as a trade organization with cash sales, an important risk is theft of cash.

Specific Risks

This part of a normative internal control description should focus on specific risks. For instance, if an organization has many sales returns, then a specific risk for this organization is that goods that are returned have been damaged by the customer. This is not necessarily inherent to trade organizations in general, but may be specific to a particular trade organization. A discussion of internal control measures to mitigate the specific risks should be deferred to the section that focuses on internal controls. However, it is useful to briefly explain each risk as it helps to prioritize the risks. Make sure that only risks are discussed that can be mitigated by internal controls.

Administrative and Organizational Conditions

Certain administrative and organizational conditions need to be met for internal controls to be effective. We distinguish the following four categories of conditions:

1. computer security;
2. segregation of duties;
3. budgets and budgeting procedures; and
4. guidelines issued by management.

These conditions apply to the organization as a whole and cut across all processes in the organization. Therefore it is efficient to discuss these in a separate section. However, to be effective these conditions should be tailored to the specific organization as much as possible.

Computer Security

This concerns general controls that relate to the automation of information provision, also called general computer controls. Four categories of computer security measures can be distinguished:

1.   measures that relate to the IT organization;
2.   measures to prevent unauthorized modification or use of files and programs;
3.   measures to ensure the continuity of business operations; and
4.   measures related to program management.

Measures in each of these categories should be considered by discussing how these should be applied in the organization under consideration.

Segregation of Duties

Under this heading two issues should be discussed:

1.   Segregation between authorization, custody, recording, execution and checking; and
2.   Assumptions made if there is not enough information about segregation in the organization at hand. For instance, in a small organization there is no human resources department, and there is no indication as to who reconciles job and shop time. The most obvious person to make this reconciliation in this case would be the manager. This should be indicated explicitly in the normative description. It is not sensible to add new functions because this implies an entirely different organizational structure which might necessitate other changes in the internal control system. This could ultimately lead to a situation where the normative internal control description is no longer applicable to the organization under consideration.

In describing segregation of duties for the organization one should indicate which officer is assigned to which tasks, and what segregated duty is involved (authorization, custody, recording, execution, or checking). The section in the normative description on internal control measures in detail (see 'Internal Control Measures' below) should cover the desired segregation of duties in each of the processes discussed.

Budgets and Budgeting Procedures

Budgets, including master budgets, form an important part of planning and control systems as they provide a normative framework in the absence of objective norms. In a proper internal control system, officers, in checking functions, will use budgets as benchmarks in a number of controls with which to compare recordings of actual transactions. However, to be able to use budgets as benchmarks, these will have to meet a number of criteria as well. Depending on the type and size of the organization, budgets will be prepared by different work units (e.g. departments), which the accounting department or another department specifically designated for that purpose consolidates for the organization as a whole. The quality of the budgets is strongly dependent on the quality of the process that creates the budget, as well as issues such as arithmetical correctness, completeness in representing the operational activities of the organization and authorization by management.

   Budgets often consist of fixed and variable cost components. These form the basis for standard cost prices and rates, and the way in which these prices and rates are determined should be included in a normative internal control description. The master budget often consists of a long-range plan, a short-term (annual) plan, functional budgets, standard cost prices and rates. A description of the budgets should include the various functional budgets. Depending on the type and size of the organization, these can include budgets for purchasing, sales, investment, production and human resources.

Management Guidelines

All procedures and other guidelines should be authorized by management. These procedures and guidelines effectively delegate tasks to lower levels and mandate the effected officers to make certain decisions independently. To make sure that the nature of this mandate is clear, management should authorize these procedures and guidelines. Management can do this by signing a delegation register, but also by communicating the internal control procedures by sending a signed memo through the organization. Most likely there will be detailed guidelines for issues such as allowable discounts on sales prices, dealing with return sales, quality checks of goods received, hedging against currency fluctuations and so on. In many cases it is more efficient to discuss the applicable management guidelines in the section on internal control measures and to merely indicate under the section on administrative and organizational conditions that management authorizes guidelines that will be further specified in the section on internal control measures.

Internal Control Measures

This section is the heart of a normative internal control description. An important starting point here is that internal control solutions should be provided for every risk identified earlier. The order of discussing the internal control measures depends on the type of organization, but usually the description of the organization in the assignment provides sufficient direction. The most common structure is a description per process, starting with sales and ending with purchasing. At a minimum, the following should be discussed for each process: the duties that are to be segregated, the appropriate reconciliations to be made, the necessary procedures and the data collections that are to be used.

Data to be Recorded to Meet Management's Information Requirements

Every description of an organization should include sufficient clues as to the nature of the organization's operational activities and the information that is necessary to properly carry out these activities and/or information on the performance of these activities. In doing so one should never go beyond the description of the organization that is provided, but of course application of theoretical internal control knowledge is helpful to assess the relevance of particular types of information. For instance, the management of an organization that repairs high-tech consumer electronics has entered into long-term contracts with large electronics producers, taking over all warranty obligations at a fixed price. This organization will want information on the actual costs per contract compared to this fixed price to assess the viability of this activity. This should be included in the normative internal control description of the organization.

Also to be included is a description of the data elements to be recorded in data collections to provide information desired by management. These data collections can be included in an appendix to the actual internal control description, organized by process, to make sure all essential elements are included.

The Internal Control Manual

The ultimate purpose of documenting and evaluating internal controls is to improve the performance of the organization (see the introduction to this chapter). To achieve this objective the internal controls need to be documented appropriately. We have discussed several methods of doing so in this chapter. To be able to communicate the documented internal controls, all documentation needs to be made available to the users in a systematic way. To this end many organizations develop an internal control manual.

The internal control manual provides a description of the organization as it is and the internal control system as it should be. Such a manual usually contains all or part of the following components:

1. Introduction including the purpose, structure and audience of the manual, as well as reading instructions.
2. A description of the organization, including the structure of the organization, its strategy, its culture (including the control environment) and its information systems.
3. Risks for the organization with respect to information provision.
4. An assessment of the likelihood and impact of certain risks.
5. A description of the internal controls per process, including:
   a. the administrative procedures;
   b. controls to be performed;
   c. data flows;
   d. data collections; and
   e. departments or offices involved in the procedures, controls, data flows and data collections.
6. The information that is to be available for decision-making, accountability and functioning of the organization.

Appendices describe the symbols used in diagrams and flowcharts and their meaning, explain the documentation methods and the software that is used to this end, and provide additional information about the nature and size of the organization in the form of reports, forms and other documents.

An internal control manual does not necessarily come in paper format. It may also be in the form of a number of computer files that are selectively accessible to users via competency tables, based on the users' positions and/or functional levels. This allows the description to be tailored to the needs of the user and his or her level in the organization. It also improves the maintainability since changes are more easily processed in electronic than in paper data carriers. Accessibility is also improved when the manual is made available through the organization's intranet.

The internal control manual should be considered as the final step in every project to set up or improve an organization's internal control system. However, the actual success of an internal control manual depends on the degree to which users accept the manual. Table 5.3 below provides tips to increase user acceptance.

Table 5.3 shows that implementing an internal control manual as the final stage of a project to develop or improve an internal control system is a process of change management. This is not to be underestimated and it is therefore recommended to use a systematic approach. In practice, junior employees or interns are

Table 5.3   Tips to increase user acceptance of the internal control manual in an organization.

Communication:
- Distinguish between user groups and try to find out who are proponents and who are opponents.
- Strive for a simple description.
- Use communication channels that are appropriate for the specific users.
- Clearly communicate that a good internal control system is beneficial for both the organization and the individuals in that organization.

Leadership:
- Find proponents of formally describing the internal control system and use them to promote the implementation of the manual.
- Set up a project organization and appoint both line and staff employees.
- Try to enforce acceptance by realizing small improvements early on in the project.

User participation:
- Involve future users in the development of the manual by inviting them to provide advice on problems that occur, and by asking them to read and comment on conceptual text, diagrams and flowchart.
- Express the internal control measures as recommendations and not as dogmatic instructions.
- Collect information on user needs, experiences and responses in relation to the manual implementation project.

often employed in these projects. This implicitly signals that management does not consider the internal control manual to be sufficiently important and is therefore to be advised against, if management wants the organization to take the internal control manual seriously.

Summary

This chapter discusses important issues relating to documenting internal control systems. Such documentation helps to map out an existing internal control system (analytical documentation), or a desirable internal control system (normative documentation). The objectives of these documentation efforts can always be related to the cells in the integral control framework, as they are to contribute to:

- a better information system;
- a more efficient and effective organization; and
- achieving strategic gains.

Internal control documentation comes in many forms (narrative or graphic) and may use many different media to communicate the constituent parts (automated or manual). Each of these forms has its own advantages and disadvantages. Narratives are form-free and use a natural language. Therefore a person who speaks that language should be able to understand the narrative. Graphic documentation (in the form of diagrams or flowcharts) usually has a fixed methodology, requiring the reader to first understand this methodology before he or she can understand the diagrams or flowcharts. We have discussed two main categories of graphic documentation: data flow diagrams and systems flowcharts. Various software packages are available for making these diagrams and flowcharts. We have also shown that graphic documentation can be complemented by an internal controls checklist that allows us to assess the quality of the process's internal control system. Ultimately all internal control documentation will end up in the internal control manual. The purpose of the internal control manual is to communicate the internal control system of an organization as a coherent set of administrative procedures, controls, data flows, data collections and officers or departments that have to follow the procedures and perform the controls. An internal control manual can be communicated on paper, but it is preferable to do so electronically, via the intranet of an organization.

II

Internal Control in Various Organizational Processes

Organizational Processes

Introduction

We distinguish the following processes in organizations:

- purchasing;
- inventory;
- production;
- sales;
- human resources management;
- investment in fixed assets;
- cash management; and
- accounting and general ledger.

There are many more organizational processes. However, we only give an in-depth discussion of the most important ones. Processes can be categorized as primary or as secondary. We use the value cycle as a coherent framework to show the interrelationships between these processes. This chapter is an introduction to Chapters 7 to 11, which describe the risks and internal controls in various organizational processes.

Learning Goals of the Chapter

After having studied this chapter, the reader will understand:

- the difference between primary and secondary processes;
- the different types of processes in organizations; and
- the interrelationships between the different types of processes in organizations.

Primary and Secondary Organizational Processes

Primary organizational processes give meaning to an organization. They provide an organization's *raison d'être*. An organization that does not have any primary processes cannot survive because it will not generate any revenues. Examples of primary processes are purchasing, inventory, production and sales. Secondary organizational processes are meaningless without the primary processes that they support. Examples of secondary processes are human resources management, investments in fixed assets, cash management, accounting, IT management, judicial affairs, logistics, marketing and research and development.

Primary Processes

In most organizations the following processes can be considered primary:

- purchasing;
- inventory;
- production; and
- sales.

Each of these processes consists of a number of steps. In combination with the appropriate controls these steps should lead to effective and efficient functioning of the process in question.

The purchasing process generally consists of requesting the purchase of a certain good by user departments such as production or sales departments (purchase requisitioning), sending purchase orders to designated vendors, receiving the goods ordered, validating the invoices received, updating accounts payable and making payments.

The inventory process generally consists of receiving goods in the warehouse, recording the receipt of goods, storing the received goods, release of goods from the warehouse and inventory counts.

Production generally consists of designing the product, annual planning, cost calculation and production planning, job preparation, releasing raw materials from the warehouse, the actual production of goods, and production accountability and post calculation.

The sales process generally consists of preparing offers, receiving orders and deciding on order acceptance, billing, picking the goods from the warehouse and shipping these to the customer, updating accounts receivable and receiving cash.

Secondary Processes

In most organizations the following processes can be considered secondary:

- human resources management;
- investment in fixed assets;
- cash management; and
- accounting and general ledger.

Like the primary processes, each of the secondary processes consists of a number of steps that, in combination with the appropriate controls, should lead to the effective and efficient functioning of that process.

The human resources management process generally consists of recruiting and selecting employees, educating and training employees, assigning tasks to employees, evaluating employee performance, remunerating employees and firing employees.

Investment in fixed assets generally consists of assessing the need for investment in fixed assets, analysing investment possibilities, making the investment decision, delivery/construction and operation of the fixed asset, paying for fixed assets and disinvesting.

The cash management process generally consists of receiving cash, keeping cash in custody, safeguarding the value of the cash position and making payments.

The accounting and general process generally consists of collecting and categorizing financial transaction data, recording financial transaction data, processing financial transaction data and providing information.

Organizational Processes in the Value Cycle

As discussed above, there are many different processes in organizations. As also discussed above, we will not describe all the possible processes. Instead we focus on those that occur in most organizations and that have some important characteristics from an internal control perspective. Figure 6.1 gives an overview of the processes that will be discussed in detail in the next chapters. We visualize the interrelationship between the various processes by means of the value cycle introduced in Chapter 2.

Purchasing services may be considered a primary process and hence be organized in an identical way to the purchase of goods. Services may be acquired by outsourcing certain tasks to service providers, such as public accounting firms, cleaning companies, IT providers and repair shops. In these cases purchasing services is comparable to purchasing goods and can be organized in much the same way as the purchase of goods. However, services can also be purchased by hiring employees. In this case the employee in

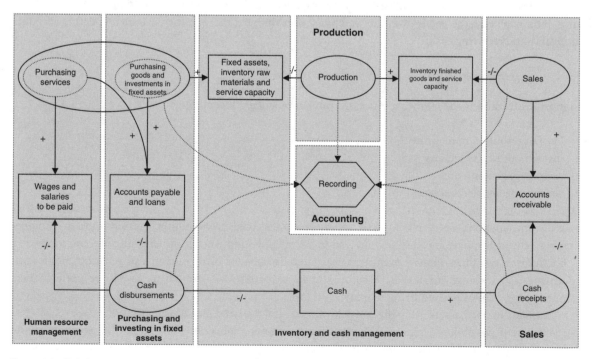

Figure 6.1   Relationships between processes in organizations.

question is entered in the payroll system and becomes subject to human resources management within the organization. This leads to significantly more involvement by the organization than when services are outsourced, particularly in the form of management controls. In Chapter 3 we discussed the distinction between bureaucratic control (in organizations putting control systems in place to purposely solve control problems) and market control (leaving control to the market and its price mechanism). Market control is especially relevant when tasks are outsourced to third parties whereas bureaucratic control is especially relevant when hiring employees to make sure they perform certain tasks. There are many management controls that apply to human resources management, with the purpose of influencing employee behaviour. This is in contrast to internal controls that mainly focus on providing the right information to enable management controls.

When goods or services that are received are not paid for in cash on delivery, the invoices received can only be paid when a designated authorization function authorizes the payment. This authorization can be given by the head of the purchasing department or the (head of the) requisitioning department. The payroll department prepares payroll, and hired employees are paid via the cash disbursements department. Authorization for payroll disbursement is usually given by the human resources department, but again the responsible (head of the) requisitioning department may also authorize these payments. A special type of purchasing is investment in fixed assets. This is rarely a routine process and generally investment decisions are made at a higher level in the organization as the investment progressively becomes more significant. For most organizations, investment in fixed assets is a secondary process.

Inventories of raw materials and other goods are maintained to be used in production or to sell directly to customers. Inventories of man hours that are used as resources are obviously not physically present in a warehouse. Effectively, this is virtual inventory embodied by the employee labour contracts. Such contracts will for example contain clauses about the number of hours an employee must work per week and the number of vacation days. If there is an inventory of man hours that can be directly sold to an organization's customers, such as in a law firm, then the inventory represents the organization's service capacity. This too is virtual inventory that is embodied by the labour contracts of the organization's employees. Besides the inventories of goods, man hours and service capacity, an organization can also have inventories of cash. This inventory consists of money that is physically present in the organization such as petty cash, but it also consists of money in the bank. Obviously cash management is an important issue since no organization can survive if money continuously exits the organization without receiving anything in exchange.

In a production process, raw materials, man hours and other resources are used to manufacture finished goods. A technical process transforms one inventory into another inventory that becomes directly saleable as a result.

Cash sales lead to direct cash receipts whereas sales on account must result in sales invoices that are sent to the customers in question and must eventually lead to cash receipts.

Ultimately transactions from all organizational processes need to be recorded in the general ledger. The general ledger is at the heart of the accounting process, in which financial transaction data are recorded. In addition to financial data, nonfinancial data are also recorded. Often this is still done in a separate system and may be quite primitive, in the form of a spreadsheet. Information provision may be undertaken by a central department at corporate level, but also by decentralized departments.

Summary

Basically there are two types of processes in organizations:

- primary organizational processes; and
- secondary organizational processes.

Primary processes, such as purchasing and sales, contribute directly to revenue generation. Secondary processes, such as human resources management or accounting, contribute indirectly to revenue generation. However, an important contingency factor to this distinction is the type of organization. Human resources management generally is a secondary process, but in service organizations that hire people and sell man hours to their customers, human resources management effectively is a purchasing activity and hence a primary process. This chapter has clarified the differences and similarities between various types of processes and has demonstrated their coherence by describing these as components of the value cycle. This chapter therefore serves as an introduction to the following chapters, where we discuss the risks and internal controls in the organizational processes presented in this chapter.

The Purchasing Process

In this chapter:

Introduction

Purchasing may pertain to raw materials, merchandise, supplies, investments, foreign currencies and services. In many organizations purchasing of raw materials and merchandise will be assigned to the purchasing function. The other purchasing tasks are usually performed by the accounting department, general management, or the management of the department that needs a particular service. In these latter cases, the formal, more operational purchasing tasks will still be performed by the purchasing function. The purchasing function is an authorization function and is usually perormed by the purchasing department. This department's main task is to purchase in the best way possible.

From a strategic and tactical point of view the purchasing department needs guidelines related to vendors, make-or-buy guidelines, information about technological developments, distribution alternatives, price developments for goods and services and inventory levels of goods.

To perform the operational purchasing tasks, purchasing clerks need information for preparing and processing purchase requisitions and placing purchase orders. This information is necessary for progress and execution control and may also be used for accountability purposes.

An important risk in the purchasing process relates to bonuses, provisions, large Christmas gifts, or even kickbacks offered to purchasing clerks by vendors if they buy from these vendors. This may induce the purchasing clerk to buy from the vendor that offers him the best personal advantages, and no longer from the vendor that offers the best price–quality relationship. Therefore, the risk of fraudulent actions needs to be taken into account. Measures to mitigate this risk are:

- proper screening of purchasing clerks;
- rewarding purchasing clerks when they meet their purchasing targets in relation to the desired price–quality relationship;
- setting up a code of conduct which prohibits accepting gifts by purchasing clerks;
- making use of guidelines for tender procedures;
- comparing purchase prices and market data in detail; and
- comparing average purchase prices between purchasing clerks.

Learning Goals of the Chapter

After having studied this chapter, the reader will understand:

- the risks in the purchasing process and the exposures to those risks;
- the internal controls to be implemented in the purchasing process; and
- the stages in the purchasing process.

Risks, Exposures and Internal Controls in the Purchasing Process

Generally, the most important risk in the purchasing process is considered to be undue influence over purchasing clerks due to gifts or even kickbacks, resulting in too high costs of goods sold. A number of internal controls can mitigate this risk. A preventive measure is appropriate screening and rewarding of purchasing clerks, supplemented by a code of conduct which prohibits accepting kickbacks and the like. Purchasing clerks should be confronted with noncompliance with the code of conduct in the form of sanctions, thus improving their purchasing ethics. Another preventive internal control measure is the use of a tender procedure which effectively precludes influence over the purchasing clerks since multiple vendors are invited to make offers and two or more employees of the purchasing department subsequently select the vendor offering the best terms. This decision should always be documented and is therefore traceable.

Furthermore, the controller or the head of the accounting department can perform detailed checks on the purchase prices and analytical reviews of the purchasing clerks' purchase prices, allowing detection of price irregularities. Although these are detective measures, they also have a preventive function since purchasing clerks are aware that such checks will be performed afterwards.

A related risk is purchasing at inflated prices, not due to influence on the purchasing clerks, but because purchases are not made on the most optimal terms. Similar controls can help mitigate this risk, such as tender procedures where the vendor that offers the best price/quality ratio is selected, comparison of each purchase price with the price list before each purchase is made and rewarding purchasing clerks based on the purchase result so that they benefit from purchasing at the best terms.

Another risk in the purchasing process is purchasing too much or too little. The risk related to purchasing too much can be mitigated by making sure that the purchasing department cannot decide independently how much is purchased. Instead, the amount to be purchased should be determined based on the inventory levels, such that purchases are made only when re-order points are reached. The risk associated with purchasing too little – which could result in having to decline customers – can be reduced by periodically evaluating vendor delivery performance. Furthermore, to mitigate both risks, proper inventory records are indispensable. Only when reliable information on the exact inventory level is available can appropriate decisions as to the amount to be purchased be made and can the organization be sure that neither too much nor too little is bought.

Other risks in the purchasing process relate to purchasing goods of inferior quality, resulting in dissatisfied customers or delays in the production process due to too little or bad quality raw materials; suboptimal use of purchasing discounts when invoices are not paid in time, resulting in overly high purchasing costs; and finally payment of invoices for goods that have not or only partially been received.

Table 7.1 provides an overview of risks, related exposures and applicable controls in the purchasing process. This list is not exhaustive but representative of the most important risks.

Table 7.1   Risks, exposures and internal controls in the purchasing process.

Risk	Exposure	Internal controls
Influence purchasing clerks by means of kickbacks, secret commissions, or other forms of inducement from vendors	Cost of goods sold too high in relation to quality of the goods or services	• Adequate screening and rewarding of purchasing clerks • Code of conduct prohibiting acceptance of gifts from vendors • Use of tender procedure • Detailed sample-based checks of purchase prices by controller or head of accounting department • Analytical review of purchase prices
Purchasing too much	Inventory costs are too high	• Authorization of purchases not by purchasing department, but by the requisitioning department • Proper perpetual inventory records
Purchase goods at inflated prices	Purchase costs are too high	• Use of a tender procedure • Comparison of purchase price with price list before purchase is made • Rewarding purchasing clerks based on purchase result
Purchase goods of inferior quality	Dissatisfied customers or production delays	• Purchase from previously screened vendors • Periodic price and quality assessment of vendors
Purchasing too little	Dissatisfied customers or production delays	• Periodic assessment of vendors on delivery terms • Proper perpetual inventory records
Not taking advantage of purchase discounts	Purchase costs are too high	• Automated procedure which makes the invoices payable when due
Payment for goods that have not been received	Loss of money	• Reconciling invoices with goods received by controller or head of accounting department

Purchase Requisitions

The purchasing process is triggered by the purchase requisition. Such a requisition can be made by for example the production department or the sales department. In a production organization purchases are aligned with planned production, and in a trade organization purchases are determined based on expected sales.

Below we discuss the creation of a purchase requisition in a production organization. In trade organizations purchase requisitions are effectively created in the same way, the main difference being that purchase requisitions are based on expected sales information supplied by the sales department.

In a production organization, the operations office (or production planning department) decides which and how many goods are needed by the production departments. It is the duty of the operations office to coordinate received orders and inform the production department about which products to produce, when and in what amounts. Based on the production planning the operations office orders the purchasing department to purchase certain goods. Since the amount and type of materials to be purchased are based on the use of these materials straight after receipt of the goods, the risk of too large or obsolete raw and auxiliary materials inventories is strongly mitigated.

The purchase prices should usually be known when a pre-calculation of the sales price is made. The purchase prices used in these pre-calculations are generally based on invited tender offers.

In an organization that produces to stock, the operations office decides on the re-order points together with the purchasing department. Re-order points specify at what level of inventory goods should be ordered and therefore determine *when* to order. These re-order points should be set taking into account the level of raw and auxiliary materials that should be in stock to facilitate production during the delivery of new inventory of these materials. The order quantity, which specifies *how much* to order, is based on materials consumption, average delivery time, purchasing prices, purchasing costs and carrying costs.

Information as to when the re-order point is reached can come from three sources:

1.   the warehouse clerk in the raw and auxiliary materials warehouse;
2.   the inventory records; or
3.   the purchasing clerk.

The Warehouse Clerk

The warehouse clerk can do the following:

- He can inform the operations office when the re-order point is reached. The operations office verifies if and, if so, how much should be available when, and if necessary submits a purchase requisition to the purchasing department.
- The warehouse clerk informs the purchasing department directly that the re-order point has been reached. Based on this information, the relevant quantity is ordered. This implies that the warehouse clerk effectively submits the purchase requisition. A disadvantage of this approach is that the warehouse is authorized to submit purchase requisitions to the purchasing department directly. If the warehouse clerk makes a mistake in observing re-order points, either intentionally or unintentionally, this will not be discovered in the short run. The warehouse clerk is therefore able to order at an earlier moment than is strictly necessary and can, as such, prevent inventory shortages from being discovered. For example, if there is a shortage of 100 items, this will be discovered when production requests these 100 items that, according to the inventory records, should still be in stock. To prevent this discovery, the warehouse clerk will intentionally indicate that the re-order point is reached at (re-order point + 100 items) and submit a purchase requisition to the purchasing department at that (incorrect) point in time. By automating the notification of re-order points such control problems are avoided and these human mistakes are no longer made.

Not being able to detect mistakes in time may also be disadvantageous for the organization in case of unintentional mistakes (e.g. calculation errors). Ordering too soon due to a mistake will result in an inventory level that is unnecessarily high. Ordering too late may result in production delays because certain materials turn out not to be in stock. These advantages are mitigated when the next option is used.

Inventory Records

Inventory records that are always up-to-date and accurate can be used to submit purchase requisitions to the purchasing department. If, however, inventory records are not up-to-date, the warehouse clerk will have to notify the purchasing department that the re-order point has been reached. The purchasing department will examine the inventory records to verify this claim. In this way, mistakes in the inventory records are discovered before the purchasing department makes a purchase order.

Purchasing Clerk

The purchasing department itself can also create purchasing requisitions. In these cases the automated system should notify the purchasing department via a programmed procedure that the re-order point in the inventory records is reached. In effect, deciding on the re-order point is a policy decision that is made by a higher level management rather than the manager of the purchasing department.

Purchase Orders

After the purchasing department has received the purchase requisitions, they process these by doing the following:

1. verifying which vendors can deliver the required goods;
2. examining the vendor's delivery terms;
3. selecting the vendor(s); and
4. preparing a purchase order and sending it to the vendor(s).

Vendors

To verify which vendors can deliver the requested goods the purchasing department will consult the purchasing sources files. Product documentation in these files contains product-related information, such as product description, purchase price and sales price, as well as information related to potential vendors that supply these products. Vendors are identified by means of a vendor code. This code refers to vendor documentation, which contains the following information per vendor: name and address, product range, delivery time, delivery and payment terms, and past experiences with the vendor. A purchasing clerk has obtained this vendor information by consulting purchasing sources, documentation and putting out tender offers. The purchasing clerk will assess the acceptability of the vendor and product data.

Vendor's Delivery Terms

To examine the delivery terms of the eligible vendors, it may be necessary to invite these vendors to submit a tender. The related data need to be input into the information system and a programmed procedure assigns a sequential number to the request for tender. The purchasing clerk that receives the tenders and verifies whether a tender has been received from all vendors that have received a request is preferably different from the purchasing clerk that has sent out these requests. This segregation assures that sufficiently reliable vendor information is available to impartially select a vendor. If this segregation were not present, the purchasing clerk might manipulate the tenders in such a way that he forced a biased decision. For example, he could withhold or modify tenders from certain vendors, even though these vendors' tenders are better for the organization. He could collude with certain vendors by agreeing to let these vendors supply to the organization in exchange for a certain fee. By segregating the activities related to sending out the requests for tender and those related to processing the tenders collusion between vendors and purchasing clerks can be largely prevented.

Vendor Selection

After the purchasing clerk has established that responses have been received from all vendors that have been asked to submit a tender, the purchasing manager will select a vendor based on information in the vendor file. For relatively important purchases the purchasing manager will submit his well-founded selection to management for approval.

Preparation and Sending of Purchase Order

The purchasing department prepares the purchase orders and sends these to the selected vendor(s). The purchasing department subsequently also monitors the timely and correct processing of purchase orders based on the receipt of goods.

If the purchasing department has put out requests for and received tenders, they will prepare a purchase order based on the tender that is signed for approval by management or the purchasing manager. The original purchase order is sent to the vendor after management or the purchasing manager has signed it.

The purchasing manager also inputs the purchase order data in a purchase order file. This file contains at least the following information per purchase order:

- purchase order number;
- purchase order data;
- product code;
- vendor code;
- quantity;

- price;
- delivery date; and
- other terms.

The product code refers to the product file which contains all product information, and the vendor code refers to the vendor file which contains all vendor information. In the automated system these files are integrated in the purchasing database. The following information can be retrieved from these files:

- overviews to prepare journal entries (general ledger, accounts payable subsidiary ledger, value added tax);
- overviews per vendor, per product, per delivery date and/or combinations thereof;
- overviews of ordered goods in the inventory records, for sales or production;
- comparison of ordered and received quantities;
- comparison of purchase order data and invoiced amounts; and
- historical overviews per vendor.

The automated system can also indicate when deliveries are late. It also provides overviews of goods to be received by the warehouse, which are instrumental in planning the warehouse activities. However, a potential disadvantage of the availability of this type of information to the warehouse manager is that, especially during busy times, the quantities, types and, if necessary, quality of goods received is not independently established since the warehouse manager already knows what these are. Purchase order information should also be supplied to the accounts payable department, which validates the vendor invoices.

Receipt of Goods

The receipt of ordered goods is a vital link in the value cycle and is therefore of great importance to the internal control system. Receipt of goods should confirm that the vendor has delivered what the purchasing department has ordered. Upon receipt of the goods the warehouse manager, or a separate receiving department, needs to establish:

- The validity of the goods that are received; are these the goods that were ordered?
- The completeness of the execution of the order by the vendor; were all the ordered goods received? and
- The correctness of the time of delivery against the delivery terms that were agreed upon; was the delivery on time?

Goods may be received by the warehouse manager or by a separate receiving department. The vendor has an interest that is opposed to that of the warehouse manager (custody function), resulting in reasonable assurance that the warehouse manager will supply valid information on received goods to the accounting department, and reasonable assurance that the correct goods have been received.

In larger organizations goods are not received by the warehouse manager but by a separate receiving department. This department establishes that quantities and weights reported by the vendor are in accordance with the vendor packing slip. The warehouse department subsequently unpacks the goods, inputs relevant data, provides detailed receipt information and stores the goods in the warehouse.

Validation of Invoices

Purchase of goods results in the receipt of vendor invoices. The accounts payable department needs to establish the validity of these invoices. From the point of view of segregation of duties it is essential that the purchasing department, which has an authorization function, and the warehouse manager, who has a custody function, do not validate invoices because this is a checking function. If the purchasing department were to validate invoices, adverse differences between the agreed price and the price on the invoice may not be noted intentionally. Because of his contacts with suppliers, the purchasing clerk may collude with one or more suppliers to invoice a higher price than that on the purchase order and share the difference. If another department validates invoices, this type of collusion is possible only if the validating department is involved in the collusion as well.

For similar reasons invoice validation by the warehouse manager is not to be recommended. In addition, the warehouse manager could accept goods with lower than agreed quality.

To properly validate invoices, the accounts payable department needs the following information:

1. the purchase order, and sometimes the tender;
2. the receiving report; and
3. the invoice.

The Purchase Order

Via the automated system, purchase order data should be received directly from the purchasing department, who authorized the order. The purchase order contains information on quantity, product names, price, quality and other delivery terms and the vendor's name and address.

The Receiving Report

The automated receiving report should be received directly from the function that has received the goods. In most cases this will be the warehouse manager. In organizations with a separate receiving department, this latter department will supply the accounts payable department with the receiving report. The receiving report contains information on the date of receipt, quantity, quality, product names and vendor name.

There is no receiving report when services instead of goods are received. To substitute, the service recipient will supply signed job time records. For example, if a temp has worked in an organization for a certain amount of time, this organization should appoint an employee that is authorized to check and sign the temp's job time records. The temp agency should be informed of this employee's name and signature, and copies of the job time records should remain in the organization to update accounts payable.

The Invoice

The invoice is a document that reflects the vendor's delivery of a number of specific goods at a certain point in time and thus his right to receive payment of the agreed price. The invoice should contain at least the following data:

- invoice date;
- vendor name; and
- invoiced amount.

After scanning the invoice, the automated system automatically assigns a sequential number to the scanned invoice. If there is no scanning system for received invoices in place, then the mail department manually applies the numbering using a stamp, simultaneously keeping a record of the invoice numbers, invoice dates, vendors' names and invoiced amounts. By means of a programmed procedure the invoice data are directly sent to the accounts payable department to document the invoice in the accounts payable subsidiary ledger to establish the invoice's validity, and to enable progress control on the processing of invoices. Invoices are also sent to the accounting department for recording in the general ledger. If upon processing the invoices in the general ledger it is noticed that a number is missing, the record from the mail department can help to identify the invoice with the missing number.

Based on the receiving report the accounts payable department verifies whether the goods have indeed been received and if quantities and qualities according to the invoices match those of goods that have actually been received. Based on the purchase order the accounts payable department establishes whether goods received are in line with the quantity, quality and type that was ordered. Based on the same purchase order they also verify the validity of the price and other terms on the invoice. They then establish the validity of the invoice calculations and document this in a checking file that is also accessible by the purchasing department. If differences are noted in the quantities or qualities delivered the purchasing department will contact the vendors. This could lead to an additional delivery or a credit note. Differences in calculation may be processed by the accounts payable department. The accounts payable department will monitor progress of the resolution of the differences.

By requiring the employees of the accounts payable department to provide an electronic signature after the validation of each invoice, the controller or the head of the accounting department can verify if all invoice checks have been performed. Timely processing of invoices is of the utmost importance for proper transaction processing. It also facilitates timely payment of invoices, allowing the organization to take advantage of any discounts. Validated invoice data is subsequently provided to the purchasing department to update their files.

Figure 7.1 shows the process of invoice validation.

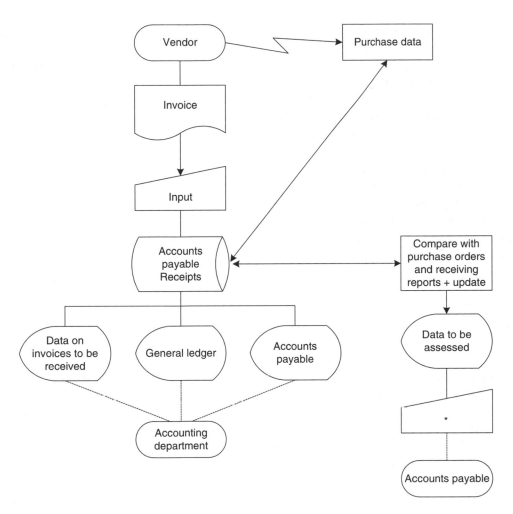

Figure 7.1   Invoice validation.

Accounts Payable

The accounting department records the totals of the approved invoices and the related payments in the general ledger, sometimes subdivided into groups of creditors. The accounts payable department is responsible for safeguarding and monitoring individual accounts payable, keeping track of the approved invoices and related payments per individual creditor. The accounts payable department thus has a custody function, and its main activities consist of documenting vendor invoices and payments.

Updating the accounts payable administration is usually part of the integrated processing of purchases, and the transaction is not processed until the related invoice is validated. Furthermore, by means of programmed procedures the automated system facilitates selection of payable invoices, preparation of payment orders and journalizing these.

Per individual creditor, the accounts payable department should contain information on the creditor's code, name and address. In addition, the invoice amount and due dates have been documented at the receipt and validation of the invoice. If the accounts payable department is able to issue payment orders, information related to payment method (in cash or via bank) and the bank account is required.

Information in the accounts payable administration allows the preparation of the following statements:

- overview of invoices (and amounts) payable;
- overview of individual payment orders;
- overview of liquidity position to support financial control activities, taking into account invoices due;
- automated notification of vendors' discount terms;
- counts per currency for financial control purposes; and
- historical overviews of creditors' positions.

Payment of Vendor Invoices

After invoices have been validated, they need to be made payable. In general only those invoices should be made payable where it is certain that the invoice amount is correct. To this end validated invoices should be authorized for payment by a designated employee who is generally part of the cash disbursements department. This employee should verify whether the required controls have been performed and whether the related purchase order and receiving report do indeed exist (i.e. a three-way check). After he has thus established the validity of the invoice he will approve the invoice for payment.

By consistently requiring that only invoices that contain purchase order and receipt data should be paid the organization avoids paying duplicate invoices or invoices that are improperly sent. After all, for every invoice there is only one purchase order and one receiving report.

By means of a programmed procedure the automated system filters invoices due from the accounts payable file based on invoice data and payment terms. These invoices are included in an overview that contains the following information per vendor: payable invoices, invoice amount and due date. After the cash disbursements clerk has verified and, if necessary, adjusted this information, he authorizes payment. He does so by entering their authorization code or signing the payment list. By means of a programmed procedure the automated system generates the payment list or a collection of payment orders. These orders are subsequently transferred to the bank. This can be done electronically – via the Internet, a CD-rom, or a data tape – or by using paper documents. Every time payment information is transferred to the bank the cash disbursement clerk calculates a batch total and inputs this together with, or adds it to, the detailed payment information.

When paying invoices, it is crucial that the correct amount is paid on the correct date. If a payment term was agreed on, early payment will lead to loss of interest, and late payment may result in a late payment fine. Therefore, the cash disbursements clerk should have access to information on unpaid invoices and desired payment dates in the accounts payable administration.

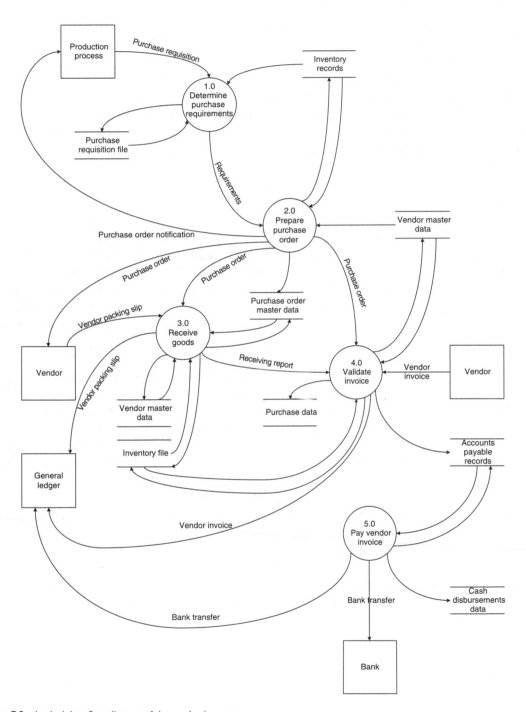

Figure 7.2   Logical data flow diagram of the purchasing process.

A Generic Logical Data Flow Diagram of the Purchasing Process

The purchasing process can be summarized by means of a data flow diagram (DFD) as introduced in Chapter 5. We draw a logical DFD – instead of a physical DFD – because the physical file organization and the departments may differ per organization, whereas the required data and activities are usually comparable between organizations (see Figure 7.2).

Summary

This chapter discusses internal controls in the purchasing process. We first discuss risks, exposures and applicable controls. We then discuss several stages in the purchasing process: purchase requisitions, purchase orders, receipt of goods, validation of invoices, accounts payable and finally payment of invoices.

The risks in the purchasing process include undue influence on purchasing clerks by means of presents or even kickbacks, resulting in the costs of goods sold being too high; purchasing at inflated prices; purchasing too much or too little; purchasing goods of inferior quality; not taking advantage of payment discounts when invoices are not paid on time, resulting in goods being sold at too high a price; and payment of invoices for goods that have not, or only partially, been received.

The purchasing function is performed by the purchasing department. This department's task is to purchase at the best possible terms. The purchasing department cannot buy of its own accord. The department should receive purchase requisitions from other, authorized, departments (e.g. the operations office in a production organization). Purchase policies may include requesting tenders from several vendors by the purchasing department. The purchasing department further generates and submits purchase orders to the selected vendors. It also monitors the correct and timely processing of purchase orders based on the receiving reports.

The accounts payable department validates the vendor invoices. To prevent collusion with vendors, the accounts payable department should be independent from the purchasing department and the warehouse manager. Invoices are validated based on the corresponding purchase orders and receiving reports.

The accounts payable department documents the payables per creditor. The accounts payable administration facilitates proper settlement of invoices by supplying the cash disbursements clerk with information on unpaid invoices and payment facilities to determine the optimal time of payment. It also facilitates the verification of the validity and timeliness of establishing payables by the controller or the head of the accounting department.

The Inventory Process

Introduction

Many organizations hold inventories of goods. A trade organization has inventories of finished goods to meet current customers' demand and to show goods to potential customers. A production organization has inventories of raw and auxiliary materials to facilitate smooth progress of their production process and timely execution of production orders.

However, holding inventory also entails costs and risks. Holding inventory may result in interest costs since inventories capture part of the organizational capital and carrying costs because inventories take up physical space. Organizations will therefore have to weigh up the costs and the benefits of holding inventory. Furthermore, inventories represent value and require safeguarding to prevent theft. Of course this risk is strongly affected by the nature and size of the organization. A jeweller's inventories are more prone to theft than a brickyard's. Other inventory risks relate to obsolescence, write-downs and quality decreases. Considering these risks and costs, organizations will generally want to minimize their inventories.

By implementing adequate internal controls, inventory risks can be reduced to acceptable levels. To this end we distinguish general and specific controls. Examples of specific controls are physical inventory counts and destruction procedures. Examples of general, organizational, controls are segregation of duties between authorization, custody and recording functions and creating appropriate procedures for receiving, safeguarding, releasing and recording inventory. Segregation of duties related to inventory consists of installing a designated function for safeguarding goods and separating these goods from other organizational activities. This function is performed by a warehouse manager with a custody function, who safeguards goods in a warehouse that is closed to third parties.

Learning Goals of the Chapter

After having studied this chapter, the reader will understand:

- the risks in the inventory process and the exposures to those risks;
- the internal controls to be implemented in the inventory process, including organizational security measures to safeguard inventory; and
- the stages in the inventory process.

Risks, Exposures and Internal Controls in the Inventory Process

The most important risk in the inventory process concerns theft of goods. Both probability and impact (in terms of loss of assets) of this risk increases with the value of the goods. A number of controls can mitigate the risk of theft. First, the creation of a closed warehouse that is accessible only to warehouse employees prevents unauthorized personnel from entering the warehouse and makes sure that the warehouse is closed after hours. Second, to make sure that all warehouse movements are recorded and hence traceable based on discharge documents, management can implement a procedure that requires discharge of all inventory releases and goods receipts, documentation of all releases and receipts in the warehouse manager's inventory file and recording of these releases and receipts in the general ledger inventory records. Finally, inventory variances can be discovered on a timely basis by periodic physical inventory counts conducted by the controller or the head of the accounting department. This detective control may also act as a deterrent to theft.

Another risk in the inventory process relates to write-downs, obsolescence, or decrease in the quality of goods, resulting in loss of assets. Controls to mitigate this risk include the preparation of overviews of goods that have not been released over a certain period of time (to assess obsolescence), periodic inventory counts to assess quality decrease and periodic comparison of book and market values to assess write-downs. Furthermore, goods need to be stored in appropriate warehouses to minimize quality decreases. Finally, management needs to implement appropriate procedures to reject and destroy obsolete or damaged goods. Rejection of goods should not be done by the warehouse manager but by an accounting clerk, who is not involved in safeguarding the goods. If the warehouse manager were authorized to reject and destroy goods he could conceal inventory variances by rejecting goods that are no longer present, resulting in a decrease in inventory for these goods. Goods should be destroyed in the presence of two employees from two different departments, a warehouse clerk and an accounting clerk. They should draw up a destruction protocol in the inventory records. Both employees should confirm the protocol by entering a status code in the automated system.

Other risks in the inventory processes concern receipt of goods of inferior quality for which regular prices are paid; recording goods as being cheaper or of lower quality than actually received, resulting in loss of assets; delaying the recording of goods receipts (lapping), also resulting in loss of assets; and finally inventory records that are not up-to-date, which could result in inefficiencies, problems in sales or production due to inventory shortages, or excessive purchasing and large inventories.

Table 8.1 provides an overview of risks, related exposures and applicable controls in the purchasing process. This list is not exhaustive but representative of the most important risks.

Table 8.1   Risks, exposures and internal controls in the inventory process.

Risk	Exposure	Internal controls
Theft of goods	Loss of assets	• Closed warehouse accessible only to warehouse employees • Discharge of all goods releases and receipts • All releases and receipts are recorded in the inventory records • Periodic inventory counts
Write-down, obsolescence, or quality decrease of goods	Loss of inventory value	• Periodic overviews of goods that have not been released over a certain period of time (to assess obsolescence)

(Continued)

Table 8.1   (Continued)

Risk	Exposure	Internal controls
		• Periodic comparison of book and market value of goods to assess write-downs • Periodic inventory counts to assess quality decrease • Storing goods in appropriate warehouses • Rejection of goods by controller or head of accounting department
Receipt of goods of inferior quality	Loss of inventory value	• Quality checks of all received goods by warehouse manager or separate quality inspector
Recording goods as being cheaper or of lower quality than actually received	Loss of inventory value and unreliable inventory records	• Segregation of duties between purchasing and warehouse departments • Automatic updates of inventory records based on authorized purchases
Delaying the recording of goods receipts (lapping)	Loss of inventory value; no or insufficient knowledge of actual inventory levels	• Automatic updates of inventory records based on authorized purchases and sales • Segregation of duties between the purchasing, sales and warehouse departments • Surprise inventory counts
Inventory records are not up-to-date	Inventory shortages or surpluses	• Automatic updates of inventory records based on authorized purchases • Programmed input controls in updating inventory records

Receiving Goods

When goods are delivered to the warehouse, the warehouse manager verifies that the number and type of goods are in line with the information on the packing slip. Subsequently the warehouse manager compares the delivery with the corresponding purchase order. To this end the purchase order number is entered in the automated system. If the delivered goods are present in the purchase order file, the warehouse manager is authorized to accept the goods. The warehouse manager signs the packing slip as evidence to the carrier that goods have been released.

Upon receipt of the goods the warehouse manager establishes the quantity and, if required, quality of the goods. If certain quality standards are set, the warehouse manager will have to be informed and instructed about these standards. If the quality assessment of the delivery is very complex, a designated quality inspector, with a checking function, will have to judge the quality of the received goods.

The warehouse manager enters the relevant information related to the goods receipt so as to update the inventory file. A programmed procedure automatically assigns the receipt date to the goods receipt. The inventory records are subsequently updated based on notification of the receipt in the inventory file, and the receipt is linked to the related purchase order. By means of a programmed procedure the automated system checks quantities using the purchase order data. Differences are noted and submitted to the purchasing department for further processing.

Independently verifying the type, quantity and quality of the received goods provides more assurance that the receipt data are valid. If data on the packing slip are used for this, it is possible that receipt data are not accurately checked.

Recording of Goods

In the inventory records quantity and value information is recorded per product so that at any point in time it is possible to know what quantities should be present in the warehouse. Inventory records are kept by the accounting department, which has a recording function. Although the warehouse manager documents all goods receipts and releases in the automated system, the actual recording of inventory in the inventory records is not assigned to the warehouse manager, who, after all, has a custody function. After entering changes in inventory into his inventory file, the warehouse manager no longer has authority over the data and thus has no recording function. The inventory records are necessary to check whether inventory is actually present, to control inventory and to monitor inventory control.

The function, form and content of inventory records require careful consideration. Inventory records keep track of the organization's physical inventory. Physical inventory is inventory that is actually present in the organization. Economic inventory includes the goods for which the organization runs the risk of changes in market prices. Economic inventory is comprised of physical inventory, ordered but not yet received goods (pre-purchases) and already sold but not yet delivered goods (pre-sales), as follows:

$$\text{Economic inventory} = \text{physical inventory} + \text{pre-purchases} -/- \text{pre-sales}$$

If the organization has goods that are subject to relatively large price changes, it is important that the inventory records also reflect the pre-purchases and the pre-sales.

Inventory records should:

1. record inventory quantities and values per product;
2. indicate re-order points;
3. identify obsolete products; and
4. identify excessive inventory amounts.

Record Inventory Quantities and Values Per Product

Recording of quantities and values is based on the release and receipt data from the warehouse manager. Inventory records are generally kept per product, but if this is not economically feasible or possible, these records can also be kept per product group, product type, or batch.

Indicate Re-order Points

By means of programmed controls the automated system compares actual inventory to the re-order point level and, if required, either initiates a purchase order or informs the purchasing department that the re-order point has been reached.

Identify Obsolete Products

To identify obsolete products programmed controls can periodically generate overviews from the inventory records that show which products have not been released over a specified period of time (e.g. three months). It should be noted that the warehouse manager is not responsible for goods becoming obsolete. Based on indications of obsolescence from the inventory records management can examine if, and if so why, certain products are obsolete. The warehouse manager should not be allowed to reject obsolete products by himself. The warehouse manager might be tempted to conceal inventory variances by rejecting products that are no longer present in the organization, so that inventory is decreased for these goods. An accounting clerk, who has no interest in rejecting goods, should approve rejection first.

Obsolete products should only be destroyed in the presence of two employees from two different departments: a warehouse clerk and an accounting clerk. By engaging two employees (the so-called four-eye principle) the probability that goods are not destroyed but are appropriated by the employee is reduced. The two employees should draw up a destruction protocol in the inventory records. Both employees should confirm the protocol by entering a status code in the automated system.

Identify Excessive Inventory Amounts

By means of programmed controls the automated system compares the actual with the maximum amount of inventory and indicates whether there are excessive amounts of certain products, based on which management may decide to take action.

To perform the tasks above a wealth of product-related information should be recorded in the inventory records. However, the standing data that can be used by multiple departments (planning, accounting, purchasing and sales) can be relatively minimal: the product code and description.

Other relevant data include:

- detailed product description;
- code of potential replacement product;
- warehouse location;

- standard price; and
- date of last inventory count and any variances and causes of these variances (in code form).

Dependent on the function or department using inventory-related information, the following data can be added:

- To prepare purchase orders in the purchasing department:
    - vendor code;
    - purchasing clerk code;
    - purchase price (if necessary);
    - re-order point;
    - order quantity;
    - maximum inventory level (if necessary); and
    - vendor delivery time.
- To prepare invoices in the billing department:
    - sales clerk code;
    - fixed sales price;
    - value-added tax code; and
    - number of items per packing unit.

Storage

Inventory is held in the warehouse. Since inventory has a certain value for the organization, the warehouse needs to meet the following two requirements:

1. Goods need to be stored in the best way possible. This means that goods need to be treated by knowledgeable employees and that they be kept in the most appropriate state during the time of storage; and
2. Goods cannot be retrieved from the warehouse without authorization from an authorized officer.

The warehouse manager is charged with the proper storage and correct handling of goods in the warehouse. This warehouse manager therefore has a custody function. He is also responsible for the presence of the goods. This means that he is responsible for any variances between inventory according to the inventory records (beginning inventory + goods received in the warehouse −/− goods released by the warehouse) and inventory that is actually present in the warehouse.

To carry this responsibility, the organization of the warehouse needs to meet the following requirements:

- Goods need to be stored in an enclosed space, and no one else besides the warehouse managers should be able to retrieve goods from the warehouse. If goods are not stored in an enclosed space or if someone other than the warehouse manager has access to the warehouse keys, the manager cannot oversee retrieval of goods and he can therefore not be held responsible for any inventory variances;

- Goods should only be released in exchange for documents that are authorized by appropriate officers. To account for released goods the warehouse manager should be able to show that he released the goods by order of authorized officers; and
- The warehouse manager should have access to inventory-related information, either via a terminal that is linked to the automated system or by means of his inventory files.

These three requirements do not apply for storage of all goods. For (a) goods that have low value, or (b) goods that are always used in relation to other goods, goods are not recorded per product and the warehouse manager is not responsible for inventory. In such cases, open warehouses are used.

Goods of Low Value

For goods that have low value it may not be worthwhile to store these in a closed warehouse and to record releases separately, since the latter would require subsequent processing of these releases by the warehouse manager and by the accounting department. It may turn out that the recording costs are higher than the value of the associated goods. This problem can be overcome by storing these goods in an open warehouse. Goods that qualify for this type of storage are stored outside the warehouse, in the departments that regularly use these goods.

To establish whether this type of storage is still appropriate, periodical evaluation of quantities retrieved from the warehouse is required. By means of the so-called retrograde method the normative quantities for production are calculated and compared with the difference between the beginning and ending inventory in the open warehouse, corrected for supplies from the closed warehouse. Any differences may be due to goods that have become unusable during production, or theft. If differences are too large and/or cannot be explained it may be too expensive for the organization to use an open warehouse. If costs due to these differences are higher than the recording costs that were saved the organization may consider storing goods in closed warehouses again.

Goods of High(er) Value in Open Warehouses

In production organizations many goods are used in relation to other goods, such as finished goods or other parts of the finished goods. For a bicycle factory the number of spokes, chain guards, wheels and so on per bicycle frame is fixed. If the number of frames is accurately recorded, but not the related parts, then the use of many parts can be accurately deduced based on the number of bicycles that are produced.

In such cases, even with an open warehouse the accounting department can exactly determine the normative parts consumption. This requires accurately calculated production standards, to determine the theoretical parts consumption by means of multiplication. Open warehouses can be maintained as long as the actual ending inventory of each part sufficiently matches the ending inventory calculated based on purchased quantities and theoretical consumption.

Application of open warehouses in organizations is increasing thanks to systems of authorized purchasing and purchasing in the most exact way at the right time. In open warehouses custody of inventory is in effect assigned to the production workers or the operations office.

Release of the Goods

Goods cannot be released from the warehouse without proper authorization. Since he has a custody function the warehouse manager has no authorization over goods in the warehouse and therefore cannot independently initiate release – only the sales or production departments can do so.

When the sales department has entered a new sales order or the production department has entered a new production order in the automated system, the system generates a picking ticket for goods release by means of a programmed procedure. This picking ticket authorizes the warehouse manager to release the related goods. Upon release of the goods the warehouse manager enters the product code, the quantity and the customer code. Similar to the procedure for goods receipt, the automated system assigns the release date by means of a programmed procedure. Based on the picking ticket the inventory records are updated.

Inventory Counts

Inventory counts complete the internal controls in the inventory process. To verify whether inventory according to the inventory records is valid, the existence and value of the goods should be established. Inventory counts help establish existence, but can only partly verify value – more specifically, the completeness of the product, any damage and sometimes the price code on the product.

Below, we first discuss inventory counts for goods with detailed inventory records. We then discuss inventory counts for goods without detailed inventory records.

For goods with detailed inventory records, inventory is counted to verify whether inventory per product in the warehouse matches the product data in the inventory records. In such cases products that are somehow related need to be counted simultaneously. This applies to the same goods in different packaging, or goods that are made from the same fabric or in the same colour (e.g. men's trousers).

The entire inventory does need to be counted integrally because inventory can be distinguished by product. In these cases partial inventory counts can be performed on a sample basis.

Inventory counts consist of inspecting inventory. The warehouse manager performs the count and is observed and checked by the controller, the head of the accounting department, or an accounting clerk who is not involved in maintaining the inventory records. Related data (product code, quantity, price, damage, decay, where applicable) are noted on an inventory list generated from the automated system, and are signed by both officers. Subsequently the count data are entered into the automated system and compared to the inventory records by an accounting clerk. Any variances may be due to theft, (administrative) errors, decay or damage, and need to be investigated. Both the accounting clerk and the warehouse manager need to be involved in this investigation. Any final variances between inventory present in the warehouse and inventory in the inventory records need to be adjusted in the inventory records. Goods that are decayed or damaged need to be destroyed. Finished goods should only be destroyed in the presence of two officers from two different departments: a warehouse clerk and an accounting clerk. They should draw up a destruction protocol in the inventory records. Both employees should confirm the protocol by entering a status code in the automated system.

Goods without detailed inventory records need to be integrally counted. The purpose of such an inventory count is to establish the value of inventory on the balance sheet. This value is established as follows:

Beginning inventory + purchases −/− sales = expected ending inventory = counted inventory

Any variances between the expected ending inventory and counted inventory could be due to theft, damage, decay or administrative errors, and should be adjusted in the inventory account and the associated profit or loss. Finally, decayed or damaged products need to be properly destroyed.

Summary

This chapter discusses internal controls in the inventory process. We first discuss risks, exposures and applicable controls. We then discuss several stages in the inventory process: receipt of goods, recording of goods, storage, release and finally inventory counts.

The most important risk in the inventory process relates to theft of goods. When the value of goods increases, the loss of assets due to theft increases as well and therefore the probability of theft is higher in such cases. We have discussed controls to mitigate this important risk. Other risks in the inventory process relate to write-downs, obsolescence and decrease in the quality of goods during storage, resulting in loss of assets; receipt of goods of inferior quality even though regular sales prices were paid; recording goods as being cheaper or of lower quality than actually received, resulting in loss of assets; delaying the recording of goods receipts (lapping), resulting in loss of assets and insufficient knowledge about actual inventory levels; and finally the risk that inventory records are not up-to-date, which could result in inefficiencies, problems in sales or production due to inventory shortages, or excessive purchasing and large inventories.

Inventory is held in the warehouse, where it is safeguarded by the warehouse manager who has a custody function. He is responsible for appropriate storage and handling of all goods in the warehouse. For the warehouse manager to carry this responsibility, goods need to be stored in enclosed spaces that are not accessible to others. In this way, goods cannot be removed from the warehouse by anyone other than the warehouse manager.

The warehouse manager should not accept goods into the warehouse without proper authorization from the purchasing department. To this end the warehouse manager compares the received goods with the corresponding purchase order in the automated system. Upon receipt the warehouse manager establishes the quantity and, if so required, the quality of the goods. He enters relevant information in the inventory file. By means of a programmed procedure the inventory records are updated based on the receiving report in the inventory file.

In the inventory records per product the quantity and value are recorded. Maintaining the inventory records is a recording function that is usually assigned to the accounting department. Inventory records are used to record inventory quantities and values per product, indicate re-order points, identify obsolete products and identify excessive inventory quantities.

Goods are stored in the warehouse. A proper warehouse should store goods in the best way possible and keep them in the most appropriate state during storage. Furthermore, goods cannot be retrieved from the warehouse without authorization by the warehouse manager. Only goods that have low value or are used in relatively fixed proportions to other goods should be stored in open warehouses. In such cases, usually no record is kept of goods consumption.

The warehouse manager should not be able to release goods from the warehouse without proper authorization from either the production or the sales department. The warehouse manager should enter every release into the automated system.

Inventory counts complete the internal controls in the inventory process. To verify the validity of inventory in the inventory records, the existence and value of the related goods need to be established. During inventory counts inventory is inspected to establish that the recorded quantities are indeed present in the warehouse.

The Production Process

In this chapter:

Introduction

Production organizations are characterized by a technical transformation or production process in which they transform raw and auxiliary materials, man hours and machine hours into finished products. Besides producing products, production organizations also need to purchase materials, store raw and auxiliary materials and finished products and sell these finished products. They therefore also have a purchasing, inventory and sales process. However, in this chapter we will focus on the production process only. From an internal control perspective, a transformation process represents a disruption in the flow of goods. Due to the occurrence of waste and breakdown in the transformation process, it is not easy to directly relate the amounts of raw and auxiliary materials used (offers) to the amounts of finished goods obtained (yields). For production organizations with a strong relationship between offers and yields, it is easier to predict the revenues (yields) that ought to be generated given a certain amount of raw and auxiliary materials (offers). Internal controls mainly focus on efficiency analyses per department. That is, given the strong relationship due to the tight production standards, any deviations are caused by inefficiencies in the production process. The weaker the relationship between offers and yields, the more additional controls are needed to establish the completeness of revenues. Due to the weaker production standards, in such cases deviations may not only be caused by production inefficiencies but also by inappropriate standards for that production run. Therefore, the inefficiency analyses are focused on orders or production runs and distinguish between production inefficiencies and insufficiently reliable production standards.

From an internal control perspective, the utilization of production capacity is important because this directly relates to the costs of a production process. Therefore, the use of man and machine hours needs to be recorded and checked for acceptability. Furthermore, production organizations often produce multiple types of products. Thus, cost control, cost allocation and cost price calculation are important features of the internal control system.

As we discuss in more detail in Chapter 14, we distinguish three types of production organizations: organizations that produce to stock, organizations with mass customization and organizations that produce to order. Although most production process-related issues discussed in this chapter apply to all types of production organizations, some apply to only one or two types. Where necessary we will make that distinction below.

The main risks within the production process relate to production inefficiencies, unauthorized production, unreliable production standards and theft of work-in-progress. For organizations that produce to stock, an additional risk is the insufficient alignment between production and demand, leading to dissatisfied customers and loss of revenues in case of underproduction, or increasing stocks in case of overproduction. When production organizations produce to order, a major additional risk relates to the shifting of revenues and costs between projects.

Learning Goals of the Chapter

After having studied this chapter, the reader will understand:

- the risks in the production process and the exposures to those risks;
- the internal controls to be implemented in the production process; and
- the stages in the production process.

Risks, Exposures and Internal Controls in the Production Process

The main risk within the production process relates to inefficiencies in the production process resulting in production costs which are too high. To mitigate this risk, production organizations need to segregate duties between the operations office (pre-calculation; authorization), the production department (production; execution) and the accounting department (post-calculation; recording) in order to make sure that efficiency results are determined independently from the standard setting party (operations office) and the production party (production department). Furthermore, to calculate inefficiencies, the production departments must keep track of actual usage (hours; materials) and actual production output, and production standards need to be strict and detailed.

A further risk includes unreliable production standards, leading to flawed decision-making regarding production targets and production efficiency. The controls to mitigate this risk are segregation of duties between the product design department (execution) and the operations office (authorization), implementation of management guidelines with respect to standard setting and quality checks on the product development process and performance of technical post-calculations to ensure optimized product standards.

Unauthorized production is another risk in the production process, resulting in unnecessary production costs for products for which there is no or insufficient demand. Hence, production should not be authorized by the production department but by either the sales department or the warehouse. Moreover, production orders should always be based on sales forecasts and/or inventory levels.

Another risk in the production process relates to the theft of work-in-progress, leading to a loss of assets. Production organizations need to maintain physical access controls to minimize entry to production facilities by non-production personnel and lock production facilities outside production hours. They also need to implement a system of granting discharge when work-in-progress is transferred between production departments or work centres and they need to undertake periodic physical inventory counts of work-in-progress.

Furthermore, especially when producing to stock, there is the risk of insufficient alignment between production and demand, resulting in dissatisfied customers and loss of revenues in case of underproduction, and increased stocks, obsolescence and increased inventory costs in case of overproduction. Organizations can mitigate this risk by performing adequate market research on customer needs, using reliable sales forecasts by the sales department, using an adequate production planning system which allows for periodic realignment of production output levels and adequate cash planning in order to survive periods of low demand.

A risk that is specific to organizations that produce to order relates to shifting costs between projects (from fixed-fee to cost-reimbursement contracts) so that cost-reimbursement customers are overbilled. To mitigate this risk, organizations need to segregate duties between the production department (execution) and the accounting department (recording), allocate projects to project managers on a sequential and not on a simultaneous basis and perform periodic analytical reviews of project efficiency.

Table 9.1 provides an overview of risks, related exposures and applicable controls in the production process. This list is not exhaustive but representative of the most important risks.

Table 9.1 Risks, exposures, and internal controls in the production process.

Risk	Exposure	Internal controls
Inefficient production	High production costs	• Segregation of duties between the operations office (pre-calculation; authorization), the production department (production; execution), and the accounting department (post-calculation; recording) • Documentation of actual usage (hours, materials) and actual production output by production department • Tight and detailed product and production standards • Performance of pre- and post-calculations to determine efficiency results
Insufficiently reliable production standards	Flawed decision-making with respect to production targets and production efficiency	• Segregation of duties between the product design department (execution) and the operations office (authorization) • Management guidelines with respect to product standard setting and quality checks on product development • Technical post-calculation in order to optimize product standards
Unauthorized production	Incurring costs for products for which there is no or insufficient demand	• Authorization of production orders not by production department but by sales or warehouse • Production orders are always based on sales forecasts and/or inventory levels
Theft of work-in-progress	Loss of assets	• Minimize entry to production facilities by non-production personnel by means of physical access controls • Locking production facilities outside production hours • A system of granting discharge when work-in-progress is transferred between production departments or work centres • Periodic inventory counts of work-in-progress

Insufficient alignment between production and demand	Dissatisfied customers and loss of revenues (underproduction); increasing stocks, obsolescence, and increased inventory costs (overproduction)	• Adequate market research on customer needs • Use of reliable sales forecasts by sales department • Use of an adequate production planning system which allows for periodic realignment of production output levels • Cash planning in order to survive periods of low demand
Shifting of costs between projects (from cost-reimbursement to fixed-fee contracts)	Cost-reimbursement customers are overbilled, unreliable production records and unreliable input for new pre-calculations	• Segregation of duties between production department (production; execution) and accounting department (cost allocation to projects; recording) • Allocation of projects to project managers on a sequential and not on a simultaneous basis • Analytical review of project efficiency

Product Design

The product design department is responsible for designing new products. This department performs an execution function. When designing a new product, the product design department needs to take into account the functional, technical and quality requirements and the estimated production cost. The functional and quality requirements and the potential selling price of a product are defined based on market research conducted by the marketing department. The technical product requirements are based on client demands but also on the technical knowledge of the design department.

Since the design of a product usually involves huge research and development costs, management needs to authorize the investment in a new product. After authorization by management and the outcomes of the market research by the marketing department, the product design department can start the design of a new product. When the product design department has developed the new product after sufficient testing, it needs to make graphical representations of the design and a detailed manufacturing plan. This detailed plan consists of a bill of materials and an operations list. The bill of materials indicates which raw and auxiliary materials are needed to produce the product. The operations list specifies the manual and mechanical processes necessary to produce the new product. The design department inputs all information from the graphical product representations, bills of materials and operations lists in corresponding files in the information system.

Annual Planning, Cost Calculation and Production Planning

For organizations that produce to stock, the operations office derives the annual planning from the organization's strategic plan, set by management. Based on the annual planning, the operations office derives the utilization rates of machinery and calculates man and machine hour rates. Organizations that produce to order have to deal with more uncertainty regarding annual planning, cost calculation and production planning. For these organizations, the operations office will develop a more general planning and will adjust the planning and the rates accordingly when production activities deviate from planning.

Based on the bill of materials and an operations list, the operations office determines the standard usage of raw and auxiliary materials, man hours and machine hours. Because the operations office determines the standard usage before the start of the production process, this is called a pre-calculation. And because this pre-calculation only specifies the amounts of materials and hours, but not the associated prices and rates, it is a quantitative or technical pre-calculation. In addition, the cost accounting department prepares a financial pre-calculation, based on the prices of raw and auxiliary materials and the man and machine hour rates. This pre-calculation forms the basis for the cost price of the product. For production to stock, quantitative and financial pre-calculations have to be performed at the start of a new production process and any time prices for materials and labour change. In contrast, for production to order, these calculations have to be made for each order since each order is unique.

After the quantitative and financial pre-calculations, the operations office specifies, based on the annual planning, the desired production levels in an annual production plan. This planning encompasses capacity planning (what production capacity is necessary to satisfy expected sales according to the annual planning?), occupancy or utilization planning (relating (expected) orders to available capacity, which may result in over-staffing or understaffing, necessitating additional measures, such as employing temporary workers or asking regular staff to do temporary periods of overtime in case of understaffing) and detailed production orders (allocating people and machinery to activities).

Hence, the operations office is responsible for the annual planning, the quantitative pre-calculation and the production planning, including job preparation and production order issuance. Given these planning responsibilities, the operations office has an authorization duty with respect to production and is independent of the production department. The operations office's tasks further include production progress controls.

All information about the man and machine hours and the quantitative pre-calculations is input into the information system by the operations office and recorded by the accounting department. Furthermore, the financial pre-calculations are input by the cost-accounting department and recorded by the accounting department.

Job Preparation

In this stage of the production process, the operations office informs the production manager about new production orders via the information system. Production orders are always based on sales forecasts and/or inventory levels and are therefore initiated by either the sales department or the warehouse, to mitigate the risk of unauthorized production.

The production information system contains the information on the production orders. Production orders are detailed descriptions of what must be produced, and in what quantity, in the next production run. A production order also contains the required authorizations for using specified quantities of raw materials and equipment (e.g. bills of materials), an indication of who should be working on what order (staffing), starting and ending time of the production run, as well as task descriptions for production personnel if the activities to perform are nonroutine. The production manager will subsequently assign production personnel, equipment and machinery to each production order. Figure 9.1 shows an example of a production order.

Raw and auxiliary materials may be supplied from a closed or an open warehouse depending on the value of the goods and potential constraints on the production process. For instance, if the production process will be delayed because of a queue at the warehouse desk, having a closed warehouse may cost more than the related internal control benefits. In this case the constraint is the inventory process. If another process constitutes the constraint, warehouse waiting time is acceptable up to the time that the inventory process becomes the most prominent constraint. At any time, the operations office needs to make sure that the required materials are available on time.

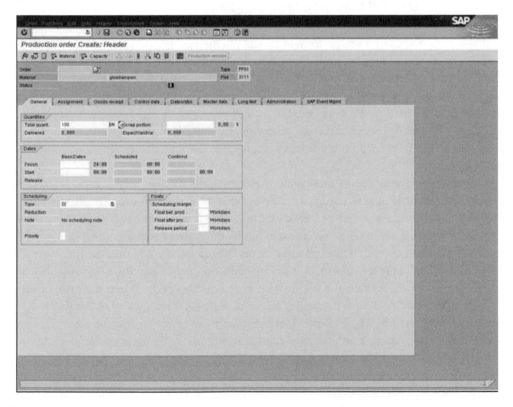

Figure 9.1 Production order.

Raw Materials Release

Goods cannot be released from the raw materials warehouse without proper authorization, in this instance from the production department. Since the warehouse manager has a custody function, he has no authorization over the raw and auxiliary materials in the warehouse and therefore cannot independently initiate the release of raw and auxiliary materials. The warehouse manager only releases raw and auxiliary materials from the warehouse against a materials requisition. A materials requisition specifies the types and quantities of materials to be released by the warehouse for each production order. For each new production order, the system generates picking tickets for raw and auxiliary materials release by means of a programmed procedure. Upon release of the raw and auxiliary materials the warehouse manager enters the product number, the quantity and the production code. Analogous to the procedure for the receipt of raw and auxiliary materials, the automated system assigns the release date by means of a programmed procedure. Based on the picking ticket the inventory records are updated.

Production and Production Records

The actual production activities are performed by the production department, which has an execution function. Per production order, the production personnel keep track of the actual man and machine hours spent, the actual amounts of raw and auxiliary materials used and the amount of products and waste produced. Production personnel input this information per production order into an (automated) production report. All production reports need to be authorized by the production manager (via a status code: authorized). By means of a programmed procedure, the information about actual usage is automatically transferred to and recorded in the inventory records. An example of a production report is shown in Figure 9.2 below.

Via these production reports the operations office automatically receives information about the progress of production orders and is able to assess whether or not the production order is on schedule. When a production order is finished, the finished goods are transferred from the production department to the finished goods warehouse. The production manager inputs the delivery of the goods to the warehouse into the production report and the warehouse manager inputs the receipt of goods into the inventory file. A programmed procedure compares the information in the production report and the inventory file and updates the inventory records to ensure that the information is recorded properly. When the price of the finished goods depends on the quality, a separate quality inspector will assess the quality of the finished goods and report this in the inventory file. The quality inspector is part of the receiving department finished goods and has a checking function. Again, a programmed procedure automatically updates the inventory records to ensure that the information is recorded properly.

To properly manage the production process, large projects are technically subdivided into sequential stages. This is done as early as the pre-calculation. The subdivision into sequential stages may also be

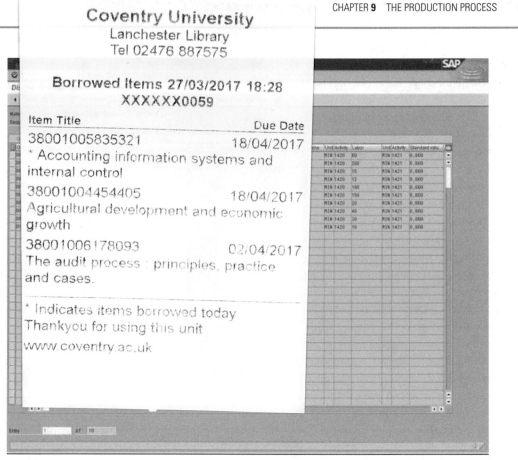

Figure 9.2   Production report.

helpful to determine valuation of work-in-progress and revenue recognition. For instance, work-in-progress may be valued as follows:

Value at the beginning of the period + directs costs −/− billed installments.

Instalments are billed at pre-defined stages in the production process. At the end of each stage a certain percentage of the work is considered completed, at which point revenues are recognized.

Post-calculation

Within production organizations, post-calculations must be compared to pre-calculations to evaluate production efficiency, reliability of production standards and the fairness of cost prices. To properly conduct this comparison, segregation of duties needs to be in place. Therefore, quantitative or technical pre-calculation should be performed by the operations office (authorization), actual production activities by the production department (execution) and quantitative post-calculation by the controller or the head of the accounting department (checking). Financial pre-calculation should be performed by the cost accounting department (execution) and financial post-calculation by the controller or the head of the accounting department (checking). Comparisons of pre-calculations and post-calculations are also conducted by the controller or the head of the accounting department.

For production to stock, pre-calculations and post-calculations are performed per production department, which is a form of process costing. For production to order, pre-calculations and post-calculations are performed per production order, a form of job-order costing. A potential risk here is the invalidity and incompleteness of the production data. Therefore, controls must be put in place to provide reasonable assurance that the production data as well as the production standards used are valid and complete. For instance, the production software must have been tested thoroughly before implementing, the standards as recorded in the standards file must be periodically reviewed for reasonableness, and offers and yields must be reconciled by means of the retrograde method, which calculates standard usage of materials and hours as well as standard costs based on actual production levels.

Comparison of quantitative or technical pre-calculations and post-calculations help to identify inefficiencies and/or inappropriate production standards by means of variance analyses. Differences due to inappropriate production standards are denoted budget variances, whereas differences caused by inefficiencies are appropriately called efficiency variances. The production manager is considered primarily responsible for efficiency variances, whereas the operations office is responsible for budget variances.

Comparison of financial pre-calculations and post-calculations helps to identify price variances. Price variances are the differences between standard prices of raw materials, man hours and machine hours, and actual prices based on vendor invoices. These differences are the primary responsibility of the purchasing department and help to assess the fairness of cost prices. Cost prices are important for determining the sales price and the margin to be realized on each of the products produced by the organization. This may influence the composition of the organization's product lines.

A Generic Data Flow Diagram of the Production Process

The production process can be summarized by means of a data flow diagram (DFD) as introduced in Chapter 5. We draw a logical DFD – instead of a physical DFD – because the physical file organization and the departments may differ per organization, whereas the required data and activities are usually comparable between organizations (see Figure 9.3).

Summary

This chapter discusses internal controls in the production process. We first discuss risks, exposures and applicable controls. We then discuss several stages in the production process: product design; annual planning; cost calculation and production planning; job preparation; raw materials release; production and production records; and post-calculation.

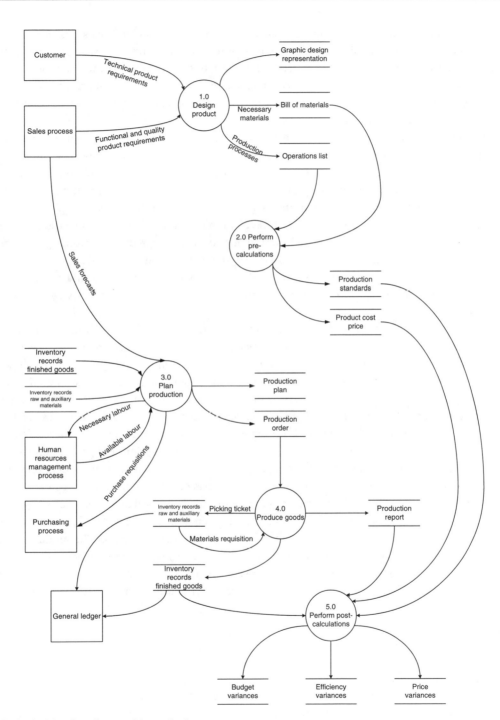

Figure 9.3   Logical data flow diagram of the production process.

The major risks within the production process relate to production inefficiencies, unauthorized production, unreliable production standards, theft of work-in-progress and, when producing to stock, the insufficient alignment between production and demand, leading to dissatisfied customers and loss of revenues in case of underproduction, or increasing stocks in case of overproduction. When organizations produce to order, a major risk relates to the shifting of costs between projects. The chapter also discusses the exposure of these risks and controls to mitigate these risks.

The product design department is responsible for the design of new products. This department performs an execution function. Because the design of a product is usually associated with huge research and development costs, management needs to authorize the investment in new products. Based on the organization's strategic plan, the operations office drafts the annual planning. Based on the annual planning, the operations office subsequently prepares the quantitative pre-calculation and the production planning, including job preparation and production orders. Given these planning responsibilities, the operations office has an authorization duty with respect to production. In the next stage of the production process, job preparation, the operations office informs the production manager about new production orders via the information system. The production manager then assigns production personnel, equipment and machinery to each production order and authorizes the warehouse manager to release raw and auxiliary materials from the raw materials warehouse.

The actual production is performed by the production department, which has an execution function. Per production order, the production personnel input the actual man and machine hours spent, the actual number of raw and auxiliary materials used and the amount of products as well as waste produced. Via these production reports, the operations office automatically receives information about the progress of production orders and is able to assess whether or not the production order is on schedule. When a production order is finished, the finished goods are transferred from the production department to the finished goods warehouse.

Based on the production information in the information system, the controller or the head of the accounting department performs the post-calculation, which is a checking function. For production to stock, pre-calculations and post-calculations are performed per production department and for production to order pre-calculations and post-calculations are performed per production order. Differences between pre-calculations and post-calculations are identified by variance analyses and can be caused by inefficiencies and/or by using inappropriate standards in the pre-calculation. The latter differences are denoted budget variances, whereas differences caused by inefficiencies are appropriately called efficiency variances. The production manager is considered primarily responsible for efficiency variances, whereas the operations office is responsible for budget variances. Price variances, the differences between standard prices of raw materials, man hours and machine hours, and actual prices based on vendor invoices, are the primary responsibility of the purchasing department.

The Sales Process

In this chapter:

Introduction

The sales function is aimed at generating revenues from products and/or services delivered by the organization. Therefore this function is very important within an organization. This importance is best illustrated by means of the master budget, which is based on sales. Sales expectations determine required inventory levels, production volumes (in case of production organizations), and purchasing amounts. Thus, the sales budget determines the inventory, production and purchasing budgets.

Because the sales function decides on the acceptance of customer orders it is to be qualified as an authorization function. Within an organization the sales function is performed by the sales department. This department acquires and executes customer orders and takes care of customer relations. To acquire orders the sales department needs information on sales from various perspectives, on sales activities and sales promotions and on the sales staff, both in a qualitative and quantitative sense, including recruitment and training. For effective processing of customer orders the sales department needs information about the customers, as well as on the number and types of products ordered.

In addition, to properly perform the sales function the sales department also needs information on the back orders, rejected orders (including the reason for rejection), possible customer complaints, and analyses of unsuccessful offers. Customer relations activities involve providing product information and promotional activities.

To properly perform the sales function the sales department also needs information about new markets and new market strategies, analyses of competitors and (large) customers, competitors' products, consumer research, population prognoses, income prognoses and technological developments. This information is partly external in nature and/or obtained via market research. In these cases the sales function is usually assisted by the marketing function that takes care of sales promotion.

An important sales-related risk is the pressure on salespeople to offer products at lower prices and/or better terms. Another risk is salespeople creating a shop within a shop, engaging in transactions on their own account and for their own benefit instead of the organization's, resulting in a loss of profit margin on these transactions for the organization. An organization runs a number of other specific sales-related risks. These include product liability, price and currency changes between the moment of order acceptance and delivery. In particular for construction and similar projects this latter period can be very long. Relevant risks also relate to saturation and changes in customer demand. Collecting and evaluating information on product and debtors' risks is therefore essential.

To reduce sales-related risk, management has to decide on the delivery conditions of products and services. A trade organization and an organization that produces to stock usually have fixed sales prices. In addition, management will issue guidelines for additional conditions related to credit terms, discounts for certain groups of customers and bulk discounts. For organizations that produce to order prices per order are determined by the operations office (or production planning department). Sales can be conducted as credit sales or as cash sales.

For credit sales it is important to verify customer creditworthiness and inventory availability. In addition, specific measures are required to make sure that all deliveries are invoiced at the correct prices. Cash sales require specific measures to ensure that no products are delivered without receiving payment and that receipts transfers are complete and timely.

Thus, different internal control measures are required for credit sales compared to cash sales.

Learning Goals of the Chapter

After having studied this chapter, the reader will understand:

* the general risks in the sales process, and the exposures to those risks;
* the internal controls to be implemented in the sales process; and
* the stages in the sales process.

Risks, Exposures and Internal Controls in the Sales Process

An important risk in the sales process relates to salespeople charging sales prices that are too low or granting discounts that are too high, resulting in loss of assets and profit margin. Relevant internal controls include the use of price lists with fixed discount percentages or discount tables to prevent salespeople from granting overly large discounts, sample-based checks by the controller or the head of the accounting department of a number of sales transactions where discounts were granted and analytical review of discounts given by the sales department. These last two measures facilitate assessment of the size of the discount, subsequently allowing management to call the relevant salespeople to account for the discounts they have granted.

Another important risk concerns the shop within a shop. In this case salespeople conduct transactions on their own account instead of on behalf of the organization, causing the organization to miss out on the profit margin on these transactions. This risk can be mitigated by segregating the sales department from the purchasing department, and clear communication of the sales procedures to customers. If there is a separate purchasing department sales staff are not responsible for purchasing products, which makes it harder for them to exclude the organization in sales transactions with their customers. By communicating the sales procedures to customers the organization wants its customers to realize that regular deliveries can only take place via the organization's warehouse. Furthermore, the sales clerk cannot gain control of the goods in the warehouse without being noticed.

A further risk relates to shifting of sales between periods (they are either accounted too early or too late) because of bonus contracts, which could result in bonuses that are unjustifiably high. To mitigate this risk the sales department (authorization function) should not be responsible for recording sales transactions. This task should be allocated to an independent department instead (the accounting department). This prevents salespeople from manipulating information related to sales transactions.

Sales transactions in different currencies present a risk because adverse changes in exchange rates could lead to exchange losses. The organization could engage in forward contracts to mitigate this risk. In this case the currencies in which the transactions are conducted are sold at the current exchange rate (this is because the organization may receive currencies due to the sales transaction) to ensure that potential exchange rate fluctuations do not erode the profit on the sales transaction.

A specific credit sales risk relates to customer creditworthiness. Sales transactions with noncreditworthy customers may result in undesirable uncollectable accounts. If the size of the organization allows it, tasks related to credit checking and documenting customers' credit positions should not be assigned to the sales department. The sales department may be motivated to sell as much as possible and may therefore be inclined to sell to less creditworthy customers. This inclination is nonexistent for a separate credit department, which has only one objective: to assess the creditworthiness of the customers. In addition, appropriately documenting customers' credit positions also facilitates the proper assessment of these customers' creditworthiness. If the organization is too small to put a separate credit department in place, then the controller or the head of the accounting department must regularly check whether the sales department complies with the organization's credit policy.

Two other risks related to sales on account are an excessive accounts receivable position, leading to high related financing costs, and incomplete billing of sales, leading to loss of assets, revenues and profit margin. The first risk can be mitigated by periodic ageing of open accounts receivable, dunning procedures, using short payment terms and giving discounts for prompt payment. The second risk can be mitigated by segregating the department that initiates the billing (e.g. the sales department or a separate billing department) and the department that releases the goods (the warehouse). In addition, the organization may use a pre-billing system, sequentially number the bills of lading and periodically reconcile the bills of lading with the retained invoice copies. In this way, the organization can establish whether an invoice has been sent for every bill of lading.

Table 10.1 provides an overview of risks, related exposures and applicable controls in the sales process. This list is not exhaustive but representative of the most important risks.

Table 10.1   Risks, exposures and internal controls in the sales process.

Risk	Exposure	Internal controls
Discounts granted by salespeople are too high	Loss of revenues and profit margin	• Management guidelines for allowing discounts (discount tables) • Sample-based detailed checks on allowed discounts by controller or head of accounting department • Analytical review of discounts granted by salespeople
Use of incorrect sales prices	Loss of revenues and profit margin	• Use of fixed price lists and fixed discount percentages • Sample-based detailed checks on sales prices by controller or head of accounting department • Analytical review of sales prices billed by salespeople
Shop within a shop	Loss of profit margin	• Segregation of duties between sales and purchasing • Clear communication of sales procedures to customers, with deliveries always taking place via warehouse
Shifting of sales transactions between periods due to bonus contracts	(Too) high bonus contract costs	• Segregation of duties between sales department (authorization) and accounting department (recording)
Sales transactions in foreign currencies	Exchange rate losses	• Reduction of exchange rate risk by engaging in forward transactions

Credit sales to noncreditworthy customers	Losses on sales	• Assessment of customer creditworthiness preferably not by sales department but by separate credit department • Adequate recording of accounts receivable by accounting department • Checking compliance with organization's credit policy by accounting department
High accounts receivable position	High financing costs	• Periodic ageing of accounts receivable, subsequent active dunning of the related debtors by the accounts receivable department • Prompt billing • Stimulating customers to pay on time by giving discounts for prompt payment • Short payment terms
Failure to bill customers	Loss of assets and profit margin	• Segregation of duties between initiation of billing (sales department) and release of goods (warehouse) • Automatic sequential numbering of bills of lading and periodic reconciliation of bills of lading with invoices • Employing a pre-billing system

Preparing Offers

The sales process starts with receipt of a customer order to deliver goods or a customer's request to provide an offer for the delivery of goods. Customers may approach the organization themselves, for instance because they are an existing customer of the organization, or because they are familiar with the organization through advertising and promotions. Alternatively, customers may have been approached by the organization's sales department, for instance by a sales representative visiting (potential) customers. Both order receipts and requests for offers are processed by the sales department. If a client places an order straight away, an offer procedure is not necessary. The order receipt is discussed in the next section. If a customer places a request for an offer first, then the following sequential steps are usually followed.

After requests for offers have been received by the sales department the related data are put into the offer file by the sales department. These data include name and address of the customer, quantity, quality, credit terms and desired delivery date. The system automatically assigns a sequential number and the date to each request that is entered. The sales department subsequently prepares the offers based on the sales terms (prices, credit terms, discounts and so on) set by management.

To prepare an offer the sales department needs to answer the following three questions:

1. Can we deliver the products on time?
2. At what prices and on what conditions can we make an offer? and
3. Is the customer creditworthy?

Can We Deliver the Products on Time?

To answer this question the sales department needs to have inventory information. In an automated system the sales department will be authorized to view this information in the inventory records. If the products are not in stock then the sales department has to consult the purchasing department (for trade organizations) or the operations office (for production organizations) to verify whether the goods can be delivered on time.

At What Prices and on What Conditions Can We Make an Offer?

If different discounts and/or different terms of delivery have been agreed upon with customers then for each request the agreement per customer has to be consulted. Related information in the customer master data file includes the customer's name and address information, the agreed upon terms of delivery, discounts and so on.

Is the Customer Creditworthy?

For every customer a maximum credit amount, a credit limit, should be set. These limits should be authorized and included in the accounts receivable master data. Using the automated information system the sales department will compare the available credit in the accounts receivable master data (the balance of the credit limit and open accounts receivable for the debtor) with the sales value of the products desired by the customer. Based on this information the sales department can decide if, and if so how much, credit is to be granted on which conditions and for what term.

The sales department or a separate credit department should establish the credit limit per customer. To this end the department will have to collect the necessary information, differentiating between existing and new customers.

For existing customers the credit limit should be established as follows:

- Assess the development of revenues generated by the customer in the past three to five years based on information in the accounts receivable administration. Also assess the accompanying gross and net profit margins. Use all related information available in the organization, including information on the customer's payment discipline and information from salespeople.
- If the customer is important and large enough, related information can be bought from commercial information providers (such as Dun & Bradstreet). Of course this requires the organization to be a customer of such providers.
- Ask the customer for financial information. Investigate whether the customer owns real estate and whether it is mortgaged (land register).
- If the customer does own real estate, there is a possibility of requiring corporate or personal collateral from the customer to provide additional assurance. This will affect the size of the credit limit. However, any collateral provided should not render the organization careless since sale under distress takes time and may put off other customers.

Credit limits for new customers are set differently. As a policy, many organizations grant a limited amount of credit sales to new customers on which they have little or no information. In the meantime as much information as possible is collected from sources discussed above. Based on this information a definite credit limit is set, or credit is refused. Collateral is even more important here than for existing customers.

If a customer asks for a high credit limit in exchange for important prospects, careful consideration of risks is required.

If collateral is acquired related information is to be collected in a collateral file. Periodically (at least once a year) the value of the collateral needs to be (re-)examined.

One needs to be aware of the fact that setting credit limits may also mean limiting sales possibilities, since additional sales are not possible once the credit limit has been reached. The credit and sales departments have opposing interests, which is beneficial for the organization as long as it does not lead to lasting conflicts. However, if the size of the organization does not allow for a separate credit department, then a higher management function must decide on the credit limits per customer.

After the three questions above have been answered a programmed procedure updates the offer file and the sales department prepares an offer based on information in the file, signs the offer and sends it to the potential customer.

Order Receipt and Order Acceptance

Sales orders are received by the sales department and entered in a sales order file. By means of a programmed procedure the automated system assigns a sequential number to each order. Customers can place an order via the sales representatives or directly at the sales department. The sales department subsequently needs to assess the feasibility of the order, establishing that:

- the products can be delivered on a timely basis;
- the price and other conditions stipulated by the customer in the order are acceptable; and
- the customer is creditworthy.

These activities are conducted in much the same way as when preparing offers, described in the previous section. If an order is based on an offer that was prepared earlier, then the issues discussed above have already been examined. The sales department should establish that the offer is still valid and that the information in the sales order (quantity, quality, price, delivery time, terms of payment and so on) are in accordance with that in the offer extended to the customer.

If the sales department accepts an order, a sales clerk enters this decision in the automated system. By means of a programmed procedure the data on accepted orders are subsequently sent to the billing department (see 'Billing', below) and the warehouse (see 'Picking and Shipping', p. 195).

Billing

Based on order information received from the sales department – and based on the type of billing system possibly also based on release information from the warehouse – the billing department or the sales department prepares and sends the invoice to the customer. In a fully integrated system the invoices can also be created directly based on the accepted order information. Whatever the case, the content of the invoice always needs to be decided on by an authorization function. Generating the invoice based on information received from an authorization function and physically sending it to the customer is an execution function.

An invoice contains the following information: invoice number, customer number, customer's name and address, invoice date, invoice amount and terms of payment. A number of billing systems can be distinguished:

1. pre-billing
2. post-billing
3. interim billing.

Pre-billing

In a pre-billing system, invoices are created based on approved sales orders. An invoice copy is subsequently used to pick goods in the warehouse and prepare these for shipment to the customer. This form of billing can be used only when it is certain at the moment of order acceptance that all goods can be delivered. The advantage of pre-billing is that it assures the organization that no goods are shipped for which no invoice was created.

Post-billing

In a post-billing system invoices are created after goods have been prepared for shipment. Post-billing is necessary when it is not possible to gather all necessary information on goods ordered beforehand. This may occur when the price depends on the quality or the weight of the goods, which cannot be established until goods are picked in the warehouse. In this case billing takes place based on information related to goods shipped, for instance based on the picking ticket or the bill of lading.

Interim Billing

In an interim billing system an invoice is created at order acceptance, together with a picking ticket. Ideally, the controller or the head of the accounting department reconciles the goods picked and transferred to the shipping department (by the warehouse) on the one hand and the invoices sent (by the sales department or a separate billing department) on the other. Differences should lead to a signal either to the sales department (or the separate billing department) that the invoice should not be sent to the customer yet, or to the warehouse not to transfer the goods to the shipping department for shipment to the customers yet.

The decision to use one of these billing systems is based on the availability of information necessary to create invoices, as well as the custom of the industry in which the organization operates. Although the terms pre- and post-billing suggest otherwise, the difference between both billing systems has nothing to do with the time of sending the invoice and the goods, but with the document on which the invoice is based: the sales order (pre-billing), or the packing slip or bill of lading (post-billing).

In some industries it is customary to bill the customers not on a daily basis, but at the end of a certain period (e.g. each month), using a cumulative invoice. This is called cyclical billing, and an advantage is that the preparation of cumulative invoices can be staggered over time, for instance each day. This overcomes the disadvantage of the pile-up of work at the end of the period.

After the creation of invoices the billing information is transferred via the automated system to the accounts receivable department and the accounting department by means of a programmed procedure. The actual, physical sending of the invoices to the customers (execution function) may take place at several places in the organization, as long as the billing department keeps a register of the invoices to be sent and the controller or the head of the accounting department establishes (or is able to establish) after sending the invoices that these invoices match with information in this register. As an additional control the controller or the head of the accounting department periodically checks whether the goods shipped to customer, multiplied by the sales prices (taking discounts into account), is equal to the invoiced amounts according the accounts receivable subsidiary ledger.

Picking and Shipping

The warehouse is the location where raw materials and other products are received, safeguarded and released. The warehouse manager is responsible for proper storage and treatment of all goods kept in the warehouse. This is a custody function. The warehouse manager is not allowed to receive and release goods unless he or she has been authorized to do so by an authorization function. In case of a goods release an accepted sales order, a sales invoice or a picking ticket authorizes the warehouse manager to pick and release the relevant goods. If a picking ticket is used then the picking ticket is generated based on the sales order file – which includes at least the customer number, the product codes and the quantities ordered per order – based on accepted sales orders. Such a picking ticket contains product codes, product descriptions, quantities and location codes. If orders are serially processed then the sales order file generates invoice copies that function as picking tickets. The location codes can be ordered in such a way that an optimal route through the warehouse is generated and goods can be picked much more efficiently. The warehouse department subsequently generates packing slips for the shipping department, which specify the destination and contents per shipment. The packing slips are accumulated in a packing list, which specifies the delivery route, sorting goods picked in the warehouse per delivery address (i.e. the customer's address). Based on the packing list shipping checks the goods transfer from the warehouse. If there is no separate shipping department then the warehouse will prepare orders for shipment and ship the goods to the customers itself. Upon transfer of goods to the shipping department or to the customer the warehouse manager enters the product code, the quantity and the customer code. By means of a programmed procedure the inventory records and the sales order file are updated based on the input.

Accounts Receivable

Credit sales result in accounts receivable. Customers are informed of the creation of an account receivable by means of an invoice. Because the organization now has a claim against the customer, the customer is referred to as a debtor. Two organizational departments are involved in keeping accounts of debtors: the accounts receivable department and the accounting department. The accounts receivable department is responsible for safeguarding and monitoring individual accounts receivable, and the accounting department is responsible for recording these accounts receivable.

As part of its custody function, the accounts receivable department is responsible for managing the customer accounts and documenting the receivables per debtor. This is done based on received billing information and information regarding cash receipts from debtors.

Receivables per debtor are captured in the accounts receivable subsidiary ledger. This subsidiary ledger contains the following information: debtor code, name and address of the debtor, credit limit, terms of payment, annual sales, payment discipline, information on the sales invoices (billed amount and due date), cash receipts and (outstanding) balances.

The accounting department records the totals of the invoices sent and cash received in the general ledger. This department has a recording function with respect to the accounts receivable administration. The controller or the head of the accounting department needs to regularly reconcile the totals of the receivables per debtor (accounts receivable department) and the totals for the accounts receivable account in the general ledger.

The accounts receivable subsidiary ledger is primarily used to facilitate monitoring the timeliness of payments by debtors. To monitor the accounts receivable the accounts receivable department will periodically examine which accounts receivable are overdue beyond term. A programmed control can help to identify these open accounts receivable.

The accounts receivable department will subsequently demand payment from these debtors by notifying them in writing that the payment term has passed and requesting them to pay. Before doing so the accounts receivable department should contact the sales department to decide on the best way to demand payment from the customer, taking into account the size and length of the organization's relationship with the customer. If after a while the debtor still has not paid, the organization can consider engaging a collection agency.

Although an organization may have good credit control, there will always be accounts receivable that are difficult to collect or even uncollectable. These are so-called doubtful accounts. Since uncollectability implies financial losses, provision needs to be made. There are two methods for doing so:

1. the static approach; and
2. the dynamic approach.

Static Approach

At least once a year the collectability of accounts is examined, incorporating all available information. If an account is deemed uncollectable the organization attempts to express the associated risk as a percentage of the amount owed. The resulting amount is added to the provision for doubtful accounts. Since the assessment of individual accounts is made at a certain moment in time this is called the static approach to building a provision for doubtful accounts.

An advantage of this approach is the assessment of credit risk per individual debtor. An associated disadvantage is that a lot of information per individual debtor is required to make this assessment. Therefore, this method is only economic for 'large' debtors. A debtor is generally considered 'large' when it is part of the 20% of debtors that collectively account for about 80% of the organization's annual revenues.

Dynamic Approach

Conversely, there are about 80% of debtors that account for about 20% of the annual turnover of the organization. These are mainly smaller debtors, for which it is not economic to apply the static approach to adding to the provision for doubtful accounts. A different approach is applied instead: depending on the amount of (for instance monthly) revenues obtained from a debtor a small percentage (0.5–1%) of those revenues is added to the provision for doubtful accounts. Because the revenues obtained are the starting point, this approach is called the dynamic approach.

Most organizations simultaneously apply both the static and the dynamic approach. A frequent (re)evaluation of the provision is therefore appropriate.

Like any asset, accounts receivable can be insured. If an organization insures its accounts receivable, it will have to pay premiums over all outstanding balances except those relating to debtors that have been refused by the insurance company. The insurance company will also set its own credit limits per debtor. These limits are usually lower than those set by the organization itself, and therefore the organization will always have a residual credit risk. As a result the organization will have to reduce the relation with the debtor to such a level that the associated financial risk is acceptable again. Most of the time the customer will not accept this and he may move to a competitor if he considers the credit limit to be too low.

Accounts receivable can also be sold. Sale of accounts receivable for cash is called factoring. The advantage for the selling organization is that it no longer has to wait for its money, which improves the organization's liquidity position. An associated disadvantage is the interest and costs that the organization will have to pay the factor. Factoring always entails additional effort for the accounts receivable department. This is caused by the fact that the factor never finances more than 80% of the accounts receivable that have been sold. The other 20% thus remains to be collected. Because the factor collects the entire account receivable, however, the associated debtor needs to be kept in the accounts receivable subsidiary ledger. After collection the factor settles the remaining 20%. If the factor has trouble collecting, he will transfer the account receivable back to the organization, while at the same time calling in the amount paid by the factor in the past, plus costs.

Cash Sales

In the previous sections we have assumed and discussed credit sales. However, many sales transactions relate to cash sales. This includes sales with payment by means of smart cards. Cash sales require specific internal control measures to ensure that products are not handed over without payment and that cash receipts are deposited in a timely fashion and completely. Cash sales are common in organizations where products are stored in locations that are specifically accessible to customers, such as shops or department stores, and in service organizations like transportation companies, cinemas and theatres.

In shops products are usually stored in publicly accessible locations. The customer selects the desired products by himself and takes these to a cash register. The cash register clerk enters the product prices in the cash register. Alternatively, the product codes are read in a cash terminal and the automated system subsequently and automatically generates the prices and produces proof of payment in the form of a receipt. By assigning value to the receipt, e.g. the possibility of exchanging sold goods or warranty rights, customers will want to get a receipt when they pay. Since receipts are not generated unless the clerk enters the products in the cash register or cash terminal, chances are reduced that sales are not recorded.

Use of a cash register or a cash terminal facilitates mechanically totalizing the amounts to be received per customer. This is generally faster than manual totalizing and reduces the chances of error in doing so. Furthermore, the amounts entered are totalized and captured in a file with control totals that is inaccessible to the cash register clerk. This way there is a mechanically generated total of amounts received in cash and checks. This total can be used to check the cash accounted for by the cash register clerk. The cash controller (e.g. an accounting clerk) is present when the cash register clerk counts the cash. A protocol of the cash count is drawn up, specifying the total amount of cash, and signed by the cash controller and the cash register clerk. The controller subsequently reconciles the amount of cash and the control total.

A final control measure related to cash sales is supervision of customer payment in the store itself (using mirrors and/or cameras or otherwise).

The above measures are aimed at preventing shoplifting as much as possible. However, it can never be ruled out altogether, particularly since statistics indicate that employee theft is a considerable source of fraud.

A Generic Logical Data Flow Diagram of the Sales Process

The sales process can be summarized by means of a data flow diagram (DFD) as introduced in Chapter 5. We draw a logical DFD – instead of a physical DFD – because the physical file organization and the departments may differ per organization, whereas the required data and activities are usually comparable between organizations (see Figure 10.1).

Summary

This chapter discusses internal controls in the sales process. We first discuss risks, exposures and applicable controls. We then discuss several stages in the sales process: preparing offers, order receipt and order acceptance, billing, picking and shipping, accounts receivable and cash sales.

Risks in the sales process relate to salespeople charging sales prices that are too low or granting discounts that are too high to increase their sales; salespeople creating a shop within a shop; shifting sales transactions between periods, resulting in unjustifiably high bonuses; exchange rate risk for sales in foreign currencies; customer creditworthiness in case of credit sales; and (excessively) high accounts receivable positions and failure to bill customers for sales conducted, resulting in a loss of assets and profit margin. Appropriate internal control measures have been suggested to mitigate each risk.

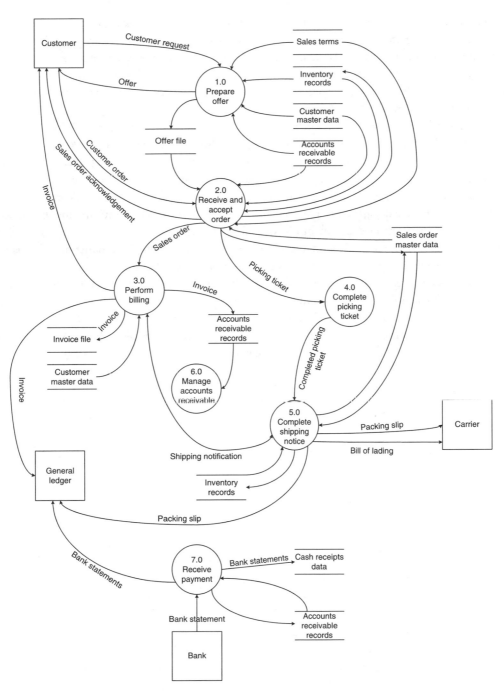

Figure 10.1 Logical data flow diagram of the sales process.

The sales department is responsible for making offers to customers and executing sales orders received from customers. To prepare an offer and/or to assess the feasibility of a sales order the sales department needs information on inventory availability, sales prices, and other terms of delivery, as well as customer creditworthiness. If the sales order is accepted and considered feasible, a sales clerk enters this decision into the automated system. By means of a programmed procedure the data on accepted orders are subsequently sent to the billing department.

For each approved sales order the sales department has to prepare picking tickets and invoices. Creation of picking tickets depends on the time of billing. In a pre-billing system, goods are picked based on the invoice (copy). In an interim billing system invoices are created while goods are being picked. Also in this case invoices (or invoice copies) may be used as picking tickets. In a post-billing system invoices are created after goods have been picked. Copies of approved sales orders are usually used as picking tickets in this case.

The accounts receivable department is responsible for safeguarding and monitoring individual accounts receivable, while the accounting department is responsible for recording accounts receivable. To manage uncollectable accounts, which represent a financial loss, a provision for doubtful accounts needs to be created. We also discuss the possibility of factoring or insuring accounts receivable.

In case of cash sales specific internal controls need to be implemented to make sure goods are not transferred without payment in exchange, and to make sure receipts are accounted for in a timely fashion and completely. By using cash registers or cash terminals automatic entry of amounts that were keyed into the cash register or read into the cash terminal is enforced and captured in a file with control totals, which is inaccessible to the cash register clerk. Based on these entries the validity of deposited cash can be verified.

11

Secondary Processes

Introduction

This chapter discusses the secondary organizational processes that relate to human resources management, investment in fixed assets, cash management, and accounting and general ledger activities. The previous chapters in this Part on internal control in various organizational processes focused on the primary organizational processes related to purchasing, inventory, production and sales. As explained in Chapter 6, the primary processes directly contribute to revenue generation, while the secondary processes indirectly contribute to revenue generation.

In many organizations, human resources management, investment in fixed assets, cash management (or treasury) and accounting and general ledger activities, do not directly contribute to revenue generation, and we therefore consider them to be secondary processes. However, there are exceptions to this rule. For law firms or accounting firms, for example, their ability to generate revenues crucially and directly depends on the knowledge and skills of their employees and revenues are generated based on the hours spent by their employees. For these types of organizations, which we discuss in more detail in Chapter 17, human resources management is strongly integrated with the purchasing process and should therefore be considered as part of the primary processes of these organizations. Similarly, organizations that put space or electronic capacity at their clients' disposal, such as transportation companies and telephone operators, crucially depend on investment in fixed assets for their ability to generate revenues. In these cases, investment in fixed assets is strongly related to these organizations' purchasing process, and should therefore be considered a primary process. Organizations that put space and electronic capacity at their clients' disposal are further discussed in Chapter 16.

For each secondary process, this chapter will discuss the most important internal controls.

The human resources management process generally consists of recruiting and selecting employees, educating and training employees, assigning tasks to employees, evaluating employee performance, employee remuneration and employee termination.

The process of investment in fixed assets consists of assessing the need for investment in fixed assets, analysing investment possibilities, making the investment decision, delivery/construction and operation of the fixed asset, paying for fixed assets and disinvesting. The cash management process consists of receiving cash, cash custody, safeguarding the value of the cash position and making payments. Finally, the accounting and general ledger activities consist of collecting and categorizing financial transaction data, recording financial transaction data, processing financial transaction data and providing information.

Learning Goals of the Chapter

After having studied this chapter, the reader will understand:

- the general internal controls to be implemented in the human resources management process;
- the general internal controls to be implemented in the investment process;
- the general internal controls to be implemented in the cash management process; and
- the general internal controls to be implemented in the accounting and general ledger process.

Human Resources Management

The human resources management process generally consists of recruiting and selecting employees, educating and training employees, assigning tasks to employees, evaluating employee performance, employee remuneration and employee termination.

Recruitment and Selection

Recruitment and selection is the first step in the human resources management process. The human resources process is either triggered by one of the functional departments indicating a need for additional employees, or by the personnel plan. The personnel plan is part of the strategic plan of the organization. Based on the estimated activity level (e.g. sales forecast) of the organization, the personnel plan details the need for employees, specifying the different types of skills and knowledge required.

When the human resources manager receives a recruitment request he examines whether the request fits the personnel plan. Based on this examination, the human resources manager decides whether to start the recruitment procedure. When a recruitment procedure is started, the recruitment request is input into the information system. The human resources manager subsequently identifies the minimum qualifications required for the position and prepares a description for the vacant position. The human resources manager then prepares screening criteria, invites and receives applications, and screens received applications. Together with the functional manager who initiated the vacancy, and based on the screening criteria, the human resources manager then selects and invites the top-ranking candidates for interviews. All these steps are also documented in the personnel files in the information system. After interviews are conducted, a candidate is selected and offered an employment contract. If the candidate accepts the job offer, the human resources manager authorizes the wages and the employment contract. The hiring decision and all related employment contract information are captured in the personnel files. All information in these files is automatically updated in the system by means of a programmed procedure.

Per newly hired employee, the following information is documented in his personnel file:

- employee number;
- address;
- position in the organization;
- employment contract information (e.g. salary, length of the appointment etc.);
- specific knowledge and skills (e.g. college degree); and
- career plan (including information on career development, education and training).

After the employee starts his work in the organization, the following data is documented in his personnel file as well:

- employee performance;
- employee evaluation;

- payroll; and
- career advancement.

Education and Training

Organizations need to offer education and training facilities to further the development of both newly hired employees and incumbent employees. The human resources manager needs to make sure that the employee's education and training continuously fit with his career plan. Together with the human resources manager, the functional manager authorizes any education and training requests of employees. The human resources department needs to document all employees' education and training activities in their personnel files.

Task Assignment

Employees should have the appropriate amount of knowledge and skills to perform a task. To this end the personnel files should contain information about an employee's education and experience. Managers will consult the personnel files to assign tasks to their employees. Before a manager assigns a task, he must determine whether the task fits the functional specification of the employee's position. Task assignment occurs within a structure of delegation and accountability. This implies that a manager delegates a task to an employee, and that this employee needs to account for his task performance.

Performance Evaluation

Performance evaluation affects employee behaviour and is intended to provide employees with periodic feedback about job effectiveness, as well as career guidance. To this end, the evaluation should result in a fair and balanced assessment of the employee's performance. Based on the outcome of the evaluation, career plans are adjusted and employees are rewarded (promotion; pay rise), or punished (demotion; dismissal). The employee's performance is evaluated by the functional manager, together with the human resources manager, and the outcomes of the evaluation are documented in the personnel files.

Organizations can evaluate and reward employees to manage either organizational output (e.g. profit) or organizational processes. In the first case, performance should be measurable, employees should be able to influence performance, employees should know the related performance target and their pay should be related to this performance target. For example, when a manager receives part of his salary based on the profit of his business unit, the business unit profit needs to be measurable, the manager should be able to influence the profit, he should know what the desired profit target is and his salary should depend on the profit of his business unit. This relates to output controls as discussed in Chapter 3. Organizations can also evaluate employees to manage organizational processes. In particular, this concerns the delegation of tasks to employees and holding them accountable for the quality of the performed activities. Chapter 3 discusses process controls more extensively.

In either case, performance evaluation is intended to align the employee and organizational goals to improve organizational output.

Remuneration

The remuneration process depends on the type of remuneration that employees receive. Employees may receive a fixed salary, variable compensation based on employee performance or both. When employees receive fixed wages, only the employee time and attendance (number of hours worked or job time) needs to be documented, and reconciled with the required working hours as specified in the employment contract (shop time). However, when employees (also) receive performance-based compensation, the quality of their work also needs to be evaluated and documented.

There are several ways to document employee time and attendance. For example, in many organizations employees can punch in and out of work using a time clock located at the entrance to the employee's workplace. However, in most cases, employees fill out time cards that need to be authorized by their supervisors. The payroll clerk receives the authorized time cards from the various department supervisors at the end of each pay period. These time cards indicate regular and overtime hours, vacation and sick leave. The payroll clerk compares the information on the time cards (job time) with the employment contract information (shop time) in the personnel files, and establishes that job time equals shop time. For hourly workers (temporary employees) or employees with overtime hours, the payroll clerk compares the employee's hourly wage rate with the employment contract information in the personnel files.

The payroll clerk subsequently prepares payroll, which is authorized by the cash disbursements clerk who initiates payment to the employees.

Termination

Organizations also need to have procedures in place for terminating dysfunctional employees. When performance evaluation indicates that employees do not function appropriately, a plan for improvement is prepared by the employee's superior and the human resources manager and communicated to the employee. Related employee performance should be closely monitored by both officers. Both the improvement plan and subsequent employee performance should be documented in the employee's personnel file. When the employee continues to be dysfunctional, a termination procedure is started. The decision to start such a procedure, as well as the actual termination, needs to be documented in the related personnel file by the human resources manager.

Investment in Fixed Assets

Investment in fixed assets generally consists of assessing the need for investment in fixed assets, analysing investment possibilities, making the investment decision, delivery/construction and operation of the fixed asset, paying for fixed assets and disinvesting.

Investment Need

From an internal control perspective, investments in fixed assets are quite similar to regular purchases. The main differences, however, are that investments in fixed assets are costly and capital intensive, have a longer planning horizon and are made less frequently and at a higher hierarchical level within the organization. Given these attributes and their impact on the organization, investments in fixed assets need to be based on a formal investment plan. This investment plan should incorporate the current year's sales forecast, taking into account last year's figures; market developments including competition; long-term sales targets and current capacity and expected capacity usage. All investments should occur in conformity with the investment plan, and any budget overruns should be authorized by management.

Investment Analysis and Decision

All investment possibilities should be documented and analysed extensively to allow management to make a well-founded decision. Decisions are usually made based on financial criteria. Therefore, the following information is required per investment alternative:

- the investment amount;
- the expected cash inflows and outflows, current capacity, and expected capacity usage during the life of the asset invested in; and
- the economic useful life of the asset.

Based on the financial conditions and the technical attributes of the investment, management selects the alternative they want to invest in.

Delivery or Construction, Operation and Payment

After delivery or construction, the asset will be put into operation. The asset will be put into operation in the department that identified the need for the investment. Furthermore, the asset needs to be paid for. Since payment can have important consequences for working capital, investment planning is needed. All investments should occur in conformity with the investment budget and applicable management guidelines, and any budget overruns should be authorized by management. In this way the organization can properly manage the consequences of its investments for working capital. Payment is usually spread out over multiple payments, and the terms of payment and the due dates should be included in the investment plan.

Disinvestment

When a capital asset becomes obsolete, the organization will disinvest in the asset. The disinvestment decision is usually based on information in the investment plan, which also specifies the economic useful life of the asset. The organization depreciates the asset over the asset's life, and when the asset is fully depreciated, the investment plan will suggest disinvestment. The actual disinvestment decision will be made by an authorization function, in most cases management. The disinvestment decision needs to be documented in the fixed asset records and recorded in the general ledger. The controller or the head of the accounting department should check all related information and should assess whether the decision was appropriately made. He should also reconcile the flow of goods and the flow of money with respect to the disinvestment:

Fixed assets at t_0 + investments in fixed assets $-/-$ depreciation of fixed assets = fixed assets at t_1

The controller or the head of the accounting department establishes fixed assets at t_0 and at t_1 by means of physical inspection of the related fixed assets. He establishes investments and disinvestments by consulting the contract register which details all investment and disinvestment contracts.

Cash Management

The cash management process generally consists of receiving cash, keeping cash in custody, safeguarding the value of the cash position and making payments.

Receiving Cash and Making Payments

Particularly in trade organizations, many sales transactions involve cash sales. Cash sales require specific internal controls to ensure that goods do not change hands without corresponding payment, and that cash receipts are transferred in a timely fashion and completely. When customers want to make cash payments, they take the desired products to a cash register. The sales clerk enters the product prices in the cash register. Alternatively, the product codes are entered in a cash terminal and the automated system automatically generates the associated prices and produces proof of payment in the form of a receipt. By attaching value to the receipt, e.g. the possibility of exchanging goods sold or warranty rights, customers will want to get a receipt when they pay. Since receipts are not generated unless the clerk enters the products in the cash register or cash terminal, chances are reduced that sales are not documented and recorded.

At the end of each day, the cash received needs to be counted. The use of a cash register or a cash terminal facilitates mechanical or electronic totalization of the amounts received. This is generally faster than manual totalization and reduces the chance of errors. The amounts of cash received are documented in a file with control totals that is inaccessible to the sales clerk who operates the cash register or cash terminal, resulting in a mechanically or electronically generated total of cash received. These totals should be compared with the cash that is accounted for by the sales clerk. The cash controller (e.g. an accounting clerk) is present when the sales clerk counts the cash. A protocol of the cash count is drawn up, specifying the total amount of cash, and signed by both the cash controller and the sales clerk. The cash controller then hands over the cash to the cashier who signs for receipt. The total of the cash count and the transfer to the cashier is documented in the cash journal and recorded in the general ledger. The controller or the head of the accounting department subsequently reconciles the amount of cash and the control total.

An important risk regarding cash transactions is lapping. If the cashier is responsible for both cash custody and cash recording, he will have the opportunity to record cash receipts later than they actually occurred or record cash disbursements before they actually occurred. For example, assume that customer A pays €100 to the cashier in payment of invoice X. The cashier accepts this money, but does not record the cash receipt in the general ledger. When later on customer B pays €150 in payment of invoice Y, the cashier does not record this cash receipt as a payment by customer B of invoice Y, but as the payment by customer A of invoice X instead. Later, when customer C pays invoice Z, this is recorded as the payment of customer B on invoice Y. When this process continues in this way, the cashier continually enjoys illegitimate credit from his employer. This scheme is called lapping and can be mitigated by segregation of duties between the cash custody, cash recording and cash authorization functions, surprise cash counts, and by rotating the cash custody function.

Finally, the cashier should not make payments until he receives authorization to do so from the cash disbursement clerk. All payments are ultimately recorded in the general ledger by the accounting department.

Cash Custody

The cashier has custody over cash and is responsible for the presence of cash. Assurance of receipts and disbursements is possible since a cashier should only perform transactions for which he is authorized by another officer within the organization. This is evident for cash disbursements, but also applies to cash receipts. The cashier documents cash transactions in a cash journal. All cash transactions are also recorded in the general ledger by the accounting department. The controller or the head of the accounting department is responsible for periodically reconciling the general ledger and the cash journal. For example, the opening cash balance of a certain day plus the cash receipts minus the cash disbursements during that day must be present in the cash register, which is verified by means of a cash count.

Safeguarding the Value of the Cash Position

An important activity within banks is treasury management. This involves attracting financial resources for the organization, cash-flow management, controlling currency and interest risks, and asset liability management.

Organizations need to implement tight internal controls over the treasury function. Management will have to define guidelines specifying the financial risk that the treasury is allowed to take, the employees that are responsible for implementing the treasury guidelines and the limits of their responsibility, and the hedging techniques which are acceptable for treasury to use. Furthermore, the treasury department has to see to it that the management guidelines are implemented in all parts of the organization by establishing and maintaining communications with those departments that incur risks, establishing and maintaining relationships with banks and financial institutions, defining employees' responsibilities of employees, and limits to those responsibilities, and supervising the control of access to dealing and back office functions.

Accounting and General Ledger Process

The final secondary process that we discuss in this chapter is the accounting and general ledger process. This process generally consists of collecting and categorizing financial transaction data, recording financial transaction data, processing financial transaction data and providing information to both internal and external stakeholders.

Collection and Categorization of Financial Transaction Data

Organizations generate large amounts of information through the activities within the various organizational processes. This information is ultimately collected by the accounting department in the general ledger. The accounting and general ledger activities consist of (1) accumulating and classifying data by general ledger account and recording data in those accounts, and (2) feeding the financial and managerial reporting process by providing information needs to prepare external and internal reports.

Recording and Processing Financial Transaction Data

Ultimately, all organizational transactions need to be recorded in the general ledger. The trigger for general ledger recording is the manager or clerk who performs the transaction, e.g. a sales or purchase transaction. The clerk or manager performing the transaction needs to enter all relevant information relating to that transaction in the organization's information system. For self-checking purposes, the clerk or manager is still able to change the information he entered as long as he has not completed the entry (by pushing the 'enter' button). This is to ensure that all information that is entered into the system is as accurate as possible, and to ensure efficiency of operations (e.g. to check before invoices are paid that the corresponding goods or services are actually ordered and received). In all cases, the manager or clerk preferably enters the information about that transaction into the information system immediately after the transaction has occurred.

After the clerk or manager has performed a self-check on the information entered, he completes the entry by pushing the 'enter' button. After that, the clerk or manager can no longer alter information about the transaction, resulting in the final recording of that transaction in the general ledger. The accounting department is ultimately responsible for recording all organizational transactions in the general ledger. The accounting department should have no other operational, responsibilities to ensure that all transactions are independently recorded and cannot be altered once each transaction has occurred.

The general ledger is thus updated for each regular, routine transaction. In addition, the treasurer can make entries of nonroutine transactions such as the purchase of securities. Based on all information about routine and nonroutine transactions, the accounting department produces an initial trial balance which lists all the balances for all general ledger accounts. Subsequently, the controller or the head of the accounting department can post adjusting entries resulting from corrections, revaluations, accruals or deferrals. After the adjusting entries have been made, the accounting department produces an adjusted trial balance. From the adjusted trial balance, the financial statements are prepared. Furthermore, from the same information in the general ledger and other parts of the information system, various managerial reports are prepared, such as budgets and performance reports.

Information Provision

All information that is collected must be organized and stored in the information system in such a way that it meets the demands of users. Within the organization, employees need information for self-checking purposes, e.g. to check whether the goods sent are actually invoiced. Managers need information about the results of the activities or operations that are their responsibility. The controller or the head of the accounting department needs information for checking the activities performed within the organization. Furthermore, investors, other outside parties, but also inside parties such as employees, require periodic financial statements to assess the organization's performance, and regulators require information on the organization's compliance with applicable laws and regulations. Therefore, the information system needs

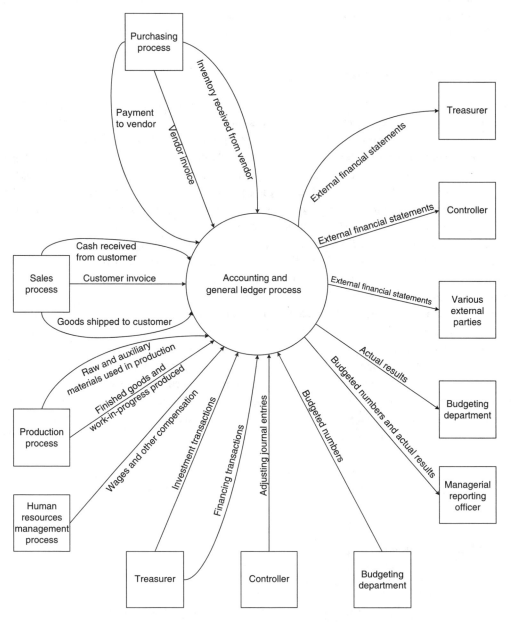

Figure 11.1   A generic logical data flow diagram of the general ledger and accounting process.

to be designed to be able to produce periodic reports and to provide for the information needs of users in a timely fashion.

A Generic Logical Data Flow Diagram of the Accounting and General Ledger Process

From the previous chapters (7–10) and sections ('Human Resources Management', p. 203; 'Investment in Fixed Assets', p. 205 and 'Cash Management', p. 207) we have learned that various primary and secondary processes fuel the general ledger which is maintained by the accounting department. Information from the processes related to purchasing, inventory, production, sales, human resources management, investment in fixed assets and cash management is collected, categorized and stored in the general ledger by the accounting department. Furthermore, the accounting and general ledger activities supply information to various (external and internal) parties for financial reporting and managerial reporting purposes. Hence, the accounting and general ledger activities play a pivotal role in organizations. The information flows to and from the accounting and general ledger process are depicted in the logical data flow diagram in Figure 11.1.

Summary

This chapter discusses internal controls in the secondary organizational processes that relate to human resources management, investment in fixed assets, cash management, and accounting and general ledger activities. The previous chapters on internal control in various organizational processes have discussed internal controls in primary organizational processes such as purchasing, inventory, production and sales, which directly contribute to revenue generation. In contrast, secondary processes indirectly contribute to revenue generation. However, as we have noted, in organizations that put skills and knowledge at their clients' disposal, such as law or accounting firms, human resources are of such direct importance to revenue generation – and revenue assurance – that the related process is strongly integrated with the purchasing process and should thus be considered a primary rather than a secondary process. Similarly, for organizations that put space or electronic capacity at their clients' disposal, such as transportation companies or telephone operators, investment in fixed assets is at the heart of their service provision and the related process is therefore considered to be part of the primary organizational processes of such organizations.

Internal Control in Various Types of Organizations

Typology of Organizations

Introduction

An organization can be considered a unique collection of processes. Identifying risks, the exposures to these risks and the potential controls to mitigate each risk *per process* is the common approach to designing and evaluating internal control systems. Although this may seem an adequate approach, it does not consider the idiosyncrasies of the combination of processes within one organization, which may result in different and/ or additional risks and controls for an organization as a whole rather than the sum of the individual risks, exposures and controls per process. Therefore, we develop a typology of organizations on the basis of internal control criteria. Similar to the process approach, we identify risks, exposures and mitigating controls. However, in the typology approach we do not identify these per process but for each type of organization as a whole.

The typology of organizations provides a framework to help classify organizations or parts of organizations in such a way that for each type a set of standard internal control measures can be derived. Classifying an organization in the appropriate category(ies) of the typology provides decision-makers with a sound basis for developing and evaluating the organization's internal control system, as it helps to identify the most important risks, exposures and controls for the organization. The purpose of this chapter is to introduce a typology of organizations that has proved to be instrumental in designing and evaluating organizations' internal control systems.

Learning Goals of the Chapter

After having studied this chapter, the reader will understand:

- the importance of a typology of organizations for the design and evaluation of internal control systems;
- the composition of a typology of organizations that is a fair representation of our current economical environment;
- the main risks that are inherent in each type of organization distinguished in the typology; and
- the main internal controls that are applicable to each type of organization distinguished in the typology.

Typology of Organizations

An organization that purchases and sells tangible goods or manufactures certain products from raw materials is characterized by a flow of goods. From an internal control perspective the presence of a flow of goods is generally considered helpful because it allows for relatively easy application of a number of strong and straightforward internal controls. For example, goods can be counted when they are in stock or when they are transferred from one department or person to another, and inventory, purchases and sales can be reconciled with each other. When a flow of goods become less distinctive, e.g. in organizations that provide services or put space, electronic capacity, knowledge or skills at their customers' disposal, measurement points such as inventory counts and transference moments will also become less visible. Therefore, these organizations require different and additional internal controls compared with organizations with a more distinctive flow of goods.

Considering the importance of the value cycle – including segregation of duties and reconciliations – for internal control, we base our typology of organizations on the coherence between the flow of goods and the flow of money. More specifically, the presence of a flow of goods results in a higher position in the typology. Because every organization has a flow of money, but not every organization has a flow of goods, the two main categories distinguished are organizations with a dominant flow of goods, and organizations without a dominant flow of goods. The typology presented here has many similarities with some well-known industry classifications. However, the main difference is that existing industry classifications are based on some kind of natural distinction between organizations without having made an unambiguous choice for any criterion, whereas our classification is based on the criterion of whether or not there is a dominant flow of goods that complements a flow of money. A special position is taken by governmental institutions, which mainly generate revenues from taxes, and other not-for-profit organizations such as foundations, associations and nongovernmental organizations (NGOs). These organizations may very well offer products and services that are similar in nature to those offered by organizations in other categories in the typology, yet the relationship between goods or services sold and cash received is often nonexistent. For instance, a province that engages a contractor to build a road will have to pay him, but will not normally receive any cash for the usage of the road by cars. Rather, the province will collect taxes from all people that have cars, or receive governmental contributions, as a result of which there is no direct relationship between expenditures and revenues. Therefore, these organizations are considered in a separate category in the typology. The typology of organizations that will be discussed in the following chapters is depicted in Figure 12.1.

It should be stressed that many organizations may fall into more than one category. The recommended approach is to first identify the revenue categories, and then identify the type of organization for each revenue category. For instance, a municipality that issues passports and hence collects legal dues has characteristics of a service organization with a limited flow of own goods. When this municipality also has a library for its citizens and collects revenues from loaning various media, it also has characteristics of an organization that puts specific space (loaning a book is comparable in nature to renting an apartment) at its customers' disposal. Another example is a transportation company that, in addition to having trucks on the roads to carry goods (disposition of specific space), has a petrol station where cars and trucks can fill their tanks (trade with cash sales) and a car wash (disposition of specific space).

When classifying organizations in the typology, we have to be aware of the problem of ecological fallacy, which occurs when we assume that every organization in a certain category exhibits all the characteristics of that particular category. This is not necessarily the case. For instance, a telecom provider may also sell mobile phones and other mobile devices. This is an activity that cannot be labelled disposition of specific electronic capacity, but is merely cash or credit sales. Hence, the typology must be applied sensibly, and the reasons for using it should always be taken into consideration, creating a model of a complex reality to help us better understand this reality.

Classification			Examples
Organizations with a dominant flow of goods	Trade organizations	Cash sales	Supermarkets, department stores, petrol stations
		Credit sales	Mail order companies, wholesalers
	Production organizations	Production to stock	Brickyards, beer breweries, paper mills
		Mass customization	Computer assembly companies, car assembly companies, single cut clothing manufacturing
		Agrarian and extractive organizations	Dairy farms, mines, oil companies
		Production to order	Shipyards, aircraft factories, contractors, film companies
Organizations without a dominant flow of goods	Service organizations with a limited flow of goods	Limited flow of own goods	Restaurants, newspaper publishers
		Limited flow of goods owned by third parties	Auctioneers, dry cleaners, bicycle repair stores, garages
	Service organizations that put space and electronic capacity at their customers' disposal	Disposition of specific space	Hotels, hospitals, oil pipeline companies, airlines, water companies, gas companies, transportation companies
		Disposition of specific electronic capacity	Internet providers, telecom providers, electricity companies
		Disposition of nonspecific space	Swimming pools, cinemas, concert halls, railway companies
	Service organizations that put knowledge and skills at their customers' disposal	Selling man hours	Public accounting firms, law firms, cleaning service companies
		Deployment of intellectual property	Software producers, car navigation companies, information brokers, traders of bitable goods
		Sale of financial products	Banks, insurance companies, investment companies, pension funds
	Governmental and other not-for-profit organizations		Ministries, government agencies, police organizations, prisons, universities, municipalities, foundations, associations and nongovernmental organizations (NGOs)

Figure 12.1   Typology of organizations.
(Adapted from Starreveld *et al.* 1998)

Trade Organizations

Trade organizations purchase goods, temporarily store them and eventually sell them, either through cash or credit sales. An important risk in these types of organizations is goods leaving the organization without a subsequent corresponding inflow of money. This may occur as a result of unintentional errors. For instance, when goods are delivered to a customer but the billing department does not prepare an invoice, most likely there will not be any inflow of money to compensate for the outflow of goods. Goods may also exit the organization without an accompanying inflow of money as a result of fraudulent actions. For instance, an employee takes goods from the warehouse, does not make proper payment and takes the goods home for his own use or sells these on his own account. An outflow of goods without a corresponding inflow of money results in increasing costs and decreasing profits. Internal controls to be put in place include:

- storage of goods in a closed warehouse under the custody of a warehouse manager;
- inspections at the gate to detect misappropriated goods;
- periodic physical inventory counts and reconciliation with the perpetual inventory records;
- use of pre-numbered packing slips and reconciliation of the number of packing slips to the number of invoices produced; and
- periodic reconciliation of the cash inflows and the sales according to the sales ledger.

The above risks and controls apply regardless of whether a trade organization generates cash or credit sales. An important additional risk applies for organizations with credit sales. Credit sales may turn out to be uncollectable if customers are not creditworthy. In this case, accounts receivable that are doubtful must be depreciated and the revenues must be reduced by the same amount. Controls that must be put in place include a creditworthiness check when a sales order is received, assigning credit limits to customers, billing as soon as possible after the sales transaction and systematically sending follow-up letters to defaulting debtors.

On the purchase side, received invoices may not be in agreement with received goods. Obviously, from the buyer's viewpoint an important risk is that the amount billed exceeds the value of the received goods. If this is not discovered and the invoice is paid, the cash outflow is too high compared with the revenue-generating capacity of goods that are received. An independent three-way match between the invoice (e.g. by the controller or the head of the accounting department), the goods receipt note and the order should mitigate this risk.

From an internal control perspective, a trade organization should make sure that the checking function (e.g. the controller or the head of the accounting department) maps the flow of goods and subsequently makes the following reconciliation:

$$\text{Inventory at } t_0 + \text{purchases} -/- \text{sales} = \text{inventory at } t_1$$

Inventory is counted applying the so-called four-eye principle, which means that at least two people – for example a warehouse clerk and an accounting clerk – do the inventory counts. Purchases and sales are taken from the general ledger or from the subsidiary purchase and sales ledgers. Should there be any deviations, the controller or the head of the accounting department should further analyse each of the components of the reconciliation above to detect potential causes of these deviations.

Production Organizations

Production organizations transform raw materials, man hours and machine hours into finished products through a technical transformation process. Thus, there are at least two types of inventory: inventory of raw materials and inventory of finished products. Therefore, many of the risks faced by trade organizations apply to production organizations as well. However, in addition there are various planning problems that are significantly more complex than comparable planning problems in trade organizations. A common risk in production organizations is the gradually declining accuracy of standards for raw materials, man hours, and machine hours when production is more tailored to the requirements of specific customers, such as for production to order. As a result, progress control on production processes becomes more difficult, suboptimal production targets may be set and erroneous production decisions may be made. Applicable controls include information provision on actual usage, procedures for adjustments of production standards and comparison of pre- and post-calculations, including analyses of any deviations by finance and control experts within the firm, such as controllers, business analysts and management accountants.

The operations office plays an important role in production organizations. This department makes the operational production decisions (authorizing function) and ensures that all necessary conditions are fulfilled to start and continue producing, including job preparation, production order issuance, progress control and nonfinancial (technical) pre- and post-calculation. Production orders are detailed descriptions of what and how much must be produced in the next production run. A production order also contains the required authorizations for providing specified quantities of raw materials and equipment that are to be used, an indication of who should be working on each order, starting and ending time of the production run, as well as task descriptions for production personnel if the activities to perform are nonroutine. It is important that actual expenses are reliably recorded and that these are regularly compared to the associated pre-calculations. Whereas the analysis of deviations between nonfinancial pre- and post-calculations can conveniently be made by the operations office, the analysis of deviations between nonfinancial and financial pre- and post-calculations is a designated task for the controller or the head of the accounting department (checking function). Pre- and post-calculations are generally less accurate when producing to order rather than producing to stock. If in that case the organization has fixed-fee contracts as well as cost plus contracts (based on actual costs billed), two risks arise. First, when actual exceed budgeted costs for a fixed-fee contract (i.e. the post-calculation exceeds the pre-calculation), the organization is set to suffer losses on the order. This increases the risk of (fraudulent) administrative re-allocation of costs from fixed-fee contracts to cost plus contracts, resulting in unreliable cost information per production order. Second, when the post-calculation exceeds the pre-calculation in the case of cost plus contracts, the organization will not suffer losses on the order since all costs (plus the targeted profit) are billed. However, in the long run this may lead to unsatisfied customers, reputation loss and potentially a loss of customers, because they were billed greater costs than budgeted. Internal controls to mitigate these risks mainly include segregation of duties between independent recording of production order costs on the one hand and order execution on the other.

In our discussion of production organizations, we include agrarian and extractive organizations because of the many similarities between these types of organizations and general production organizations. However, there are some risks that apply to agrarian and extractive organizations rather than to any other type of production organization. For instance, agrarian and extractive organizations are heavily dependent on environmental circumstances, such as weather conditions, (crop and animal) diseases and environmental laws. As a result, yields are difficult to predict. For example, due to weather conditions, the harvest may be extremely rich one year and extremely poor in another. Controls to be put in place include grow plans that are adjusted during the growing process, use of external yield forecasts and industry ratios, and pre-calculations of expected crops.

A special category of production organizations is formed by organizations that assemble products from standardized components based on specific customer orders. This type of production is generally referred to as mass customization. Dell computers are a typical example. On Dell's website customers can order a certain type of PC via an extensive menu, choosing specific components such as the hard disk, processor(s), monitor, memory, installed software or keyboard. In this type of organization it is not the finished products that are kept in stock, but the various components. Because this type of organization has many characteristics of production to stock, yet only has modest inventories, the risks that apply here are of a different nature, which justifies a separate category in the typology of organization. The main risk in mass customization is delivering a product that is not in agreement with the order as specified by the customer. Many errors in this field are a matter of deficient quality checks, which may lead to customer complaints, reputation loss and forgone revenues. Hence, there must be proper quality check procedures that result in integral quality assurance by an independent checking function such as a quality inspector. In addition, customer complaints must be reliably documented and progress checks on the settlement of complaints must be put in place.

Service Organizations with a Limited Flow of Goods

Service organizations with a limited flow of goods generate income by complementing a flow of goods with services. These services would not exist if there were no flow of goods, such as in restaurants (without food and beverages, customers will not want to pay, no matter how good service quality is) or repair shops (without objects to be repaired, service is not possible). From an internal control perspective it is of the utmost importance that a relationship is established between the service and the flow of goods.

An important risk in service organizations with a limited flow of goods is that services do not meet the customers' demand because the primary documentation of the customer order was inadequate. As a result either customers do not get what they ordered, or they get something they did not order. As a consequence the organization may develop a bad reputation and work inefficiently because order execution has to undergo numerous revisions before the customer is satisfied. Another risk is that employees report more hours on a certain project than they actually spent. This risk is comparable to the risk in production organizations that costs are re-allocated from one order or project to another. Controls that can be put in place here include:

- procedures for order confirmation to customers;
- sequential numbering of orders;
- segregation of duties between order acceptance (e.g. an attendant in a restaurant) and order execution (e.g. the chef and his team in a restaurant);
- periodic analytical review by a checking function of the relationship between the usage of raw materials, materials and man hours, and reported revenues;
- direct supervision on order acceptance and order execution; and
- using test buyers.

Service Organizations that Put Space and Electronic Capacity at their Customers' Disposal

Service organizations that put space and electronic capacity at their customers' disposal generate income by transferring the power of disposal of that capacity to the customer during a designated time frame. This may pertain to seats in a theatre, hotel rooms, apartments, admittance to a swimming pool, space in a truck, the use of a telephone network or sending fluids and gases through pipelines. From an internal control perspective it is important that a relationship is established between the service and the capacity that enables the service, i.e. between the volume or surface area, the time this capacity has been in use by customers and the revenues that are generated by providing the service.

An important risk in service organizations that put space and electronic capacity at their customers' disposal is that services that are provided are not billed. Hence, the service does not generate income whereas costs are incurred, leading to insufficient coverage of capacity costs. To mitigate this risk, vacancy must be checked by a checking function (e.g. the controller or the head of the accounting department) through personal inspection. Subsequently this checking function reconciles available occupancy reports with his personal inspection reports, relating total capacity to (inspected) vacancy and reported occupancy.

Service organizations that put specific electronic capacity at their customers' disposal, such as Internet service providers or mobile telephone operators, rely heavily on their computer systems. Hence, an important risk in this type of organization is impaired quality of their computer systems. As discussed in Chapter 4, IT adds its own dynamics to organizations and their controls. If the computer systems of a provider of high-tech services goes down, either no transactions are possible or the capacity put at each customer's disposal cannot be measured. Hence, all kinds of general controls aimed at business continuity must be put in place, including:

- sound procedures for back-up and recovery of software and data, and safe storage facilities;
- a programmed procedure for making recovery points in files;
- storing hardware in physically secured rooms that are fire- and waterproof;
- data-processing hot sites or cold sites;

- logical and physical access controls; and
- procedures (software) and hardware for secure electronic data communication, to prevent viruses, denial of service attacks and other IT related risks.

In addition, various controls to protect data integrity must be put in place, including:

- input and output checks;
- networks of control totals; and
- analytical review of actual performance benchmarked against forecasts and budgets.

To assure validity and completeness of revenues, these types of organizations often have a dedicated revenue assurance function. Revenue assurance should make sure that all services that were provided are actually billed and at the correct rates. For that purpose at least three groups of data should be appropriately linked: customer data, tariffs data and capacity usage data. For example, a mobile phone operator maintains a customer file, a rate file and a usage file that contain the following data: customer code, name, address, bank account, connection type, subscription rate, description (code for text message, voice call, data transfer), rate per text message, rate per voice call minute, rate per kilobyte of data transfer, transaction code, start time call, end time call and number of kilobytes of data transfer. To produce a correct invoice, reliable usage records must be appropriately related to the customer and rate files so that the services used by the customer are completely billed at the applicable rates.

If available capacity is not capped or if capacity usage cannot be reliably determined, for instance in organizations that put nonspecific space at their customers' disposal, a reconciliation of the capacity and the revenues as generated by that capacity is meaningless or simply impossible. A feasible alternative is to develop a so-called quasi-goods flow. Real goods and quasi-goods have in common that they both have value. However, a quasi-good takes its value from the fact that it entitles the holder to a service or good, whereas a real good has intrinsic value that is contained in its physical characteristics. For instance, a ticket that provides access to a swimming pool represents a certain value, but it is merely a piece of paper that is virtually worthless. To apply a quasi-goods movement as a control instrument, certain criteria apply to the production and handling of the quasi-goods:

- to produce the quasi-goods the organization must make use of reliable software provided by a trustworthy company;
- the software must assign a sequential number to each quasi-good that is printed;
- the quasi-good must be invalidated upon entry to the nonspecific space (e.g. a swimming pool). This invalidation must be performed by a function (e.g. a ticket inspector) that is separate from the function that sold the quasi-good to the customer (e.g. the ticket office of a swimming pool);
- the paper on which the quasi-good is printed must be safeguarded by a separate custody function; and
- at the end of a sales period (e.g. the end of a day at a swimming pool), a checking function (e.g. the controller or the head of the accounting department) determines the number of quasi-goods sold by comparing the starting and ending sequential quasi-good numbers as contained in the software log. Multiplied by the price of the quasi-good, this should equal the cash that has been collected (the so-called 'Soll' position).

The checking function then determines the *'Ist'* position by counting the cash that was actually collected in the cash register. If *'Soll'* and *'Ist'* do not match, the checking function should perform a further analysis to determine the nature of the deviation.

Service Organizations that Put Knowledge and Skills at their Customers' Disposal

Organizations that put knowledge and skills at their customers' disposal generate revenues by selling man hours, deploying intellectual property or selling financial products. The sale of man hours relates, for example, to hours spent by cleaning personnel in an office building or hours spent by auditors and lawyers on behalf of their clients. The deployment of intellectual property for example relates to the development and selling addresses of software, MP3 files, PDF files or address files. The sale of financial products relates to the provision of banking and insurance services.

When selling man hours, the difference between hours spent by a lawyer or a cleaner is not relevant from an internal control perspective. In both cases there must be a system that records the job time. However, a risk occurs if both fixed-fee and cost reimbursement (i.e. actual hours spent times the hourly rate) arrangements are provided. As we have illustrated for production organizations, shifting hours and costs from one order or project to another may lead either to forgone revenues or to unsatisfied clients and reputation loss, as well as unreliable order and/or project records. Somewhat related to re-allocating hours is the risk that recorded hours are invalid (overreporting) or incomplete (underreporting). This may lead to invalid or incomplete invoices without the financial records showing this. Controls that could be put in place here include:

- budgeting and analytical review by the controller or the head of the accounting department;
- a checking function that reconciles shop time (based on an independent record of the time an employee arrives at the site where he executes his job, and the time he leaves), job time (based on the job time ticket filled out by the employee) and pay time (according to his labour contract);
- calculation of batch totals of the hours spent per order or project by the employee, input of the batch totals together with the hours spent per order or project and a programmed procedure calculating the same batch total and comparing this to the batch total as calculated by the employee; and
- direct supervision of employees' presence, using time clocks at the gate and time cards, or having a door-keeper keep track of arrival and departure times.

Although there is a wide variety of organizations that deploy intellectual property, from an internal control perspective they have three features in common. First, similar to organizations that put electronic capacity at their customer's disposal, organizations that deploy intellectual property, such as software companies or digital information brokers, often rely heavily on their computer systems. Organizations that use IT as an enabler of their primary processes (e.g. fully web-based organizations) will suffer from business continuity problems if their computer systems go down. Therefore these organizations should pay substantial attention to computer security. Second, the production process is costly and evolves on a project basis. Hence, an adequate project management system is necessary to manage product development and the costs and progress of the development process. Third, the deployment costs of the product are low. To recover the development or production costs, therefore, the sales price of intellectual property has to be substantially larger than the deployment costs (e.g. the disk that contains the software).

Organizations that sell financial products also rely heavily on their computer systems. Imagine a bank, pension fund or insurance company without computers. These types of organizations always engage in massive data processing, which often entails extremely complex organizational processes. The main risk is that information about clients (insurance policies, damage claims, bank deposits, invested capital, etc.) is invalid and/or incomplete. This information represents direct monetary value and hence requires high reliability, while at the same time being prone to internal and external fraud. Controls that must be put in place here are largely comparable to the information security controls as applied in organizations that put specific electronic capacity at their customers' disposal and organizations that deploy intellectual property. However, the main difference lies in the nature of the services that are provided and the traceability of these services from provider to customer. Whereas controls in organizations that put specific electronic capacity at their customers' disposal and organizations that deploy intellectual property rely heavily upon segregation of duties within the IT organization, controls in organizations that sell financial products focus more on segregation of duties within the user departments and clearly defined responsibilities. A designated internal control function is responsible for the reconciliation of various data collections. The actual checks will normally be done in the form of programmed procedures.

Governmental and Other Not-for-profit Organizations

Within the category of organizations without a dominant flow of goods, governmental and other not-for-profit organizations have a special position. These organizations do not have profit goals and will primarily have an income spending role as opposed to an income generating role that is common for commercial organizations. In line with this limited role, therefore, the accounting systems of these organizations are often cash- rather accrual-based (i.e. they record receipts and expenditures rather than revenues and costs). As a result, budgeting is the main control tool. Another characteristic of this type of organization is that there is often no direct relationship between offers and yields. Therefore, other controls are needed for cost control. The budget plays an important role here too. An important risk in this type of organization is that there is unsatisfactory compliance with procedures, contracts, laws or regulations. When a governmental organization is noncompliant, this is considered illegitimate. Of course this is no different in commercial organizations, but since the government is accountable to citizens and spends taxpayers' money, this is considered a very serious offence that erodes the government's credibility. Controls that can be put in place include:

- monitoring of all activities by independent functions such as the internal control department, the accounting offices or the various internal audit departments of ministries or municipalities, with a focus on legitimacy of expenditures and obligations;
- clear internal and external reporting on policies that precede budgets, long-range estimates and activity plans, performance and effects of decisions, financial slack with respect to policies, assets, liabilities, accounts receivable, accounts payable, cash flows and liquidity;

- segregation of duties between those who decide upon the spending of money and those who verify this, such as the General Accounting Office or various decentralized accounting offices that operate at the level of municipalities, provinces or other public jurisdictions;
- analysis of differences between budgets and actuals by a checking function (e.g. an internal auditor); and
- oversight by independent representatives of citizens (e.g. municipality council, Parliament).

When classifying organizations as governmental we must again be aware of the ecological fallacy issue discussed earlier and recognize that not all the processes in governmental organizations have all the characteristics of this type of organization. An interesting example in this respect is the tendency for governmental organizations to operate in a more corporate fashion. In such cases governmental organizations should also put controls in place that are comparable to the controls that commercial organizations would employ in similar processes. This is particularly relevant for governmental institutions that supply specific products for which they receive direct payments. Examples include the city administration office where the production of passports and drivers' licences is somewhat comparable to the work of a printing company, or a city's parks and public gardens department that can be compared to a landscaping firm. Governments also try to apply the planning and control cycle to processes that traditionally are difficult to control in a corporate fashion. For example, the Dutch government has been using a methodology that looks back at the realization of plans and the relationship between the resources employed and the results obtained, in addition to the formation of future plans and putting an organization in place that facilitates the execution of these plans.

Foundations and associations often provide services instead of tangible products. Therefore the most important risks are comparable to those of organizations without a dominant flow of goods. However, there are some specific characteristics of foundations and associations that distinguish them from many other organizations without a dominant flow of goods. First, workers in foundations and associations are often volunteers. On the one hand this may have positive effects on the control environment since there is more congruence between the organization's goals and the individual employees' goals. On the other hand this may lead to a situation where controls are not accepted by the workers because this is perceived as undermining the trust in their voluntary work. Second, any foundation or association has a board that consists of a chairman, a treasurer and a secretary as a minimum. The degree of involvement of the board in the daily activities of the organization as well as its size are important determinants of the organization's capability to put proper segregation of duties in place. An important risk in this respect is that small foundations and associations with many volunteers often have very powerful boards that may find themselves in a position where they can make intentional or unintentional errors without being discovered. For this reason it is advisable to put the same types of controls in place and provide the same types of management reports as in comparable commercial organizations. A typical example is the cash checking committee in an association that has tasks similar to those of an internal audit department. Third, foundations and associations often finance their activities with governmental subsidies. This necessitates external oversight of the board and key executives similar to external oversight in commercial organizations, showing that the gap between *corporate governance* in commercial organizations and *government governance* in governmental and other not-for-profit organizations is only small.

Introduction to the Following Chapters

In the next chapters we will discuss the categories of organizations as distinguished in the typology: organizations with a dominant flow of goods in Chapters 13 (trade organizations) and 14 (production organizations), and organizations without a dominant flow of goods in Chapters 15 (service organizations with a limited flow of goods), 16 (service organizations that put space and electronic capacity at their customers' disposal) and 17 (service organizations that put knowledge and skills at their customers' disposal). We discuss the internal controls for governmental and other not-for-profit organizations in Chapter 18. We follow a similar approach in each of these chapters by systematically and sequentially discussing for each type of organization its characteristics, the risks, exposures and internal controls, the administrative and organizational conditions that apply, and the main processes that occur in that type of organization.

Summary

This chapter introduces a typology of organizations in line with the requirements of our contemporary economic climate. A typology is a model and thus provides a simplified representation of reality. Because of this feature the typology as presented in this chapter enables a decision-maker conveniently to identify a number of key characteristics of an organization, its exposure to certain risks and certain internal controls to be put in place to mitigate these risks. This chapter thus provides a useful introduction to the next chapters that each discuss a specific type of organization as specified in the typology.

13

Trade Organizations

In this chapter:

Introduction

Trade organizations purchase goods, store these goods for a certain period of time and then sell the goods to customers. The typology of organizations distinguishes two types of trade organizations: (1) trade organizations with cash sales and (2) trade organizations with credit sales. Trade organizations with cash sales are organizations that predominantly sell to final consumers, such as supermarkets or clothing retailers. Trade organizations with credit sales are predominantly wholesalers that sell goods to other organizations, or organizations that sell on account to final customers, such as internet retailers or mail-order businesses.

From an internal control perspective, we distinguish three main processes within trade organizations: the purchasing process, the inventory process and the sales process. For each of these processes, internal controls need to be implemented to mitigate the risks to achieving the organizational objectives. Risks with respect to trade organizations relate, for example, to the attractiveness of the goods (theft), creditworthiness of customers, kickbacks or unreliable inventory records. Internal controls that can be implemented to mitigate these risks range from segregation of duties to implementing management guidelines for performing analytical review.

The internal controls that are put in place will only be effective if certain administrative and organizational conditions are met. These conditions can be summarized under the following headings: computer security, segregation of duties, management guidelines and budgeting. The computer security measures as discussed in Chapter 4 are generally applicable to all types of organizations. Therefore, in this chapter, and all following chapters on the typology of organizations, we will only discuss segregation of duties, management guidelines and budgeting, tailored to the type of organization under consideration.

Learning Goals of the Chapter

After having studied this chapter, the reader will understand:

- the internal control consequences of classifying organizations as trade organizations with cash sales and trade organizations with credit sales;
- the risks for trade organizations with cash sales and for trade organizations with credit sales from an internal control perspective;
- the administrative and organizational conditions of trade organizations with cash sales and trade organizations with credit sales;
- the main processes of trade organizations with cash sales and trade organizations with credit sales; and
- the internal controls that can be put in place in trade organizations with cash sales and trade organizations with credit sales.

Characteristics of Trade Organizations with Cash Sales

From an internal control perspective, trade organizations with cash sales are the least complex types of organization. Often, these organizations are retailers. Typically, customers will visit the store, pick the goods they want to buy and pay the store personnel, whereas suppliers will deliver the goods and receive cash on delivery. Here, the value cycle as introduced in Chapter 2 will only consist of two events (purchasing/cash disbursement and selling/cash collection) and two positions (inventory and cash). The reconciliations between the flows of goods and the flows of money will therefore be limited to:

$$\text{Inventory at } t_0 + \text{purchases} -/- \text{sales} = \text{inventory at } t_1$$
$$\text{Cash at } t_0 + \text{sales} -/- \text{purchases} = \text{cash at } t_1$$

In practice, most purchases will not be paid cash on delivery but on account when a truck driver delivers the goods and an invoice is sent separately. In that case accounts payable will come into existence at the moment goods are delivered. The second reconciliation will then be replaced by the following two:

$$\text{Cash at } t_0 + \text{cash receipts} -/- \text{cash disbursements} = \text{cash at } t_1$$
$$\text{Accounts payable at } t_0 + \text{purchases} -/- \text{cash disbursements} = \text{accounts payable at } t_1$$

We will continue our discussion of trade organizations with cash sales under the following assumptions: (1) purchases are delivered by the vendor and are paid on invoice, (2) sales take place in the organization's store and are paid in cash on delivery.

Risks, Exposures and Internal Controls of Trade Organizations with Cash Sales

In trade organizations with cash sales we distinguish risks in the purchasing process, the inventory process and the sales process. The most important risk in the purchasing process relates to officers receiving kickbacks, secret commissions or other forms of inducement from vendors resulting in overly high costs of sales. The internal controls that must be implemented to mitigate this risk are the use of tender procedures, detailed checks of purchase prices by the controller or the head of accounting department and analytical review of purchase prices.

With respect to the inventory process, physical access controls to the store (such as protected gates, security cameras and security personnel), supervision by store personnel and periodic physical inventory counts are important controls to mitigate the risks related to the inventories on display. These controls are aimed at reducing theft of inventory by customers.

In the sales process, the theft of cash is a significant risk. Internal controls to mitigate this risk are segregation of duties between recording, custody and authorization of cash, and surprise cash counts.

An overview of risks, exposures and internal controls identifiable for trade organizations with cash sales is provided in Table 13.1.

Table 13.1 Risks, exposures and internal controls of trade organizations with cash sales.

Risk	Exposure	Internal controls
Kickbacks, secret commissions or other forms of inducement from vendors	High cost of goods sold	• Use of tender procedure • Detailed checks of purchase prices by controller or head of accounting department • Analytical review of purchase prices

(Continued)

Table 13.1   (Continued)

Risk	Exposure	Internal controls
Goods received are not in agreement with purchase orders	Obsolete inventory High cost of goods sold	• Quality and quantity checks on receipt of goods • Recording of quality and quantity of goods received on receipt of goods • Segregation of duties between warehouse (custody) and purchasing (authorization) • Reconciliation of purchase orders and receiving reports by cash disbursement department
Vendor invoices are not in accordance with goods received	High cost of goods sold	• Quality and quantity checks on receipt of goods • Recording of quality and quantity of goods received on receipt of goods • Segregation of duties between warehouse (custody) and accounts payable (custody) • Reconciliation of vendor invoices with receiving reports by cash disbursement department
Accuracy of purchase prices	High cost of goods sold	• Integrity controls over vendor files containing price information • Segregation of duties between accounting department (recording) and purchasing department (authorization) • Sample-based checks by checking function on purchase prices in relation to agreed upon prices with vendors
Shifting of purchase transactions between periods	High cost of goods sold	• Integrity controls over vendor files containing price information • Segregation of duties between accounting department (recording) and purchasing department (authorization) • Sample-based checks by checking function on purchase prices in relation to agreed upon prices with vendors, purchase requisitions, orders, receipt of goods and vendor invoices • Appropriate purchase requisitioning procedures
Unreliable accounts payable records	Inadequate account payable management, resulting problems with creditors and loss of reputation	• Primary recording of vendor invoices immediately at receipt • Checking accounts for goods to receive and invoices to receive
Wrong vendor choice	Opportunity costs	• Adequate vendor information system with detailed vendor information
Capital intensive inventories	Continuity of business	• Reliable and timely information about goods ordered and received, goods sold and delivered, and market expectations
Shifting of inventory between locations	Incompleteness of revenues is concealed	• Simultaneous inventory counts
Unreliable inventory records	Suboptimal ordering moments, high costs of holding inventory, stockouts, resulting loss of customers and forgone revenues	• Periodic inventory counts • Analytical review of inventory recordings by controller or head of accounting department • Adequate procedures for backorders

Shop within a shop	Loss of revenues	• Segregation of duties between sales (authorization) and purchasing (authorization) • Clear communication of purchasing and sales procedures to vendors and customers
'Ready to sell' products	Theft of products by employees	• Closed warehouse accessible only to warehouse employees • Discharge of all goods releases and receipts • All releases and receipts are recorded in the inventory records • Periodic inventory counts • Supervision by warehouse manager
Inventories on display	Loss of assets because of theft of inventory by customers	• Physical access controls to the store such as protected gates, security cameras and security personnel • Supervision by store personnel • Periodic inventory counts
Accuracy of sales prices	Loss of revenues	• Integrity controls over price files • Segregation of duties between accounting department (recording) and sales department (authorization) • Sample-based checks on prices billed
Shifting of sales transactions between periods	Loss of revenues	• Integrity controls over price files • Segregation of duties between accounting department (recording) and sales department (authorization) • Sample-based checks on billed prices
Discounts	Forgone revenues	• Management guidelines for allowing discounts (discount tables) • Sample-based detailed checks on allowed discounts according to sales invoices
Cash transactions	Loss of assets because of theft of cash by employees	• Segregation of duties between recording, custody and authorization with respect to cash • Surprise cash counts
Lapping	Loss of interest revenues and eventually potential complete loss of cash	• Segregation of duties between recording, custody and authorization with respect to cash • Surprise cash counts • Rotating the cash custody function
Relatively simple sales transactions	Sales order, shipping order, bill of lading, picking and packing lists, invoices and other documents are generally not prepared	• Use of a cash register • Secondary segregation of duties between cash register operators (e.g. sales personnel) and head cashier
Many customers	Difficult to obtain detailed customer information	• Adequate controls over the customer master files
Tight margins	Low fault tolerance, strong need for efficient processes	• Tight controls over the purchasing and sales prices • Daily analytical review of margins at product level
Relatively unpredictable product demands	Decision what and when to buy is critical to the continuity of the business	• Market research

In trade organizations, the value cycle is instrumental in assuring the completeness of revenues. In these types of organization, there is a strong link between the flow of goods and the flow of money. Goods that are purchased are subsequently sold, implying that the revenues are strongly linked to the goods purchased and goods sold. Therefore, reasonable assurance about the completeness of revenues is obtained through appropriate segregation of duties and reconciliations performed by the controller or the head of the accounting department.

Administrative and Organizational Conditions in Trade Organizations With Cash Sales

Segregation of Duties

Trade organizations with cash sales must segregate the functions that are involved in purchasing goods, receiving goods and preparing receiving reports, checking the quality of received goods, safeguarding goods, selling goods, safeguarding cash, recording transactions and checking whether transactions have been properly recorded.

Table 13.2 gives an overview of the system of segregation of duties in trade organizations with cash sales.

Table 13.2   Segregation of duties in trade organizations with cash sales.

Officer	Department	Task	Duty
Purchase clerk/manager	Purchasing department	Purchasing goods	Authorization
Receiving clerk	Receiving department	Receipt of goods, preparation of receiving report	Execution
Quality inspector	Receiving department	Checking quality of received goods	Checking
Warehouse clerk/manager	Warehouse department	Safeguarding goods	Custody
Store personnel	Shop floor	Replenish the store inventory and serving customers	Execution
Sales clerk/manager	Sales department	Selling goods (including receipt of customer payments)	Authorization
Sales clerk/manager	Sales department	Temporary safeguarding of cash	Custody
Cashier	Cash department	Safeguarding cash	Custody
Cash disbursements clerk/ manager	Cash disbursements department	Payment of vendor invoices	Authorization
Accounts payable clerk/ manager	Accounts payable department	Safeguarding accounts payable	Custody
Accounting clerk	Accounting department	Recording transactions	Recording
Controller or head of accounting department	Accounting department	Checking transactions	Checking

Budgeting

For trade organizations, budgeting revolves around the annual master budget and some constituent budgets, including:

- the sales budget;
- the cost budget per department;
- the cash budget; and
- the purchase budget.

Management must approve budgets and standards and the controller or the head of the accounting department should periodically report to management on any deviations of actual results from budgeted results. Internal control systems use budgets as '*Soll*' positions in analytical review procedures.

Management Guidelines

Trade organizations with cash sales need to develop authorized management guidelines with respect to cash and the safeguarding of goods, including:

- the maximum amount of cash in the cash drawers;
- the acceptance of various forms of cash, including credit cards, debit cards, electronic wallets and cheques;
- the deposit of cash received into a safe;
- access to ready-to-sell goods by employees; and
- the movement of goods between the closed warehouse and the store.

Case Study 13.1: Shop within the Shop

Repeatedly, the importance of clear-cut management guidelines for a purchasing department is shown, not just for the purchasing clerks, but also for the vendors, to know exactly how to order, deliver and pay. Unfortunately, for the purchasing department of one of our clients these guidelines did not exist for the suppliers, due to which the purchasing clerk placed orders with various suppliers, which were immediately resold to acquaintances and friends. Obviously, revenues were pocketed by the purchasing clerk, while the purchases were allocated to a number of his employer's cost centres. Some suppliers had had to wait a long time for their money. Since the purchasing clerk was their contact person, he was able to stall them with all kinds of excuses. Amazingly, not only did the patient suppliers continue with new deliveries, but they also delivered goods that did not belong to the ordinary set of goods of our client. Even more so, a number of shipments were delivered directly to the purchasing clerk's home address. In a final discussion, the purchasing clerk admitted to having his own shop within the shop.

(Continued)

All goods he had ordered this way he had always resold. Our client is now looking for a new purchasing clerk. The new purchasing clerk definitely needs to operate differently from his predecessor. The organization's suppliers will receive written guidelines, explaining how orders are to be placed, who will be authorized to do so and to what addresses deliveries are to be made. In addition, these guidelines will also contain instructions for dealing with arrears or departures from the established ordering methods. Obviously, the last two issues need to be reported to management, not to the purchasing department.

(*Source*: Hoffmann, Detective tips for business. nr 117. May 1997 [Recherchetips voor het bedrijfsleven].)

The Main Processes in Trade Organizations with Cash Sales

In trade organizations with cash sales we distinguish three main processes: the purchasing process, the inventory process and the sales process. Since we have already discussed details of the internal controls of each of these processes in Chapters 7, 8 and 10, respectively, we will focus on specific risks and applicable controls in this section.

Purchasing Process

Purchase prices may fluctuate because the goods in question may be bought on a market where prices are dictated by the equilibrium between supply and demand. When purchase prices fluctuate strongly, the moments at which purchases are made must be recorded by an officer independent of the officer that has custody over cash. A risk that may occur here is the shifting of transactions through time; for example by administratively shifting purchases made in a period with low market prices to a period with high prices, the differential monetary amount can be withdrawn from the organization. In this case, proper segregation of duties between recording, cash custody and purchase authorization is an essential preventive measure. In addition, the purchase requisition procedures need to be tightened such that purchase requisitions must be followed up within a limited period of time. Further, the trail of documents from purchase requisition to vendor invoice must be investigated on a sample basis.

When purchase prices are more stable, fixed administrative prices can be used. In that case, scrutinizing the differences between actual purchase prices and fixed administrative rates in combination with sample-based detailed checks on individual transactions are important control measures to be performed by the controller, the head of the accounting department or a designated internal control function.

Inventory Process

In the inventory process periodical physical inventory counts are necessary to determine whether the stocks according to the perpetual inventory records are actually present in the warehouses. Therefore, proper inventory count procedures, as determined by management, are important controls to mitigate the risks of ready to sell products, unreliable inventory records, billing errors and many other risks that have an impact on the completeness of revenues. During inventory counts, receipt or distribution of goods should not take place, since existing stocks need to be determined as accurately as possible. In addition, the inventory counter must be independent from the custody function. However, as a custody function the warehouse manager must be present during inventory counts since he is responsible for inventory, and he needs to observe possible differences between actual inventory and inventory according to the perpetual inventory records. Moreover, with his knowledge he can advise the inventory counter on technical issues. The type of counting method is dependent on the way inventory records are kept. One type of inventory counting is integral inventory counting, where the entire stock is counted at the same time. If inventory records contain a specification of for example the article type, inventory counts can be done separately for each article, at a time when regular business is least disrupted or when stock is at a minimum level, such as after a sales promotion action. This counting method is denoted cycle counting. Inventory is counted in such a way that within a certain period all articles are counted at least once. If there are multiple locations where similar stocks are kept, inventory counts in all these locations must be done at one and the same time, to prevent shifting of stocks between locations. This is called simultaneous counting. For example, when an organization has multiple branches, a deficit in location A may temporarily be replenished from the inventory of location B. If an inventory count in location B is done subsequently to a count in location A, the inventory shifted from location B to location A may be moved back to location B in order to prevent the counters detecting the shifting of stocks. Simultaneous counting will mitigate this risk.

Sales Process

The importance of cash transactions has decreased in the last few decades since credit cards, electronic wallets and other forms of virtual money have gradually replaced cash. Some even expect a completely cashless society in the near future. However, especially in many small retail organizations, there are still a lot of cash transactions, and hence internal controls regarding the function of the cashier are still important. The cashier has custody over money and is responsible for the presence of cash. Control of receipts and disbursements is possible since a cashier should only perform transactions for which he is authorized by either the cash receipts manager (in case of cash receipts) or the cash disbursement manager (in case of cash disbursements). This is obvious for cash disbursements, but also applies to cash receipts. The cashier documents cash transactions in a cashbook. All cash transactions are also recorded in the general ledger by the accounting department. The controller or the head of the accounting department is responsible for periodically reconciling the general ledger with the cashbook. For example, the opening cash balance of a certain day plus the cash receipts minus the cash disbursements during that day must be present in the cash register which is checked by means of a cash count.

A serious risk regarding cash transactions is lapping. If there is a pairing of duties between cash custody and cash recording, the cashier will have the opportunity to record cash receipts later than they actually took place or record cash disbursements before they have actually taken place. For example, customer A pays € 100 to the cashier in payment of invoice X. The cashier takes this money and to conceal the theft, he does not record the cash receipt in the general ledger. When customer B later on pays €150 in payment of invoice Y, the cashier does not record this cash receipt as a payment by customer B of invoice Y, but as the payment by customer A of invoice X. Later, when customer C pays on invoice Z, this is recorded as the payment by customer B of invoice Y. When this process continues in this way, the cashier continually enjoys illegitimate credit from his employer. This scheme is denoted lapping and can be mitigated by segregation of duties between the cash custody, cash recording and cash authorization functions, surprise cash counts and by rotating the cash custody function.

Case Study 13.2: After a Season of Cutting, Stores Sweeten Discounts

By Stephanie Rosenbloom

For weeks, reluctant consumers have forced retailers to lower their prices – and lower them again and again – before they even considered opening tight wallets and purses.

Now shoppers are expecting even better deals, as they do every year, in the post-Christmas clearance sales.

Industry analysts say consumers will not be disappointed, though the deals will most likely come with a twist. Rather than seeing merchandise marked down even more from the 75 percent-off stickers, shoppers should expect more combined discounts – or 'bundling,' as it is known in the industry.

'Buy a laptop, get a free printer, ink cartridges – and paper,' explains Marshal Cohen, chief industry analyst for the NPD Group, a retailing industry consulting company. Retailers have no choice but to find creative ways to clear their store shelves, because they have to make room for spring merchandise. And persuading consumers to take their goods off their hands is increasingly their only option, since other avenues, like discount Web sites, already have full inventories of their own.

After all, retailers had one of the worst holiday shopping seasons in decades, with sales falling by double digits in nearly all categories, including apparel, luxury goods, furniture and electronics and appliances, according to SpendingPulse, a report by MasterCard Advisors that estimates retail sales from all forms of payment, including checks and cash.

Even worse for retailers, consumers bought fewer gift cards than last year – 10 to 40 percent fewer, according to various estimates. Gift cards provide an added bonus for retailers; they tend to drive sales in January, with shoppers buying other things once they are in the store.

As a result, retailers will have to work that much harder to clear Christmas inventory, which many stores were unable to trim enough ahead of the quickly softening economy. Mr. Cohen and other analysts said retailers would need popular brands and unique fashions to lure traffic in the future, not just low prices.

Many chains bundled products on the first day of their after-Christmas sales, a tactic that worked for them on Black Friday, the blockbuster shopping day after Thanksgiving. At J. C. Penney, a $988 leather sofa (reduced from $2,858) came with a free wing chair, normally $899. At Old Navy, T-shirts were $10.50, or $6 each if you bought two or more. At Bath and Body Works, the company's signature collection of creams, gels and scents carried buy-two-get-one-free deals.

But all this sustained discounting has industry professionals worried not only about erosion of profits – in general, discounting merchandise more than 50 percent is a losing proposition for retailers – but also about consumer spending habits.

'Many of the senior executives we've talked to are worried about how we retrain the customer to pay full price,' said Joseph Feldman, a retailing analyst with Telsey Advisory Group, an equity research and consulting company.

Hana Ben-Shabat, a partner in the retail practice of the A. T. Kearney consulting company, said the storewide discounting that took place this holiday season was a result of retailers' being blindsided by an economy that was far worse than they had anticipated. Come spring, she said, they will be more selective when choosing which products and categories to offer at lower prices.

'It's just not sustainable to keep selling everything at a 50, 60, 70 percent discount,' she said.

In their most recent earnings calls, retailers like Saks and Neiman Marcus admitted their profit margins were taking a beating.

'It's not anything we like,' Burton M. Tansky, president and chief executive of the Neiman Marcus Group, said of all the promotions. 'It's a necessity.' Typically, retailers wait about eight weeks before putting merchandise on sale, but analysts said that given the economy, this spring they may wait only about two or three weeks. 'There is no more patience,' Mr. Cohen of the NPD Group said. 'The rules have changed.'

Liz Robbins contributed reporting.

Source: New York Times, December 27, 2008.

Characteristics of Trade Organizations with Credit Sales

Trade organizations with credit sales form the basis for the value cycle introduced in Chapter 2. Often, these organizations are wholesalers where customers do not visit the store; goods are delivered by a carrier and customers pay at another time than on delivery. In addition to purchases that lead to accounts payable we therefore also see sales that lead to accounts receivable here. The reconciliations between the flows of goods and the flows of money will therefore be somewhat more elaborate than for trade organizations with cash sales:

$$\text{Inventory at } t_0 + \text{purchases} -/- \text{sales} = \text{inventory at } t_1$$
$$\text{Accounts receivable at } t_0 + \text{sales} -/- \text{cash receipts} = \text{accounts receivable at } t_1$$
$$\text{Cash at } t_0 + \text{cash receipts} -/- \text{cash disbursements} = \text{cash at } t_1$$
$$\text{Accounts payable at } t_0 + \text{purchases} -/- \text{cash disbursements} = \text{accounts payable at } t_1$$

We will continue our discussion of trade organizations with credit sales under the following assumptions: (1) purchases are delivered by the vendor and are paid on invoice, (2) sales are delivered to the customer and billed separately.

Risks, Exposures and Internal Controls of Trade Organizations with Credit Sales

As with trade organizations with cash sales, for trade organizations with credit sales we can identify risks in the purchasing process, the inventory process and the sales process. Most of the risks in these processes that apply to trade organizations with cash sales also apply to trade organizations with credit sales. This is particularly true for risks related to the purchasing and inventory processes since these generally do not differ between the two types of trade organizations. The differences are in the sales process where cash sales are replaced by credit sales and delivery is made through shipment instead of having customers come to the organization's store to collect goods. This implies that cash-related risks are generally not present in trade organizations with credit sales. However, for trade organizations with credit sales there are also additional risks that are not present in trade organizations with cash sales. First, the creditworthiness of customers is a prominent risk that can lead to invalid sales and subsequent loss of revenues. Therefore, trade organizations with credit sales must put procedures in place to check customer creditworthiness at order acceptance. This check must be performed by the credit department. Second, the mere existence of accounts receivable leads to uncertainty about the organization's cash position. Follow-up letters, urging customers to pay on time by giving discounts for prompt payment and charging fines for overdue payments, periodic ageing of accounts receivable and integrity controls on the accounts receivable files are part of the solution. Third, when goods are shipped, errors may occur and customers may lodge complaints. Internal controls to mitigate this risk include well-designed picking and packing lists, segregation of duties between warehousing and shipping, customer complaints procedures and reconciliations of sales orders, picking tickets and invoices by the controller or the head of the accounting department. Fourth, billing errors could lead to a loss of revenues (understating invoices) or customer complaints (overstating invoices). Various detective controls can be put in place to mitigate this risk, including reconciliation of orders with shipments and invoices, and re-performance of invoice calculations. Applicable preventive controls include segregation of duties between billing, accounts receivable and the general ledger. A specific preventive measure is a pre-billing system (see 'Billing', in Chapter 10, p. 193) to avoid shipping goods without creating an invoice. Finally, as a result of the relative complexity of sales transactions, there is a high administrative burden on the organization involving the creation of sales orders, shipping orders, bills of lading, picking and packing lists, and invoices. Preventive controls include segregation of duties between sales, the accounting department, accounts receivable, warehousing and shipping. Detective controls include reconciliations of sales orders, shipping orders, bills of lading, picking and packing lists, and invoices by the controller or the head of the accounting department.

An overview of the additional risks identifiable for trade organizations with credit sales is provided in Table 13.3. Note that, apart from the cash-related risks, most of the risks in Table 13.1 also apply to trade organizations with credit sales.

Table 13.3   Risks, exposures and internal controls of trade organizations with credit sales.

Risk	Exposure	Internal controls
Creditworthiness of customers	Invalid sales and hence loss of revenues	• Procedures for checking customer creditworthiness by credit department at order acceptance • Adequate documentation of accounts receivable • Segregation of duties between recording, custody and authorization with respect to accounts receivable • Periodic ageing of accounts receivable
Uncollectability of accounts receivable	Uncertainty about cash position Loss of revenues	• Follow-up procedures • Urging customers to pay on time by giving discounts for prompt payment and fines for overdue payments • Periodic ageing of accounts receivable • Integrity controls on accounts receivable files
Shipping errors	Customer complaints Loss of revenues	• Well-designed picking and packing lists • Segregation of duties between warehousing (custody) and shipping (execution) (note that sales department provides information to both) • Adequate customer complaints procedures • Reconciliation of sales orders, picking tickets and invoice
Billing errors	Loss of revenues (understatements) Customer complaints (overstatements)	• Pre-billing system • Reconciliation of sales orders with shipments and invoices • Re-performance of invoice calculations • Segregation of duties between billing (execution), accounts receivable (custody) and the accounting department (recording) • Adequate customer complaints procedures
Relatively complex sales transactions	High administrative burden on the organization	• Segregation of duties between sales (authorization), the accounting department (recording), accounts receivable (custody), warehousing (custody) and shipping (execution) • Reconciliations of sales orders, shipping orders, bills of lading, picking and packing lists and invoices by controller or head of accounting department
Unreliable accounts receivable records	Inadequate account receivable management, resulting problems with debtors, and loss of reputation	• Primary recording of customer invoices immediately at creation of invoices • Input controls on accounts receivable information

Administrative and Organizational Conditions in Trade Organizations with Credit Sales

Segregation of Duties

Trade organizations with credit sales must segregate virtually the same functions as trade organizations with cash sales. There are, however, five additional functions that trade organizations with credit sales need to segregate: (1) a function for checking customer credit, which we refer to as the credit clerk or

Table 13.4   Segregation of duties in trade organizations with credit sales.

Officer	Department	Task	Duty
Purchase clerk/manager	Purchasing department	Purchasing goods	Authorization
Receiving clerk	Receiving department	Receipt of goods, preparation of receiving report	Execution
Quality inspector	Receiving department	Checking quality of received goods	Checking
Warehouse clerk/manager	Warehouse department	Safeguarding goods	Custody
Sales clerk/manager	Sales department	Selling goods	Authorization
Credit clerk/manager	Sales department or separate credit department	Checking the creditworthiness of customers	Checking
Shipping clerk/manager	Shipping department	Shipping goods to customers	Execution
Billing clerk/manager	Billing department	Billing customers	Execution
Accounts receivable clerk/manager	Accounts receivable department	Safeguarding accounts receivable	Custody
Cash receipts clerk/manager	Cash receipts department	Receipt of customer payments	Authorization
Cashier	Cash department	Safeguarding cash	Custody
Cash disbursements clerk/manager	Cash disbursements department	Payment of vendor invoices	Authorization
Accounts payable clerk/manager	Accounts payable department	Safeguarding accounts payable	Custody
Accounting clerk	Accounting department	Recording transactions	Recording
Controller or head of accounting department	Accounting department	Checking transactions	Checking

manager; (2) a function for shipping goods sold, a shipping clerk/manager; (3) a function for billing customers, a billing clerk/manager; (4) a function for safeguarding accounts receivable, an accounts receivable clerk/manager; and finally (5) a function for receipt of customer payments, a cash receipts clerk/manager.

Table 13.4 gives an overview of the system of segregation of duties in trade organizations with credit sales.

Budgeting

No additional budgets must be created when compared to trade organizations with cash sales. However, there will be more uncertainty about the amounts of cash that will be collected since there is an additional risk of uncollectable amounts. This results in a less predictable cash budget. Another complicating factor is the organization's discretion regarding payment of creditors. The organization may develop a policy for paying creditors that incorporates postponing payments when debtors default, leading to slightly more complex administrative procedures with respect to budgeting and cash planning.

Management Guidelines

The policy for making payments to creditors and balancing these with receipts from debtors must be formalized via management guidelines. Further, there must be management guidelines for shipping goods when payment is not yet effected. The other management guidelines as discussed for trade organizations with cash sales also apply here.

The Main Processes in Trade Organizations with Credit Sales

As in trade organizations with cash sales, within trade organizations with credit sales we distinguish three main processes: the purchasing process, the inventory process and the sales process. The purchasing and inventory processes are similar to those of trade organizations with cash sales. With respect to the sales process, however, there are some notable differences, which we discuss below.

When the sales department accepts a customer order because the potential customer is deemed creditworthy (creditworthiness check) and the required goods are in stock (inventory availability check), this will result in an instruction to pick the goods in the warehouse and send the associated invoice to the customer. How the picking ticket is produced depends on the billing system that the organization uses. A distinction can be made between pre-billing, post-billing and interim billing. Management's choice between these systems is largely determined by the organization's commercial policy. For example, the required speed of delivery, customer expectations, competitive position and industry customs determine the time the organization can spend on internal controls that may delay the time of delivery. In addition, it is important that all data necessary for billing are known by the billing department before the warehouse is notified. The various billing systems differ with respect to the document that forms the basis for the invoice.

In a pre-billing system, invoices are prepared based on authorized sales orders. A copy of the invoice is subsequently printed in the warehouse, serving as a picking ticket for the warehouse manager. Note that pre-billing does not imply that the invoice is *sent* to the customer prior to the picking and delivery of goods. Rather, it indicates that administratively, the invoice is *prepared* prior to picking the goods. An advantage of pre-billing is that there is reasonable assurance that no goods are shipped without an invoice being produced. After all, the reconciliation between the sales invoice to be sent and the warehouse picking ticket is built into this billing system. However, pre-billing is only possible when inventory availability is known before picking and packing. All products carried by the organization need to be in stock, and the measurement unit for warehouse distribution needs to equal the measurement unit for billing. For example, a cheese wholesaler uses kilograms as its measurement unit for billing whereas the measurement unit for warehouse distribution is the number of cheeses. Pre-billing cannot be applied in this case, since the amount of kilograms of cheese to be shipped cannot be determined in advance.

In a post-billing system the warehouse picks and packs the goods based on copies of authorized orders, and the invoice is prepared on the basis of the shipping notice. Billing takes place after the order is reconciled with the shipping notice as entered into the system or approved by the shipping department after they have shipped the goods. Usually post-billing is used when not all information on the goods to be shipped is available in advance. The cheese wholesaler mentioned above is an example, as is a situation in which a specific article number needs to be stated on the invoice because of warranty obligations. It would be most efficient to have these numbers printed on the picking tickets used in the warehouse, but for reasons of segregation of duties the warehouse should receive only the minimally required amount of information.

A billing system that combines pre-billing and post-billing features is interim billing. In the case of interim billing, invoices are prepared based on the customer order. At the same time, the goods ordered by the customer are picked and packed by the warehouse based on a copy of the customer order. By means of a copy of the sales invoice the shipping department checks if all packed and shipped goods have been billed by matching the packing slips with the invoices. Because of the increasing availability of integrated information systems, interim billing is now rarely encountered in practice.

The controller or head of the accounting department is responsible for checking the validity and completeness of billing. An important check here is the reconciliation between the goods shipped according to the perpetual inventory records and the total of the amounts billed according to the accounts receivable administration. In addition, samples of sales transactions are examined for use of correct prices, discounts and other delivery conditions.

Credit sales result in accounts receivable records. Ideally, these should be kept by two departments. The accounting department records the accounts receivable at an aggregate level in the general ledger, thus performing the recording function. In addition, the accounts receivable department documents accounts receivable in the accounts receivable subsidiary ledger, thus performing the custody function. The accounts receivable subsidiary ledger contains information on each account receivable in a lot more detail than the general ledger. After all, accounts receivable are important for trade organizations, and besides the total of customer account balances, information on a more detailed level is needed such as the sales per expiration date for each debtor. In this way, insight can be gained into the composition of account balances in terms of the relative importance of each debtor in the accounts receivable total, the average term of credit allowed and ageing of accounts receivable. In addition, timely payment by debtors can be monitored. As part of accounts receivable control, periodically debtors are identified for which the credit term allowed has expired without receipt of payment. Measures need to be taken to collect these potentially bad debts. In general, the accounts receivable department will take care of the follow-up towards the debtors involved. However, they will not do this until the sales department has been consulted for advice on the potential causes, potential sensitivities with the debtors involved and the importance of maintaining these specific customer relationships. For example, a customer may want to discuss possible deviations in the quality or quantity of the delivered goods or misstatements in the invoices. Follow-up to bad debts can be done via various methods, including: writing follow-up letters, contacting the debtor by telephone, contacting the debtor by e-mail, visiting the debtor or ultimately handing over the outstanding receivables to a debt collection agency. By documenting the methods used and the effectiveness of each of these methods, statistics are obtained on the most effective way of following up on bad debts.

The form of accounts receivable documentation depends on the information needs of the organization. The nature of the sales relation is important as well. For payments in periodical instalments recording per debtor in the general ledger or a subsidiary ledger is necessary. This form of accounts receivable documentation is also preferable in case of recurring sales transactions between a customer and the organization since the sales information system needs to provide information on terms of payment, outstanding receivables and payment records. In contrast, when sales transactions are nonrecurring, sporadic or of minor financial importance, documenting receivables at the individual debtor level is less efficient, and chronological documentation per invoice number or date, or a ledgerless accounts receivable administration on the basis of sales invoices might be a better option. However, these latter forms of administration are less and less common now that IT has facilitated input and recording per individual debtor in such situations as well.

The accounts receivable administration per debtor helps the sales department to rate the debtors' creditworthiness when making offers or accepting orders for credit sales. This rating compares information on the credit limits and the applicable payment conditions with the actual customer account balances. Determining the credit limit per customer is a complex task because many variables may be of importance. These credit limits along with the credit policy must be set by a credit manager. She advises management on the implementation of management guidelines – preferably embedded in applicable software – that must provide a benchmark for the sales department to approve or to reject a sales transaction with a certain customer. Low credit limits result in enhanced credit control, but may result in sales transactions being rejected and hence forgone revenues. Generous credit limits stimulate sales, but also increase the likelihood of bad debts. The performance of sales clerks is often evaluated on the basis of the turnover generated and rewarded by means of promotion prospects or variable pay. Should they be authorized to set credit limits, they will be in a position to boost sales just by increasing credit limits. Therefore, sales clerks should never be able to determine credit limits. However, because customer relationships may be damaged, sales clerks must have some discretion in applying the credit policies as set by the credit manager. A secondary segregation of duties within the sales department between the department head and the sales clerks and representatives usually provides a solution to this dilemma.

Summary

This chapter has discussed the internal controls that must be put in place in trade organizations. In the typology of organizations, we distinguish two types of trade organizations: (1) trade organizations with cash sales and (2) trade organizations with credit sales. For each type, we have discussed the risks, exposures and internal controls, the administrative and organizational conditions, such as segregation of duties, budgeting and management guidelines, and the main processes, i.e. the purchasing process, the inventory process and the sales process.

In trade organizations with cash sales, risks are mainly associated with the use of cash to complete sales transactions and the fact that goods to be sold are on display. Hence, theft of cash and theft of goods are significant risks. Internal controls to mitigate these risks are segregation of duties between recording, custody and authorization with respect to cash and goods, and surprise cash counts and physical inventory counts. Other more general risks are officers receiving kickbacks, secret commissions or other forms of inducement from vendors, and unreliable inventory records. Trade organizations with cash sales must segregate the functions that are involved in purchasing goods, receiving goods and preparing receiving reports, checking the quality of received goods, safeguarding goods, selling goods, keeping custody of cash, recording transactions and checking whether transactions have been properly recorded. Trade organizations with cash sales need to develop authorized management guidelines with respect to handling cash and safeguarding goods.

In trade organizations with credit sales, specific risks relate to credit sales and delivery by shipment rather than having customers visit the organization's store to collect goods. Therefore, the creditworthiness of customers, the existence of accounts receivable, shipping errors and billing errors are prominent risks in these types of firms. Furthermore, organizations with credit sales have a separate credit department that checks the creditworthiness of customers based on specifically issued management guidelines.

Production Organizations

Introduction

To a large extent production organizations are comparable to trade organizations. After all, both types of organizations have a dominant flow of goods and a related flow of money. In principle, the risks with respect to the control of the purchasing, inventory and sales processes do not differ. A major difference between production and trade organizations is the fact that production organizations have a technical transformation process creating added value. From a control point of view this has three important implications:

- There is a disruption in the flow of goods. It is not easy to directly relate the amounts of raw and auxiliary materials used to the amounts of finished goods obtained, because of waste and breakdown;
- Occupation of production capacity is important. Therefore, use of man hours and machine hours needs to be documented and checked for acceptability; and
- Often, production organizations produce multiple types of products. Thus, cost control, cost allocation and cost price calculation are more important and more complex here than in trade organizations.

In the typology of organizations we distinguish four types of production organizations: (1) organizations that produce to stock, (2) organizations with mass customization, (3) agrarian and extractive organizations and (4) organizations that produce to order. Organizations that produce to stock usually produce standard goods for an impersonal market with generally applicable wishes. Examples are beer breweries, brick manufacturers or producers of consumer goods. Organizations with mass customization produce goods by assembling standard parts according to individual customer wishes. Examples of mass customization are computer manufacturers that assemble computers according to their customers' preferences (e.g. Dell computers), or car manufacturers that assemble cars based on their customers' choices from a standard set of options or alternative parts (e.g. Smart). Agrarian and extractive organizations are quite similar to organizations that produce to stock, although the yields are more difficult to predict due to environmental circumstances, such as weather conditions, (crop and animal) diseases and environmental laws. Examples of agrarian and extractive organizations are dairy farms, agricultural farms, mines and oil companies. Production to order concerns production according to individual, specific customer wishes, such as the construction of large infrastructural projects (i.e. bridges, office buildings), a boat wharf for luxury yachts or film studios making movies.

From an internal control perspective, we distinguish four main processes within production organizations: the purchasing process, the inventory process, the production process and the sales process. For each of these processes, internal controls need to be implemented to mitigate the risks to achieving the organizational objectives. Specific risks with respect to production organizations relate, for example, to unreliable production standards, insufficient product quality, a complex flow of goods or the attractiveness of the produced goods (theft). Internal controls that can be implemented to mitigate these risks range from segregation of duties to implementing management guidelines for performing analytical review.

The internal controls that are put in place will only be effective if certain administrative and organizational conditions are met. These conditions can be summarized under the following headings: computer security, segregation of duties, management guidelines and budgeting. The computer security measures as discussed in Chapter 4 are generally applicable to all types of organizations. Therefore, we will only discuss segregation of duties, management guidelines and budgeting tailored to production organizations.

Learning Goals of the Chapter

After having studied this chapter, the reader will understand:

- the internal control consequences of classifying organizations as organizations that produce to stock, organizations with mass customization, agrarian and extractive organizations and organizations that produce to order;
- the risks for organizations that produce to stock, organizations with mass customization, agrarian and extractive organizations and organizations that produce to order from an internal control perspective;
- the administrative and organizational conditions of organizations that produce to stock, organizations with mass customization, agrarian and extractive organizations and organizations that produce to order;
- the main processes of organizations that produce to stock, organizations with mass customization, agrarian and extractive organizations and organizations that produce to order; and
- the internal controls that can be put in place in organizations that produce to stock, organizations with mass customization, agrarian and extractive organizations and organizations that produce to order.

Characteristics of Organizations that Produce to Stock

From an internal control perspective, organizations that produce to stock are the least complex types of production organizations. In principle, production to stock relies on standard conditions. This implies that standard amounts are produced to stock, standard procedures are followed, planning, job preparation, production and production progress control are relatively simple and the technical transformation processes is straightforward. In contrast, with respect to these issues mass customization, agriculture and extraction, and production to order are more complex.

Production organizations use production standards in their technical transformation processes. Based on these standards, the amount of raw and auxiliary materials, man hours and machine hours to be used for a certain quantity of finished goods can be determined. After production this standard use should be compared to actual use, and the controller or the head of the accounting department should analyse possible differences and report thereon to management. Due to the repetitive character of production to stock processes, production standards are usually stricter than in production to order processes and because of the tightness of the standards, the relationship between offers and yields is easy to recognize.

The reconciliations between the flows of goods and the flows of money are similar to those of trade organizations. In addition, for production organizations the following reconciliations related to the transformation process apply:

$$\text{Inventory raw materials at } t_0 + \text{purchases} -/- \text{delivered to production department}$$
$$= \text{inventory raw materials at } t_1$$
$$\text{Raw materials delivered to production} * \text{production standard} = \text{finished goods delivered by production}$$
$$\text{Inventory finished goods at } t_0 + \text{delivered by production} -/- \text{sales} = \text{inventory finished goods at } t_1$$

As in trade organizations, in production organizations the value cycle is instrumental in assuring the completeness of revenues owing to the strong link between the flow of goods and the flow of money. Raw materials that are purchased are transformed into finished goods and subsequently sold, implying that the revenues are strongly linked to the raw materials purchased and the finished goods sold. Reasonable assurance about the completeness of revenues is achieved through appropriate segregation of duties and reconciliations by the controller or the head of the accounting department.

Risks, Exposures and Internal Controls of Organizations that Produce to Stock

The risks for organizations that produce to stock mainly relate to production planning and measuring production inefficiencies. Regarding production planning, risks for organizations that produce to stock relate to unauthorized production, the complex flow of goods, work-in-progress, insufficient alignment between production and demand and misalignment between product design and sales. These risks are caused by the fact that (1) production organizations in general have a more complex flow of goods than trade organizations and (2) organizations that produce to stock specifically first produce the goods and then sell them to customers, which requires proper alignment between demand and production.

Probably one of the most important risks with respect to production planning is unauthorized production, resulting in additional costs for products for which there is no or insufficient demand. An internal control measure that can mitigate this risk is requiring authorization of production orders by the sales or warehouse department instead of by the production department. Furthermore, production orders always need to be based on sales forecasts and/or inventory levels.

Another risk is insufficient alignment between production and demand, leading to dissatisfied customers and loss of revenues (in case of underproduction), or increasing stocks which may lead to obsolescence and increased inventory costs (in case of overproduction). Controls to mitigate this risk are an adequate production planning system which allows for periodic realignment of production output levels and using reliable sales forecasts by the sales department.

Production inefficiencies can lead to inappropriately high production costs. There are several internal controls to mitigate this risk. First, organizations need to implement segregation of duties between the operations office (pre-calculation; authorization), the production department (production; execution) and the accounting department (post-calculation; recording) so that efficiency results are determined independently from the standard setting party (operations office) and the production party (production department). Second, in order to calculate inefficiencies, the production departments need to document actual usage (hours, materials) and actual production output per production department. Third, tight and detailed product and production standards need to be used. Fourth, pre- and post-calculations are performed per production department or per activity as in Activity-based Costing (ABC).

An overview of risks for production to stock is provided in Table 14.1. Note that most of the risks related to the purchasing, inventory and sales processes as discussed for trade organizations in Chapter 13 (see Tables 13.1 and 13.3) also apply to production organizations.

Table 14.1 Risks, exposures and internal controls of organizations that produce to stock.

Risk	Exposure	Internal controls
Investments in production facilities	Overinvestments and/or underinvestments	• Investment planning
Insufficiently reliable production standards	Inadequate decision-making with respect to production targets and production efficiency	• Segregation of duties between the product design department (execution) and the operations office (authorization) • Management guidelines with respect to product standard setting and quality checks on product development • Technical post-calculation in order to optimize product standards
Insufficiently reliable pre-calculation by operations office	Inadequate decision-making with respect to production targets and production efficiency	• Segregation of duties between the operations office (authorization) and the production department (execution) • Management guidelines with respect to cost calculation and production rates • Post-calculations in order to optimize pre-calculations
Unauthorized production	Incurring costs for products for which there is no or insufficient demand	• Authorization of production orders not by production department but by sales or warehouse department • Production orders are always based on sales forecasts and/or inventory levels
Inefficient production	High production costs	• Segregation of duties between operations office (pre-calculation; authorization), production department (production; execution), and accounting department (post-calculation; recording) • Documentation of actual usage (hours, materials) and actual production output by production department • Tight and detailed product and production standards • Department-based pre- and post-calculation

(Continued)

Table 14.1 (Continued).

Risk	Exposure	Internal controls
Complex flow of goods	Loss of inventories or loss of revenues	• Permanent checks by the operations office, the production department and the warehouse department on the flow of goods • Progress controls on the flow of goods by operations office • Uniquely identifiable production orders in the information system
Theft of work-in-progress	Loss of assets	• Minimize entry to production facilities by non-production personnel by means of physical access controls • Locking production facilities during out-of-production hours • A system of granting discharge when work-in-progress is transferred between production departments or work centres • Periodic inventory counts of work-in-progress
Valuation of work-in-progress	Valuation of work-in-progress enhances risk of erroneous business performance reporting	• Segregation of duties between accounting department (recording), operations office (authorization) and production department (execution) • Progress controls by the operations office on production and reporting on work-in-progress • Procedures for cost price calculation
Insufficient product quality	Customer complaints and loss of reputation	• Independent quality checks on raw materials and finished goods • Implementation of destruction procedure of rejected goods • Implementation of a customer satisfaction measurement system
Insufficient alignment between production and demand	Dissatisfied customers and loss of revenues (under-production); increasing stocks, obsolescence and increased inventory costs (overproduction)	• Adequate market research on customer needs • Use of reliable sales forecasts by sales department • Use of an adequate production planning system which allows for periodic realignment of production output levels • Cash planning in order to survive periods of low demand

Administrative and Organizational Conditions

Segregation of Duties

To achieve optimal production efficiency, organizations that produce to stock, but also production organizations in general, need to segregate the functions involved in designing products, production planning, pre-calculation, purchasing raw materials, receiving raw materials and preparing receiving reports, checking the quality of raw materials, safeguarding raw materials, production of finished goods, checking the quality of finished goods, safeguarding finished goods, selling goods, performing post-calculations, recording transactions and checking if transactions have been properly recorded.

Particularly important for achieving a desired level of production efficiency is the segregation between pre-calculation (standard setting), actual production (on which efficiency tests are performed), and post-calculation (assessing production efficiency). This segregation is necessary since production inefficiencies may not only be due to inefficient production by the production department, but also to inadequate standard setting by the operations office. Therefore, we need to segregate all three functions. Table 14.2 provides an overview of the desired segregation of duties for organizations that produce to stock.

Table 14.2   Segregation of duties in organizations that produce to stock.

Officer	Department	Task	Duty
Product designer	Product design department	Designing new products	Execution
Production planner	Operations office (or production planning department)	Performing technical pre-calculations and production planning	Authorization
Cost accountant	Cost accounting department	Performing financial pre-calculations	Execution
Purchase clerk/manager	Purchasing department	Purchasing raw materials	Authorization
Receiving clerk	Receiving department raw materials	Receipt of raw materials, preparation of receiving report	Execution
Quality inspector raw materials	Receiving department raw materials	Checking quality of received raw materials	Checking
Warehouse clerk/manager raw materials	Warehouse department raw materials	Safeguarding raw materials	Custody
Production worker	Production department	Production finished goods	Execution
Technician	Technical or maintenance department	Maintaining the technical/ production facilities	Execution

(*Continued*)

Table 14.2   (Continued).

Officer	Department	Task	Duty
Quality inspector finished goods	Receiving department finished goods	Checking quality of finished goods	Checking
Warehouse clerk/manager finished goods	Warehouse department finished goods	Safeguarding finished goods	Custody
Sales clerk/manager	Sales department	Selling goods	Authorization
Credit clerk/manager	Sales department or separate credit department	Checking the creditworthiness of customers	Checking
Shipping clerk/manager	Shipping department	Shipping finished goods to customers	Execution
Billing clerk/manager	Billing department	Billing customers	Execution
Accounts receivable clerk/manager	Accounts receivable department	Safeguarding accounts receivable	Custody
Cash receipts clerk/manager	Cash receipts department	Receipt of customer payments	Authorization
Cashier	Cash department	Safeguarding cash	Custody
Cash disbursements clerk/ manager	Cash disbursements department	Payment of vendor invoices	Authorization
Accounts payable clerk/ manager	Accounts payable department	Safeguarding accounts payable	Custody
Accounting clerk	Accounting department	Recording transactions	Recording
Controller or head of accounting department	Accounting department	Checking transactions and performing quantitative (technical) and financial post-calculations	Checking

Budgeting

In production organizations, budgeting starts with the sales forecast since sales should determine the production level. The sales forecast is based on sales levels of previous years, market developments and seasonal patterns. This should result in a sales budget detailing expected sales per product. Based on the sales budget the inventory budget is drawn up, both of which inform the production and purchase budgets. On the basis of the production budget the machinery and labour occupancy rates, and – based on the cost of capital, labour and materials (the latter based on the purchase budget) – the labour and machinery cost rates are determined. Management must approve budgets and standards and the controller or the head of the accounting department should regularly report to management on any deviations of actual results from the budgeted results. Internal control systems use budgets as '*Soll*' positions in analytical review procedures.

Management Guidelines

Most management guidelines for trade organizations discussed in Chapter 12 also apply to production organizations. There are a number of additional guidelines that specifically pertain to organizations that produce to stock. These are guidelines related to the organization of the production process, the control of the production costs, the purchasing and storing of raw materials and the selling of finished goods. Hence, additional management guidelines to be implemented by organizations that produce to stock should concern:

- pre- and post-calculation;
- minimum occupancy rates of machinery;
- calculation of production efficiency;
- maintenance of the machinery;
- safety and environmental issues;
- quality of raw materials purchased;
- determination of insufficient quality of raw materials and finished goods;
- destruction or sale of waste products or rejected finished goods; and
- calculation of sales prices of finished goods.

The Main Processes in Organizations that Produce to Stock

We distinguish four main processes in organizations that produce to stock: the purchasing process, the inventory process, the production process, and the sales process. Because we have already discussed these processes extensively in Chapters 7 to 10, we will focus on specific risks, exposures and applicable controls of the production process here. Since many risks are related to production planning, we will start our discussion with production planning, followed by the assessment of production efficiency (pre- and post-calculation), and a discussion of reconciliations related to production to stock. Note that the risks, exposures and internal controls related to the purchasing, inventory and sales processes for organizations that produce to stock are similar to those for trade organizations and we therefore refer to Chapter 13 in this respect.

Production Planning

Based on an organization's strategic plan and the thereof derived annual plan, desired production levels are specified in an annual production plan. This planning encompasses capacity planning (what production capacity is necessary to satisfy expected sales according to the annual planning), occupancy planning (relating (expected) orders to available capacity, which may result in over- or understaffing, necessitating additional measures, such as employing temporary workers or asking regular staff to do temporary periods of overtime in case of understaffing) and detailed production plans (allocating people and machinery to activities).

Production planning must be carried out by the production planning department, or the operations office, which should be independent of the production department. The tasks of the operations office include job preparation, production order issuance, progress control and technical post-calculation. Production orders are detailed descriptions of what must be produced and in what quantity in the next production run. A production order also contains the required authorizations for using specified quantities of raw materials and equipment, an indication of who should be working on what order (staffing), starting and ending time of the production run, as well as task descriptions for production personnel if the activities to perform are nonroutine. Raw materials and equipment may be supplied by a closed or an open warehouse depending on the value of the goods and potential constraints to the production process. For instance, if the production process will be delayed because of the unavailability of a specific item as a result of a queue at the warehouse desk, having a closed warehouse may cost more than the related internal control benefits will yield. In this case the constraint is the warehouse ordering process. If there is another process constituting the constraint, warehouse waiting time is acceptable up to the time that the warehouse ordering process becomes the most prominent constraint.

Production Efficiency

Within production organizations, post-calculation must be compared to pre-calculation to evaluate production efficiency. There are two types of pre- and post-calculations: the quantitative or technical pre- and post-calculation and the financial pre- and post-calculation. For both calculations, proper segregation of duties needs to be in place. Therefore, the pre-calculation needs to be separated from production and from the post-calculation. The technical pre-calculation is performed by the operations office or production planning department, production by the production department and the technical post-calculation is performed by the accounting department. Furthermore, the financial pre-calculation is done by the cost-accounting department, and the financial post-calculation is the task of the controller or the head of the accounting department. For production to stock, pre- and post-calculation are performed per production department, which is a form of process costing. For production to order pre- and post-calculation are performed per production order, a form of job-order costing. A potential risk is the invalidity and incompleteness of the production data. Therefore, before the controller or the head of the accounting department can perform the post-calculation, controls must be put in place to provide reasonable assurance that the production data as well as the production standards used are valid and complete. For instance, the production software must have been tested thoroughly before implementing, the standards as recorded in the standards file must be periodically reviewed for reasonableness, and offers and yields must be reconciled by means of the retrograde method (see Chapter 9).

Differences identified by variance analyses might not just be caused by inefficiencies but also by using inappropriate standards in the pre-calculation. These latter differences are denoted budget variances, whereas differences caused by inefficiencies are appropriately called efficiency variances. Primarily, the head of the production department is considered responsible for efficiency variances, whereas the operations office is responsible for budget variances. Price variances, the differences between standard prices of raw materials, man hours and machine hours, and actual prices based on vendor invoices, are the primary responsibility of the purchasing department.

Reconciliations

Each production department reports the results of the production process in a production report. This report contains:

- raw and auxiliary materials received from the warehouse and used in the production process;
- man and machine hours used in the production process;
- amount of produced finished goods; and
- amount of waste and breakdown.

The controller or the head of the accounting department compares these actual results to the standards from the pre-calculation and prepares a performance report for the organization's management. Other data on the progress of the production process are obtained from the warehouse, the maintenance or technical department and the quality inspector. Validity and completeness of production data is established by means of reconciliations. Examples include the following:

- raw and auxiliary materials received by the production department should equal the delivery of these materials by the warehouse;
- the number of man hours reported in the production reports (the job time) should equal the hours workers were present at the shop floor according to the payroll records (shop time);
- the number of machine hours reported is compared to statements from the maintenance or technical department on the number of available machine hours; and
- the amount of finished products according to the production report should equal the amount of products received by the finished products warehouse, the amount of shipped goods according to the shipping documents and the amounts checked by the quality inspector.

Characteristics of Organizations with Mass Customization

Nowadays many production organizations are confronted with two seemingly conflicting challenges. On the one hand, they need to deliver high-quality products, specifically tailored to the needs of their customers, while on the other they need to produce at low cost. Production to stock usually implies lower production costs, but products cannot be tailored to specific customer needs. With production to order, products can be tailored to customer needs, but the individual character of the production process usually implies higher production costs. The solution to this dilemma is mass customization: products are specifically tailored to customer needs by assembling components that are produced to stock. Therefore, mass customization is comparable to production to stock, but from an internal control perspective it is slightly more complex due to the more complicated technical transformation process in which components are assembled into final products. Due to its repetitive character, mass customization has relatively tight production standards. Therefore, the relationship between offers and yields is easy to recognize. The reconciliations between the flows of goods and the flows of money are therefore similar to those of production to order, except for the fact that the reconciliations are applied to components rather than raw materials.

Risks, Exposures and Internal Controls of Organizations with Mass Customization

From a risk perspective, organizations with mass customization are quite similar to organizations that produce to stock. Many risks associated with production to stock, such as investments in production facilities, insufficiently reliable product standards, insufficiently reliable pre-calculation by the operations office, unauthorized production, inefficient production, complex flow of goods and theft and valuation of work-in-progress, also apply to organizations with mass customization. We therefore do not discuss these again in this section, and only focus on the specific risks related to mass customization. We distinguish the following risks: misalignment between produced goods and customer orders, insufficient quality of the components used, insufficient inventory of components and fluctuation in product demand.

The risk related to the misalignment between goods produced and customer orders can be mitigated by adequate recording of product specifications per order. Further controls to mitigate this risk are independent checks on alignment between customer orders and product specifications, independent quality checks on finished goods, the implementation of a customer complaints procedure with independent recording of complaints and follow-up procedures, and the implementation of a customer satisfaction measurement system.

Another risk specifically related to mass customization is insufficient quality of components. Appropriate controls to moderate this risk are independent quality checks on the components used to assemble the finished goods, the implementation of a destruction procedure of rejected components and the implementation of a customer satisfaction measurement system.

The risk associated with insufficient inventory of components can be mitigated by adequate inventory planning of components based on sales forecasts of customized products, reliable inventory records, the use of appropriate re-order points and by purchasing components only from reliable vendors.

Fluctuation in product demand resulting in overcapacity or undercapacity can be mitigated by using reliable sales forecasts from the sales department and adequate capacity planning by the operations office or production planning department, which allows for interim adjustments of production capacity.

An overview of the risks specifically related to mass customization is provided in Table 14.3. As stated, many of the risks for organizations that produce to stock as shown in Table 14.1 also apply to mass customization. Further, many of the risks related to the purchasing, inventory and sales processes discussed for trade organizations in Chapter 13 (Tables 13.1 and 13.3) also apply to production organizations.

Table 14.3 Risks, exposures and internal controls of organizations with mass customization.

Risk	Exposure	Internal controls
Misalignment between goods produced and customer orders	Customer dissatisfaction	• Adequate recording of product specifications per order • Independent checks on alignment between customer orders and product specifications • Independent quality checks on finished goods by the quality inspector • Implementation of a customer complaints procedure • Implementation of an information system where customer complaints are independently recorded • Follow-up procedures on customer complaints • Implementation of a customer satisfaction measurement system
Insufficient quality of components	Insufficient product quality, leading to customer dissatisfaction	• Independent quality checks on components by the quality inspector • Implementation of destruction procedure of rejected components • Implementation of a customer satisfaction measurement system
Insufficient inventory of components	Inability to produce goods ordered by customers, resulting in customer dissatisfaction	• Adequate inventory planning of components based on sales forecasts of customized products • Reliable inventory records • Use of sufficiently high re-order points • Purchase of components from reliable vendors
Fluctuation in product demand	Overcapacity or undercapacity	• Use of reliable sales forecasts by sales department • Adequate capacity planning which allows for interim realignment of production capacity • Cash planning in order to survive times of low demand

Administrative and Organizational Conditions

The administrative and organizational conditions of organizations with mass customization are virtually the same as those of organizations that produce to stock. Hence, we will only discuss these in so far as they deviate from those for production to stock.

Segregation of Duties

Since organizations with mass customization must segregate the same functions as organizations that produce to stock, we do not present a separate table here but refer to Table 14.2.

Budgeting

Compared with organizations that produce to stock no additional budgets must be created. However, there will be more uncertainty about product demand and the specific (assembled) products that are ordered, rendering the sales and inventory budgets less predictable.

Management Guidelines

Organizations with mass customization require additional guidelines on the use of re-order points and the purchase of components from reliable vendors since it is essential for an efficient production process that components are readily available in inventory. The other management guidelines are the same as those discussed for production to stock.

Case Study 14.1: BUSINESS TECHNOLOGY; Industry Is Learning to Love Agility

By John Holusha
New York Times May 25, 1994,

The Ford Motor Company's electronic components plant here is a complicated place, producing 124,000 engine controllers, anti-lock brake sensors and speed-control units a day. Since each product has 400 to 500 parts, managers have to keep track of more than five million individual pieces daily.

Nevertheless, Dudley C. Wass, the plant's manager, says that when an order to change a product is received, the altered units usually can be shipped within 24 hours.

The reason is that the two-year-old plant has been designed with a high level of flexible automation, extensive computer controls and lean inventories in an effort to emphasize fast response time.

`We are more of a software business than hardware,' Richard A. Chow-Wah, an engineer at the plant, said. 'When we get changes, the software allows us to accommodate it.'

Mr. Wass and his associates say they are trying to become 'agile' manufacturers – able to switch quickly and economically from one product to another with very little disruption. They are also working to establish closer relationships with suppliers and customers in an effort to react more quickly to shifts in markets.

It is a philosophy that is being acted upon throughout Ford, which intends to rely heavily on its international computer networks to combine its North American and European automotive operations into a single organization by the end of this year.

Such an approach, being adopted by a growing number of corporations, is a change from the old mass production model that sought to reduce costs by carefully tuning a process and then churning out products in large numbers. That time-honored technique – elevated to an industrial art form by Ford Motor's founder, Henry Ford – reduced the amount of fixed cost in each copy of the product. But it also tied up a lot of resources in inventory and partly finished products and made it less likely that defects would be found before a large volume of production was affected.

Making extensive use of bar-code technology to label and track virtually every circuit board, and relying heavily on computerized equipment that can be reprogrammed on the fly, factory managers like Mr. Wass are able to pare inventories, reduce turnaround times and respond more quickly to customer demands.

`Our model is the cheetah,' Mr. Wass said. 'We want to be able to stop on a dime, direct all our energy toward a goal, turn quickly and accelerate rapidly.'

The approach is meeting with favor in the higher ranks at Ford. 'The plant is on the leading edge; it's one of our best,' said Charles W. Szuluk, the company's vice president for process leadership. He said the Lansdale plant's ability to respond quickly to customers allowed it to bid for added business and its ability to manufacture different products on the same assembly line reduced investment requirements.

The concept of agile manufacturing has been taking shape in industrial America as companies struggle to compete with foreign producers, particularly in areas like electronics. Although there are no statistics on how many companies are adopting agile ways, the approach has the enthusiastic backing of the Government. The Defense Department recently sought bids for $30 million in projects incorporating agile manufacturing.

Unlike traditional manufacturers, with their hierarchical management and emphasis on sheer output, agile companies stress sharing of information and power across the organization, alliances with suppliers and customers, and fast responses to changing market conditions. Engineers at Ford's headquarters in Dearborn, Mich., can put design changes into a computer system, then send the information electronically to production plants like the one here in Lansdale.

Some researchers of industrial organizations say that this new agility may lead to 'virtual' enterprises, in which several companies come together to make a specific product for a certain length of time, and then dissolve as the participants go on to other projects. The central concept is that each organization would do what it does best, with one company designing the product, another manufacturing it and others handling marketing and sales.

The Main Processes in Organizations with Mass Customization

As with production to stock, we distinguish four main processes in organizations with mass customization: the purchasing process, the inventory process, the production process and the sales process. The purchasing, inventory, production and sales processes are discussed extensively in Chapters 7 to 10, and the specific production process for mass customization is comparable to organizations that produce to stock. We will therefore not discuss the production process for mass customization separately.

Characteristics of Agrarian and Extractive Organizations

From an internal control perspective, agrarian and extractive organizations are considered production organizations, and they posses characteristics of production to stock and production to order. That is, agrarian and extractive organizations produce vegetables, dairy products, meat, wood, minerals (e.g. salt, copper, gold), oil and gas to stock but due to environmental circumstances, such as weather conditions, diseases and environmental laws, yields (revenues) are difficult to predict.

Within the category of agrarian and extractive organizations, we distinguish agriculture, horticulture, cattle breeding, forestry, fishery, mineral exploration and oil and gas exploration. There seems to be much variation within these different types of organizations. However, they all belong to the category of agrarian and extractive organizations as they have three characteristics in common:

1.   These organizations are subject to heavy and detailed regulation;
2.   Due to environmental circumstances and (technical) capabilities, agrarian and extractive organizations are subject to a high degree of uncertainty in the relationship between offers and yields; and
3.   Long-range planning is difficult as these organizations are heavily influenced by external factors, such as the political climate, environmental pressure and diseases that reduce or disable production completely.

Sub 1. Heavy and detailed regulations

Regulations in this sector vary from production quotas to environmental laws regulating the exploration of minerals and oil and gas. Quotas exist in the fishing sector, where there are catch limitations for certain types of fish, and in dairy farming as dairy farmers are subject to milk quotas to mitigate the overproduction of milk. The mineral and oil and gas industries are subject to environmental regulation with respect to the environmentally friendly exploration of minerals and oil and gas. These regulations aim for ecological and sustainable exploration to protect the environment.

Sub 2. High degree of uncertainty in the relationship between offers and yields

Revenues or yields of agrarian and extractive organizations are difficult to predict due to weather conditions and (technical) capabilities. The weather conditions heavily influence the relationship between offers (sowing seeds, seed potatoes, flower bulbs) and yields (corn, potatoes, flowers). For example, due to weather conditions, the harvest may be extremely rich one year and extremely poor in another. Furthermore, the (technical) capabilities of a farmer or fisherman are another crucial component in the ultimate yield. Although the fishing industry depends heavily on technological advances such as radar to detect fish, it is the fisherman who evaluates the (radar) information and decides in which part of the waters he will fish.

Sub 3. External factors

Since agrarian and extractive organizations impact the environment, they are often faced with environmental pressure groups, and these groups can have an impact on the agrarian or extractive yield or production (e.g. animal protection groups that release animals). Also the political climate influences agrarian and extractive organizations as governments can behave in a more or less protectionist fashion (e.g. in the case of foreign firms exploring minerals or oil and gas) or a more or less environmentally friendly fashion (e.g. they constantly weigh the [environmental] costs and [economic] benefits of agrarian and extractive organizations). Another external factor is the diseases that affect agrarian organizations. Various diseases can, for example, result in the sanitary slaughter of livestock after the outbreak of diseases such as bird flu or blue tongue. Also, consumer markets can decrease (e.g. because of mad cow disease) or harvests can be lost (e.g. in the case of potato late blight).

Case Study 14.2: Shell's Chief Reaffirms Goal of 30 % More Output by 2015

By Heather Timmons
New York Times June 23, 2005

LONDON, June 22 – Jeroen van der Veer, chief of the Royal Dutch/Shell Group, said Wednesday that the company would spend more on research, focus on big technology-driven projects and possibly acquire other oil producers and reserves to increase production by 30 percent as planned by 2015.

Mr. van der Veer, who took the helm 15 months ago after Shell was forced to admit it had overstated its oil and gas reserves, said earlier this year that the company planned to produce 5 million barrels of oil a day in a decade, up from about 3.5 million to 3.8 million now. This week, he presented his top managers with more details of that 10-year plan, and on Wednesday, he briefed journalists about it at Shell's London headquarters.

Most of the shift in strategy focuses on making the company an indispensable partner to countries rich in oil and natural gas. Several of the world's top energy companies are quietly following this plan, as oil in geographically accessible areas dries up and exploration shifts to remote locales, or to countries where governments are reluctant to cede control of their resources to Western oil companies.

Crucial changes at Shell include increasing the company's participation in what Mr. van der Veer calls elephant projects, or projects requiring several billion dollars in investment. To date, Shell is involved in three such projects with government and industry partners: at Sakhalin island, in Russia; Bonga, off the coast of Nigeria; and in Nanhai, China. By 2015, the company plans to be involved in 10 such projects, he said.

(Continued)

In a related move, Shell is starting an internal program to generate more creative proposals to encourage joint ventures with government-owned oil companies and countries with big reserve bases. The company also plans to increase its research and technology budget, currently $553 million a year, by an unspecified amount.

`Shell is spelling out what a lot of oil companies are already doing,' said Lucas Herrmann, a Deutsche Bank analyst in London. 'If it helps them gain access, when access is an issue, I think it's a positive move.' Shell has generally had good technology, Mr. Herrmann said, and 'can use its expertise and ability to arbitrage markets to appear the more attractive partner.'

Mr. van der Veer also underscored that Shell would have the means to make acquisitions in the future. Shell is in the process of melding the Shell Transport and Trading Company and the Royal Dutch Petroleum Company, the two publicly traded companies that make up the Royal Dutch/Shell Group.

If the combination is approved by shareholders next week, as expected, Shell will be able to issue equity or debt when it wants, Mr. van der Veer said, providing financing for an acquisition. 'The board has a duty not to have a disadvantaged relationship to other companies,' Mr. van der Veer said.

He said that Shell was not looking at any specific acquisition target at the moment and added that consolidation historically occurred when oil prices fell.

Along with its growth efforts, Shell will be paring in some areas, Mr. van der Veer said. The company will be involved in about 100 countries by 2015, down from about 140 now.

To establish the completeness of revenues of agrarian and extractive organizations, three common factors are distinguished. First, the value cycle is instrumental in reconciling the completeness of revenues by linking the flow of goods and the flow of money. Second, agrarian and extractive organization need to have a system of lot recording. Third, these organizations need to have contract files including all contracts with suppliers. We will discuss these three common factors more extensively.

The Value Cycle

The reconciliations between the flows of goods at agrarian and extractive organizations will be performed according to the following formula:

$$\text{Amount of natural resources} * \text{production standard} = \text{amount of finished goods}$$

The natural resources and finished goods differ however per type of agrarian and extractive organization. For dairy farms, for example, the production of milk (i.e. the finished good) will be related to the number of cattle (i.e. the amount of natural resources). Moreover, for agricultural farms, the corn revenues will be related to the amount of land on which the corn was cultivated. By subsequently multiplying the amount of finished goods with the applicable market price, the amount of revenues that ought to be reported (*Soll* position) can be calculated. Nevertheless, the production standard is rather weak due to the various uncertainties in the production process. To facilitate the reconciliation between the flow of goods and the flow of money, some agrarian and extractive organizations can use an instrument that transforms the offers and yields to a basic component, such as lard or nitrate. We provide three examples of such an instrument:

* For dairy farming, a lard-balance is used to indicate the relationship between the raw milk produced and the dairy products obtained.
* For the production of farmyard manure, a nitrate-balance is used to indicate the relationship between the manure produced and the metastasized manure.
* For wood production, a wood-balance is used to indicate the relationship between the cut-down trees and the wood produced.

Lot Recording

Since the finished good with agrarian and extractive organizations is a natural product, it will exhibit quality differences. And because high-quality goods will lead to higher revenues than low-quality goods, agrarian and extractive organizations need to distinguish these quality differences. Therefore, these organizations record their production per production run or lot (i.e. harvest, catch, drilling run) and calculate profits per lot (by considering the offers and yields). Hence, the reconciliations between the flows of goods at agrarian and extractive organizations (amount of natural resources * production standard = amount of finished goods) is actually performed per lot.

Contract Files

To facilitate the checks on the completeness of revenues of agrarian and extractive organizations, these organizations need to have contract files including all contracts with suppliers. Due to the uncertainly in the production standards, it is not possible to calculate the amount of natural resources from the amount of finished goods (multiplied by the production standard) or to calculate the amount of finished goods from the amount of natural resources. Consequently, all contracts with suppliers (indicating the amount of natural resources purchased) and customers (indicating the amount of finished goods sold) need to be recorded in contract files.

Risks, Exposures and Internal Controls of Agrarian and Extractive Organizations

Many of the risks for production to stock and mass customization also apply to agrarian and extractive organizations, mostly those associated with investments in production facilities, insufficiently reliable production standards, inefficient production, product quality and misalignment between production and demand. Specific to agrarian and extractive organizations are the risks of the uncertainty of revenues, seasonal production patterns, noncompliance with applicable laws and regulations, political, social and environmental pressure, disturbances in climate control systems, changing weather conditions and the availability of minerals to be less than expected or more difficult to extract.

Almost certainly one of the most important risks with respect of agrarian and extractive organizations is the uncertainty of revenues, resulting in financial problems, possibly leading to going concern problems. In order to mitigate this risk, agrarian and extractive organizations (1) need to conduct scenario planning, indicating all possible production scenarios the organization can encounter, (2) collect information on external factors that can influence the revenues, such as weather forecasts, (3) perform extensive analytical reviews of revenues in order to benchmark the organizations' output with industry averages, and (4) conduct adequate cash planning in order to survive in times when revenues are low.

Another risk is that of production following a seasonal pattern, creating temporary over- or undercapacity, production inefficiencies and possible financial problems in low season. Agrarian and extractive organizations therefore need to conduct adequate capacity planning given the nature of the seasonal production pattern (such as harvest seasons or bans on fishing during certain times of the year), implement management guidelines with respect to outsourcing in times of low season and investments in a maximum production capacity to handle production in high season, and adequate cash planning in order to survive when production (and thus income) is low.

A further risk to agrarian and extractive organizations is the noncompliance with applicable laws and regulations, resulting in fines and possibly legally required discontinuation of activities when the violation is severe. To respond to this risk, agrarian and extractive organizations can appoint a compliance officer who constantly monitors (non)compliance, conducts periodic internal audits on compliance with applicable laws and regulations (e.g. milk and fishing quotas, production of manure, the extraction of oil, gas and minerals), stimulates compliance by educating on the applicable laws and regulations, and segregates duties between the authorization of production, the actual production (e.g. fishing, extraction), the recording of production output and checking of compliance with laws and regulations to optimally monitor noncompliance.

An overview of risks, exposures and internal controls for agrarian and extractive organizations is provided in Table 14.4. Note that most of the risks related to the purchasing, inventory and sales processes as discussed for trade organizations in Chapter 13 (see Tables 13.1 and 13.3) also apply to production organizations.

Table 14.4   Risks, exposures and internal controls of agrarian and extractive organizations.

Risk	Exposure	Internal controls
Uncertainty of revenues	Financial problems, possibly leading to going concern problems	• Scenario planning, indicating all possible (positive and negative) scenarios • Collection of information on external factors that can influence the revenues, such as weather forecasts • Analytical review of revenues (benchmarking with industry averages) • Cash planning in order to survive in times when revenues are low

Seasonal pattern	Temporary over- or under-capacity, production inefficiencies and possible financial problems in low season	• Capacity planning taking into account the seasonal pattern • Management guidelines with respect to outsourcing and maximum production capacity • Cash planning in order to survive in low season
Noncompliance with applicable laws and regulations	Fines and possibly legally required discontinuation of activities	• Appointment of a compliance officer • Periodic internal audits on compliance with applicable laws and regulations (e.g. milk and fishing quotas, production of manure, the extraction of oil, gas and minerals) • Educate personnel on the applicable laws and regulations • Segregation of duties between authorization of production, the actual production (e.g. fishing, extraction), recording of production output and checking compliance with laws and regulations
Political, social and environmental pressure	Losses and possibly forced discontinuation of activities	• Collect information on potential and actual political, social and environmental issues and adjust production accordingly (interactive control system)
Disturbances in climate control systems	Unsuccessful harvest	• Back-up climate control system and power supply • Maintenance contract for the climate control system
Changing weather conditions	Unsuccessful harvest	• Production to stock of nonperishable products • Investments in stronger crops • Outsourcing of production to countries with a more stable or predictable climate • Use of climate control systems
Available minerals are less than expected	Lower revenues	• Perform geological research and development • Perform test drilling
Available minerals are more difficult to extract	Increased extraction cost	• Perform geological research and development • Perform test drilling

Administrative and Organizational Conditions

The administrative and organizational conditions of agrarian and extractive organizations are practically similar to those of organizations that produce to stock. Hence, we will only discuss those that deviate from production to stock.

Segregation of Duties

Because organizations that produce to order must segregate the same functions as organizations that produce to stock, we again do not present a separate table with segregated duties here but refer to Table 14.2 instead.

Budgeting

The main difference from organizations that produce to stock is the degree of uncertainty about the production standards and the quantity of goods produced. Therefore, the production budget will be less predictable, and will thus contain various scenarios (from no production output to a high or maximum production output). Per scenario (from loss-generating to highly profitable), the cash budget will be determined. Furthermore, the controller or the head of the accounting department will use external information sources such as weather forecasts and industry production data to benchmark the production output, and report to management on any deviations of actual results from the scenario result.

Management Guidelines

Most of the management guidelines that apply to production to stock also apply to agrarian and extractive organizations, such as guidelines with respect to pre- and post-calculation, calculation of production efficiency, maintenance of the machinery, quality of raw materials (e.g. sowing seeds, flower bulbs), determination of insufficient quality of raw materials and finished goods (e.g. corn, flowers), destruction or sale of waste products or rejected finished goods and the calculation of sales prices of finished goods. Agrarian and extractive organizations will have additional or more specific management guidelines with respect to how to deal with environmental conditions such as rainfall, draught, and crop and animal diseases. Furthermore, they will also have additional guidelines on the compliance with applicable laws and regulations (such as environmental laws) and on the calculation of production efficiency as they need to correct for weather circumstances, production quotas etc.

The Main Processes in Agrarian and Extractive Organizations

As with organizations that produce to stock, agrarian and extractive organizations distinguish four processes: the purchasing process, the inventory process, the production process and the sales process. Nevertheless, for agrarian organizations, the purchasing process relates to the purchase of so-called raw materials such as sowing seeds, flower bulbs or cattle. And for extractive organizations the purchasing process relates to the acquisition of extracting capacity such as fishing boats, drilling and other extraction machinery. Because we have already discussed the purchasing, inventory, production and sales processes extensively in Chapters 7 to 10, we will focus here on two specific issues of the production process of agrarian and extractive organizations: the detailed production planning and the high degree of uncertainty in the relationship between offers and yields.

The production process of an agrarian organization starts with a cultivation plan in case of agricultural and horticultural organizations, or a breeding plan in case of cattle farming. These plans indicate the production output that needs to be achieved in a certain period of time, and the actions that need to be taken to achieve that output. For example, a cultivation plan for cabbage lettuce will indicate the planting of seedlings or rooted cuttings in a nursery in early February, transplanting the seedlings into rows in a nursery bed by the end of February, planting the grown seedlings in a greenhouse in March and harvesting the crop in May. Furthermore, the cultivation plan indicates the estimated yield of cabbage lettuce, based on the amount of seedlings planted and production standard for that type of cabbage lettuce. Also, the cultivation plan will take into account the potential deviations from standard production due to weather conditions and diseases (i.e. how the yield will be affected in case of a certain type of disease or certain weather conditions).

Production plans of extractive organizations are of a similar nature and exactly specify for example how minerals (such as salt, copper, gold) need to be extracted. Furthermore, these production plans take into account the potential deviations from planned production due to weather conditions (in particular over-ground level extraction can be affected by bad weather – e.g. the evacuation of a drilling platform in case of a heavy storm), disruptions of extraction machinery or changes in extraction rights (i.e. when governments determine to decrease the extraction amount of oil or gas).

Next to the planning stage of the production process, the high degree of uncertainty in the relationship between offers (e.g. flower bulbs) and yields (flowers) is another specific issue in the production process of agrarian and extractive organizations. Due to environmental circumstances such as weather conditions, crop and animal diseases, extraction complexities (e.g. wrong judgements by fishermen, technical complexities of mineral extraction), environmental laws and regulations, and political, social and environmental pressure, the relationship between offers and yields is rather weak and therefore less useful to establish the completeness of revenues. The controller or the head of the accounting department, who must reconcile the relationship between offers and yields, actually has to use a higher outcome range and needs to benchmark the outcome with industry averages and yield information from previous years and from competitors. For example, given the number of cattle, the milk production will be compared with the average milk production in the industry, with the milk production of dairy farms nearby and with the previous year's milk production of the dairy farm. Hence, these reconciliations actually have the character of analytical review.

Characteristics of Organizations that Produce to Order

From an internal control perspective, the most complex type of production organization is an organization that produces to order. Compared with production to stock, agriculture and extraction, and mass customization, production planning, job preparation, production and production progress control are more complex due to the nonrepetitive nature of the technical transformation process. The project-based character of production to order results in softer standards and a less detailed production planning, compared with production to stock and mass customization. The global annual planning results in flexible production planning and a production budget with larger tolerances. Man and machine hour rates are determined based on the production budget as well as the expected capacity utilization of production workers and machinery in the production departments. Compared with the tight rates for production to stock, the production to order rates will need to be adjusted more often. Hence, because of the softer standards, the relationship between offers and yields is more difficult to recognize.

Nevertheless, the transformation process of production to order is similar to production to stock. Based on the relatively soft production standards, the amount of raw and auxiliary materials and man and machine hours to be used for a certain amount of finished goods can be determined. This standard use is compared to the actual use, and differences are reported. Therefore, these reconciliations are similar to those of production to stock and mass customization, except for the weaker transformation standards.

Risks, Exposures and Internal Controls of Organizations that Produce to Order

Many of the risks for production to stock, agriculture and extraction, and mass customization also apply to organizations that produce to order, particularly those associated with investments in production facilities, insufficiently reliable production standards, inefficient production, work-in-progress, product quality and misalignment between production and demand. The nonrepetitive or project-based character of the production process for organizations that produce to order renders some of these risks even more prominent. This applies particularly to the reliability of production standards and efficiency of production. Internal controls to mitigate the latter risk are segregation of duties between the technical and financial pre-calculation (operations office and cost accounting respectively), production (production department) and the post-calculations (accounting department); documentation of actual usage (hours, materials) and actual production output per order by the production department; using product and production standards which are as detailed as possible; and conducting pre- and post-calculation per order. The main difference with production to stock is that for production to order all calculations concerning production efficiency are performed per order since that is the unit of production, compared to production to stock where calculations are performed per department since inefficiencies cannot be attributed to individual products, but only to departments.

Some risks apply only to production to order, and these relate to the shifting of revenues and costs between projects, excessive processing time of projects and the potential complexity of projects. Focusing on the first of these, when an organization that produces to order undertakes some projects for a fixed price (fixed-fee contract) and bills others based on the costs made (cost plus contract) this increases the risk of shifting revenues and costs between projects. When actual exceed budgeted costs for a fixed-fee contract, the organization will suffer losses on the order. However, by (administratively) shifting costs from fixed-fee contracts to cost plus contracts, a project manager can still bill his costs and realize a profit on the fixed-fee contract. Although this is initially profitable for the firm and increases the project manager's bonus, this practice is undesirable since customers with cost plus contracts are overbilled, and unreliable production records are created, which could lead to unreliable future production standards. There are several internal controls to mitigate this risk. First, segregation of duties between the production department (production; execution) and the accounting department (cost allocation to projects; recording) needs to be created. Second, allocation of projects to project managers needs to be done on a sequential rather than a simultaneous basis. Third and last, the controller or the head of the accounting department should perform an analytical review of project efficiency and profitability.

An overview of these, and other, risks for organizations that produce to order is provided in Table 14.5. As discussed, many of the risks for production to stock (Table 14.1), mass customization (Table 14.3), and – although to a lesser extent – agriculture and extraction (Table 14.4) also apply to production to order. Also, many of the risks related to the purchasing, inventory and sales processes for trade organizations (Tables 13.1 and 13.3) also apply to production organizations.

Table 14.5 Risks, exposures and internal controls of organizations that produce to order.

Risk	Exposure	Internal controls
Insufficiently reliable product standards	Inadequate decision-making with respect to production targets and production efficiency	• Segregation of duties between product design (execution) and the operations office (authorization) • Management guidelines with respect to product standard setting and quality checks on product development • Detailed post-calculations per order to distinguish between production inefficiency and unreliable product standards
Inefficient production due to the project-based character of production	High production costs	• Segregation of duties between operations office (pre-calculation; authorization), production department (production; execution), and accounting department (post-calculation; recording) • Documentation of actual usage (hours, materials) and actual production output per order by production department • Product and production standards as detailed as possible (although they will be relatively loose compared with production to stock) • Pre- and post-calculation per order
Misalignment between good produced and customer order	Customer dissatisfaction	• Adequate recording of product specifications per order • Independent checks on alignment between customer orders and product specifications • Independent quality checks by the quality inspector finished goods • Implementation of a customer complaints procedure • Implementation of an information system where customer complaints are independently recorded • Progress controls on customer complaints • Implementation of a customer satisfaction measurement system

(*Continued*)

Table 14.5   (Continued)

Risk	Exposure	Internal controls
Shifting of revenues and costs between projects (from fixed-fee to cost-reimbursement contracts)	Cost plus customers are overbilled, unreliable production records and unreliable input for new pre-calculations	• Segregation of duties between production department (production; execution) and accounting department (cost allocation to projects; recording) • Allocation of projects to project managers on a sequential basis, not on a simultaneous basis • Analytical review of project efficiency (revenues and costs) of projects
Excessive processing time of projects	Projects not finished in time leading to customer complaints, loss of reputation and financial losses	• Adequate production planning by operations office • Progress controls on projects by operations office
Potentially complex projects	Incorrect billing and incorrect valuation	• Management guidelines for partial billing in accordance with project progress and valuation of work-in-progress • Detailed checks by head of accounting department on agreement between billing information and actual project progress • Analytical review of valuation of work-in-progress

Administrative and Organizational Conditions

The administrative and organizational conditions of organizations that produce to order are virtually the same as those of organizations that produce to stock. Hence, we will only discuss these in so far as they deviate from production to stock.

Segregation of Duties

Because organizations that produce to order must segregate the same functions as organizations that produce to stock, we again do not present a separate table with segregated duties here but refer to Table 14.2 instead.

Budgeting

No additional budgets are required compared with organizations that produce to stock. However, since there is more uncertainty about the production standards and the costs of goods sold, the production budget will be less predictable.

Management Guidelines

Organizations with production to order will issue additional management guidelines with respect to the acceptance of large projects and the calculation of project costs. There will also have to be additional guidelines on the calculation and valuation of work-in-progress of large projects. The other management guidelines as discussed for production to stock also apply here.

The Main Processes in Organizations that Produce to Order

In organizations that produce to order we distinguish four main processes: the purchasing process, the inventory process, the production process and the sales process. For a discussion of the purchasing, inventory, production and sales processes we refer to Chapters 7 to 10. We discuss the production process for production to order below in so far as it differs from the production to stock discussed in 'The Main Processes in Organizations that Produce to Stock' (p. 255). In doing so we focus on cost calculation and cost allocation per order, as these apply specifically to production to order.

For organizations that produce to order, acquisition is important because orders trigger the production process. Orders received by the sales department are communicated to the operations office. The operations office prepares a detailed technical pre-calculation, incorporates every order in the short-term planning and thus prepares the execution of the orders. This includes having designs made of the product and product parts, preparing bills of materials, ordering raw and auxiliary materials which are not part of the organization's regular stock, preparing the short-term planning based on available man and machine hours, reserving stocks, machines and personnel, and calculating the ultimate date at which operational activities need to begin with reference to the delivery date that is set. Based on the detailed calculation the capacity that was tentatively reserved can then be definitively allocated to each particular order.

To maintain a grip on the production process, large projects are technically subdivided into sequential stages. This is done as early as the pre-calculation. During execution, the controller prepares the post-calculation and provides a variance analysis per stage. The subdivision into sequential stages may also be helpful to determine valuation of work-in-progress and revenue recognition. For instance, work-in-progress may be valued as follows:

Value at the beginning of the period + directs costs −/− billed installments

Installments are billed at predefined stages in the production process. At the end of each stage a certain percentage of the work is considered completed, at which point revenues are recognized.

Determination of a product's or project's cost price is important for the planning and control of production processes. By comparing the pre- and post-calculations of these cost prices, the efficiency of the production processes, the reliability of standards used and the fairness of prices can be determined. Specifying a cost price is also important for determining the sales price and the margin to be realized on each of the products produced by the organization. This may influence the composition of the organization's product lines.

Summary

This chapter discusses internal control for production organizations. According to the typology of organizations, we distinguish four types of production organizations: (1) organizations that produce to stock, (2) organizations with mass customization, (3) agrarian and extractive organizations and (4) organizations that produce to order. For each of these, we discuss the risks, exposures and internal controls, the administrative and organizational conditions – such as segregation of duties, budgeting and management guidelines – and the main process, i.e. the production process.

Organizations that produce to stock usually produce standard goods for an impersonal market with generally applicable wishes. Examples are beer breweries, brick manufacturers or producers of consumer goods. Organizations with mass customization, such as computer manufacturers, produce goods by assembling standard parts according to individual customer wishes. Agrarian and extractive organizations also produce to stock, although yields are more difficult to predict due to various natural and regulatory circumstances as compared with mass customization or organizations that produce to stock. Examples are dairy farms, cattle breeding and oil and gas companies. Production to order concerns production according to individual, specific customer wishes, such as large infrastructural projects or the construction of luxury yachts.

From an internal control perspective, the most important difference between the four types of organizations related to (differences in) the tightness of the production standards, affecting the way production efficiency is determined. Organizations that produce to stock determine production efficiency per department and can use relatively tight production standards in doing so. Organizations with mass customization calculate production efficiency per department and per order and are also able to use tight standards to do so. Agrarian and extractive organizations determine production efficiency per so-called 'production run', being either a harvest season, a flock of cattle or a period of mineral, oil or gas extraction. Agrarian and extractive organizations are however not able to use tight production standards due to environmental circumstances (e.g. weather conditions), crop and animal diseases and regulation. Organizations that produce to order calculate production efficiency per order and can only use relatively weak production standards to calculate production efficiency.

The risks for organizations that produce to stock mainly relate to production planning and measuring production inefficiencies. These risks result from the fact that (1) production organizations in general have a rather complex flow of goods compared with trade organizations, and (2) organizations that produce to stock specifically first produce the goods and then sell them to customers, which requires proper alignment between sales and production.

Specific risks that we distinguish for mass customization are misalignment between produced goods and customer orders, insufficient quality of the components used, insufficient inventory of components and fluctuation in product demand.

Agrarian and extractive organizations are specifically subject to the risk of yield uncertainty, seasonal patterns, political, social and environmental climate and noncompliance with applicable laws and regulations.

Specific risks for production to order are insufficiently reliable product standards, inefficient production, misalignment between produced good and customer order, shifting of revenues and costs between projects, excessive processing time of projects and potentially complex projects.

Segregation of duties is rather similar across the four types of production organizations. Given the importance of production efficiency in production organizations, it is essential to segregate pre-calculation (technical standard setting by the operations office and financial standard setting by the cost accounting department), actual production (by the production department) and post-calculation (technical and financial assessment of production efficiency by the accounting department). These duties need to be segregated since production inefficiencies can be due not only to inefficient production by the production department, but also to inadequate standard setting by the operations office or cost accounting.

Service Organizations with a Limited Flow of Goods

Introduction

To some extent, service organizations with a (limited) flow of goods are comparable to trade and production organizations. The flow of goods is the starting point for controlling a major part of the information flows within these service organizations. These organizations are usually characterized by some kind of transformation process (e.g. in a restaurant, meals are produced using all kinds of ingredients), and there are similarities with the production processes in production organizations. However, there are also some significant differences, and the most important relate to capacity employment and the relationship between usage of goods and revenues generated. In service organizations, capacity is put directly at the customers' disposal, whereas in production firms it is only indirectly employed to satisfy customers' needs by using it in technical transformation processes. Moreover, the relationship between capacity usage and revenues is usually less tight in service organizations. Because capacity plays an important role in controlling this type of service organization, additional attention should be paid to the planning of activities that contribute to an optimization of capacity usage on the one hand, and to an enhanced alignment between capacity and revenues on the other (e.g. reservations in a restaurant).

In the typology we distinguish two types of service organizations with a limited flow of goods: (1) organizations that have a limited flow of their own goods, and (2) organizations where these goods belong to third parties. This difference only affects the risks, exposures and internal controls stemming from the absence of a cash outflow to pay vendor invoices in the second category of service organizations. However, for organizations in both categories, the primary documentation of the service request is crucially important to assuring the completeness of revenues. The primary documentation is compared with data obtained from other departments or officials within the organization. For example, in a restaurant the primary documentation of the order made by the waiter can subsequently be compared with the documentation of the kitchen (including purchasing), the reception, and payment to the waiter or the cashier. In general the control system in organizations with a limited flow of goods must be designed such that employees charged with executing duties (e.g. the kitchen where meals are prepared) and authorization (the reception or the cashier in a restaurant) cannot influence the primary documentation (e.g. the waiter in a restaurant). If such segregation of duties is not possible, alternative control measures should be taken to ensure that completeness of revenues is established by using sequentially pre-numbered tickets (e.g. job time tickets or move tickets). When the exposure of a risk to the completeness of revenues is substantial, both measures may be put in place simultaneously.

From an internal control perspective, we distinguish three main processes within service organizations with a limited flow of goods: a purchasing process, a service process (comparable to a production process in production organizations) and a sales process. For each of these processes, internal controls need to be implemented to mitigate the risks to achieving the organizational objectives. Risks for service organizations with a limited flow of goods relate, for example, to the incomplete documentation of orders, theft of cash or service products or unreliable inventory records. Internal controls that can be implemented to mitigate these risks range from segregation of duties, management guidelines and strict procedures, to performing analytical reviews.

As for any organization, internal controls that are put in place will only be effective if certain administrative and organizational conditions are met. These conditions relate to computer security, segregation of duties, management guidelines and budgeting. The computer security measures discussed in Chapter 4 are also applicable to service organizations with a limited flow of goods. Hence, this chapter will only discuss segregation of duties, management guidelines and budgeting as applicable to service organizations with a limited flow of goods.

Learning Goals of the Chapter

After having studied this chapter, the reader will understand:

- the internal control consequences of classifying organizations as service organizations with a limited flow of own goods and service organizations with a limited flow of goods owned by third parties;
- the risks for service organizations with a limited flow of own goods and service organizations with a limited flow of goods owned by third parties from an internal control perspective;
- the administrative and organizational conditions of service organizations with a limited flow of own goods and service organizations with a limited flow of goods owned by third parties;
- the main processes in service organizations with a limited flow of own goods and service organizations with a limited flow of goods owned by third parties; and
- the internal controls that can be put in place in service organizations with a limited flow of own goods and service organizations with a limited flow of goods owned by third parties.

Limited Flow of Own Goods

This section discusses service organizations with a limited flow of own goods. We distinguish a huge variety of organizations with a limited flow of own goods, ranging from fast-food chains and à la carte restaurants to publishers. A common feature of these organizations is that they all have a purchasing process, a service process (akin to a production process) and a sales process. The nature of these processes is, nevertheless, dependent on the particular type of service organization with a limited flow of own goods. We therefore do not provide a universal discussion of service organizations with a limited flow of own goods but discuss a specific type of organization with a limited flow of own goods: a restaurant. In the next sections, the characteristics, risks, exposures and internal controls, administrative and organizational conditions and the main processes in restaurants are discussed.

Characteristics of Restaurants

From an internal control perspective, restaurants are comparable to production organizations with respect to the transformation process. Production companies transform raw materials into finished goods, while restaurants transform ingredients into meals. And in both transformation processes, standards are used based on which the efficiency of the transformation process can be determined. More specifically, based on standards, the amount of raw materials (ingredients) to be used for a certain amount of finished goods (meals) can be determined. This standard use is compared with actual use, and differences are analysed and reported to management. Restaurants are nevertheless regarded as service organizations because the relationship between offers (ingredients) and yields (revenues) is less strict compared to production organizations, certainly organizations that produce to stock. The price for a meal is generally about three to four times higher than the price paid for the ingredients. This relatively high added value is necessary to cover the more costly transformation process: restaurants need to hire a cook and waiters, purchase equipment, pay rent or a mortgage for the restaurant building needed to create a restaurant atmosphere. However, because there is a relationship between offers and yields, the reconciliations between the flows of goods and the flows of money are quite similar to those of production organizations:

$$\text{Inventory ingredients at } t_0 + \text{purchases} -/- \text{ingredients delivered to kitchen}$$
$$= \text{inventory ingredients at } t_1$$
$$\text{Ingredients delivered to kitchen} * \text{standard (recipe)} = \text{meals prepared by kitchen} = \text{meals sold}$$

Furthermore, if we assume that all transactions are in cash, in the sales process a further reconciliation can be made between the flows of goods and the flows of money:

$$\text{Cash at } t_0 + \text{sales (meals sold * price per meal)} -/- \text{purchases (ingredients)} = \text{cash at } t_1$$

As these reconciliations show, the value cycle is instrumental in assuring the completeness of revenues. In restaurants, there is still a link between the flow of goods and the flow of money. Ingredients that are purchased are subsequently sold (as meals), implying that the revenues are associated with the ingredients purchased and meals sold. Hence, reasonable assurance about the completeness of revenues can be acquired through appropriate segregation of duties and reconciliations by the controller or the head of the accounting department.

Case Study 15.1: Chan Yan-tak: China's First Three Michelin Star Chef

At last someone cooking one of the world's most popular cuisines has made the top grade of the gastronome's bible

Guardian, Thursday 4 December 2008
Alex Renton

Congratulations to Chan Yan-tak, the first Chinese cook to win three Michelin stars: he's head chef at Lung King Heen – View of the Dragon – a restaurant serving contemporary Cantonese food in Hong Kong's Four Seasons Hotel.

Terry Durack of *The Independent* appears to be the only British reviewer who's sat down there – he was impressed, particularly by the frogs' legs with spicy salt (£12, served in a basket fashioned from hundreds of tiny crisped whitebait). 'Yauatcha and Hakkasan, I love you still, but you have serious competition here,' he writes in his piece. Alan Yau's Hakkasan was of course the first British Chinese to grab a rosette from Michelin.

Of course, it hasn't been easy for a China-based chef to get anything from the man with the spare tyres – until last month, there was no Michelin guide to anywhere in Asia except Tokyo. Which does expose the bias in Michelin. The media (us) too often lazily see the Guide and its awards as the Olympics (Nobels? Oscars?) of commercial cuisine. But this is nonsense – Michelin hardly ventures outside Western Europe and the United States.

Also Michelin is skewed by the fact that its palate is overwhelmingly western. Only two of the 12 judges of the new Hong Kong and Macau guide were Chinese. Unsurprisingly, the other three-rosette award they made was to Joel Robuchon's restaurant in the Hotel Lisboa, Macao (a five star flop-house for gamblers); half the rest of the rosettes went to non-Chinese restaurants in the two cities, most of them operating out of global brand hotels.

The Szechuan-trained English chef Fuchsia Dunlop asked (on BBC Radio Four last night) whether Asian and European cuisines could fairly be judged side-by-side: Chinese cooking being about some very different things – not least with its interest in texture.

Dunlop told how she once took three top chefs from Szechuan province to eat at the Californian shrine-restaurant Chez Panisse. They were 'baffled and disturbed' by the food. 'It's interesting,' said one of them, 'but I don't know if it's good or bad.'

Risks, Exposures and Internal Controls of Restaurants

For restaurants, we distinguish risks in the three main processes: the purchasing process, the service process, and the sales process.

The most important risk in the purchasing process is probably that restaurants work with perishable products, which can lead to a loss of value of ingredients when the ingredients are not used in time. Internal controls to mitigate this risk are an adequate warehouse facility (i.e. a cold store) to store the perishable ingredients, daily consultation between the purchaser and the chef de cuisine about perishable ingredients that are needed for that day, implementation of a destruction procedure for rejected ingredients and analytical review of the quantity of rejected ingredients.

In the service process, misalignment between meals ordered by guests and meals prepared by the kitchen is a major risk. Such misalignment creates customer dissatisfaction and results in a loss of assets (i.e. meals are returned to the kitchen and the appropriate meal needs to be prepared from scratch) that should be avoided. Controls to mitigate this risk are the (eye-ball) observation by the manager/owner of misaligned orders, documentation of meals that are returned to the kitchen, appropriate guidelines for waiters about the careful acceptance of orders and the implementation of a customer satisfaction measurement system.

The incomplete documentation of orders by waiters (also called 'shop within the shop') is a prominent risk in the sales process of restaurants. Internal controls to mitigate this risk are (1) segregation of duties between order acceptance (waiters; authorization), the preparation of meals (kitchen; execution) and the recording of all activities (accounting department; recording); (2) supervision by the manager/owner of the proper documentation of orders by waiters; (3) attaching value to the bill (e.g. offer guests a discount on their next visit in exchange for the bill) or informing guests that they should receive a bill when they pay; (4) the implementation of a code of conduct regarding the documentation of orders; and (5) analytical review by the controller or the head of the accounting department of revenues and order size per waiter.

An overview of risks applicable to restaurants is provided in Table 15.1.

Table 15.1 Risks, exposures and internal controls of restaurants.

Risk	Exposure	Internal controls
Insufficient quality of ingredients	Customer complaints and loss of reputation	• Independent quality checks of ingredients by a quality inspector and the chef de cuisine • Implementation of a customer satisfaction measurement system
Fresh products (ingredients are perishable)	Loss of value of ingredients	• Adequate facilities to store perishable ingredients • Daily consultation between purchaser and chef de cuisine about perishable ingredients • Implementation of a destruction procedure for rejected ingredients (by chef de cuisine and accounting clerk) • Analytical review of the quantity of rejected ingredients
Insufficient inventory of ingredients	Inability to serve meals ordered by customers resulting in customer complaints and loss of revenues	• Adequate inventory planning of ingredients • Periodic reviews by controller or head of accounting department of customer orders that were not executed because of insufficient inventory of ingredients • Purchase of ingredients from reliable vendors
Misalignment between customer orders and meals prepared	Customer dissatisfaction and loss of assets because of meals returned to kitchen	• Supervision by manager/owner of misaligned orders • Documentation of returns (meals returned) to kitchen

		• Appropriate guidelines for personnel (waiters) about careful acceptance of orders • Implementation of a customer satisfaction measurement system
Incomplete documentation of orders by waiters (shop within the shop)	Loss of assets and/or revenues	• Segregation of duties between order acceptance (waiters; authorization), preparation of meals (kitchen; execution) and recording of all activities (accounting department; recording) • Observations by manager/owner of order documentation by waiters • Attach value to bill (e.g. bill will give customers discount for next visit) or informing guests they should receive bill on payment • Implementation of a code of conduct regarding order documentation • Analytical review by controller or head of accounting department of revenues and order-size per waiter
Theft of ingredients by personnel	Loss of assets	• Minimize entry to the storage facility by other than storage personnel (large restaurant) or kitchen personnel (smaller restaurant) • Documentation of all receipts of ingredients and deliveries to kitchen • A system of granting discharge when ingredients are transferred between storage facility and kitchen • Periodic inventory counts of ingredients
Theft of cash	Loss of assets	• Cash needs to be stored in a locked cash drawer • Daily cash-counts • Observation by manager/owner of cash collection by waiters
Incomplete cash collection by waiters	Loss of assets	• Observation by manager/owner of cash collection by waiters • Analytical review of cash deficits per waiter
Relatively simple sales transactions	Personnel usually performs more than one duty (taking orders, serving meals, collecting cash)	• Use of a cash register, which records all transactions • Segregation of duties between waiters (authorization) and kitchen (execution)

Administrative and Organizational Conditions

Segregation of Duties

From an internal control perspective, restaurants have to segregate a number of functions relating to the purchasing of ingredients, quality checks of received ingredients, storage of ingredients, preparation of meals, taking orders, serving meals, collecting cash from customers, safeguarding cash, recording transactions and performing checks on all processes. Segregation of all these duties will only be possible and is only efficient in larger restaurants. In most restaurants, however, the owner will supervise his personnel and perform many duties himself, ranging from purchasing ingredients to preparing the meals or taking orders and serving meals. This (partially) compensates for the incomplete segregation of duties. Table 15.2 provides an overview of the system of segregation of duties in restaurants, assuming the restaurant is large enough to achieve optimal segregation of duties.

Table 15.2   Segregation of duties in restaurants

Officer	Department	Task	Duty
Purchase clerk/manager	Purchasing department	Purchasing ingredients	Authorization
Quality inspector (or chef de cuisine together with manager/owner)	Receiving department	Checking the quality of received ingredients	Checking
Storage clerk	Storage department	Safeguarding ingredients	Custody
Waiter	Waiting staff department	Taking customer orders	Authorization
Cook	Kitchen	Preparing meals	Execution
Chef de cuisine	Kitchen	Deciding on the menu	Authorization
Waiter	Waiting staff department	Serving meals	Execution
Waiter	Waiting staff department	Receipt of customer payments	Authorization
Cashier	Cash department	Safeguarding cash	Custody
Cash disbursements clerk/manager	Cash disbursements department	Payment of vendor invoices	Authorization
Accounts payable clerk/manager	Accounts payable department	Safeguarding accounts payable	Custody
Accounting clerk	Accounting department	Recording transactions	Recording
Controller or head of accounting department	Accounting department	Checking transactions	Checking
Manager/owner	Management	Managing all processes	Checking/Overall authorization

Budgeting

In restaurants, budgeting revolves around the annual master budget and some constituent budgets, including the sales budget; the purchase budget; the cost budget split into personnel costs, accommodation costs, depreciation and costs of ingredients; and the cash budget. Taking into account a required profit margin, the prices for meals are determined based on these budgets. Management subsequently authorizes the budgets and the prices. Furthermore, periodically – e.g. every week – the controller or the head of the accounting department should report to management on any differences between the budgets and the actual results.

Management Guidelines

Management guidelines for restaurants relate to meal prices, handling of cash, purchasing of ingredients and storage of perishable ingredients. More specifically, in restaurants, management will issue guidelines with respect to:

- prices for meals and drinks (price list);
- use of discounts for meals and drinks;
- level of re-order points for ingredients and drinks;
- storage of perishable ingredients and related destruction procedures;
- access to ingredients by employees;
- selection of suppliers of ingredients (mainly with respect to quality issues);
- order acceptance by waiters;
- dress code for waiters;
- maximum amount of cash in the cash drawers;
- acceptance of various forms of cash, including credit cards, debit cards, electronic wallets and cheques;
- handling of tips;
- cash procedure and the deposit of received cash into a safe;
- health and hygiene regulation; and
- dealing with customer complaints.

The Main Processes in Restaurants

We distinguish three main processes in restaurants: the purchasing process, the service process (preparation of meals and drinks, akin to a production process) and the sales process. Since our discussion on internal controls in the purchasing and sales processes in previous chapters applies equally to restaurants, we focus on some specific issues related to the service process below.

For restaurants, the service process mainly consists of a transformation process in which meals are produced using all kinds of ingredients. As indicated, this is similar to the production process in a production organization, and also from an administrative and internal control perspective. While production organizations use standards, restaurants use recipes for the preparation of each meal and these recipes specify the ingredients to be used. As with organizations that produce to stock, efficiency is determined per department, in this case for the kitchen as a whole, but the 'production' standards are less tight. The process, however, is comparable.

An important difference with production organizations, however, is the fact that restaurants work with perishable ingredients. Therefore, a rejection and destruction procedure needs to be implemented. Each day, the chef de cuisine should determine which ingredients can no longer be used the next day. The chef de cuisine and an accounting clerk should make sure that the rejected ingredients are either destroyed or handed over as forage to a transport company. They should draw up a protocol of destruction, which is documented in the warehouse file. The protocol contains information on the ingredients destroyed and contains the electronic signature of both the chef de cuisine and the accounting clerk. The controller or the head of the accounting department should regularly perform analytical reviews of the ingredients that are destroyed. For example, he calculates the ratio of ingredients destroyed to the total number of ingredients purchased and the revenues generated in that period (day). This analysis should be performed both on the total number of ingredients destroyed and per type or category of ingredient. The outcomes of these analyses can help improve the efficiency of the purchasing process, since ingredients that have to be destroyed can form a substantial cost for restaurants.

Limited Flow of Goods Owned by Third Parties

As with organizations with a limited flow of own goods, there is a great variety of organizations with a limited flow of goods owned by third parties, ranging from garage businesses and bicycle repair shops to auctioneers. In all these organizations we can again distinguish three main processes: a purchasing process, a service process (again similar to a production process) and a sales process. The exact nature of these processes depends, however, on the specific type of service organization. Again, therefore, we do not provide a general discussion of service organizations with a limited flow of goods owned by third parties, but discuss a typical type of service organization with a limited flow of goods owned by third parties instead: a garage business. More specifically, we focus on the car repair activities of garages. In the next sections, we discuss the characteristics, risks, exposures and internal controls, administrative and organizational conditions and the main processes in garage businesses.

Characteristics of Garage Businesses

Revenues of garage businesses generally come from two sources: man hours and spare parts. That is, when customers bring their car to a garage for repairs, the repair costs usually relate to spare car parts necessary for the repair job and the man hours spent on that job by the mechanic(s).

Completeness of revenues from man hours worked can be established based on the documentation of hours worked by the mechanics who deliver the services. That is, each mechanic has an employment contract that specifies the required working hours per week (shop time), and each mechanic needs to document the time he or she spends on each repair job (job time). The difference between shop time and job time is the number of hours that cannot be billed to customers (indirect hours). The controller or the head of the accounting department should perform the following reconciliations:

$$\text{Shop time (time in the shop)} -/- \text{indirect hours} = \text{job time (time spent on repair job)}$$
$$\text{Job time} * \text{rate} = \textit{Soll} \text{ position of revenues}$$

These reconciliations can only be made when there is proper segregation of duties between the reception desk (acceptance of orders; authorization), the car mechanics (performing the repairs; execution) and the accounting department (recording all transactions).

As with trade organizations, completeness of revenues from spare parts can be established based on the relationship between offers and yields, captured in the value cycle. For a garage business, the value cycle consists of two events, purchasing/cash disbursement and selling/cash receipts, and two positions, inventory and cash. The reconciliation between the flow of goods and the flow of money is as follows:

$$\text{Inventory spare parts at } t_0 + \text{purchases} -/- \text{sales} = \text{inventory spare parts at } t_1$$

As this reconciliation shows, the value cycle is instrumental in assuring the completeness of revenues from spare parts. Spare parts are purchased and subsequently sold. Therefore, revenues from spare parts are related to parts purchased and parts sold (i.e. used in the repair process).

Hence, by reconciling both the man hours and the spare parts used in the repair process, the completeness of revenues can be established.

Risks, Exposures and Internal Controls of Garage Businesses

We identify risks in the three main processes in garage businesses: the purchasing process, the service process and the sales process.

A significant risk in the purchasing process relates to insufficient inventory of spare parts since this can result in inability to execute repairs. Internal controls to mitigate this risk are adequate inventory planning of spare parts, the use of sufficiently high re-order points and the selection of reliable vendors who can make daily deliveries on request (for at least the more expensive spare parts).

Unreliable pre-calculation by the foreman responsible for planning the repairs, might lead to inadequate decision-making with respect to targets and efficiency. This risk can be mitigated by proper segregation of duties between planning of repairs by the foreman (authorization) and execution of repairs by the mechanics (execution). Furthermore, post-calculations on repair jobs need to be performed to optimize pre-calculations, since inefficiencies could not only be due to inefficient execution of the repairs but also to overly strict pre-calculations (i.e. standards). Finally, management should issue guidelines on how to perform cost calculations and on the workshop rates and prices for spare parts that are used.

Another important risk for garage businesses is the incomplete documentation of repair orders by the reception, which could result in a loss of assets and/or revenues. This sales risk can be mitigated by segregation of duties between order acceptance (reception; authorization) and execution of repairs (mechanics in the repair workshop; execution) such that repairs cannot be accepted by the car mechanics. Therefore, the organization should clearly communicate to customers that repair jobs are only accepted by the reception. Furthermore, the manager/owner needs to supervise this process personally and implement a code of conduct regarding the initial documentation of orders. Finally, the controller or the head of the accounting department should perform analytical reviews of revenues and types of repair jobs.

These and other risks for garage businesses are provided in Table 15.3.

Table 15.3   Risks, exposures and internal controls of garage businesses.

Risk	Exposure	Internal controls
Insufficient inventory of spare parts	Inability to execute repairs	• Adequate inventory planning of spare parts based on forecasts per type of repair • Use of sufficiently high re-order points • Purchase of spare parts from reliable vendors who can deliver daily at request (expensive spare parts)
Insufficiently reliable pre-calculation by foreman (repair planning)	Inadequate decision-making with respect to targets and efficiency	• Segregation of duties between repair planning (foreman; authorization) and actual repairs (car mechanics in workshop; execution) • Management guidelines with respect to cost calculation, and workshop rates and prices for spare parts • Post-calculations to optimize pre-calculations
Accuracy of rates for man hours and spare parts prices	Loss of revenues and profit margin	• Use of predetermined fixed workshop rates (man hours) and price lists for spare parts with predetermined discounts • Integrity controls over price files • Sample-based checks on prices billed by controller or head of accounting department • Analytical review of prices for repair jobs by controller or head of accounting department
Theft of spare parts	Loss of assets	• Closed warehouse that is accessible to warehouse personnel only

		• Documentation of all receipts of spare parts and deliveries to workshop • Granting discharge when spare parts are transferred between warehouse and workshop • Periodic inventory counts of spare parts
Incomplete documentation of repair orders by reception (shop within the shop)	Loss of assets and/or revenues	• Segregation of duties between order acceptance (reception; authorization) and execution of repairs (car mechanics in workshop; execution) • Clear communication to customers that repair jobs are to be accepted by reception only • Supervision by manager/owner of repairs by car mechanics • Implementation of a code of conduct regarding documentation of orders • Analytical review of revenues and types of repair jobs by controller or head of accounting department
Misalignment between repair orders and repairs executed	Customer dissatisfaction and loss of assets because of additional costs to (re-) perform the appropriate repair job	• Supervision by manager/owner of misaligned orders • Documentation of additional repairs • Appropriate guidelines for reception, foreman and mechanics about careful acceptance and execution of orders
Inefficient execution of repairs	High repair costs	• Segregation of duties between repair planning/pre-calculation (foreman; authorization), actual repairs (car mechanics in workshop; execution) and post-calculation (accounting department; recording) • Documentation of actual usage (hours, spare parts, materials) per repair job by mechanics
Insufficient quality of repairs	Customer complaints and loss of reputation	• Independent quality checks on spare parts and finished repair jobs by quality inspector • Implementation of a customer satisfaction measurement system
Fluctuation in demand for repairs	Overcapacity or undercapacity	• Use of reliable forecasts of repair demand, taking into account seasonal patterns • Adequate capacity planning which allows for interim realignment of repair capacity

Administrative and Organizational Conditions

Segregation of Duties

Garage businesses need to segregate the following functions to assure the completeness of revenues: purchasing of spare parts, safeguarding spare parts, acceptance of repair orders, planning repairs, executing car repairs, quality checks of the repairs, billing customers, receipt of customer payments, transaction recording and checking all processes.

Table 15.4 provides an overview of the segregated duties in garage businesses, assuming that the garage is able to achieve optimal segregation. Segregation of all these duties is possible and efficient only in larger garage businesses.

Table 15.4 Segregation of duties in garage businesses.

Officer	Department	Task	Duty
Purchase clerk/manager	Purchasing department	Purchasing spare parts	Authorization
Warehouse clerk/manager	Warehouse department	Safeguarding spare parts	Custody
Reception clerk	Reception department	Accepting repair orders	Authorization
Foreman	Workshop	Assessment of repair jobs and planning of repairs	Authorization
Car mechanic	Workshop	Executing repairs	Execution
Quality inspector	Workshop	Checking quality of executed repair jobs	Checking
Reception clerk	Reception department	Billing customers	Execution
Reception clerk	Reception department	Receipt of customer payments	Authorization
Cashier	Cash department	Safeguarding cash	Custody
Cash disbursements clerk/manager	Cash disbursements department	Payment of vendor invoices	Authorization
Accounts payable clerk/manager	Accounts payable department	Safeguarding accounts payable	Custody
Accounting clerk	Accounting department	Recording transactions	Recording
Controller or head of accounting department	Accounting department	Checking transactions	Checking

Budgeting

Garage businesses determine their master budget based on the goals to be achieved (expected revenues), the activity level of past years (revenues in previous years) and the available repair capacity. The investment and cash budgets are derived from the master budget, and subsequently the annual sales, purchase and cost budgets are drafted. The cost budget incorporates personnel costs, housing costs, depreciation and other overhead costs. The workshop rates are determined based on the cost budget, taking into account a target profit margin. Management subsequently authorizes the budgets and the rates. Furthermore, periodically – e.g. every week – the controller or the head of the accounting department should report to management on any deviations of actual results from the budgeted results.

Management Guidelines

Garage businesses should develop management guidelines on workshop rates, prices for spare parts, purchasing and storage of spare parts, quality (check) of repairs and the handling of cash. More specifically, management should issue guidelines with respect to:

- workshop rate and prices for spare parts (price list);
- use of discounts for repair jobs;
- level of re-order points for spare parts;
- access to spare parts by employees;
- selection of suppliers of spare parts (mainly with respect to the quality of spare parts);
- quality checks on repair jobs;
- maximum amount of cash in the cash drawers;
- acceptance of various forms of payment, including cash, credit cards, debit cards, electronic wallets and cheques; and
- cash procedure and deposit of cash receipts into a safe.

Case Study 15.2: AAA Offers Consumer Checklist For Getting Quality Auto Repair

Auto News from October 10, 2008, InternetAutoguide.com
www.aaa.com/news.

Checklist helps head off vehicle repair problems before they start

ORLANDO, Fla., Oct. 10 /PRNewswire-USNewswire/ – Auto repair questions create major headaches for consumers, often causing motorists to dread taking their vehicle in for service.

(Continued)

Which shop should I go to? Can I trust them?, Will the repairs be done right?, How much will it cost?

In fact, AAA research shows roughly one out of 10 consumers was dissatisfied in their most recent visit to a repair facility, with the biggest complaints being:

– Inability to fix problems on first visit.
– Inability to diagnose problems properly.
– Work took too long.
– Low quality work.

'Many disputes between consumers and repair shops are the result of misunderstandings over what was supposed to be repaired and what was actually done,' said John Nielsen, director, AAA Approved Auto Repair Network.

To help ensure consumers receive reliable, quality auto repair service, AAA recommends motorists use the following checklist–

– Determine what type of repair facility is needed. Most vehicles can be repaired and maintained by a full-service repair facility, but if there is a major problem with a specific vehicle system, a shop specializing in that area might be the best choice. Vehicles still under warranty typically must be repaired by the dealer.

– Select a repair facility you trust. Friends, relatives and co-workers are a good source of recommendations. Also, consumers can look for one of the more than 8,000 AAA Approved Auto Repair facilities in the U.S. and Canada. Since 1975, AAA has certified repair shops as a public service. To qualify, facilities must meet and maintain stringent standards for service, training, cleanliness and equipment. AAA also regularly surveys shops' repair customers to ensure ongoing high customer satisfaction. To locate a AAA-approved facility, visit AAA.com/Repair.

– Make an appointment. If the facility manager knows a motorist is coming and has a rough idea of the problem, the right technician can be assigned to the job and allowed enough time to get it done properly.

– Describe the problem. Don't tell the technician what needs to be repaired or replaced unless it's obvious. Instead, describe the problem and its symptoms, and let the technician determine the appropriate solution.

– Read the repair order. Be wary of blanket statements such as 'check and correct transmission noise' or 'fix engine;' They could result in an unexpected and costly major repair. And never sign a blank repair order or tell the shop to 'just fix it' or 'do what's necessary' unless the problem is covered under warranty.

– Get a written estimate. Oral estimates can be disputed or forgotten. Always ask for a written estimate prior to approving work on your vehicle.

– Insist on a call if repair costs will exceed the estimate. Predicting exact repair costs can be difficult, so most written estimates allow up to a 10 percent overrun. However, motorists should make sure it's written on the repair order they want to be called if the costs will exceed this allowance.

– Carefully consider add-on repairs. If the repair facility calls to say a different part of the vehicle also needs work, it may be best to defer those repairs until a later visit unless the shop can provide clear justification for making them immediately. Don't hesitate to get a second opinion if the extra work does not appear warranted.

– Ask for replaced parts. When dropping their vehicle off for service, consumers should tell the shop they will want to see any replaced parts. Consumers are also entitled to keep those parts, unless the facility must return them under a warranty or exchange program. Replaced parts and a well-documented repair order can be useful if there is a problem later.

– Take a test drive. If a problem remains or the vehicle does not run properly after it's picked it up, don't go home. Return to the shop immediately. If a problem arises after leaving the shop, make an appointment to bring the vehicle back as soon as possible.

– Get a detailed copy of the repair order. Make sure it specifies the costs of labor and each part. Ask for the facility's warranty in writing if it's not printed on the bill. AAA Approved Auto Repair facilities offer a minimum 12-month/12,000-mile warranty.

The Main Processes in Garage Businesses

As with restaurants, within garage businesses we distinguish three main processes: the purchasing process, the service process (car repairs, similar to a production process) and the sales process. The purchasing process applies to spare parts and is identical to the purchasing process discussed in Chapter 7. The service process applies to the execution of car repairs and is comparable to production to order. We therefore do not extensively discuss these processes here. Like the service process the sales process for a garage business is comparable to that of production to order. There are however some slight differences which we discuss below.

The sales process is initiated by a customer who goes to the reception desk. The reception clerk formally accepts the car for the repair job and inputs all relevant information into the repair order file. A programmed procedure automatically assigns a (sequential) number to the repair job. The foreman then assesses the necessary repair(s) and also enters this information in the repair order file. If the chef's assessment substantially deviates from the initial assessment made by the reception clerk, this clerk contacts the customer. When the customer agrees with the assessed repair(s), the foreman then authorizes the repair job and assigns the appropriate mechanic(s) to the job. The car mechanics can then retrieve spare parts from the warehouse and start the repair job.

During and after the repair job the car mechanics enter all relevant information in the repair file under the appropriate repair order. A quality check should be performed on each repair job to assess the quality of repairs. When the garage business is large enough this check will be performed by a designated quality officer. For efficiency reasons, however, the quality check could also be performed by the foreman. Although in the latter case this quality check is not an independent check, a procedure where customers can lodge complaints and the implementation of a customer satisfaction measurement system can provide management with an additional indication of the quality of the workshop's work. As an additional management control, management can decide to (partly) base the bonus of the workshop on the number of complaints lodged.

Summary

This chapter discusses service organizations with a limited flow of goods. The typology distinguishes two types of service organizations with a limited flow of goods: (1) organizations that have a limited flow of their own goods, and (2) organizations where these goods belong to third parties. Since there is a large variety in organizations in each category, we cannot provide a universal discussion of service organizations with a limited flow of own goods or goods owned by third parties. Instead, for each typology we discuss a specific type of organization. For organizations with a limited flow of own goods we discuss a restaurant, and for organizations with a limited flow of goods owned by third parties, we discuss a garage business. For these two types of service organizations, we discuss the risks, exposures and internal controls, the administrative and organizational conditions, such as segregation of duties, budgeting and management guidelines, and the main processes, i.e. the purchasing process, the service process and the sales process.

From an internal control perspective, restaurants are comparable to production organizations with respect to the transformation process. Production companies transform raw materials into finished goods, while restaurants transform ingredients into meals. In both transformation processes, standards are applied that can be used to determine the efficiency of the transformation process. Restaurants are nevertheless regarded as service organizations because the relationship between offers (ingredients) and yields (revenues) is less tight compared to production organizations – certainly compared to production to stock, since the price for a meal is about three to four times higher than the price paid for the ingredients. Another difference is the fact that restaurants work with perishable ingredients. Specific internal controls are required to mitigate this risk.

Garage businesses resemble production organizations on the one hand and trade organizations on the other. This is because garage businesses generate revenues from two sources: hours worked by mechanics and the sale of car parts. Completeness of revenues from hours worked can be established based on the documentation of hours worked by the car mechanics who deliver the services. The efficiency of the repair process can be measured similarly to production organizations. Completeness of revenues from car parts can be assured in much the same way as in trade organizations, since the relationship between offers and yields in a garage business is quite similar to that in trade organizations. Car parts are purchased and used (sold) in the car repair process. Since each customer needs to pay for the materials used, the controls with respect to the use of car parts in the service (repair) process are similar to those of trade organizations.

16

Service Organizations that Put Space and Electronic Capacity at their Customers' Disposal

In this chapter:

Introduction

Compared to service organizations with a limited flow of goods, service organizations with disposition of space or capacity are characterized by providing resources – space or capacity – rather than physical goods. Therefore, the available capacity and the utilization of that capacity are important starting points for establishing the completeness of revenues. Hence, the primary recording of capacity and a system of checks and balances to check capacity usage requires specific attention.

The typology distinguishes three types of service organizations that put space and electronic capacity at their customers' disposal: (1) organizations with disposition of specific space, (2) organizations with disposition of specific electronic capacity and (3) organizations with disposition of nonspecific space. Service organizations with disposition of specific space are for example hotels, transportation companies or hospitals. Customers can reserve a specific part of the organization's capacity during a specified time period: a hotel room, a truck or a hospital bed. Service organizations with disposition of specific electronic capacity are organizations where customers can reserve a specific part of the organization's electronic capacity. Examples are Internet providers and telephone operators, since customers customarily pay a rate per time period for the use of Internet or phone capacity. Service organizations with disposition of nonspecific space are organizations where the use of capacity frequently changes since customers can use the organization's capacity for a certain amount of time, but cannot reserve a specific part of that capacity. Examples are swimming pools, museums, cinemas or public transport companies.

From an internal control perspective, we distinguish two main processes within service organizations with disposition of space or electronic capacity: investment in fixed assets, which is strongly integrated with the purchasing process in these organizations, and the sales process. Service organizations invest in (purchase) space or capacity and generate revenues by putting that space or capacity at the customers' disposal (selling space or capacity). For each of the processes, internal controls need to be implemented to mitigate risks to achieving the organizational objectives. Important risks are for example the incomplete recording of capacity use, inadequate control of investments and investment planning as services cannot be kept in stock, and inefficient use of capacity, that is, suboptimal occupation. These risks require control activities that are mostly short-term orientated. In addition, depending on the specific type of service organization, capacity does not necessarily result in revenues. For example, whether a swimming pool or a bus is completely occupied or completely empty does not change the capacity that is available and the capacity costs to be incurred. As a result, there is only a remote relation between capacity and costs on the one hand and revenues on the other hand. Therefore, controls should not just focus on financial information, as this might induce management to concentrate only on cost savings without considering other objectives that may be strategically important, but on nonfinancial information too. Nonfinancial measures that management could use for assessing performance include measures of customer satisfaction (e.g. through interviews and customer complaints systems), direct measures of the service provided (e.g. by means of test buyers and personal inspections) and proxies of customer satisfaction (e.g. measuring customer waiting time as an approximation of customer satisfaction).

As for any organization, internal controls that are put in place will only be effective if certain administrative and organizational conditions are met. These conditions relate to computer security, segregation of duties, management guidelines and budgeting. The computer security measures as discussed in Chapter 4 also apply to service organizations with disposition of space and capacity. Hence, this chapter will only discuss segregation of duties, management guidelines and budgeting as they apply to service organizations that put space and electronic capacity at their customers' disposal.

Learning Goals of the Chapter

After having studied this chapter, the reader will understand:

- the internal control consequences of classifying organizations as service organizations with disposition of specific space, service organizations with disposition of specific electronic capacity and service organizations with disposition of nonspecific space;
- the risks for service organizations with disposition of specific space, service organizations with disposition of specific electronic capacity and service organizations with disposition of nonspecific space from an internal control perspective;
- the administrative and organizational conditions of service organizations with disposition of specific space, service organizations with disposition of specific electronic capacity and service organizations with disposition of nonspecific space;
- the main processes in service organizations with disposition of specific space, service organizations with disposition of specific electronic capacity and service organizations with disposition of nonspecific space; and
- the internal controls that can be put in place in service organizations with disposition of specific space, service organizations with disposition of specific electronic capacity and service organizations with disposition of nonspecific space.

Disposition of Specific Space

Similar to organizations with a limited flow of goods, we can distinguish a huge variety of organizations that make specific space available to their customers. These organizations range from hotels and hospitals to transportation companies. A common feature of these organizations is that they all distinguish an investment/purchasing process and a sales process. However, the nature of these processes is dependent on the type of space disposition. We therefore do not provide a general discussion of service organizations with disposition of specific space, but focus on a particular type of organization: a transportation company. The next sections discuss the characteristics, risks, exposures and internal controls, administrative and organizational conditions and the main processes in transportation companies as an example of organizations that put specific space at their customers' disposal.

Characteristics of Transportation Companies

Organizations that put specific space at their customers' disposal, such as transportation companies, strive for optimal usage of their maximum capacity. In terms of internal control, capacity and usage (maximum capacity minus vacancy) and the documentation of the primary request (transport request) require special attention. To assure revenue completeness the following reconciliations are generally applicable:

$$\text{Available transport capacity} -/- \text{Vacancy} = \text{Occupation}$$
$$\text{Occupation} * \text{Rate per capacity unit} = \text{Revenues} \, (\textit{Soll} \text{ position})$$

The ability to determine available capacity is instrumental in verifying completeness of revenues since maximum revenues are affected by the expansion or reduction of that capacity. Therefore, important controls are investment and disinvestment procedures, as well as segregation of duties between authorization of investments and disinvestments on the one hand and recording of cash flows on the other. Determining available capacity is more complicated when maximum capacity can be expanded without making significant investments, e.g. an additional truck is purchased. Measures to be taken to mitigate the risk of unauthorized capacity expansion include segregation of duties between custody of trucks (the organization's available capacity) and authorization of transport services to be provided based on the organization's available capacity, and reconciliation of the recorded sales with related expenses.

Risks, Exposures and Internal Controls of Transportation Companies

In our discussion of transportation companies we distinguish risks in the two main processes: investment in fixed assets, which in these companies is strongly integrated with the purchasing process, and sales.

The most important risk in the investment/purchasing process is probably that transportation companies need to make significant investments in transport facilities. These investments matter as they can have important consequences for working capital. Therefore, transportation companies need to prepare an investment and maintenance plan and the investment budget. Furthermore, all investments should occur in conformity with investment budget and applicable management guidelines, and any budget overruns should be authorized by management. By implementing these internal controls the organization can properly manage the consequences of its investments for working capital.

A major risk in the sales process is drivers transporting goods for their own gain (shop within the shop). Internal controls to mitigate this risk are proper segregation of duties between order acceptance (order acceptance; authorization), transport planning (planning and logistics; authorization), transporting goods (drivers; execution) and billing (billing; execution); clear communication to customers that transport orders should always (and only) be accepted by the order acceptance department; supervision of drivers' transport routes by means of GPS; a Code of Conduct for drivers prescribing segregation between acceptance of transport orders and execution of those orders; and finally analytical review of capacity usage and unexpected mileage per driver by the controller or the head of the accounting department.

An overview of these and other risks applicable to transportation companies is provided in Table 16.1.

Table 16.1   Risks, exposures and internal controls of transportation companies.

Risk	Exposure	Internal controls
Significant investments in transport facilities	Incorrect investment decisions for necessary working capital	• Preparation of investment and maintenance planning • All investments should occur in conformity with investment budget • Investment guidelines as set by management • Management should authorize budget overruns
Capacity cannot respond immediately to received orders	Overcapacity or undercapacity, resulting in losses due to underusage or having to decline customers	• Careful market analysis by sales department of customer demand for the medium range, and annually per season and moment of the day • Adequate capacity planning by planning and logistics department, with sufficient flexibility to allow interim adjustments to transport capacity • Analysis of capacity usage of trucks (per order, outward journey, return journey, route, driver etc.) by controller or head of accounting department
Unreliable pre-calculation by order acceptance	Ineffective decision-making regarding transport efficiency, resulting in efficiency losses	• Segregation of duties between order acceptance (sales department; authorization), transport planning (planning and logistics department; authorization) and transporting the goods (drivers in transport department; execution) • Management guidelines regarding cost calculations and transport rates • Optimizing pre-calculations using post-calculation differences per transport order
Drivers exceed allowed driving time, and/or violate other relevant laws and regulations	Fines because of exceeding allowed driving time, speed limits, other fines etc.	• Incorporation of margins in planning of rides by planning and logistics • Management should issue clear guidelines for drivers regarding breaks, speed limitations • Speed limiting devices and tachographs installed in trucks
Drivers transport goods for their own benefit (shop within the shop)	Loss of revenues	• Segregation of duties between order acceptance (sales department; authorization), transport planning (planning and logistics department; authorization), transporting the goods (drivers in transport department; execution) and billing (billing department; execution) • Clear communication to customers that transport orders should be accepted by the order acceptance department • Supervision of drivers' transport routes by means of GPS • Code of Conduct for drivers prescribing segregation between acceptance of transport orders and execution of those orders • Analysis of capacity usage and unexpected mileage per driver by controller or head of accounting department
Theft of trucks, cargo and/or fuel	Loss of assets	• Trucks and cargoes secured by means of garaging on lockable company premises or in parking garages, and by using modern technologies such as GPS, RFID-chips and alarm systems

(Continued)

Table 16.1   (Continued)

Risk	Exposure	Internal controls
Transport of perishable goods	Efficiency losses due to perished cargo	• Trucks should be properly equipped to transport perishable goods (e.g. cooling facilities) • Adequate planning by separate planning and logistics department using advanced planning software
Transport of hazardous materials	Environmental damage resulting in loss of reputation and permit	• Trucks should be properly equipped to transport hazardous materials • Compliance with environmental regulations during transport • Adequate planning by separate planning and logistics department taking transport limitations into account
Underusage of capacity due to empty return journeys	Efficiency losses	• Use of advanced logistic planning software • Correct documentation of transport orders by sales department • Central planning and progress control by separate planning and logistics department

Administrative and Organizational Conditions

Segregation of Duties

From an internal control perspective, transportation companies must segregate the functions relating to making investments, investment calculations, safeguarding trucks, vans, buses and other transportation means, maintenance of transportation means, order acceptance and order execution (driving from A to B). Besides these duties, as in any organization order acceptance, accounts receivable, accounts payable, cashier, authorizing payments, recording of transactions and checking of transactions must be separated. Table 16.2 shows the desired segregation of duties in transportation companies.

Table 16.2   Segregation of duties in transportation companies.

Officer	Department	Task	Duty
Investment calculator	Fleet acquisition department	Making investment calculations	Execution
Head of investments	Fleet acquisition department	Making investments in transport capacity	Authorization
Fleet manager	Fleet maintenance department	Safeguarding and maintenance of trucks, vans and buses	Custody
Sales clerk/manager	Sales department	Order acceptance	Authorization
Credit clerk/manager	Sales department or separate credit department	Checking the creditworthiness of customers	Checking
Planning and logistics officer	Planning and logistics department	Transport planning	Authorization

Drivers	Transport department	Driving the trucks, vans, buses or other vehicles	Execution
Billing clerk/manager	Billing department	Billing customers	Execution
Accounts receivable clerk/ manager	Accounts receivable department	Safeguarding accounts receivable	Custody
Cash receipts clerk/manager	Cash receipts department	Receipt of customer payments	Authorization
Cashier	Cash department	Safeguarding cash	Custody
Accounts payable clerk/manager	Accounts payable department	Safeguarding accounts payable	Custody
Cash disbursements clerk/ manager	Cash disbursements department	Payment of vendor invoices	Authorization
Accounting clerk	Accounting department	Recording transactions	Recording
Controller or head of accounting department	Accounting department	Checking transactions	Checking

Budgeting

As in most other organizations, the budgeting process of transportation companies starts from the sales forecast. The sales forecast incorporates the quantities (numbers, weights, surface area or volumes) that are expected to be transported, the locations at which to pick up and drop off goods or passengers and the timing of transportation activities. The forecast is based on sales in prior years, received orders, market developments, competition and any other information that will make this forecast more reliable. The sales forecast informs the following plans:

* investment plan (including disinvestments and depreciations);
* maintenance plan; and
* personnel plan.

Along with the fixed capacity costs of transportation means and the expected variable costs of personnel and energy, these plans are used to calculate and negotiate with the responsible functions the various cost budgets. Overheads – including housing and administrative staff – are calculated as a percentage of the budgeted direct costs and added to the applicable budgets.

Management Guidelines

For transportation companies, management guidelines relate to the acceptance of transportation orders, the transport rates (including discounts), maintenance of fixed assets, compliance with labour laws and investments in transportation means. More specifically, in transportation companies, management will issue guidelines with respect to:

* the rates per capacity unit (count, kilo, m^2 or m^3) and per transportation means;
* customer discounts;

- order acceptance;
- investments or disinvestments in transportation capacity;
- maintenance of trucks, vans, buses, cars and other transportation means deployed by the company;
- compliance with laws and regulations, e.g. those governing driving hours;
- procedures regarding route planning; and
- acceptance of hazardous materials.

The Main Processes in Transportation Companies

We distinguish two main processes within transportation companies: investment in fixed assets, which is strongly integrated with purchasing, and sales. The investment/purchasing process in transportation companies pertains to purchasing capacity (trucks) and combines a regular purchasing process with the secondary process of investment in fixed assets. We will not discuss the purchasing process further here, but focus on some specific items in the sales process instead. This particularly relates to the acceptance and planning of transport orders.

Transport orders are received by the order acceptance department. Clerks enter every order into the order file after which a programmed procedure automatically assigns a sequential order number to the order and records the order in the information system. Per order, the order acceptance calculates the transport fee based on the transport rate, transport capacity needed and transport time or distance. The clerk then enters the transport fee in the order file and a programmed procedure automatically updates the information system. After confirmation of the order by the customer (by means of an e-mail or signed contract) the transport order becomes definite. An order acceptance clerk then changes the status code of the order from preliminary to definite. A programmed procedure then automatically updates the information system with this new information.

The planning department receives all accepted orders. They plan the transport orders by determining which truck and driver are needed at what time to transport the goods. They enter the planned transports in the planning file. Based on the planning file, the truck drivers receive the information of planned orders and transport the goods from A to B. During transport, the planning department keeps track of the trucks by means of GPS and onboard computers. The drivers enter the relevant transport data, such as departure time, arrival time and transported goods into the planning file via the onboard computer. A programmed procedure then automatically updates the information system with the new information and indicates in the planning file that the order is completed.

Case Study 16.1: Upgraded XATANET Software Delivers Enhancements for Improved Fleet Operations Visibility and Control.

PR Newswire, Tuesday, January 13, 2009

MINNEAPOLIS, Jan. 13 /PRNewswire-FirstCall/ – XATA Corporation today announced the release of the next version of its on-demand fleet operations software. The new features and enhanced tools in XATANET 4.3 give fleet managers a clearer view of the day-to-day operations of their fleets to improve vehicle utilization and performance. This release also delivers enhanced mapping capabilities and customer-defined reporting.

'The release of 4.3 demonstrates our commitment to listening to our customers and continually providing flexible functionality to help them optimize their fleets,' said Tom Flies, senior vice president, product management, XATA Corporation. 'The new components of the upgraded XATANET help companies reduce costs and create efficiencies – key savings at any time, but particularly in today's economy.'

In addition to the enhanced mapping and customer-defined reporting tools, XATANET 4.3 also includes the following new features:

- Two new reports, a Driver Fuel Analysis Summary report and Fleet Utilization Summary report, which provide management easy access to important fleet data.
- Additional Point of Delivery (POD) functionality that delivers both POD and XATANET on a single, handheld device.
- New dashboard option that allows XATANET users to view idle time during a route, excluding all other non-trip time. This new reporting option allows fleet managers to monitor the driver's impact on vehicle idling.
- Four new Smart Checks and Exceptions, which help gauge actual -vs.- planned leg time and stop time.
- Enhanced data-capture, which provides fleet managers increased visibility on fuel economy changes.

Furthermore, to assure completeness of revenues for transport companies, and for service organizations with specific reservation of capacity in general, vacancy needs to be considered because expected revenues depend on it. After all, expected revenues equal occupation times the transport rate, where occupation is calculated as the difference between maximum capacity and vacancy. An employee independent from the order acceptance and planning department should check vacancy. In a transport company, an accounting clerk should check in irregular instances whether truck space that should not be in use according to the planning file is indeed not in use, i.e. is on the transport company's premises or at a specified other location. In the latter case, vacancy should be checked at that particular site.

Disposition of Specific Electronic Capacity

This section discusses service organizations that put specific electronic capacity at their customers' disposal. We again focus on a particular type of organization, a telephone operator, rather than providing a general discussion of service organizations with disposition of specific electronic capacity. The next sections discuss the characteristics, risks, exposures and internal controls, administrative and organizational conditions and the main processes of telephone operators as an example of organizations that put specific electronic capacity at their customers' disposal.

Characteristics of Telephone Operators

Telephone operators collect revenues from two sources: phone calls and subscriptions. The main driver of revenues generated from phone calls is used network capacity. At least two issues complicate verification of completeness of these revenues. First, if capacity is available in material form, such as transportation capacity in the form of trucks, it is possible, at least during transport, to trace capacity usage even when the initial capacity request is not properly documented. This is not possible for telephone operators, however, since their capacity is available in electronic rather than material form. For telephone operators, therefore, the reliability of the information system is essential to establish capacity usage. Second, compared, for example, to transportation companies, it is almost impossible for telephone operators to check vacancy of the telephone network because the frequency of transactions is very high. Therefore, the initial documentation of each phone call (transaction) is essential to establish completeness of revenues of telephone operators, reinforcing the importance of a reliable information system for such organizations. To establish the completeness of revenues from phone calls the following reconciliation is generally applicable:

$$\text{Documented time of phone calls} * \text{rate per phone call} = \text{Revenues from phone calls}$$

Verifying the completeness of revenues from subscriptions requires information on the number of subscriptions as contained in the subscriptions file. Hence, the following reconciliations apply:

$$\text{Number of subscriptions at } t_0 + \text{new subscriptions} -/- \text{terminated subscriptions}$$
$$= \text{Number of subscriptions at } t_1$$
$$\text{Number of subscriptions at } t_1 * \text{subscription rate} = \text{Revenues from subscriptions}$$

Risks, Exposures and Internal Controls of Telephone Operators

We focus on two main processes within telephone operators when analysing risks: the investment/purchasing process and the sales process.

The most important risk with respect to the investment/purchasing process is probably overload or underuse of the telephone network. An overloaded network might lead to network breakdown, resulting in loss of revenues and dissatisfied customers. When a network is underused sales may not be sufficient to cover fixed capacity costs. Therefore, a telephone operator must perform a careful market analysis of customer demand per year, month and ultimately per moment of the day. In doing so, organizations should take the types of services into account since nowadays most telephone operators offer both fixed and mobile services, the latter available through pre-paid or post-paid (subscription) contracts. Furthermore, seasonal effects, average occupation and peak-load must also be taken into account. Finally, the telephone operator should also analyse network capacity usage and consider entering into contracts with other telephone operators for flexible capacity to allow the temporary use of their capacity.

In the sales process, the interruption of the automated system is a prominent risk as this could lead to a situation where no telephone traffic and/or recording of transactions are possible. Such cases might result in a loss of revenues since the telephone operator cannot charge customers for phone calls as caller and/or call time are unknown. Therefore, there must be back-up procedures for the automated system and files, recovery procedures for programmes and files, fallback arrangements to have (shadow) systems on standby, adequate physical and logical access controls for the automated system and computer facilities, and computer facilities and files must be stored in (physically) secured places.

An overview of these and other risks applicable to telephone operators is provided in Table 16.3.

Table 16.3 Risks, exposures and internal controls of telephone operators.

Risk	Exposure	Internal controls
Significant invest-ments in network facilities	Consequences of incorrect invest-ment decisions for necessary working capital are severe	• Preparation of investment and maintenance planning • All investments should occur in conformity with investment budget • Investment guidelines as set by management • Management should authorize budget overruns
Overburdening or underusage of telephone network	Network down, resulting in loss of revenues and dis-satisfied customers; or capacity loss	• Careful market analysis of customer demand for the medium range and annually per season and per moment of the day • Analysis of network capacity usage by controller or head of accounting department • Contracts with other telephone operators for flexible capacity to allow temporary use of their capacity
Subscriptions and call charges with different rates	Use of incorrect rates resulting in a loss of revenues and profit	• IT controls to secure the integrity of rates in the price file • Use of fixed rates • Random detailed checks on subscription and call rates charged by controller or head of accounting department • Analysis of rates charged by controller or head of accounting department
Granting discounts via subscriptions and special discount offers	Loss of revenues and profit	• Management guidelines on granting of discounts (discount tables) • Random detailed checks by controller or head of accounting department on discounts granted • Analysis by controller or head of accounting department of discounts granted by salespeople
Subscribers are not creditworthy	Uncollectable receivables	• Creditworthiness check not by sales department but by separate credit department • Adequate recording of customers' credit position
Large accounts receivable position	High financing costs	• Encourage early payment by granting discounts • Strict payment terms • Management guidelines regarding maximum accounts receivable position • Periodic check on ageing of accounts receivable, subsequent active dunning of subscribers • Procedures to disconnect phone if debtors are in default

(*Continued*)

Table 16.3   (Continued)

Risk	Exposure	Internal controls
Complex technology regarding international settlement of telephone services provided (roaming)	Loss of revenues and profit	• Adequate recording of international calls in usage file • Reconciliation by controller or head of accounting department of amounts billed by international network providers and amounts charged to subscribers for international calls
Interruption of automated system	No transactions possible and/or no recording of transactions possible, leading to a loss of revenues and profit	• Back-up procedures for automated system and files • Recovery procedures for programs and files • Fallback arrangements to have (shadow) systems on standby • Adequate physical and logical access controls • Computer facilities and storage of files in (physically) secured spaces
Interruption of telephone network	No transactions possible, resulting in dissatisfied subscribers and loss of revenues	• Adequate network maintenance procedures • Fallback arrangements to have (shadow) systems on standby • Implementing complaints procedures to allow customers to lodge their complaints

Administrative and Organizational Conditions

Segregation of Duties

From an internal control perspective, telephone operators must segregate functions related to investment calculations, making investments in transponders and other IT devices, network management, information system management, customer services, technical customer support and revenue assurance. Besides these specific functions, as in any organization, functions related to order acceptance, accounts receivable, cashier, authorizing payments, transaction recording and checking must be segregated. Table 16.4 provides an overview of the desired segregation of duties in telephone operators.

Table 16.4   Segregation of duties for telephone operators.

Officer	Department	Task	Duty
Investment calculator	Network acquisition department	Making investment calculations	Execution
Head of investments	Network acquisition department	Making investments in telephone capacity	Authorization
Network manager	Network maintenance department	Safeguarding and maintenance of the telephone network	Custody
IT officer/manager	IT department	Safeguarding and maintenance of the organization's information systems	Custody

Sales clerk/manager	Sales department	Sales of new subscriptions and pre-paid contracts	Authorization
Credit clerk/manager	Sales department or separate credit department	Checking potential customers' creditworthiness	Checking
Help desk clerk/manager	Help desk	Handling customers' technical questions and giving on-line support	Execution
Customer service clerk/manager	Customer service department	Handling of customer complaints	Execution
Revenue assurance auditor	Revenue assurance department	Reconciling services provided with services billed	Checking
Billing clerk/manager	Billing department	Billing customers	Execution
Accounts receivable clerk/manager	Accounts receivable department	Safeguarding accounts receivable	Custody
Cash receipts clerk/manager	Cash receipts department	Receipt of customer payments	Authorization
Cashier	Cash department	Safeguarding cash	Custody
Cash disbursements clerk/manager	Cash disbursements department	Payment of purchase invoices	Authorization
Accounts payable clerk/manager	Accounts payable department	Safeguarding accounts payable	Custody
Accounting clerk	Accounting department	Recording transactions	Recording
Controller or head of accounting department	Accounting department	Checking transactions	Checking

Budgeting

For telephone operators budgeting starts with a sales forecast, specifying the expected net number of connections per type of service. This forecast should incorporate last year's figures, market developments including competition and sales targets, and ultimately results in a sales budget. Based on the sales budget, the capacity and personnel plans are made. The capacity plan specifies the planned investments and disinvestments in telephone capacity and other key fixed assets, given current capacity and expected capacity usage. The personnel plan contains required personnel taking into account current personnel. As the drivers of a significant part of the company's cost, the capacity plan and personnel plan are then fed into the overall cost budget. The sales budget and cost budget together with the overhead surcharges are the basis for the rates to be charged to customers. An important issue for telephone operators is their dynamic environment, which could render budgets obsolete – and therefore irrelevant – at a faster pace than in many other organizations. For this reason, telephone operators maintain elaborate budgeting systems that include budgeting cycles and pre-budgeting cycles to update the budgets in accordance with changing circumstances. Two more budgets of a more operational nature that will need to be developed are the investment budget and the liquidity budget. The former provides the discretionary bandwidth to the head of investments to make investments, the latter specifies the expected cash flows. All plans and budgets must be authorized by the company's management.

Case Study 16.2: Sprint Mobile Plan could Spark US Price War

By Paul Taylor in New York
January 15, 2009
The Financial Times

Boost Mobile, Sprint Nextel's prepaid mobile unit, launched a $50-a-month nationwide unlimited calling plan on Thursday, raising fears of a US pricing war and sending shares of rivals Leap Wireless and MetroPCS Communications tumbling.

Leap dropped $2.47, or 8.9 per cent, to $25.23 in Nasdaq Stock Market trading. MetroPCS fell $2.10, or 13 per cent, to $13.87 in New York Stock Exchange composite trading.

Boost is targeting the nationwide plan, available to customers from next week, at budget-conscious consumers concerned about the cost of operating a mobile phone.

It will provide customers unlimited voice, text and web access and, unlike the regional unlimited plans offered by Boost's rivals, has no roaming charges. Boost believes the new offering will be attractive to its existing customers and those of rival carriers, including the leading monthly contract providers such as Verizon Wireless, AT&T's Mobile unit and Deutsche Telekom's T-Mobile USA.

'The price point is a new low in the wireless market, where even Sprint's own flagship brand charges $99 for its "Simply Everything" plan, and where comparable value-oriented plans from MetroPCS and Leap are in the $60 range,' said Craig Moffett, a Sanford Bernstein analyst. 'Unlike Metro and Leap, however, the new Boost plan doesn't have regional restrictions, putting it more directly in more competition with Verizon, AT&T and T-Mobile.'

Verizon Wireless – the nation's largest wireless carrier following the acquisition of Alltel at the start of this year – and AT&T both offer unlimited voice call plans for $99 a month.

'This plan is designed to be disruptive,' said Matt Carter, Boost's president. 'Wireless consumers know there's a lot of wrong out there – activation fees, overage charges and extra costs for services like voicemail and roaming.'

'Unlike some other prepaid services, our new flat-rate plan will not include any of these charges; what you see is what you get,' he said. Boost claims that once roaming and other charges are added in, comparable pre-paid plans from its rivals cost $60 or more a month.

Boost offers mobile phone services using Sprint Nextel's iDen nationwide network and is hoping that the flat rate features of the plan will appeal to current customers who spent an average of $31-a-month in the third quarter.

In contrast Leap and MetroPCS, which abandoned merger plans last year, operate regional networks but recently signed a roaming agreement that enables them to offer coverage to about 200m people in the US.

To date prepaid services in the US have been less successful than similar offerings in other markets although some analysts believe the current economic recession could fuel further growth as traditional contract customers seek to limit their spending.

Management Guidelines

For telephone operators, relevant management guidelines relate to setting telephone rates, marketing new products, information systems security and network maintenance. More specifically, telephone operators' management will issue guidelines with respect to:

- subscription and charge rates;
- discounts on subscription and charge rates;
- expansion and reduction of telephone capacity (investments);
- maintenance of the telephone network;
- information system security;
- creditworthiness of potential customers;
- customer complaints;
- helpdesk procedures; and
- revenue assurance.

The Main Processes of Telephone Operators

Like transportation companies, from an internal control perspective, telephone operators have two main processes: an investment/purchasing process and a sales process. The investment/purchasing process in telephone companies relates to purchasing telephone network capacity and combines a regular purchasing process with investment in fixed assets. We will not discuss the purchasing process here, but focus on some specific issues related to information system security in the sales process.

As already mentioned in the section on risks, the interruption of the automated system is a prominent risk as this leads to a situation where no telephone traffic is possible or no recording of transactions is possible, in which case the telephone operator cannot charge customers for phone calls as the subscriber and/or phone time is unknown. Therefore, telephone companies need to implement several information security controls. First, there need to be appropriate physical and logical access controls. Physical security is aimed at prohibiting access to hardware, data and programs for unauthorized persons by means of physical measures, such as locking computer rooms, safe storage of back-up files or using fire-resistant walls and doors for the computer room. Logical access controls are aimed at preventing logical access to the information system. Hence, telephone companies should use user-ids in combination with passwords and an access control matrix allowing employees to access/alter data files/fields. Second, telephone companies should implement back-up and recovery procedures. Back-up procedures relate to making copies of files for the purpose of data recovery. The copying of files is based on the grandfather-father-son principle, in which the copy is called the son and the original is called the father copy. When a copy is made of the son, the new copy is called son, the son is called father and the father is called grandfather copy. By following this procedure, there is always a back-up file of the back-up file, which creates the additional security that data can be recovered at a reasonable expense. Data recovery procedures then describe how data that were erroneously destroyed or modified need to be restored. In addition to back-up and recovery procedures, telephone companies should also have a disaster recovery plan, with instructions on how to act after a disaster or shut-down of the system has occurred in order to have the system work properly again as soon as possible. Finally, telephone companies should have fallback arrangements when the primary information system breaks down. This implies that a telephone company should have a data processing hot site alongside its primary system which can be made available for operation at very short notice when the primary system breaks down.

Disposition of Nonspecific Space

This section discusses service organizations that put nonspecific space at their customers' disposal. As with the previous two typologies that we have discussed, there is a huge variety of organizations with disposal of nonspecific space, ranging from museums and parking lots to public transport companies. We do not provide a general discussion of service organizations with disposition of nonspecific space, but instead focus on a specific type of organization: a museum. The next sections discuss the characteristics, risks, exposures and internal controls, administrative and organizational conditions and the main processes in museums as an example of organizations that put nonspecific space at their customers' disposal.

Characteristics of Museums

For museums, and for any other organization that puts nonspecific space at its customers' disposal, vacancy control is not practically possible. This is because change frequency in the disposed space is high, and/or because a specific space area is hard to mark out. For example, a visitor cannot reserve a certain amount of space in a museum, like one can reserve a room in a hotel. Instead, service use is made dependent upon 'goods' that serve as proof of cash receipts in payment of services. These 'goods' do not have intrinsic value, but rather an underlying nominal, or fiduciary, value, and are therefore denoted quasi-goods. Quasi-goods entitle the buyer of those goods to services provided by or on behalf of the organization that put these into circulation. Examples are coffee coins for coffee machines, or, in the case of a museum, entrance tickets that give the buyer access to the museum for a certain period of time. In the absence of a flow of physical goods, the flow of quasi-goods, entrance tickets, is the starting point for assuring the completeness of revenues. The purchasing, storage and sales of entrance tickets are related by means of the following reconciliations, which are to be made frequently, preferably daily:

Beginning inventory of entrance tickets + Inventory increase −/− Ending inventory of entrance tickets
= *Soll* position of number of entrance tickets sold
Soll position of number of entrance tickets sold * Ticket price
= *Soll* position of revenues from entrance tickets

The controller or the head of the accounting department should distinguish as many revenue categories as there are different nominal values of the quasi-goods (i.e. different ticket prices on the entrance tickets), and then perform the reconciliations above for each of these revenue categories. The sum of the *Soll* positions of revenues for each of the revenue categories should subsequently be related to cash receipts determined by the following reconciliation:

Cash at the end of the day $-/-$ Cash at the beginning of the day + Cash payments = Cash receipts

Note that these reconciliations are only valid when the use of quasi-goods is complemented by physical access controls at the entrance to the museum. To prevent more use being made of the quasi-good than was intended the quasi-goods must be invalidated after ticket inspection. For instance, the ticket inspector should tear off a part of the ticket upon entrance to the museum. This requires segregation of duties between the clerk that invalidates the ticket (checking) and the clerk that authorizes the sale of the ticket (authorization). That is, the ticket inspector should not be involved in the sale of the tickets at the ticket counter.

Case Study 16.3: Vanderbilt Museum is Fighting for its Life

Maxine Hicks for *The New York Times*, January 4, 2009

IN the courtyard of the Vanderbilt Museum's mansion, a 1999 Lincoln Navigator S.U.V. sat on display last weekend, waiting to be auctioned off to raise money to help keep the financially troubled museum open.

Inside the home where William K. Vanderbilt II once lived, the millionaire's 1928 Lincoln – not an S.U.V. – was on exhibit, along with hundreds of objects he collected during worldwide travels on his 264-foot yacht. Among the museum's preserved artifacts are fish, birds, tarantulas, two shrunken heads from Peru and an Egyptian mummy.

Now a fight is on within Suffolk County government over how to preserve the 43-acre estate, which also includes a marine museum that Willie K., as he was known, built before his death in 1944, and a more modern planetarium.

In the short term, the museum must raise $35,000 by Jan. 14 to meet its payroll, said Carol Ghiorsi Hart, the executive director. 'If we can't raise that, we'll have to shut down,' she said.

The Navigator, donated by the museum board's president, Steven Gittelman, was part of the fundraising effort, as was a party last Sunday sponsored by William J. Lindsay, presiding officer of the County Legislature, that took in nearly $17,000.

In the longer term, however, the museum needs some $800,000 to stay open this year, having lost most of its endowment income because of the stock market dive in September and October.

On Dec. 2, the Suffolk Legislature passed a bill that would have raised an array of county parks fees to provide that money, but County Executive Steve Levy vetoed it. At its Dec. 16 meeting, the Legislature failed to override the veto.

Now two legislators are planning to offer bills that they say could have a better chance of survival. Vivian Viloria-Fisher, the deputy presiding officer, said she had filed an amended bill with smaller increases in parks fees and a stipulation that they would last only one year. Jon D. Cooper, the majority leader, said he was preparing a bill to raise $500,000 by finding offsets, or unused funds, in the county budget.

(Continued)

Mr. Cooper said he thought the museum could manage with the lower amount because it has raised fees, sought donations and made plans to add a new cafe and gift shop.

Neither bill could be considered by the Legislature until early February.

But Mr. Levy said neither would meet with his approval. 'Of course, we all want to see the Vanderbilt remain viable, but I certainly don't want to see parks fees raised to do so,' he said.

Mr. Cooper's proposal, he said, would probably be based on 'phantom revenue that doesn't exist.' Mr. Levy said he would rather see any surplus funds spent on services like health care.

'The best solution, to my mind, is for them to seek a private loan to get them through this very rough year,' and three banks have shown interest, he said.

'I can't borrow money I can't pay back,' Mr. Gittelman said. 'It would be our preference that the Legislature get us through this year.'

THE museum is in trouble because Mr. Vanderbilt left an $ 8.2 million endowment stipulating that the original principal could not be spent. Until late last year, the museum was receiving $ 800,000 a year, about half of its operating expenses, from endowment income. The endowment had grown to $ 12.3 million before dropping to $ 8.3 million (now invested in bonds).

To save money, the museum has cut back on open days, now Tuesdays and weekends, though school groups may come on any day. A $ 25,000 grant from Arrow Electronics allowed it to open free Dec. 26 to 31.

Heating, insuring and guarding the contents of a shuttered museum would cost almost as much as keeping it open, said Mr. Gittelman, who vowed, 'I'm not letting it close.'

Risks, Exposures and Internal Controls of Museums

We focus on two main processes in our analysis of risks for museums: the investment/purchasing process and the sales process.

In the investment/purchasing process, the significant investment in works of art is regarded as a prominent risk. As with transportation companies, the consequences of incorrect investment decisions for necessary working capital can be severe. Hence, museums need to have proper investment and restoration planning. Moreover, all investments should occur in conformity with the investment budget and management must always authorize overruns.

A significant risk in the sales process is access by visitors without payment or at a price that is too low. This leads to an unwanted loss of revenue. Consequently, the museum needs to implement an adequate system of quasi-goods. This implies that the museum must use reliable software, provided by a trustworthy company, to produce the quasi-goods. The software must assign a sequential number to each quasi-good that is printed and differential rates (if any) should be easily recognizable. The paper on which the quasi-good is printed must be safeguarded in a lockable safe. Furthermore, the quasi-good must be invalidated upon entry to the museum, and as indicated above this invalidation must be done by a clerk that is separate from the clerk that sold the quasi-good to the customer. Finally, at the end of a sales period (e.g. the end of a day), a checking function (e.g. the controller or the head of the accounting department) determines the number of quasi-goods sold by comparing the starting and ending sequential quasi-good numbers as contained in the software log. Multiplied by the price of the quasi-good, this should equal the cash that has been collected (the '*Soll*' position). The checking function then determines the '*Ist*' position by counting the cash that was actually collected in the cash register. If '*Soll*' and '*Ist*' do not match, the checking function should perform a further analysis to determine the nature of the deviation.

An overview of these and other risks for museums is provided in Table 16.5.

Table 16.5 Risks, exposures and internal controls of museums.

Risk	Exposure	Internal controls
Significant investments in works of art	Consequences of incorrect investment decisions for necessary working capital are severe	• Preparation of investment and restoration planning by management • All investments should occur in conformity with investment budget • Management should authorize budget overruns
Access without payment or at price that is too low	Loss of revenues	• Production of quasi-goods by reputable printer • Quasi-goods should be (pre-) numbered consecutively and differential rates (if any) should be easily recognizable • Segregation of duties between ordering (management; authorization), safeguarding (custodian; custody) and recording (accounting department; recording) of quasi-goods • Quasi-goods are safeguarded by administrator of quasi-goods (custody function) in a lockable space or safe, accessible by administrator only • Daily reconciliation of amount of quasi-goods sold and cash received by controller or head of accounting department • Periodic inventory counts of quasi-goods by controller or head of accounting department • Segregation of duties between sale of quasi-goods (front desk; authorization) and admission to the museum (ticket inspector; checking)
Ticket sellers at front desk account for regular tickets as discounted tickets	Loss of revenues	• Segregation of duties between ticket sales by front desk (authorization) and recording of ticket sales by accounting department (recording) • Ticket price and discount (if any) printed on ticket • Specific check by ticket inspector on discounts applied • Museum visits by test buyers (mystery guests) • Analysis of discounts granted by controller or head of accounting department • Management guidelines regarding granting of discounts
Special discounts for specific categories of visitors and groups	Use of incorrect prices resulting in loss of revenues	• Measures to assure the integrity of admission prices in the price file • Check by ticket inspector on discounts applied on tickets • Analysis of ticket prices and discounts by controller or head of accounting department

(Continued)

Table 16.5 (Continued)

Risk	Exposure	Internal controls
Theft of cash	Loss of assets	• Securing cash by means of adequate recording in cash register by accounting department (recording) and safeguarding of cash in lockable till (cash drawer) by front desk personnel and cashier (custody) • Daily cash counts by front-desk personnel/cashier and controller or head of accounting department • Close supervision of front desk employees by management
Unauthorized granting of access to visitors	Loss of revenues	• Segregation of duties between tickets sales (front desk; authorization) and admission to the museum (ticket inspector; checking) • Supervision of ticket sales by management
Theft of works of art	Loss of assets	• Display of works of art in guarded spaces (e.g. behind glass) • Safeguarding works of art during opening hours by museum stewards (custody) • Assigning unique numbers to all works of art and keeping detailed description of each object in computer files • Installation of alarm system and cameras • Providing every object with GPS or RFID-chip • Periodic physical counts of all works of art (in warehouse and on display)

Administrative and Organizational Conditions

Segregation of Duties

From an internal control perspective, museums must segregate the functions pertaining to purchasing works of art, safeguarding the works of art in the museum and admittance to the museum. Besides these specific functions, as in any organization the functions of cashier, authorizing payments, transaction recording and checking of transactions must be segregated. Table 16.6 provides an overview of the desired segregation of duties in museums.

Table 16.6 Segregation of duties in museums.

Officer	Department	Task	Duty
Curator	Art acquisition department	Purchasing works of art to exhibit in the museum	Authorization
Warehouse clerk/manager	Warehouse department	Safeguarding works of art	Custody
Conservator	Conservation department	Restoration and repair of works of art	Execution
Front desk clerk	Sales department	Ticket sales	Authorization

Ticket inspector	Sales department	Checking entrance tickets for admittance to the museum	Checking
Steward	Museum floor	Safeguarding the works of art during opening hours	Custody
Cashier	Cash department	Safeguarding cash	Custody
Cash disbursements clerk/ manager	Cash disbursements department	Payment of invoices	Authorization
Accounts payable clerk/manager	Accounts payable department	Safeguarding accounts payable	Custody
Accounting clerk	Accounting department	Recording transactions	Recording
Controller or head of accounting department	Accounting department	Checking transactions	Checking

Budgeting

The starting point for the budgeting process in museums is the expected number of visitors per year. This forecast is based on last year's visitor numbers, market developments (including competition) and the targeted number of visitors, and ultimately results in a sales budget. Based on the sales budget, the personnel plan is developed, specifying required personnel taking into account current personnel. As a driver of a significant part of the company's cost, the personnel plan is then fed into the overall cost budget. The overall cost budget also contains estimates of other costs, such as those related to art acquisition, housing, maintenance and other overheads. Together with required profit margins and/or government funding for which the museum might be eligible, the sales budget and cost budgets are the basis for the entrance fees to be charged to visitors. All plans and budgets must be authorized by the museum's management.

Management Guidelines

Relevant management guidelines for museums refer to art acquisition, entrance fees, handling of works of art and handling of quasi-goods and cash. More specifically, in museums, management will issue guidelines with respect to:

- policy with respect to purchasing works of art;
- entrance fees per category of visitors and groups;
- discounts for categories of visitors and groups;
- safeguarding works of art;
- maintaining and restoring works of art;
- lending out works of art to other museums;
- safeguarding quasi-goods;
- maximum amount of cash in the cash-drawers;
- acceptance of various forms of cash, including credit cards, debit cards, electronic wallets and cheques; and
- depositing received cash in a safe.

The Main Processes in Museums

We distinguish two main processes in museums: investment in fixed assets, which is strongly integrated with the purchasing process, and the sales process. Within museums the investment/purchasing process pertains to purchasing works of art and combines a regular purchasing process with the secondary process of investment in fixed assets. We will not discuss the purchasing process here, but instead focus on some specific issues related to quasi-goods in the sales process.

In contrast to reservation of specific space and time capacity, no reservations are made. Service use is made dependent upon goods that serve as proof of cash receipts in payment of services. Hence, these goods are not goods in the sense that they intrinsically have value, but merely that they have an underlying nominal value. For this reason they are also denoted quasi-goods. The absence of a flow of physical goods is handled by introducing a flow of quasi-goods and trying to control that flow instead. The quasi-goods thus form the starting point for assuring the completeness of revenues. Quasi-goods can be defined as goods, typically of low intrinsic but high nominal value, that serve as proof of cash receipts in exchange for payment of services. For example, the entrance ticket of the museum entitles the owner to access the museum. To assure the completeness of revenues, the purchasing, storage and sale of quasi-goods are related by means of the following reconciliation, to be made frequently (preferably daily):

$$\text{Beginning inventory of quasi-goods} + \text{inventory increase} -/- \text{ending inventory of quasi-goods}$$
$$= \textit{Soll position of the number of quasi-goods sold}$$

The controller or the head of the accounting department distinguishes as many types of entrance fee as there are different nominal values of the quasi-goods, and calculates the *Soll* position of the number of quasi-goods sold for each of these categories. He then relates the sum of these *Soll* positions to the cash receipts according to the following reconciliation:

$$\text{Cash at the end of the day} -/- \text{cash at the beginning of the day} + \text{cash payments} = \text{cash receipts}$$

The use of quasi-goods always needs to be complemented by physical access controls at the entrance to the space where the service is provided, in this case the museum. To prevent more use being made of the quasi-good than was intended the quasi-goods must be invalidated during ticket inspection, e.g. the ticket inspector tears off a part of the ticket upon entrance to the museum. There must be segregation of duties between the role that invalidates the quasi-goods and the role that authorizes sales, e.g. the inspector in the museum should not be involved in the sale of the tickets by the ticket counter.

The presence of quasi-goods imposes a number of internal control requirements on the organization:

* to produce the quasi-goods the organization must make use of reliable software provided by a trustworthy company;
* the software must assign a sequential number to each quasi-good that is printed;

- the quasi-good must be invalidated upon entry to the nonspecific space (e.g. a swimming pool). This invalidation must be performed by a function (e.g. a ticket inspector) that is separate from the function that sold the quasi-good to the customer (e.g. the ticket office of a swimming pool);
- the paper on which the quasi-good is printed must be safeguarded by a separate custody function; and
- at the end of a sales period (e.g. the end of a day at a swimming pool), a checking function (e.g. the controller or the head of the accounting department) determines the number of quasi-goods sold by comparing the starting and ending sequential quasi-good numbers as contained in the software log. Multiplied by the price of the quasi-good, this should equal the cash that has been collected (the so-called '*Soll*' position). The checking function then determines the '*Ist*' position by counting the cash that was actually collected in the cash register. If '*Soll*' and '*Ist*' do not match, the checking function should perform a further analysis to determine the nature of the deviation.

Summary

This chapter discusses the internal control structure of service organizations that put space and electronic capacity at their customers' disposal. In the typology of organizations, we distinguish three categories of service organizations with disposition of capacity or space: (1) organizations with disposition of specific space, (2) organizations with disposition of specific electronic capacity and (3) organizations with disposition of nonspecific space. Given the variety of organizations in each category, we do not provide a universal discussion of service organizations in each of the three categories. Instead, for each category we discuss a particular type of organization. For organizations with disposition of specific space we discuss a transport company, for organizations with disposition of specific electronic capacity a telephone operator and for organizations with disposition of nonspecific space a museum. For each of these organizations, we discuss the risks, exposures and internal controls, the administrative and organizational conditions, such as segregation of duties, budgeting and management guidelines, and the main processes, i.e. the investment/purchasing process and the sales process.

Since all organizations with disposition of space or capacity invest in space or capacity and then rent out this space or capacity to customers, a common risk is the significant investment in capacity and the fact that capacity cannot respond immediately to fluctuations in demand. Other important risks for transport companies are the unreliable pre-calculation by order acceptance, drivers transporting goods for their own gain, and the theft of trucks, cargo and/or fuel. Prominent risks for telephone operators are the large variety of different rates and discounts and the relatively high accounts receivable position. Key risks for museums relate to unauthorized access to the museum and theft of cash and works of art.

Organizations that put specific space at their customers' disposal, such as transportation companies, strive for optimal usage of their maximum capacity. Therefore, assuring completeness of revenues is based on the following reconciliations:

$$\text{Available transport capacity} -/- \text{Vacancy} = \text{Occupation}$$
$$\text{Occupation} * \text{Rate per capacity unit} = \text{Revenues (}Soll\text{ position)}$$

For organizations that put specific electronic capacity at their customers' disposal, such as telephone companies, the initial documentation of each phone call (transaction) is essential to establish completeness of revenues. Therefore, the permanent availability of the information system is essential. For organizations that put nonspecific space at their customers' disposal, such as museums, assuring completeness of revenues is based on the purchasing, storage and sales of quasi-goods in combination with proper entrance control.

Service Organizations that Put Knowledge and Skills at their Customers' Disposal

Introduction

Organizations that put knowledge and skills at their customers' disposal exist in many forms. In the typology of organizations, we distinguish (1) organizations that sell man hours, (2) organizations that (electronically) deploy intellectual property and (3) organizations that sell financial products. Service organizations that sell man hours are for example accounting firms, law firms and cleaning agencies. These organizations put the knowledge and skills of their employees (accountants, lawyers or cleaners) at their clients' disposal and these clients pay for the services provided. Service organizations that deploy intellectual property are organizations that develop products based on knowledge and skills and deploy (the intellectual property of) such products electronically. Examples of such organizations are software companies, suppliers of navigation systems or organizations that supply digital information. These organizations have in common that the development of their product(s) (software package, data base, navigation system) is rather costly, while the deployment of the intellectual property is relatively inexpensive. That is, the costs of developing a software package or application are many times larger than the costs of the compact disk on which the software is stored, since a substantial amount of research and development is involved in developing the product. Organizations that sell financial products are, for example, banks and insurance companies. They sell a wide variety of financial products, such as insurance, loans, mortgages, investment and deposit-products, etc. These organizations generate revenues by charging a fixed amount per transaction (amount per insurance or investment transaction) or a surcharge (e.g. the difference between debit and credit interest). What all these organizations have in common is that their main sources of revenue are intangible goods such as labour hours, intellectual property or financial products. Therefore, the starting points for assuring completeness of revenues are either the available capacity of man hours or the usage of the products supplied (intellectual property, or banking and insurance products).

Internal controls that are put in place will only be effective if certain administrative and organizational conditions are met. These conditions are: computer security, segregation of duties, management guidelines and budgeting. The computer security measures as discussed in Chapter 4 are also applicable to these types of service organization. Hence, this chapter will only discuss segregation of duties, management guidelines and budgeting as they apply to service organizations that put knowledge and skills at their clients' disposal.

Learning Goals of the Chapter

After having studied this chapter, the reader will understand:

- the internal control consequences of classifying organizations as service organizations that sell man hours, service organizations that deploy intellectual property or service organizations that sell financial products;
- the risks for service organizations that sell man hours, service organizations that deploy intellectual property and service organizations that sell financial products from an internal control perspective;
- the administrative and organizational conditions of service organizations that sell man hours, service organizations that deploy intellectual property and service organizations that sell financial products;

- the main processes in service organizations that sell man hours, service organizations that deploy intellectual property and service organizations that sell financial products; and
- the internal controls to be put in place in service organizations that sell man hours, service organizations that deploy intellectual property and service organizations that sell financial products.

Selling of Man Hours

This section discusses service organizations that sell man hours. In doing so we focus on a typical type of organization, an accounting firm, rather than providing a general discussion of service organizations that sell man hours. The next subsections discuss the characteristics, risks, exposures and internal controls, administrative and organizational conditions and the main processes of accounting firms as an example of organizations that sell man hours.

Characteristics of Accounting Firms

For accounting firms the starting point for the assessment of completeness of revenues is documentation of hours worked by the accountants who deliver the services, which is to be related to the applicable rate in case of cost-reimbursement (cost plus) projects, or fixed fees agreed upon in the case of fixed-fee projects. To some extent, control of information flows in these service organizations is comparable to that of service organizations that put specific space and time capacity at their clients' disposal, since reconciliations are similar in nature:

$$\text{Shop time} -/- \text{indirect hours} = \text{job time}$$
$$\text{Job time} * \text{rate} = Soll \text{ position of revenues}$$

When an accounting firm, or an organization that sells man hours in general, only has cost-reimbursement orders these reconciliations are essential in verifying the completeness of revenues. This is less true when such organizations only have fixed-fee orders. In that case, job time and the number of hours charged to specific orders in the order administration must be reconciled. Further, for fixed-fee orders the pre-calculation on which the fixed fee for an order is based must be compared to the actual hours spent on that order.

Risks, Exposures and Internal Controls of Accounting Firms

We distinguish two main processes within accounting firms: the human resources management process, which in accounting firms is strongly integrated with the purchasing process, and the sales process. The most important risk with respect to the human resources management process relates to capacity not matching market demand in the qualitative (under- or overqualified personnel) and/or quantitative (too many or too few accountants) sense, resulting in a loss of revenues, dissatisfied customers and/or damaged reputation. Internal controls that can mitigate this risk are an adequate assessment of the future order portfolio, an active human resources policy to match supply and demand and a partly flexible workforce via annual contracts and outsourcing of accountants (smaller firms can cooperate so that they have a pool of employees at their disposal).

An important risk in the sales process is accountants' noncompliance with applicable legislation. This can lead to a loss of reputation and clients, legal costs, disciplinary actions against accountants and/or losing their licence to provide assurance services. Therefore, accounting firms need to introduce peer review procedures for all their activities and implement procedures for proper hiring, selection and training of accountants.

Another prominent risk in the sales process is incorrect reporting of time, leading to incorrect billing, incorrect assessment of engagement profitability and customer complaints for overcharging. To reduce this risk, an accounting firm should make sure that their partners check on employee (job) time records per engagement, that their supervisors and managers assess employee overreporting of unproductive time, that the controller or the head of the accounting department performs an analysis of and provide explanations for differences between predicted and actually billed time per engagement, and that management issues engagement codes to prevent employees from writing time to engagements to which they are not assigned.

An overview of risks applicable to accounting firms is given in Table 17.1.

Table 17.1 Risks, exposures and internal controls of accounting firms.

Risk	Exposure	Internal controls
Capacity may not match market demand in qualitative and/or quantitative sense	Loss of revenues, dissatisfied customers, damaged reputation	• Adequate assessment by management of future order portfolio • Active human resources policy to match supply and demand • Creating flexibility by having annual contracts and by outsourcing (smaller firms can cooperate so that they have a pool of employees at their disposal)
Engagements are accepted at prices that are too low	Loss on engagements	• Procedures to approve rates • Peer review of proposals (including benchmark of engagement price against the amount of work) • Data base with past proposals as a base for calculations for new proposals
Engagements are not completed within assigned time	Loss on engagements	• Progress control and early warning of overruns • Management guidelines regarding cost calculations and hourly rates • Optimize pre-calculations by means of post-calculation differences per engagement
Underreporting of time (including overtime)	Loss of revenues	• Strict procedures for time registration by employees • Check on completeness of number of employees and time per employee, based on information in personnel files • Management guidelines for time registration: all hours spent on clients should be reported in the (job) time records, and approved by engagement team supervisor and manager

Incorrect reporting of time	Incorrect billing, incorrect appraisal of engagement profitability, customer complaints for over-charging	• Responsible partners check employee (job) time records per engagement • Supervisor and manager assess employee overreporting of unproductive time • Analysis of and explanation for differences between predicted time and time actually billed per engagement • Using engagement codes to prevent employees from writing time to engagements to which they are not assigned
Auditor noncompliance with applicable legislation	Loss of reputation and customers, legal costs, disciplinary actions against auditors, losing the licence to provide assurance services	• Peer review procedures for all activities • Proper hiring, selection and training of auditors

Administrative and Organizational Conditions

Segregation of Duties

From an internal control perspective, accounting firms must separate the functions related to recruitment, selection and hiring of personnel (including determining the employees' salaries), maintaining personnel files, acquiring clients and writing contracts with clients, and providing assurance and advisory services. Besides these specific duties, like in any organization, accounts receivable, accounts payable, authorizing payments, recording of transactions and checking of transactions must be segregated. Table 17.2 provides an overview of the desired segregation of duties in accounting firms.

Table 17.2 Segregation of duties in accounting firms.

Officer	Department	Task	Duty
Human resources manager	Human resources department	Recruitment and selection of personnel, authorization of salaries and of employment contracts	Authorization
Human resources clerk	Human resources department	Safeguarding personnel, information provision on personnel-related matters	Custody
Partner, director, manager	Management	Accepting and retaining clients	Authorization
Planner	Planning office	Allocation of employees to assignments	Authorization
Auditors and advisors	Assurance and advisory	Provision of assurance and advisory services	Execution
Accounts receivable clerk/manager	Accounts receivable department	Safeguarding accounts receivable	Custody
Cash receipts clerk/manager	Cash receipts department	Receipt of client payments	Authorization *(Continued)*

Table 17.2 (Continued)

Officer	Department	Task	Duty
Cashier	Cash department	Safeguarding cash	Custody
Payroll clerk/manager	Payroll department	Preparing payroll	Execution
Cash disbursements clerk/manager	Cash disbursements department	Authorization of salary payments	Authorization
Accounts payable clerk/manager	Accounts payable department	Safeguarding accounts payable	Custody
Accounting clerk	Accounting department	Recording transactions	Recording
Controller or head of accounting department	Accounting department	Checking transactions	Checking

Budgeting

As in most other organizations, budgeting starts from the sales forecast. For an accounting firm the sales forecast refers to the future billable hours, split into various types of contracts. Accounting firms may engage in either fixed-fee contracts, in which a fixed total fee is agreed upon, or cost-reimbursement contracts, in which there is an agreed upon hourly rate per type of service at which the actual hours spent on that project are billed. The sales forecast is based on the current client portfolio, new clients and exit clients. Often accounting firms know their new and exit audit clients more than one year ahead, which makes sales forecasting for audit services relatively simple. For other services there may be more ad hoc assignments whose timing and magnitude are often difficult to predict. Therefore it is imperative that the planning function in an accounting firm makes a detailed analysis of the partners', directors' and managers' expectations regarding new accounts.

Based on the sales forecast the personnel plan is prepared, split into different types of required skills and knowledge. Together with the fixed capacity costs of tenured personnel and the expected variable costs of temporary personnel, the sales forecast and the personnel plan are used to calculate and negotiate the various cost budgets with the responsible functions. Overheads – including overheads for housing costs and costs for administrative staff – are calculated as a surcharge of the budgeted direct costs and are added to the applicable budgets.

Management Guidelines

Relevant management guidelines for accounting firms pertain to client acceptance, rates and types of contract to offer (including discounts), peer review, consultation of peers, continuing professional development, compliance with labour laws and hiring and laying off personnel. More specifically, in accounting firms, management will issue guidelines with respect to:

- required skills and knowledge of personnel;
- quality checks, including reviewing the work of others;

- reporting of hours by employees (daily, weekly, format, level of detail per client and type of activity);
- accepting new clients; and
- billing rates.

The Main Processes of Accounting Firms

As indicated, we distinguish two main processes within accounting firms: the human resources management process, which is strongly integrated with the purchasing process, and the sales process. We will focus on some specific items in the human resources management process and the sales process.

Although the human resources management process is relevant for all organizations, it is particularly important for accounting firms as their main asset is human capital. Therefore, recruitment, selection and training are essential and all fall under the responsibility of the human resources department. The human resources management process is, however, triggered by the partners of the accounting firm, who signal a need for additional personnel. The human resources manager receives the recruitment request and tests whether the request fits the personnel plan. The human resources manager then decides whether or not to start the recruitment procedure. When a recruitment procedure is started, the human resources management clerk phrases a detailed job profile and enters the vacancy in the personnel file. Based on this entry in the personnel file, the vacancy is advertised for by the human resources clerk. Upon receipt of applications candidates are subjected to an initial selection and invited for interview. Eventually, the partner together with the human resources manager select the most suitable candidate for the job and make a job offer to the candidate. If the candidate accepts the job offer, the human resources manager authorizes the salary and employment contract. The hiring decision and all related contract information is then entered in the personnel file. All information in the personnel file is automatically updated in the information system by a programmed procedure.

After bringing the human resources capacity to the required or desired level the sales process can start. Because organizations that sell man hours often define projects (for accounting firms: engagements) as their revenue drivers, there are many similarities with organizations that produce to order, for example with respect to the pre- and post-calculations per order or project, the relatively soft standards, the treatment of work-in-progress and the controls mitigating the risk of shifting revenues and costs between projects.

Since accounting firms work on a project basis, progress controls are important, and the engagement partner is responsible for the quality and the progress of the engagement. Periodically, the partner assesses whether the costs (i.e. hours) assigned to an engagement are in line with the progress of the engagement. Discrepancies between the two are an early indication of overruns. Relatedly, controls are needed on the proper reporting of time (including overtime). Therefore, accounting firms need to implement strict procedures for time registration by employees in the sales process. All hours spent on clients should be documented in the (job) time records, and approved by the engagement team supervisor and manager. Furthermore, the controller or the head of the accounting department should verify the completeness of the number of employees and time per employee, taking into account management guidelines for time registration.

Finally, analytical review is an important control instrument for service organizations such as accounting firms, and its management is interested in ratios between chargeable and nonchargeable hours per employee, and comparisons of these numbers with budgets, prior periods, comparable employees and if possible other offices of the firm.

Deployment of Intellectual Property

This section discusses service organizations that (electronically) deploy intellectual property. As with organizations with disposition of space or capacity, there is a huge variety of organizations that deploy intellectual capacity. These organizations range from software companies and suppliers of navigation systems to organizations that supply digital information. From an internal control perspective, organizations that deploy intellectual capacity have three features in common:

1. The production process is costly and evolves on a project basis. Therefore, these organizations need an adequate project management system to manage product development and the costs and progress of the development process.
2. The deployment costs of the product are low. For example, the costs to deploy a data base to a few or to hundreds of customers are almost identical. Hence, to recover the development or production costs, the sales price of intellectual property has to be many times larger than the deployment costs (e.g. the compact disk on which the software is stored).
3. The deployment of intellectual capacity is fully dependent on the use of information systems. This requires a set of information security controls to guarantee the continuity and integrity of the information system.

Although organizations that deploy intellectual property make a product based on knowledge and skills, the typology model does not consider them as production organizations. This is due to the distorted relationship between revenues and costs, e.g. software companies have relatively high software production costs and low software deployment costs. This creates the risk of illegal distribution of products (e.g. illegal access to the data base or illegal copying by users), and requires specific information security controls in the production and deployment (sales) processes since the usual controls in production companies (efficiency controls in production as well as controls over physical goods) are not appropriate. Hence, software companies are not classified as production companies but as service organizations that deploy intellectual capital.

For service organizations that deploy intellectual property we can distinguish a production process (e.g. producing software, a navigation system, a data base) and a sales process (e.g. sale of software or navigation systems, deploying the data bases or electronic information), but the nature of these processes differs based on the type of intellectual property being deployed. We therefore do not provide a general discussion of service organizations that deploy intellectual property, but instead focus on a particular type of organization: a software company. The next sections discuss the characteristics, risks, exposures and internal controls, administrative and organizational conditions and the main processes of software companies as an example of organizations that deploy intellectual property.

Characteristics of Software Companies

Given the general features of organizations that deploy intellectual property, software companies have relatively high software production costs while the direct costs of software deployment (e.g. the costs of a compact disk on which the developed application is stored, the costs of a password procedure if customers can download the software from a website) are relatively low. Since this requires specific information security controls in the software production and deployment (sales) processes, software companies are classified as service organizations instead of as production companies.

For software companies that distribute applications via compact disks we can still distinguish a flow of goods. The reconciliations between the flow of goods and the flow of money can then be based on the production process during which the original software is copied on compact disks. The number of compact disks copied and transferred to the warehouse times the sales price subsequently represents the *Soll* position of revenues. A requirement here is that there is segregation of duties between the custody function (warehouse clerk) and the authorization function (sales manager).

A complication is the risk of illegal copying of the original application. To mitigate this risk the company should implement a system of software licensing in the production process. Internal controls related to the issuance and validation of application licences can ensure that only official users of the application (those that purchased the official application) can use the software. The completeness of revenues can then be established by reconciling the number of licences issued times the price per licence on the one hand and the total revenues (or total amount invoiced) on the other.

For software companies that deploy software to customers by charging them an annual fee (subscription fee) instead of a fee per application the completeness of revenues can be established by reconciling the number of licences issued according to the licensing file times the annual subscription rate, and the total revenues (or total amount invoiced).

Risks, Exposures and Internal Controls of Software Companies

To analyse risks for software companies we focus on two main processes: the software production process and the sales or deployment process.

The main risks in the production process are both cost and time overruns on software development projects, leading to a loss of assets and customer dissatisfaction. Controls to mitigate these risks are the use of a detailed project administration, detailed checks on time and other costs per project, and frequent progress reports and controls on project progress.

With respect to the sales/deployment process a major risk is the circulation of illegal software copies, which may result in a loss of revenues if illegal copying replaces the sale of the original software. Therefore, software companies need to implement copy protection on applications and the use of a licensing system. Furthermore, procedures are needed to control the entrance and departure of employees, as well as data-processing procedures to prevent software from leaving the organization illegally.

An overview of risks applicable to software companies is given in Table 17.3.

Table 17.3 Risks, exposures and internal controls of software companies.

Risk	Exposure	Internal controls
Cost overruns on projects	Loss of assets	• Detailed project administration • Detailed checks by controller or head of accounting department on time and other costs per project *(Continued)*

Table 17.3   (Continued)

Risk	Exposure	Internal controls
Time overruns on projects	Not meeting agreements with customers on time Loss of revenues	• Frequent progress reports by controller or head of accounting department
Circulation of illegal copies	Loss of revenues	• Copy protection on applications • Use of licensing system • Employee entrance and departure procedures, electronic data processing procedures to prevent software from leaving the organization illegally
Use of incorrect prices	Loss of revenues	• Using fixed prices • Detailed checks on prices in sales contracts by controller or head of accounting department
IT necessary to develop software is not available	Loss of revenues	• Fallback facilities and procedures • Frequent testing of fallback facilities and procedures
Unauthorized access to information system	Unreliable systems	• Access controls with user identification and passwords • Implementing firewalls to prevent unauthorized access • Logging access attempts • Physical access controls

Administrative and Organizational Conditions

Segregation of Duties

From an internal control perspective, software companies must separate the functions relating to software development, application and data management, software multiplication, safeguarding of software, licence management, sales and project administration. Besides these duties, as in any organization, purchasing, accounts receivable, accounts payable, authorizing payments, recording transactions and checking transactions must be segregated. Table 17.4 gives an overview of the desired segregation of duties in software companies.

Table 17.4   Segregation of duties in software companies.

Officer	Department	Task	Duty
Software developer	Software development department	Developing software	Execution
Quality inspector	Software development department	Checking on the quality of the developed software	Checking
Application and data manager	Application management	Maintaining the source files of the applications	Custody
Cost accountant	Cost-accounting	Financial pre-calculation of developed applications	Execution

Purchase clerk/manager	Purchasing department	Purchasing CDs, DVDs and other data carriers	Authorization
Sales manager	Sales department	Selling software	Authorization
Production worker (often outsourced to CD/DVD producers)	(Re)production	Copying the source files to CDs, DVDs and other data carriers	Execution
Licence manager	Licence management	Safeguarding of licences, giving customers access to the software	Custody
Billing clerk/manager	Billing department	Billing customers	Execution
Accounts receivable clerk/ manager	Accounts receivable department	Safeguarding accounts receivable	Custody
Cash receipts clerk/manager	Cash receipts department	Receipt of customer payments	Authorization
Cashier	Cash department	Safeguarding cash	Custody
Cash disbursements clerk/ manager	Cash disbursements department	Payment of vendor invoices	Authorization
Accounts payable clerk/manager	Accounts payable department	Safeguarding accounts payable	Custody
Accounting clerk	Accounting department	Recording transactions	Recording
Project administration (particularization of accounting department)	Accounting department	Recording costs of direct man hours, machine hours, materials usage and other direct costs	Recording
Controller or head of accounting department	Accounting department	Checking transactions and performing post-calculations	Checking

Budgeting

In the budgeting process the most important costs to focus on for software companies are software development costs. To maintain a software product, software companies must continuously invest in product updates that contain new features, fewer errors and that are adapted to the most recent operating systems. For that purpose each maintenance or development process should be organized as a project. Therefore, per project, a detailed plan must be made that includes the goal of the project, the time schedule and a cost budget split into personnel costs and costs for outsourced work. Each software development project must be authorized by management since software development is the core business of the company and therefore an important strategic issue. As in most other organizations, the budgeting process starts from the sales forecast. In the case of software companies, sales forecast refers to the numbers of software packages to be sold, subdivided into single-user and multi-user items. This forecast is based on sales in prior years, orders in portfolio, market developments (including competition) and any other source of information that will make this forecast more reliable. Based on the sales forecast at a minimum the following plans are made:

- investment plan (including disinvestments and depreciations);
- maintenance plan; and
- personnel plan.

Since software development can be considered a production activity (albeit with some very specific features), to an extent these budgets are similar to production firms' budgets. Various cost budgets are calculated and negotiated with the responsible functions, based on the plans above, fixed capacity costs of human resources and computer equipment and expected variable costs of personnel and energy. Overheads – including housing and administrative staff – are calculated as a surcharge of the budgeted direct costs and added to the applicable budgets. When setting market prices of software packages and licences, management should never be tempted to start from the relatively low costs of producing additional copies of software or giving out additional licences. Software development requires huge investments in research and development and therefore any pricing system must incorporate these investments into the sales prices.

Management Guidelines

For software companies, relevant management guidelines pertain to the acceptance of sales orders, the prices of software and licences (including discounts), maintenance of computer equipment, training of personnel, compliance with anti-trust laws (see the case 'EU court upholds Microsoft Anti-trust Decision' below) and making investments in new software products. More specifically, in software companies, management will issue guidelines with respect to:

- the initiation of new projects;
- hiring and training of personnel;
- accountability regarding software product development;
- measures to combat illegal software distribution and use;
- IT controls to ensure continuous and integer operation of the organization's computer systems; and
- pricing and discounts.

Case Study 17.1: EU Court Upholds Microsoft Anti-trust Decision

By: Mayank Sharma

A European Union court on Monday dismissed Microsoft's appeal against the 2004 ruling which found the company had abused its dominant market position to score over rivals. Microsoft's lawyers failed to impress the European Court of First Instance, which not only dismissed the case but also rejected the appeal against the € 497 million ($ 690 million) fine imposed on the company. Update: Red Hat has issued a statement about the Commission's ruling.

In 2004, the European Commission (EC) ruled against Microsoft, terming its policy of including its own Media Player software as part of the Windows operating system and refusing to provide the technical information that rivals would need to offer their product instead, as illegal. Citing a change in the competitive landscape of media players, Microsoft's lawyers argued that products like Apple's iTunes and others are all making this field more competitive than it was in 2004.

A joint press release by the Free Software Foundation Europe (FSFE) and the SAMBA project welcomes the court's latest decision. 'Through tactics that successfully derailed anti-trust processes in other parts of the world, including the United States, Microsoft has managed to postpone this day for almost a decade. But thanks to the perseverance and excellent work of the European Commission, these tactics have now failed in Europe,' says Georg Greve, president of FSFE.

The decision comes close on the heels of Microsoft's failed attempt to fast-track ISO approval for its Office Open XML format. To make matters worse for Microsoft, major competitors like IBM and Sun are grouping together behind the Open Document Format, which was approved as an ISO standard last year. According to the ruling, Microsoft can still file an appeal before the EC's Court of Justice within two months.

Red Hat's statement (update):
RALEIGH, N.C.–(BUSINESS WIRE)–Red Hat (NYSE: RHT), the world's leading provider of open source solutions, today announced the following statement in regard to the Court of First Instance in Luxembourg's decision in the matter of the European Commission vs. Microsoft:

'Today's decision by the Court of First Instance in Luxembourg in the Microsoft matter is great news for innovation and consumer choice, both in Europe and around the world. The Court has confirmed that competition law prevents a monopolist from simply using its control of the market to lock in customers and stifle new competitors,' said Matthew Szulik, Chairman and CEO of Red Hat. 'In our business, interoperability information is critically important and cannot simply be withheld to exclude all competition. Given Red Hat's firm belief that competition, not questionable patent and trade secret claims, drives innovation and creates greater consumer value, we were pleased with the overall decision and look forward to examining the decision in greater detail. Red Hat would like to congratulate the European Commission, and particularly Commissioner Neelie Kroes and her services, for their persistence and courage in bringing this matter to a successful result.'

Source: http://www.linux.com/feature/119242, September 17, 2007

The Main Processes in Software Companies

From an internal control perspective, software companies have two main processes: the production process and the sales process. The production process relates to the development of the software and is comparable to a regular production-to-order process. We will therefore not discuss the production process, but focus on some specific items in the sales process revolving around the sale and distribution of software.

The sales department initiates the copying process. After receipt of each sales order, the sales department enters the sale information in the production file. A programmed procedure then informs the copying or production department that the source application needs to be copied. The application and data manager who maintains the source files of the applications then hands over the source application to the production department against discharge. The production or copying order is then executed by the production department.

During the copying process two clerks are present (four-eyes principle) to ensure that the requested number of copies is actually made. Both production clerks confirm the number of copies made in the information system. The source application is then returned to the applications and data manager against discharge. A programmed procedure then updates the information system based on the receipt of the source application.

In addition to these controls in the copying process, the software company needs to use a licensing system to prevent illegal copying of the application by users. The licensing system should have the following characteristics:

1. The software company has a licence data base that contains all licence numbers. Each licence number is composed of a reasonable number of digits and letters.
2. Each licence number is printed on a (watermarked) certificate and is included in the package with the compact disk of the application. Because the licence code only ought to be accessible to the buyer, the box needs to be sealed.
3. The software cannot be installed without entering the licence code. After entering the code, the software searches the Internet and contacts the software company. A programmed procedure then matches the licence number entered with the numbers in the licence data base and records the date of instalment and user information and assigns the standing code 'sold' to the licence number. Then the data base sends an activation code to the user to activate the application.
4. When the licence code is forwarded to the software company for a second time (i.e. when a user wants to install/activate the same software more than once), a programmed procedure then checks whether the user information is still correct, and whether the licence code permits the activation of software more than once. When there is no agreement, an activation code will not be sent and the user is asked to contact the software company.

Selling of Financial Products

This section focuses on service organizations that sell financial products. The two most important types of organizations within this category are banks and insurance companies. Since these two organizations are representative of service organizations that sell financial products we will discuss them both.

Banks

The following subsections discuss the characteristics, risks, exposures and internal controls, administrative and organizational conditions and the main processes of banks.

Characteristics of Banks

Banks offer all kinds of financial services, including acting as intermediary between demand for and supply of money (interest revenues), and security and currency trading (provision revenues). An important activity within banks is treasury management. This involves attracting financial resources for the organization, cash-flow management, controlling currency and interest risks and asset-liability management.

From an internal control perspective, banks have a flow of money, but no flow of goods to speak of. Therefore, the usefulness of the value cycle in controlling information provision is very limited. As a consequence, for organizations like banks, there is an increased risk that their information provision is not reliable when no alternative control measures are taken. The importance of preventive measures increases when detective measures based on the value cycle, such as reconciliations and analytical review, are not possible. Important internal control measures for banks therefore include segregation of duties and directives and procedures. In addition, since IT is predominant in these organizations due to the mass character of the data flows, high demands on the IT system and the processing of data and information provision are made, underlining the relevance of IT control measures.

Risks, Exposures and Internal Controls of Banks

Banks experience risks in three categories: operational risks, credit risks and market risks. Operational risk is the risk that the bank will suffer damage because of fraud (intentionally) and errors (unintentionally). Credit risk is the risk that clients are not able to repay their loans, interest or other obligations. Market risk is the risk that the banks will lose out on currency rate transactions.

A prominent operational risk is damaged security of the information system, leading to incorrect information and financial damage for bank or customer. Therefore, banks need to implement an elaborate set of computer security measures, including access controls, programmed checks and exception reporting. Furthermore, IT audits of the integrity of the information system should be performed.

Another operational risk is the occurrence of unintentional and intentional mistakes in transactions. Internal controls to mitigate this risk are manual checks on the transaction by front office employees, segregation of duties between input of data and authorization of the transaction, programmed edit checks on input data, a separate internal control department and periodical internal audits, and a complaints procedure.

The most obvious credit risk is the risk of client insolvency, resulting in a loss of assets as clients are not able to repay their loans. Therefore, banks need to implement proper acceptance procedures with layered authorities, require collateral when granting credit and perform adequate checks on issued credit and payments that are to be made.

The existence of currency fluctuations is probably the most prevalent market risk, leading to losses on currency transactions. In order to avoid this risk, banks can engage in forward transactions for foreign currencies.

An overview of these and other risks applicable to banks is provided in Table 17.5.

Table 17.5 Risks, exposures and internal controls of banks.

Risk	Exposure	Internal controls
Damaged integrity of information systems	Incorrect information, leading to financial damage for bank or customer	• Elaborate set of information system control measures, including access controls, programmed checks and exception reporting • IT audits on integrity of information systems

(Continued)

Table 17.5   (Continued)

Risk	Exposure	Internal controls
Loss of confidential client information	Damaged reputation, clients suffer financial losses and demand compensation from bank	• Identification, authentication and authorization procedures to enter the information system • Encryption of electronic data • Firewalls
Customers lose trust in the bank (see case 'Run on the Bank')	Run on the bank and ultimately bankruptcy	• Tight authorization procedures for bank loans to clients • Segregation of duties between authorizing bank loans and making these payable to clients • Monitoring the controls on granting bank loans by independent auditors and internal control functions
Interruption of information systems	Decreasing customer numbers, failed investment transactions, claims, damaged reputation	• Back-up and recovery procedures • Disaster planning • Fallback facilities • Periodic testing of fallback facilities
Unintentional and intentional mistakes in transactions	Incorrect transfers, securities purchase, loss of assets	• Manual checks of transactions by front office employee • Segregation of duties between input and authorization of transactions • Programmed edit checks on input data • Complaints procedures • Checks by separate internal control departments and periodical internal audits
Theft by employees	Loss of assets, damaged reputation	• Selection of employees, integrity check • Personal or camera supervision • Two employees present at receipt and shipment of valuables (e.g. mailroom) • Locked safes with time switches or locks that require two keys
Theft by third parties	Loss of assets	• Locked safes with time switches or locks that require two keys • Personal or camera supervision • Training employees to watch out for suspicious behaviour • Cash desk procedures
Client insolvency	Loss of assets	• Acceptance procedure with layered authorities • Requiring collateral when granting credit • Adequate checks on issued credit
Selling products to clients that do not oversee the associated risks and/or selling products that do not meet legislators' demands	Damaged reputation, clients demand compensation by bank	• Using formal client acceptance procedures • Preparing client risk profiles • Client transaction monitoring • Monitoring the controls on granting bank loans by independent auditors and internal control functions • Risk analyses for developing new products

| Currency fluctuations | Loss on currency transactions | • Forward transactions for foreign currencies |
| Noncompliance with applicable legislation (e.g. Basel II, Bank Secrecy Act, Money Laundering Control Act, Money Laundering Suppression Act, EU Third Directive, MIFID) | Loss of licence, legal problems | • Appointing a compliance officer who monitors compliance with applicable legislation
• Strict procedures to supervise compliance with applicable laws and regulation |

Case Study 17.2: Run on the Bank

Patrick Hosking, Christine Seib, Marcus Leroux and Grainne Gilmore

The jitters plaguing financial markets spread to the high street for the first time yesterday as thousands of panicking savers queued to withdraw millions of pounds from Northern Rock, Britain's eighth-biggest bank.

The rush to pull out savings followed the revelation that Northern Rock had been forced to ask the Bank of England for a rescue injection of finance.

As crowds of customers demanded their money back, shares in Northern Rock slumped by 31 per cent after it alerted shareholders to its difficulties, wiping £900 million from its value. Shares in other financial institutions were also hit, with Alliance & Leicester down 7 per cent and the specialist lender Paragon Group down 17 per cent.

The Bank of England pledged to provide unspecified liquidity support to see Northern Rock through the turbulence while it worked on an orderly resolution to its problems. The bank is braced for a fresh surge of withdrawals from its 76 branches today and last night was planning to extend its opening hours.

Adam Applegarth, the chief executive, told *The Times* that he had ordered extra deliveries of cash in expectation of the deluge.

The nerves were exacerbated yesterday when Northern Rock's computer system collapsed under the weight of on-line customers scrambling to transfer money out of the bank. Savers were blocked from seeing details of their accounts, including statements, when they tried to log in. A spokesman said accusations that the bank had shut down its system to prevent a drain on its finances were ridiculous.

Ministers, regulators and bankers tried to calm the panic by issuing reassuring statements that customers' deposits were safe. The Financial Services Authority, which supervises banks, said that Northern Rock was solvent, exceeded its regulatory capital requirement and had a good-quality loan book.

Alistair Darling, the Chancellor, who authorised the rescue, said: 'At the moment there is plenty of money in the system, the banks have got money . . . they are simply not lending in the short-term way that institutions like Northern Rock need.'

(*Continued*)

Sentiment soured further amid fresh evidence that house prices were starting to fall. Rightmove, the online property site, reported that asking prices slumped by 2.6 per cent last month. That followed a report by the Royal Institution of Chartered Surveyors showing the first fall in house prices in nearly two years.

Northern Rock customers fearing for their savings filled branches across the country, with some queues stretching down the street. At one London branch, customers queued for more than an hour. William Gough, 75, said he did not believe the bank's assurances that his savings were safe. 'They're telling us not to worry, but we've heard it before, with Marconi,' he said, referring to the collapse of the telecoms firm in 2002.

Another saver, Gary Diamond, said: 'I don't want to be the mug left without my savings.'

Another customer, an elderly woman, said that she could not afford to take any chances. 'It's my life savings we're talking about, my pension. I'll have nothing left if they go under.'

A retired hotelier and his wife barricaded the Cheltenham branch manager in her office after being told that they could not withdraw £1 million savings without notice. The situation was resolved only when police officers arrived to calm the couple down.

The British Bankers' Association said: 'Everyone should calm down and refrain from making simplistic comments in a very complex area which just causes unnecessary worry and concern. Northern Rock is a sound and safe bank and there is absolutely no reason for either mortgage customers or savers to worry.' It is the first time that the 'lender of last resort' facility has been used since the Bank of England set up the present system in 1998. Other banks, including Barclays, have called on the Bank of England for overnight funding in recent weeks, but using the lender-of-last-resort facility is regarded as a much more serious step.

Sources at the Bank emphasised that Northern Rock would pay a penal rate of interest on any borrowings and would have to lodge assets as security.

Many financial institutions have been hit by a sudden shortage of cash and other liquid assets as banks hoard money in anticipation of having to provide finance to complex investment vehicles. Triggered initially by defaults by poor Americans struggling to meet increased mortgage bills, the problem has spread.

Northern Rock has been hit particularly badly because it relies much more on funding from wholesale investors, who have been paralysed by the credit crunch, rather than ordinary depositors. But it also risks being accused of overaggressive lending after lifting new loans by 43 per cent in the first eight months of 2007.

Around 85 per cent, or £24.7 billion, of Northern Rock's business comes through mortgage brokers. National Savings & Investments, the government-backed savings institution, said that it saw a 20 per cent jump in the number of inquiries yesterday, the majority from Northern Rock savers.

Northern Rock has around £24 billion of customer deposits, though some of the money is locked up for months in long-term accounts. It said yesterday that it still expected to make an underlying profit of £500–540 million this year.

Source: *The Times*, 15 September 2007

Administrative and Organizational Conditions

Segregation of Duties   Because there is no flow of goods, segregation of duties in banks takes another form than in many other organizations. Typically, from an internal control perspective, banks must segregate the back-office from the front-office. The front-office is in close contact with the bank's clients, receiving orders for money transfers, cash withdrawals, foreign currency exchanges, cashing cheques and any other service that the bank offers. The back-office records transactions for further processing and safeguards the bank's cash and other valuable assets. The front-office's and back-office's tasks can be further decomposed into more specific tasks, including credit management, IT services, cashier services, account management, investments, internal controls and internal auditing. Besides these rather specific duties, as in any organization, the functions of accounts receivable, accounts payable, authorizing payments, recording transactions and checking transactions must be segregated. Table 17.6 provides an overview of the desired segregation of duties in banks.

Table 17.6   Segregation of duties in banks.

Officer	Department	Task	Duty
Front-office clerk/manager	Front-office	Executing various cash transactions, including money transfers and cashing cheques	Execution
Back-office clerk/manager	Back-office	Recording transactions for further processing	Execution
Cash receipts clerk/manager	Cash receipts department	Receipt of cash and financial assets	Authorization
Cashier	Cash department	Safeguarding of cash and financial assets	Custody
Cash disbursements clerk/manager	Cash disbursements department	Payment of cash and financial assets	Authorization
Credit manager	Loan department	Deciding upon granting loans to clients	Authorization
IT manager	IT department	Safeguarding of transaction and client data	Custody
Account manager	Account management	Writing contracts and maintaining good relationships with clients	Authorization
Investment manager	Treasury department	Investing excess cash in financial instruments	Authorization
Internal control	Internal control department	Various substantive tests in the primary processes	Checking
Internal auditor	Internal audit department	Monitoring the proper functioning of the internal controls	Checking
Accounting clerk	Accounting department	Recording transactions	Recording
Controller or head of accounting department	Accounting department	Checking transactions	Checking

Within the segregation as laid out in this table, further decomposition is possible. Within a management control framework, behavioural constraints are set to mitigate the risk that loans are granted that do not comply with the bank's credit policy. This entails a maximum currency amount or a specified list of products that an employee is allowed to provide to clients. Through layered decision-making authority, such a system allocates decision-making authority for complex or high-risk transactions to specialists. For example, a junior credit manager will not be allowed to decide upon consumer loans of more than € 50 000, whereas a senior credit manager is allowed to decide upon consumer loans above that amount. For business loans this system can be even more advanced, for example allowing junior credit managers to make deals with a maximum of € 100 000, senior credit managers to engage in deals with a maximum of € 500 000, a specialized credit department in cooperation with the legal department to make deals between € 500 000 and € 1 000 000 and the credit committee (consisting of directors, managers and credit specialists) to engage in deals that exceed € 1 000 000. Further segregation of duties within banks is applied in peer review systems, as follows: employee 1 enters a financial transaction from a source document, which receives the status 'preliminary'; later on employee 2 receives the same source document, checks whether employee 1 has entered the correct data and authorizes the transaction, after which the status is changed to 'final'. This methodology is not unique to banks. However, in view of the magnitude and impact of many bank transactions, this has become a standard approach in the banking industry. Nevertheless, as is demonstrated in the case 'Mizuho Gets Order to Fix Operations', not all banks have these procedures in place or apply them properly.

Case Study 17.3: Mizuho Gets Order to Fix Operations

Friday, December 23, 2005
International Herald Tribune

TOKYO: Mizuho Securities was ordered on Thursday by the Japanese financial regulator to improve its operations after a trading error this month.

The Financial Services Agency said it had told Mizuho Securities to improve compliance and systems to prevent a recurrence of a Dec. 8 mistake that cost the brokerage firm ¥40.5 billion, or $347 million. Mizuho must report what it will do to comply with the order by Jan. 20, the agency said.

'We will take the order seriously and make efforts to strengthen internal controls so as not to repeat the mistake,' said a Mizuho spokesman, Keita Onuki.

Mizuho blamed a typing error for mistakenly offering to sell 610 000 shares of the employment agency J-Com for ¥1 each, instead of one share for ¥610 000. Problems with the computer system of the Tokyo Stock Exchange prevented the brokerage firm from canceling the sell order.

The regulator said Mizuho had failed to train traders sufficiently and had not assigned senior staff members qualified in such business to oversee operations.

Mizuho Securities, the brokerage arm of Mizuho Financial Group, Japan's second-largest financial firm, after Mitsubishi UFJ Financial, must also clarify who was responsible for the erroneous trading order and designate a crisis-management team. It must also submit quarterly reports to the agency on business improvements.

The agency also ordered the 287 brokerage firms operating in Japan to inspect their stock trading systems and internal controls and to report by Jan. 20 any measures needed to prevent similar trouble.

Separately, the Tokyo Stock Exchange said it was turning to people instead of computers to try and prevent a recurrence of such a trading error.

Three officials who monitor initial share offerings at the exchange have been ordered to suspend trading if they spot irregularities, said an exchange spokesman, Mitsuo Miwa. The previous procedure required calling a broker first.

The exchange's president, Takuo Tsurushima, resigned this week after two computer problems in six weeks. One shut down trading on Nov. 1 for more than four hours, and the other failed to respond to Mizuho's request to cancel the erroneous sell order.

'At the moment,' Miwa said, 'we don't have a computer system in place that would automatically reject impossible orders like the one with J-Com. We are looking to implement something in the future, but right now if a brokerage made a similar order, the exchange would still have to process it.'

Budgeting   The budget of a bank is based on a limited number of internal factors that are not subject to major fluctuations, including the number of clients, the number of checking accounts, the number of loans and the number of savings accounts. For a substantial part, a bank's results are dependent upon developments in these factors. Since clients will not switch to another bank very frequently, a bank can make reliable estimates of future transactions based on its current portfolio of clients. In addition, while making the budget, the bank must consider some external factors that cannot easily be influenced. Examples include foreign exchange rates, interest rates and share prices. Based on its market expectations a bank may or may not take a position in, for example, foreign currencies. If the bank expects the US dollar to rise, then it will buy dollars – i.e. taking a position in dollars – to sell these at a higher rate some time in the future. Besides the expected effects of international financial market developments on a bank's results, personnel costs and IT costs have an important effect as well and form a substantial part of the budget.

Management Guidelines   Relevant management guidelines for banks mainly pertain to details of decision-making authority and safeguarding of cash and other valuable assets, including information. More specifically, banks' management should issue guidelines with respect to:

- physical security of data;
- operations that involve IT control, such as password disciplines;
- confidentiality of client-specific information;
- clean-desk policy ('never leave information on your desk, in fax machines, printers and drawers unattended');
- maximum amounts of valuable assets in stock;
- insider trading; and
- maximum operational, credit and market risks to be taken.

Case Study 17.4: Savers' Funds in Ireland 'Still Safe'

By Ellen Kelleher
Published: January 17 2009
The Financial Times

The deposits of UK savers who moved their money to Ireland in response to the credit crunch are still safe following the nationalisation of Anglo Irish Bank, writes Ellen Kelleher .

The Irish government plans to honour its pledge to offer unlimited deposit protection for customers of all Irish financial groups, including those of Anglo Irish Bank, the Republic's third-largest bank.

'I would again stress that this government decision safeguards the interest of the depositors of Anglo,' the Irish government said.

The move to nationalise Anglo Irish, which came on Thursday, ends all attempts to keep the bank in private ownership.

It was prompted by fears that the bank could be declared insolvent, which would trigger the state's guarantee, leaving the government responsible for settling close to €100bn (£90bn) of liabilities.

The government said the bank would 'continue to trade normally as a going concern'. Trading in the bank's shares was suspended yesterday in Dublin and London.

Tens of thousands of savers sought to transfer their cash out of the UK and into Irish banks – including Post Office accounts run by Bank of Ireland, during the credit crunch.

The Main Processes in Banks

Given the diversity of processes in banks, we will not provide an elaborate discussion of these processes. Instead, this subsection will discuss some specific issues regarding the main processes in banks.

The first issue is electronic banking. Private and corporate clients can use electronic banking to make payments. Usually, electronic banking software is standard software put at the clients' disposal, which is used by the bank to provide information to their clients via electronic communication (e.g. exchange rate information) and which the clients can use to send payment orders and other transactions to their banks. Data from a corporate client's financial information system and the electronic banking system are thus integrated. For example, a salary payment run from the client's financial information system is automatically sent to the bank for processing, immediately after authorization by the general manager.

Using electronic banking requires a number of computer security measures to guarantee reliable information exchange between the bank and its customers. To ensure logical access security authorizing payments in an electronic payment setting requires careful control of digital signatures, if possible combined with a smartcard. The authorizing function with respect to payment authorization must be able to check the legitimacy of the amount to be paid, e.g. by means of control totals for payment orders, which can be sent to the bank with the payment batch. Other important control measures mainly concern physical access security and guaranteeing reliable application of the software. This involves entering into a contract with the bank on mutual liability and an extensive test of the controllability of the software package.

Another specific issue in banks is the fact that information provision mainly concerns the positions (e.g. currency position, lending positions) taken by the organization, to provide insight into the financial risks that the organization faces. Thus, positions need to be valued at current value since historical information on derivatives is meaningless. This also implies that information from third parties, external information, is necessary. Internal information is necessary to assess current positions and take actions where needed based on this assessment. The current position needs to be assessed in terms of interest, currency and the like. Frequency of reporting needs to be based on the intensity of trading and the size of the positions taken. Specific controls in banks include:

- Segregation of duties between front-office and back-office. The front-office (traders; authorizing) deals with potential lenders and issues loans. The back-office (accounting department; recording) is charged with recording transactions initiated by the front-office (documenting and confirming of transactions engaged in, and keeping track of the positions taken through these transactions).
- Setting boundaries to security traders' activities by imposing monetary and quantitative limits per period, transaction type and allowed counter-parties, and providing on-line/real-time information on the position taken to the internal control department.
- Procedures requiring front-office and back-office to operate and report independently from one another, and confirmation procedures requiring the confirmation of every transaction with the counterparty, which are to be initiated by the back-office so that transactions that are possibly not documented can still be discovered.
- Programmed controls, such as existence checks, reasonableness checks, checks on mathematical accuracy on data entered into the information system for processing.

Insurance Companies

This section discusses the characteristics, risks, exposures and internal controls, administrative and organizational conditions and the main processes of insurance companies.

Characteristics of Insurance Companies

Insurance organizations sell certainty by taking over individual clients' risks and spreading these risks over many other clients. Hence, an insurance organization mediates in having its clients share their risks with others. Obviously, insuring is the primary activity of an insurance organization. Because insurance organizations receive large amounts of money from premium payments for potential future payouts like damages claims or life insurance payments, they have excess cash which should be invested in accordance with the organization's treasury policy. Hence, investment is a secondary activity of insurance organizations. Activities concerned with efficient management of an organization's cash flows are generally referred to as treasury management.

As with banks, insurance companies only have a flow of money. Therefore, the applicability of the value cycle to control information provision is rather limited. As a consequence, for insurance companies, there is an increased risk that their information provision is not reliable when no additional control measures are taken.

The importance of preventive measures increases when detective measures, such as reconciliations, and analytical review, are not possible. Relevant internal control measures for insurance companies therefore include segregation of duties and directives and procedures. In addition, since IT is ubiquitous in these organizations due to the mass character of the data flows, high demands on the IT system and the processing of data and information provision are made, emphasizing the importance of IT control measures.

Risks, Exposures and Internal Controls of Insurance Companies

Similar to banks, the dependence on the information system is a prominent risk for insurance companies. For example, the interruption of the information system can lead to a loss in trust in the insurer resulting in decreasing customer numbers, or failed investment transactions, and claims. Therefore, insurance companies need to implement back-up and recovery procedures, disaster planning and fallback facilities which are tested periodically.

Another major risk for insurance companies is unjust claims for compensation, resulting in loss of assets when these unjust claims are awarded. To mitigate this risk, management needs to issue guidelines for claims procedures, and claims should always be processed by two employees. Furthermore, proper segregation of duties and layered authorities are required, and insurance companies need to make use of experts when assessing claims and need to set up and maintain claims files to be able to reconstruct the claim. Finally, insurance companies need to record and assess policyholders' claims history to evaluate the merits of claims that are made.

An overview of these and other risks applicable to insurance companies is given in Table 17.7.

Table 17.7 Risks, exposures and internal controls of insurance companies.

Risk	Exposure	Internal controls
Damaged integrity of information systems	Incorrect information, leading to financial damage for insurance company or customer	• Elaborate set of information system control measures, including access controls, programmed checks and exception reporting • IT audits on integrity of information systems
Unauthorized access to systems	Potentially fraudulent claims and financial damage for insurance company or customer	• Identification, authentication and authorization procedures • Confidentiality procedures • Clean-desk procedures
Interruption of information systems	Decreasing customer numbers, failed investment transactions, claims, damaged reputation	• Back-up and recovery procedures • Disaster planning • Fallback facilities • Periodic testing of fallback facilities
Adverse selection	Compensation higher than desired	• Management guidelines for client acceptance • Two employees involved in acceptance of individual clients, secondary segregation of duties between first and second acceptance officer (who both have authorization functions)

Insurance agents trying to increase their fee by convincing clients to take another policy whereas there is no need to do so	Underinsured clients, dissatisfied clients, loss of clients	• Peer reviews on insurance files by auditors or internal control department • Selection of agents, integrity check
No or incorrect billing	Loss of revenues	• Programmed checks on policyholder record • Reconciliation of number of insurance policies with addition to amounts received
Policyholder record is not up to date	Loss of clients, loss of revenues	• Procedures to regularly update policyholder records • Return mail receipts serve as warning function • Use external sources to check on existence of insured policyholders
Unjust claims for compensation	Loss of assets	• Management guidelines for claims procedures • Two employees involved in processing claims, segregation of duties and layered authorities • Use of external experts • Set up and maintain claims files • Record and assess policyholders' claims history
Employee fraud by means of ghost policyholders and fictitious claims	Loss of assets	• Segregation of duties between acceptance and claims compensation • Selection of employees, integrity check
Unintentional and intentional mistakes in transactions	Incorrect transfers, securities purchase, loss of assets	• Manual checks of transactions by front office employee • Segregation of duties between input and authorization of transactions • Programmed edit checks on input data • Complaints procedures • Checks by separate internal control departments and periodical internal audits

Administrative and Organizational Conditions

Segregation of Duties As with banks, as a result of the absence of a flow of goods, segregation of duties in insurance companies differs from that in many other organizations. Typically, from an internal control perspective, insurance companies must segregate client acceptance from claims. This segregation serves to avoid the creation of fictitious policyholders who file claims by fraudulent personnel and other individuals with malicious intent. This segregation is somewhat comparable to that of other organizations which have a separate department that can create new creditors and another separate department that is allowed to enter invoices received. As with banks, insurance companies should have a system of layered decision-making authority. Depending upon the nature of the insurance product and the magnitude of the claim an officer who is higher in the organization's hierarchy will be authorized to accept a client or to award a claim. In addition to this layered system, an independent auditor – often an operational auditor – will do file reviews to monitor the proper functioning of this system. Insurance companies may work with external agents. If an agent is allowed to write policies with clients, then this agent is an authorized agent. If an agent is not allowed to do so and merely screens potential clients to enable the client acceptance manager to accept or refuse a client, and evaluates claims to enable the claims manager to decide whether or not to honour a claim, then this agent is not authorized and hence has an execution function. Besides these rather specific duties, as in any organization the functions of accounts receivable, accounts payable, authorizing payments, recording transactions and checking transactions must be segregated. Table 17.8 provides an overview of the desired segregation of duties in insurance companies.

Table 17.8   Segregation of duties in insurance companies.

Officer	Department	Task	Duty
Client acceptance clerk/ manager	Sales department	Screening and intake of potential policyholders	Authorization
Claim assessment clerk/ manager	Claim settlement department	Evaluating insurance claims, and determining the compensation	Authorization
Agents manager	Agent management	Checking the acceptance decisions of agents and the claims of policyholders	Checking
Agents	External agent	Screening and intake of potential policyholders, evaluating insurance claims	Execution
Authorized agents	External agent	Screening and intake of potential policyholders, evaluating insurance claims	Authorization
IT manager	IT department	Safeguarding of transaction and client data	Custody
Account manager	Account management	Writing contracts and maintaining good relationships with clients	Authorization
Investment manager	Treasury department	Investing excess cash in financial instruments	Authorization
Billing clerk/manager	Billing department	Billing clients	Execution
Accounts receivable clerk/ manager	Accounts receivable department	Safeguarding accounts receivable	Custody
Cash receipts clerk/manager	Cash receipts department	Receipt of client payments	Authorization
Cashier	Cash department	Safeguarding cash	Custody
Cash disbursements clerk/ manager	Cash disbursements department	Payment of claims (payouts)	Authorization
Internal control	Internal control department	Various substantive tests in the primary processes	Checking
Internal auditor	Internal audit department	Monitoring the proper functioning of the internal controls	Checking
Accounting clerk	Accounting department	Recording transactions	Recording
Controller or head of accounting department	Accounting department	Checking transactions	Checking

Budgeting   The budget of an insurance company relies heavily on the insurance policy file. Since policy-holders will not switch insurance companies very frequently, an insurance company can make reliable estimates of future premium collections using the current portfolio according to last year's policy file, corrected for expected churn (new minus cancelled policies) and current premiums as authorized by management. Claims can be estimated using experiences in prior years, correcting for trend breaches as a result of changes in consumption patterns, economic climate and risks. In life insurance companies the actuary department plays an important role in determining the necessary reserves and expected payouts to policyholders. Further, in any insurance company, the investment result is an important component of the budget, no matter how uncertain this may be. Dependent upon the diversification of the investment portfolio, developments on the stock markets will have greater or lesser effects on the company's investment results. The cost structure of insurance companies is comparable to a bank's cost structure, so personnel costs and IT costs have an important effect as well and form a substantial part of the budget.

Management Guidelines   Relevant management guidelines for insurance companies relate to details of decision-making authority and safeguarding of cash and other valuable assets, including information. More specifically, insurance companies' management will issue guidelines with respect to:

- physical security of data;
- operations that involve IT control, such as password disciplines;
- confidentiality of client-specific information;
- clean-desk policy ('never leave information on your desk, in fax machines, printers and drawers unattended');
- client acceptance and rejection standards;
- insurance claim evaluations, critical limits above which other officers must become involved, evidence and red flags for fraudulent claims and appropriate follow-up;
- selecting authorized and unauthorized agents;
- evaluating and accepting clients by authorized agents;
- information exchange between unauthorized agents and the insurance company regarding potential clients;
- insider trading; and
- investment alternatives.

The Main Processes in Insurance Companies

Since insurance companies have a more uniform process as compared to banks, we will discuss the three main processes in insurance companies. These are the acceptance process, the claim settlement process and the investment process.

Clients can apply for insurance by filling out a standard application form. A clerk of the acceptance department enters the information in the application file. Dependent upon the type of insurance (insurance amount and risk) the manager of the acceptance department can accept or reject the applicant. In the case of a high insurance amount or high risk, two employees of the acceptance department usually need to authorize the acceptance. In any case, the acceptance decision will certainly be based on management guidelines regarding for example the claim history of the applicant. After acceptance or rejection, the application will receive the standing code 'accepted' or 'rejected' in the application file. When an application is accepted, the applicant will automatically receive the insurance policy. These written policies enable the controller or the head of the accounting department to perform reconciliations on the policies, comparable to the reconciliations on a physical flow of goods:

$$\text{Inventory blank policies at } t_0 + \text{blank policies received from the printing firm}$$
$$-/- \text{ new or accepted insurance} = \text{inventory blank policies at } t_1$$

When an insurance claim is received from a client, a clerk of the claim settlement department checks whether the claim is in conformity with the policy. Then the clerk creates a new record in the claim file, which is administered per client, and follows the management guidelines with respect to the steps to take, for example whether an expert needs to be contacted. Depending on the size of the claim, either the clerk, the manager or two employees of the claim settlement department are allowed to settle the claim. The claim is settled according to the conditions of the insurance policy. When the claim is awarded, the claim file will be updated. Based on the changed status code in the claim file (from 'under assessment' to 'awarded'), the cash disbursement manager will authorize the payout to the client. Then, the cashier will pay out the awarded claim. Both actions are automatically recorded in the claim file.

An important secondary activity of insurance companies relates to the investment of revenues received from policyholders (i.e. premiums paid by the insured). For indemnity insurance, the timing and amount of claims is unknown and as such a shorter time horizon should be taken into account. In the case of life insurance the timing of the insurance benefits is usually known exactly and the investment of the life insurance premiums is a part of the life insurance policy itself. In all cases the investment process should adhere to management guidelines and in any case the conditions of the life insurance policy need to be followed (e.g. whether the life insurance policy needs to be invested in bonds, stocks etc.). The performance of the investment department will be measured by the returns on the amount invested, and will be benchmarked with other investment products and the market index.

Summary

This chapter discusses the internal control of service organizations that put knowledge and skills at their customers' disposal. In the typology of organizations we distinguish three types of service organizations with disposition of knowledge or skills: (1) organizations that sell man hours, (2) organizations that deploy intellectual property and (3) organizations that sell financial products. Given the variety of organizations in each category, we do not provide a universal discussion of service organizations with disposition of knowledge or skills. Instead, for each typology we discuss a particular type of organization. For organizations that sell man hours we describe an accounting firm, for organizations that deploy intellectual property we discuss a software company and for organizations that sell financial products we discuss a bank and an insurance company. For each of these organizations, we discuss the risks, exposures and internal controls, the administrative and organizational conditions, such as segregation of duties, budgeting and management guidelines, and the main processes.

For accounting firms, the starting point for the assessment of completeness of revenues is documentation of hours worked by the accountants who deliver the services related to the applicable rate in case of cost-reimbursement projects, or fixed fees agreed upon in case of fixed-fee projects. For software companies that distribute applications via compact disks we can distinguish a flow of money as well as a flow of goods, allowing us to base the reconciliations between the two flows on the production process in which the original software is copied onto compact disks. Furthermore, proper software licensing procedures are paramount in such organizations. Banks and insurance companies have a flow of money, but no flow of goods to speak of. Therefore, the value cycle's usefulness in controlling information provision is very limited. Consequently, detective measures cannot be used and preventive measures such as segregation of duties and directives and procedures require more emphasis.

A prominent risk in accounting firms is the incorrect reporting of time, leading to incorrect billing, incorrect appraisal of engagement profitability and customer complaints for overcharging. A major risk in software companies is the circulation of illegal software copies, which may result in a loss of revenues if the illegal copying replaces the sale of the original software. A prominent credit risk within banks is the risk of client insolvency, resulting in a loss of assets as clients are not able to repay their loans. Therefore, banks need to implement proper acceptance procedures with layered authorities, require collateral when granting credit and perform adequate checks on issued credit. A major risk for insurance companies is the existence of unjust claims for compensation, resulting in loss of assets when these unjust claims are awarded.

Governmental and Other Not-for-profit Organizations

In this chapter:

Introduction

The final category of organizations in our typology of organizations relates to governmental and other not-for-profit organizations. These are organizations that do not operate in a market and that do not have profit goals. Governmental organizations acquire their income mainly from taxes. Not-for-profit organizations are mainly foundations, associations and so-called nongovernmental organizations (NGOs). Governmental and other not-for-profit organizations may offer tangible products or designated services just like any other (for-profit) organization. However, from an internal control perspective the relationship between goods or services offered and cash received is often hard to recognize as there is no direct connection between offers and yields. For example, a municipality engages a contractor to construct a road and recovers the costs via taxes and governmental contributions rather than via direct cash collection from the users of that road.

Because of the great diversity within the category of governmental and other not-for-profit organizations, it is virtually impossible to provide a universal description of the applicable internal controls. Therefore we will discuss some common characteristics of governmental and other not-for-profit organizations, which predominantly pertain to the missing exchange relationship with third parties, the importance of the budgetary process and the focus on legitimacy and efficiency of cash disbursements. Furthermore, these types of organizations are prone to specific risks that follow from their specific characteristics. These risks include making illegitimate payments, paying prices that are too high (using the 'taxpayers' money') and budget overruns. The internal controls to be put in place will only be effective if certain administrative and organizational conditions are met. These conditions can be summarized under the following headings: computer security, segregation of duties, budgeting and management guidelines. The computer security measures discussed in Chapter 4 are also applicable to governmental and other not-for-profit organizations. Therefore, this chapter will only discuss segregation of duties, budgeting and management guidelines as they apply to governmental and other not-for-profit organizations.

Learning Goals of the Chapter

After having studied this chapter, the reader will understand:

- the internal control consequences of classifying organizations as governmental and other not-for-profit organizations;
- the risks for governmental and other not-for-profit organizations from an internal control perspective;
- the internal controls that can be put in place in governmental and other not-for-profit organizations;
- the measures to be taken to assure the completeness of revenues in governmental and other not-for-profit organizations;
- the approach to assessing the legitimacy and efficiency of cash disbursements in governmental and other not-for-profit organizations;

- the administrative and organizational conditions that form the basis of the internal control system in governmental and other not-for-profit organizations; and
- the internal control system of various governmental and other not-for-profit organizations, including hospitals, social security departments, general accounting offices and foundations without profit goals.

Characteristics of Governmental and Other Not-for-profit Organizations

We can distinguish many different types of governmental organizations, including ministries, government agencies, police and defence organizations, prisons, inspection departments, universities, provinces, municipalities and boards of public works. Within the category of other not-for-profit organizations we distinguish foundations, associations and NGOs. These organizations have many similarities to governmental organizations. For example:

- Environmental groups, usually organized as foundations, perform tasks similar to those of policy departments of a ministry.
- Nature conservation organizations, usually also organized as foundations, have tasks that are also performed by provinces or municipalities.
- Many associations collect membership fees from their members to finance products or services that are accessible to all members, which is comparable to taxation.

Foundations and associations always have a governing board that collectively performs an authorization function. Such a board will typically consist of a chairman, a secretary and a treasurer. The board's involvement and the organization's size determine to what degree segregation of duties is possible. A common risk in smaller foundations and associations with many volunteers is that the board has a lot of power, which may result in intentional or unintentional irregularities and errors that may go unnoticed by the organization. Therefore it is of the utmost importance that ample (additional) internal controls are put in place and that management information is provided as if the foundation or association were a commercial organization.

Within the category of not-for-profit organizations, the so-called nongovernmental organizations have a special position. An NGO is an organization that aims not to maximize its profit, that is independent of the government and that often has a political or societal goal. Often, an NGO can be recognized by a specific designation in its name or description, such as action committee, special interest group, pressure group or movement. NGOs may operate on a national and on an international level. Typical examples of internationally operating NGOs are the United Nations, UNICEF, Médecins sans Frontières, the International Organization for Standardization, Greenpeace and the International Committee of the Red Cross. Examples of nationally operating NGOs are political parties, trade unions and other organizations that serve the interests of certain groups in society, such as the American Automobile Association (car drivers), or an action committee opposing the construction of a highway through a rural estate (environmentalists, local inhabitants).

When discussing the internal controls of governmental and other not-for-profit organizations, the first question that comes to mind is whether indeed these must be considered as a separate category. Indeed, many governmental and other not-for-profit organizations engage in activities that are similar to those performed by commercial organizations. Especially in an era where governments want to manage their departments or branches as if they were commercial organizations – usually referred to as the entrepreneurial government – boundaries between commercial and governmental organizations become blurred. Therefore, in developing internal control systems for governmental and other not-for-profit organizations, one should also consider internal controls discussed in previous chapters. A parks and public gardens department of a municipality for example is comparable to a landscaping firm with private clients. Similarly, the research activities of a university are comparable to a commercial market research organization or poll bureau. However, many other processes of governmental and other not-for-profit organizations often cannot be directly compared to equivalent processes in commercial organizations. Prominent examples are policy preparation and policymaking activities at ministries. These are activities that are not undertaken for a designated customer but for society in general, such as national defence or reviewing subsidy requests for tax filings. Three important arguments for considering governmental and other not-for-profit organizations as a separate category in the typology of organizations are as follows:

1. In many instances there is no or only a remote relationship between funding and spending. Activities are funded by taxes, legal dues and sometimes by commercial activities in so-called private–public joint ventures, whereas money is spent on many different areas including civil servants' salaries, a contractor building a public road, subsidies for organizations or private persons and maintenance of municipal sports facilities. Hence, it can happen that one citizen pays money (e.g. through VAT or income tax) which does not benefit himself or herself but another citizen instead, for example through subsidies or scholarships, or the right to use or benefit from certain resources such as a road, police, defence, environmental protection or a dam. Many services that are provided by governments are public goods, which means that everyone is free to use these, but not everyone has to pay for them. Because of this feature, public goods are allocated using a budget mechanism. Since a direct exchange relationship is lacking, reconciliations used in internal control systems in corporate organizations cannot be applied in the same fashion as we have come to know;

2. Many processes do not have unambiguously determinable output, making it difficult to relate outputs to inputs in such situations. Examples include subsidies to promote fine arts but also policy preparation and policymaking processes where the output consists of a report or a memorandum to enable political decision-making. It is very difficult to know in advance to what extent promotion of fine arts will be accomplished – even afterwards this is virtually impossible – or how much time will be spent on preparing a memo. As a result, typical internal control tools in commercial organizations, such as production standards, pre- and post-calculations, will not be of much help; and

3. Governmental and other not-for-profit organizations have to deal with the so-called glass house effect. If a commercial organization wastes resources or its managers perpetrate fraud, society considers this the organization's sole responsibility since customers can always buy goods or services from another

organization. This is so because wastage and fraud occur at the expense of the owners of the company – including the shareholders who can choose whether or not to be active – and not at the expense of society as a whole. However, if a governmental or another not-for-profit organization wastes its resources or commits fraud, the general public feels affected because taxpayers' money is spent. As a result, governments are accountable to citizens, and inappropriate actions attract much more attention than comparable actions in commercial organizations. This has led to increased attention to the legitimacy of government spending. Hence it is imperative that spending is evidence-based and that laws and regulations are fully complied with.

Case Study 18.1: Senate Approves $1.5 Billion Plan for Metro Funding

By Lena H. Sun
Washington Post, Thursday, October 2, 2008

The U.S. Senate voted last night to authorize long-sought federal funding for Washington's cash-strapped and aging Metro system, clearing a major hurdle toward providing $1.5 billion over 10 years to help maintain the nation's second-busiest rail system. The Senate passage is the furthest the measure has advanced since Rep. Tom Davis (R-Va.) began the effort two years ago to secure a reliable source of financial support for Metro. The bill, part of a major rail safety reform package with billions of dollars for Amtrak, was passed by the House last week and goes to the president for signing. Supporters say a veto is unlikely, partly because of the veto-proof margin of last night's 74 to 24 vote.

Although several other requirements must be met before Congress begins appropriating the funds, last night's vote was critical because the Senate had never voted on the plan. With this step, officials predicted that the federal money could become available next fall. Metro is the nation's only major transit agency without a significant source of dedicated funding, such as a portion of a sales or gas tax. The money would be used to buy rail cars and buses, and repair leaky tunnels and deteriorating station platforms.

'Metro is back on track,' Sen. Benjamin L. Cardin (D-Md.) said in a statement. 'Today we have taken a giant leap forward in securing dedicated funding for Metro so that it can meet the needs of the federal government, the millions of tourists who visit our nation's Capital, and the businesses that rely on the country's second-busiest rapid transit system.'

The legislation requires that Virginia, Maryland and the District each dedicate $50 million a year for 10 years to Metro. The District has set aside a portion of its sales tax revenue for its share, and Maryland's portion is included in the state's capital transportation budget. Virginia's lawmakers have failed to come up with a statewide plan for funding transportation. This week, however, Gov. Timothy M. Kaine (D) said the state would provide its share. State law requires the commonwealth to fully match federal transportation funds, Kaine said, adding that Metro funding would be a top priority even if that meant reallocating money from other transportation projects. The developments mark

(Continued)

the most progress so far in providing $300 million a year for 10 years in federal and state funds to keep trains, buses and stations working.

'This could not come at a better time,' said a statement from Davis, who will retire from Congress in January. 'As we have learned in recent weeks, Metro is in dire need of . . . an infusion of funding. Train cars and buses must be replaced. Platforms are crumbling . . . We need to stabilize the future of Metro, and this goes a long way toward addressing its long-term needs.'

More than 1.2 million train, bus and paratransit trips are taken on Metro on an average weekday. About 40 percent of rush-hour riders are federal workers, or almost 200,000 people, and officials have long argued that Metro is vital to the federal government and therefore deserves more federal dollars.

'Securing a federal investment to ensure the safety and efficiency of this system is long overdue,' said House Majority Leader Steny H. Hoyer (D-Md).

Although the House has passed the Metro funding authorization three times, the measure had been blocked in the Senate by Tom Coburn (R-Okla.), who objected to what he considers an earmark for Metro. This year, the Metro provision was included in a broader bill with rail safety reform measures prompted by last month's commuter train crash in California that killed 25 people.

Among those voting against the bill was Sen. John McCain (R-Ariz.). Sen. Barack Obama (D-Ill.) voted for it. With Senate passage imminent, Virginia's Kaine said in a radio interview this week that state law requires that 'no federal money be left on the table.' As a result, Metro funding will automatically become a 'top-tier project.'

Federal action comes at a critical time for the 32-year-old transit agency. Ridership is surging as many parts of the system are nearing the end of their useful lives. Last week, Metro General Manager John B. Catoe Jr. outlined more than $11 billion in capital projects that the system needs over 10 years to maintain, expand and improve service. Metro has enough capital funds through July 2010. After that, the jurisdictions served by Metro will need to come up with additional funds. Dedicated funding would end Metro's yearly pleas to local jurisdictions for money to maintain the system. Fares from passengers go toward the operating budget.

Catoe and Metro board members praised yesterday's passage. Noting that almost half of the 86 Metro stations are at federal facilities, Catoe said in a statement: 'A safe, secure and reliable Metro system is also a critical component for ensuring the continuity of federal operations during an emergency.' Said Metro Board Chairman Chris Zimmerman 'This is a big step forward in addressing the needs of the Metro system.' Board member Jim Graham also praised the move, saying, 'Without this, we can do nothing.' All three jurisdictions have to amend the governance agreement on Metro to include identical language – down to the last comma – on how they would provide their dedicated funding. That means Virginia and Maryland must complete that work during their 2009 legislative sessions to take advantage of next year's federal appropriations process, officials said.

The federal legislation also shores up management of Metro by codifying the inspector general position and adding four federal representatives to the board: two voting, two nonvoting. The board has 12 members, six voting and six nonvoting.

The bill also includes a provision to improve cellphone coverage in the subway system. Within one year, the 20 busiest underground Metro stations would be required to have cellphone access for all carriers. Currently, only Verizon or Sprint roaming customers can receive signals.

Risks, Exposures and Internal Controls of Governmental and Other Not-for-profit Organizations

Governmental and other not-for-profit organizations come in a great variety. What all these types of organization have in common are the risks in the budgeting and accounting processes. If a governmental organization also has a sales process, for example when a passport is issued and legal dues are collected, there is also the risk of default on payments. Since this risk is not specific to governmental and other not-for-profit organizations, we will not discuss it in this chapter and refer to the preceding chapters on commercial organizations.

Particularly because of the glass house effect, the most important risk in governmental organizations is illegitimate spending, which implies a violation of applicable laws and regulations. The internal controls that must be put in place to mitigate this risk include imposing behavioural constraints upon officers that authorize payments – using layered decision-making authority – and applying the four-eye principle when making payments. In addition, strict procedures must be put in place for making payments (filing purchase invoices), recording payments and accountability (e.g. monthly budget statements). Important monitoring is performed by the general accounting office or an audit function. The main goal of such a monitoring mechanism is to assess the legitimacy of spending. As is often the case, although this is a detective measure it also has a preventive effect since officers who are mandated to authorize payments will take into account that their decisions will always be monitored for legitimacy.

Another risk relates to inefficient spending and hence wasting public resources. To mitigate this risk, governmental organizations will have to put procedures in place for examining the efficiency of payments. In addition, performance ('yields') must be measured in relation to offers made. A designated checking function (internal audit department or general accounting office) will evaluate the relationship between yields and offers from an efficiency point of view. The results of this evaluation are communicated to the responsible political powers to further enhance efficiency.

An important risk to consider for not-for-profit organizations that receive donations, such as charitable institutions or churches, is that their treasury function commits fraud by embezzling donated cash. This risk is less prevalent in organizations that perform a service or supply goods to generate cash since reconciling the flow of goods or services and the flow of money will relatively easily reveal potentially fraudulent activities.

Finally, governmental and other not-for-profit organizations may exceed their budget for expenditures and liabilities. Internal controls to be put in place here include an expenditure and liability matrix to give insight into the expenditures and liabilities, a strict budgetary control system that immediately signals deviations and periodic reporting.

An overview of these and other risks applicable to governmental and other not-for-profit organizations is provided in Table 18.1.

Table 18.1   Risks, exposures and internal controls of governmental organizations and other noncommercial organizations.

Risk	Exposure	Internal controls
Illegitimate spending	Not meeting nonfinancial, often idealistic, goals; Legal problems	• Limiting decision-making authority of officials charged with spending • Assign (collective) spending authorities to more than one official • Management guidelines for spending • Management guidelines for adequate recording of spending • Management guidelines for accountability • Creation of separate internal control department (e.g. a general accounting office or internal audit department)
Inefficient spending	Loss of assets, not meeting financial goals	• Management guidelines for spending by authorization function only • Performance measurement systems • Efficiency checks by designated control departments • Governmental institutions are politically accountable
Theft of resources (particularly in not-for-profit organizations like associations and foundations)	Loss of assets	• Adequate segregation of duties in managing resources between recording (accounting department) and safeguarding of resources (cashier) • Managing resources by more than one official • Valid and complete public disclosure of resources put at the organization's disposal
Liabilities exceed budget	Loss of assets above estimate	• Expenditure and liability matrix • Rigorous budgetary control system, signalling overruns immediately • Periodic accountability reports
Expenditures exceed budget	Loss of assets above estimate	• Expenditure and liability matrix • Rigorous budgetary control system, signalling overruns immediately • Periodic accountability reports

Administrative and Organizational Conditions in Governmental and other Not-For-Profit Organizations

As we already indicated, governmental and other not-for-profit organizations form a category with a wide variety of organizations which have in common that the exchange relationship with third parties is often missing, where the budgetary process is the key control mechanism, and legitimacy and efficiency of cash disbursements are the main control goals. We will discuss the administrative and organizational conditions in governmental organizations since these have the least in common with commercial organizations. If there are specific issues regarding other not-for-profit organizations, we will also discuss these.

Segregation of Duties

Segregation of duties is taken very seriously in governmental institutions, mainly due to the legitimacy requirements for incurring expenditures. Segregation of duties can be found on any governance level within a country, ranging from segregation between the government (authorization) and the parliament (checking), to segregation between cash collection by for example the revenue service (authorization) and checking if tax filings are correct (checking). Generally, the authorization function within governmental organizations requires the following additional internal controls:

1. An elaborate system of layered decision-making authorities that imposes strict boundaries on the expenditures and liabilities per hierarchical level within the organization;
2. A four-eye or even a six-eye principle, which is applied more often than in commercial organizations when effectuating payments. This is organized as a 'pipeline' of necessary approvals to authorize a payment;
3. The recording of cash disbursements takes place against a so-called budget item. A budget item is a designated part of the budget that specifies the amounts that can be spent on a certain activity. The budget item must always be approved by the responsible political decision-making authority. When recording an expense, a checking function assesses whether or not it complies with the specifications of the budget item; and
4. Several dedicated internal control functions, including the internal audit department and the general accounting office. These assess the legitimacy and efficiency of spending by means of periodic audits.

Table 18.2 provides a general overview of the system of segregation of duties in governmental organizations.

Budgeting

The budget is at the core of the internal control system within governmental organizations. In particular, developing and preempting the budget and subsequent reporting on the budget results are important focal points of internal control within governmental organizations. On the highest national budgetary level the

Table 18.2 Segregation of duties in governmental and other not-for-profit organizations.

Officer	Department	Task	Duty
Government official	Governmental department	Authorizing the budget	Authorization
Member of Parliament	Parliament	Approval of the budget	Checking
Minister of Finance or Chief Treasurer	Cabinet and Ministry of Finance	Managing and allocating resources within the budget	Custody
Various civil servants on lower hierarchical levels	Various governmental departments	Making operational expenses	Execution
Internal auditor	Internal audit department or general accounting office	Assessing the legitimacy and efficiency of spending	Checking
Accounting clerk	Accounting department	Recording transactions	Recording
Controller or head of accounting department	Accounting department	Checking transactions	Checking

authorization function resides in the Minister of Finance. In his (national) budget, he allocates the available resources to budget items. Subsequently the amounts in question are split into smaller portions as budgets for governmental organizations. These governmental organizations are not allowed to exceed the budget allotted to them. This type of budget is a so-called task setting budget. At the end of the budget period, a financial report is prepared presenting the budgeted amounts along with the actual amounts. The general accounting office (also: government accountability office) checks this report on behalf of Parliament.

Management Guidelines

Because governmental organizations often have ambiguous goals and politically determined activities, management guidelines within this category are quite diverse. Hence, we will refrain from trying to present an exhaustive list and simply present two examples. The first example pertains to guidelines for the authorization and recording of expenditures and the requisite accountability. Important here are procurement procedures, including the applicable decision-making rights. External guidelines with respect to recording and accountability are codified in a government's accounts act or comparable laws. This law includes detailed prescriptions for the recording of expenditures and liabilities. The second example relates to guidelines for the authorization function that must give guidance for the execution of the formulated policy. These guidelines may contain a level of detail where the themes or standards for subsidy allotment are prescribed. Examples are so diverse as to include criteria for review of housing subsidy requests, parameters of calculation models for pupils' financing at secondary schools, themes for spending on development aid and criteria for research grants. Issuing general guidelines, translating these into specific guidelines, and interpreting and applying these specific guidelines are typical processes in governmental institutions. Therefore, appropriate internal controls must be put in place to mitigate the risk that governments do not comply with applicable laws and regulations that form the basis of the internal guidelines. These internal controls include unambiguously determining officers' authority to develop guidelines, version management of guidelines and checks and balances on the completeness and validity of designated guidelines at a certain point in time.

Summary

Governmental and other not-for-profit organizations do not have profit goals and primarily have an income spending role as opposed to the income generating role that is common for commercial organizations. Therefore the accounting systems of these organizations often only allow recording of receipts and expenditures instead of revenues and costs. As a result, the budget is the main control tool. Another characteristic of this type of organization is that there is often no direct relationship between offers and yields. For that reason, other tools are needed for cost control. The budget plays an important role here too. An important risk in these types of organizations is that there is unsatisfactory compliance with procedures, contracts, laws or regulations. When a governmental organization is noncompliant, this is considered illegitimate. Of course this is no different in commercial organizations, but since the government is accountable to citizens and spends taxpayers' money, noncompliance is considered a very serious offence that erodes the government's credibility. Controls to be put in place include:

- monitoring by independent functions such as the internal control department, the accounting offices or the various internal audit departments of ministries or municipalities, with a focus on legitimacy of expenditures and obligations;
- clear internal and external reporting on policies that precede budgets, long-range estimates and activity plans, performance and effects of decisions, financial slack with respect to policies, assets, liabilities, accounts receivable, accounts payable, cash flows and liquidity;
- segregation of duties between those who decide upon the spending of money and those who verify the spending, such as the general accounting office or various decentralized accounting offices which operate at the level of municipalities, provinces or other public jurisdictions;
- analysis of differences between budgets and actuals by a checking function; and
- oversight by independent representatives of citizens.

Bibliography

American Institute of Certified Public Accountants (AICPA) (1949). *Committee on Auditing Procedure. Research Report*. New York, NY: AICPA.

Anthony, R.N. (1965). *Planning and Control Systems. A Framework for Analysis*. Boston, MA: Harvard Graduate School of Business.

Coase, R.H. (1937). The Nature of the Firm. *Economica* 4.

Committee of Sponsoring Organizations of the Treadway Commission (COSO) (1992). *Internal Control – Integrated Framework*. New York, NY: COSO.

Committee of Sponsoring Organizations of the Treadway Commission (COSO) (2004). *Enterprise Risk Management – Integrated Framework*. New York, NY: COSO.

Criteria of Control Board of the Canadian Institute of Chartered Accountants (CoCo) (1999). *Guidance on Assessing Control*. Toronto, ON: CoCo.

Cyert, R.M. and J.G. March (1963). *A Behavioral Theory of the Firm*. Prentice-Hall.

Fayol, H. (1949). *General and Industrial Management*. London: Pitman.

Gelinas, U.J. and R.J. Dull (2008). *Accounting Information Systems*. Mason, OH: Thomson/South Western. 7th edn.

Gorry, G.A. and M.S. Scott Morton (1971). A Framework for Management Information Systems. *Sloan Management Review*. Vol. 13. Issue 1. Fall, pp. 55–70

Hayek, F.A. (1945). The Use of Knowledge in Society. *The American Economic Review* 4 (September).

Henderson, J.C. and N. Venkatraman (1993). Strategic alignment: leveraging information technology for transforming organizations. *IBM Systems Journal*. Vol. 32. No.1. pp. 4–16.

Institute of Chartered Accountants in England and Wales (ICAEW) (1999). *Internal Control – Guidance for Directors on Internal Control*. London: ICAEW.

Knechel, W.R., S.E. Salterio and B. Ballou (2006). *Auditing: Assurance and Risk*. Mason, OH: Thomson/South Western. 3rd edn.

Maes, R. (1998). Short Outline of a Generic Framework for Information Management. *Proceedings of ECAIS*. Maastricht: Datawyse.

Merchant, K.A. (1982). The Control Function of Management. *Sloan Management Review*. Summer. pp. 43–55.

Merchant, K.A. and W.A. van der Stede (2007). *Management Control Systems: Performance Measurement, Evaluation and Incentives*. London: Prentice Hall Inc. 2nd edn.

Ouchi, W.G. (1979). A Conceptual Framework for the Design of Organizational Control Mechanisms. *Management Science*. Vol. 25. No. 9. September, pp. 833–848.

Ouchi, W.G. (1979). A Conceptual Framework for the design of Organizational Control Mechanisms. *Management Science* (September).

Public Company Accounting Oversight Board (PCAOB) (2007). *Auditing Standard No. 5: An Audit of Internal Controls Over Financial Reporting that is Integrated with an Audit of Financial Statements.* Washington DC: PCAOB.

Romney, M.B. and P.J. Steinbart (2008). *Accounting Information Systems.* Upper Saddle River, NJ: Prentice Hall. 11th edn.

Securities and Exchange Commission (2003). Release No. 33-8238, *Management's Reports on Internal Controls Over Financial Reporting and Certification of Disclosure in Exchange Act Periodic Reports*, June 5.

Simons, R. (1994). How Top Managers Use Control Systems as Levers of Strategic Renewal. *Strategic Management Journal.* Vol.15.

Simons, R. (1995a). Control in an Age of Empowerment. *Harvard Business Review.* March–April, pp. 80–88.

Simons, R. (1995b). *Levers of Control. How Managers Use Innovative Control Systems to Drive Strategic Renewal.* Boston, MA: Harvard Business School Press.

Simons, R.H. (1999). *Performance Measurement & Control Systems for Implementing Strategy.* Prentice Hall Inc. 1st edn.

Starreveld, R.W. (1963). *Leer van de administratieve organisatie, Deel 2: Toepassingen.* Alphen aan den Rijn: Samsom. 2nd edn.

Starreveld, R.W., B. de Mare and E. Joëls (1998). *Bestuurlijke Informatieverzorging.* Part a and b. Samsom. Fourth edn.

Starreveld, R.W., O.C. van Leeuwen and H. van Nimwegen (2002). *Bestuurlijke Informatieverzorging, Deel 1: Algemene Grondslagen.* Groningen/Houten: Stenfert Kroese. 5th edn.

Taylor, F.W. (1911). *The Principles of Scientific Management.* New York: Harper & Row.

Toffler, A. (1980). *Powershift: Knowledge, Wealth, and Violence at the Edge of the 21st Century.* Bantam Books. New York.

US House of Representatives (2002). The Sarbanes-Oxley Act of 2002. Public Law 107-204 [H. R. 3763]. Washington, DC: Government Printing Office.

Volberda, H.W. (1996). Toward the Flexible Form: How to Remain Vital in Hypercompetitive Environments. *Organization Science.* Vol. 7. No. 4. pp. 359–374.

Volberda, H.W. (1998). *Building The Flexible Firm: How to Remain Competitive.* Oxford: Oxford University Press.

Weber, M. (1946). *From Max Weber: Essays in Sociology*, edited by H. H. Gerth and C. Wright Mills. New York: Oxford University Press.

Glossary

Access control: All those measures aimed at preventing logical and physical access to an information system.

Access control matrix: A computerized table containing the allowed combinations of users, actions, software modules, and data.

Accounting: The process of identifying, measuring and communicating economic information to permit informed judgements and decisions by users of the information.

Accounting information system (broad view): An accounting information system (AIS) processes data and transactions to provide users with information they need to plan, control and operate their businesses.

Accounting information system (limited view): An accounting information system (AIS) is a specialized subsystem of the management information system whose purpose is to collect, process and report information related to financial transactions.

Accuracy: The quality aspect of information referring to information having the required degree of precision.

Action controls: Controls on processes that are based on monitoring the activities performed to work toward certain results.

Adjusting entries: The journal entries made at the end of the period, after the trial balance has been prepared and before the balance sheet and the income statement are prepared.

Administrative control: See Operational control.

Adverse selection: In new principal–agent relationships, agents that are in bad faith will be inclined to engage in that relationship under less favourable conditions than the agents that are in good faith.

Application service provider (ASP): A company that offers a website containing software that can be used from a distant location and that need not be downloaded in order to be able to use it.

Artificial intelligence (AI): The overall category of software that covers neural networks and expert systems.

Attributes: The elements of a record belonging to a primary key.

Authenticity: One of the threats to information quality evolving from IT proliferation, referring to the sender and receiver of a message being who they claim to be.

Availability: One of the threats to information quality evolving from IT proliferation, referring to information being at the intended user's disposal, on time and at the right place.

Batch total: The sum of a range of figures calculated for control purposes.

Beliefs systems: All those systems that define the core values of an organization, and that deal with how the organization creates value, the desired performance levels and human relations.

Benchmarking: The process of identification, familiarizing and adopting superior practices as observed in one's own or other organizations, aimed at improving one's own performance.

BIDE formulas: A set of formulas that relates a position's value at the beginning of a period (B), its increase during the period (I), its decrease during the period (D) and its value at the end of the period (E) for control purposes.

Bill of lading: The document containing the details of a shipment, including the responsible party, the party who is going to pay, the contents of the shipment, destination, source and special instructions. It has usually has the status of a legal contract.

Bill of materials: The document containing the components and raw materials used in one unit of a finished product.

Bit: A binary digit that may only take the values of 0 or 1.

Boundary systems: The formal rules that must be complied with in order to avoid sanctions.

Bureaucratic control: The idea that control can be realized by imposing hierarchy, legitimizing authority and rules onto people.

Business intelligence (BI): The category of applications that are primarily aimed at opening up the information contained in ERP data bases for managerial information provision.

Business process management (BPM): A field of knowledge encompassing methods, techniques and tools to design, enact, control and analyse operational business processes involving humans, organizations, applications documents and other sources of information.

Business process re-engineering (BPR): The thorough analysis and complete redesign of business processes and information systems to achieve dramatic performance improvements, making optimal use of the possibilities of IT.

Byte: A group of eight bits forming one character like a digit in the decimal system or a letter of the alphabet.

Check digit: A redundant digit added to a number transported via electronic communication, for control purposes.

Clan control: The idea that control can be realized by developing shared values and beliefs, and relying on the moderating role of traditions.

Clearing account: A general ledger account, established for control purposes, that must balance at zero at the end of the period under report.

Communication: The process of sending and receiving data or information.

Completeness: The quality aspect of information referring to information being in accordance with the represented part of reality, in the sense that what is reported is not too low.

Confidentiality: One of the threats to information quality evolving from IT proliferation, referring to only allowing authorized persons to have access to specific parts of information.

Contingency: A situational factor that, individually and collectively, affects the efficiency of an organizational design parameter.

Control: Continuously realizing legitimized goals.

Control activities: All those activities aimed at ensuring that management directives are carried out.

Control environment: The norms and values of the organization with respect to control consciousness.

Controllability (of information systems): The degree to which information systems provide information that is in accordance with the quality requirements of the people who make use of that information system.

Corporate governance: All those managerial activities aimed at securing the continuity of organizations by maintaining good relations with stakeholders.

Critical success factor: The limited number of factors critical to realizing an organization's goals.

Cultural controls: Controls on creating and maintaining the desired organizational beliefs and values.

Customer relationship management (CRM): The process of collecting, recording and retrieving customer-specific knowledge.

Cycle counting: Making up an inventory by periodically counting a subset of the total inventory, such that at the end of the period under reporting, each inventory item has at least been counted once.

Data: The most elementary representation of applicable parts of reality, which does not have meaning until it is processed.

Data administrator (DA): The organizational role supporting the functioning of a data base from a user's perspective. The DA must have administrative skills to handle managerial and policy issues, and to interact efficiently with data base users.

Data base: A set of interrelated data aimed at avoiding data redundancy and following a multiple logical view of data.

Data base administrator (DBA): The organizational role supporting the functioning of a data base from a systems department perspective. The DBA must have technical skills to handle the detailed data base design work and to tune it for efficient use.

Data base management system (DBMS): A specialized computer program that handles all the data traffic to and from the data base. It is the main software to operate a data base.

Data dictionary: A representation of all the information about the data elements contained in a data base.

Data directory: A represenation of the contents of a data base aimed at locating a certain data element in the data base.

Data manipulation language (DML): A language used for maintaining a data base which includes such operations as altering, adding and deleting portions of it.

Data mining: The process of reducing large data sets to manageable proportions for further analysis such as OLAP.

Data modelling: The process of defining a data base in such a manner that it represents the most important parts of an organization and its environment.

Data-processing cold site: An infrastructure identical to the infrastructure of the primary system, that allows building of a copy of the primary system within a relatively short space of time, when it breaks down.

Data-processing hot site: A redundant system, completely identical to the primary system, to be used when the primary system breaks down.

Data query language (DQL): A language used to retrieve data from the data base for further processing such as sorting, categorizing, summarizing, calculating and presenting that information in a format that is understandable to the end-user.

Data recovery: The activity of restoring data that were erroneously destroyed or modified.

Data warehouse: A large data base covering all the data needed for decision-making and accountability which is subject-oriented, integrated, time variant and nonvolatile.

Date and time stamping: Adding the date and the time to a message to give the receiver reasonable assurance that the message has not been delayed, that it is not a message that has been sent earlier and that it has been sent in the right order relative to other received messages.

Decision support system (DSS): A computerized information system aimed at the improvement of human decision-making.

Diagnostic control systems: Controls on outcomes that are aimed at realizing an effective allocation of scarce resources, defining targets, motivating people, determining guidelines for corrective measures and enabling performance evaluation.

Efficiency (of information): The quality aspect of information referring to information being produced at the lowest possible costs.

Electronic commerce: All the sales-related activities that make use of electronic communication by means of the Internet.

Electronic data interchange (EDI): The standardized business-to-business transferral of electronic messages.

Electronic funds transfer (EFT): The effectuation of payments by using electronic communication devices.

Encryption: The transformation of information by means of a specific algorithm into a format that is not understandable by those who receive it and do not know the algorithm to transform it back to the original format.

Enterprise resource planning (ERP): An integrated, process-oriented, organization-wide IT solution designed to facilitate the achievement of an organization's goals and objectives.

Environmental management system: A coherent set of policies and accounting and administrative measures aimed at gaining an insight into, controlling and reducing the effects of operations on the environment.

Event logging: Keeping a log file to record critical security incidents.

Executive information system (EIS): Software that allows end-users at the tactical and strategic managerial level to produce the information they find necessary themselves.

Expert system (ES): A computerized information system aimed at partially or entirely replacing human decision-making by presenting proposed decisions to its users.

Extended business reporting language (XBRL): An XML-based taxonomy aimed at financial accounting in a standardized format, containing tags as attached to variables and their meaning.

Extended markup language (XML): A platform-independent, expandable and self-describing language specifically designed to create web pages and links between web pages. It eliminates the need for software for translating documents that are in different formats into one uniform format.

Extranet: A network that uses the Internet protocol for making selected organizational data and information available to third parties.

Firewall: A combination of software and hardware that concentrates all the electronic communication between an internal network (usually within one organization) and the outside world (the networks of other organizations) at one point for the purpose of keeping unwanted messages out of the organization, and securing wanted information.

Fixed administrative rate: The monetary value used to record all inventory items of a specific category. The FAR is based on the estimated average purchase prices. At the end of the period under reporting, the price differences between the FAR and the actual prices are analysed to adjust the new FAR, and to prepare the financial statements.

Flexible firm: A stereotype of the contemporary organization in the new economy, which has knowledge as its main production factor and is able to adjust swiftly to changing market conditions.

Foreign key: An attribute that contains a reference to primary keys of other files.

Fraud: The deliberate action of one person gaining an unfair advantage over another person.

Fraudulent (financial) reporting: The intentional or reckless conduct, whether by act or omission, that results in materially misleading (financial) statements.

Fraudulent financial reporting (Treadway Commission): The intentional or reckless conduct, whether by act or omission, that results in materially misleading financial statements.

General journal: The journal voucher used to record infrequent or nonroutine financial facts, including adjusting entries.

General ledger: The internal statement containing summary data for every asset, equity, liability, revenue and cost account of an organization.

Governance: The process of keeping an organization on track towards legitimized goals.

Groupware: The software that enables more efficient communication within organizations, and between organizations, or more specifically within any group that works towards a certain deliverable.

Hacking: The activity of purposely trying to make one or more of the threats to information quality (confidentiality, integrity, availability, authenticity) evolving from IT proliferation become a reality.

Hypertext markup language (HTML): A language specifically designed to create web pages and links between web pages. It eliminates the need for software for translating documents that are in different formats into one uniform format.

Incremental system development approach: A system development method that abandons the strictly stepwise approach as in the SDLC in favour of a heuristic approach that makes small steps one at a time, and that favours trial and error.

Information: All the processed data that contributes to the recipients' understanding of applicable parts of reality.

Information and communication technology (IT): All the electronic media used to collect, store and process data, to produce information and to support or enable communication.

Information control: Information control can be defined as all those activities employed by or on behalf of an organization's management to ensure the reliability and relevance of information provision for internal or external use and the proper functioning of the underlying information systems; also denoted accounting control or internal accounting control.

Information management: The discipline that deals with the production of information which nowadays always makes use of IT. Traditionally this discipline is also denoted information systems.

Information strategy: Deliberately choosing between exploiting or mitigating information imperfections.

Information system: An organized way of inputting data, processing data and providing information aimed at the attainment of organizational goals; using IT, an information system conceptually consists of the content of information and the IT infrastructure.

Integral control framework: A conceptual model to describe, analyse and solve AIS problems in contemporary organizations.

Integrity: One of the threats to information quality evolving from IT proliferation, referring to protecting information from becoming invalid, inaccurate or incomplete.

Interactive control systems: The formal control systems that managers use to involve themselves regularly and personally in the decision activities of subordinates.

Interim billing: A billing system where the customer invoice is prepared on the basis of the customer order and at the same time the ordered goods are picked by the warehouse based on a copy of the customer order.

Internal accounting control: See Information control.

Internal control: Control of judgements and activities of others in so far as that control is conducted for the management of an organization by or on behalf of that management. A more detailed definition is given by the COSO report: Internal control is a process, effected by an entity's board of directors, management and other personnel, designed to provide reasonable assurance regarding the achievement of objectives in the following categories: effectiveness and efficiency of operations, reliability of financial reporting, compliance with applicable laws and regulations and safeguarding of assets.

Internet: The international network of independent computers that communicate electronically.

Internet portal: A website that is a major starting point for users when they want to find information or conclude a transaction on the Internet.

Internet protocol (IP): The method by which data are sent from one computer to another on the Internet.

Internet protocol secure (IPsec): A secure variant of the Internet protocol to make Internet connections as secure as private networks. IPsec is frequently used to create virtual private networks.

Internet service provider (ISP): A company that has an infrastructure in place to provide individuals and organizations a connection to the Internet.

Intranet: A network that uses the Internet protocol for communication within organizations via a LAN or a WAN.

ISO: International Organization for Standardization.

IT control: All those activities employed by or on behalf of an organization's management to ensure the proper functioning of an organization's information systems.

Job order costing: The determination of the costs for each customer order or production order.

Job time: The time a worker spends on an assigned task.

Job time ticket: A document containing the time a worker has spent on the each task assigned to him.

Journal voucher: A chronological statement of the financial facts that have occurred in an organization during a certain period of time.

Just-in-time (JIT) production: A production planning system that tries to minimize inventories by producing in response to customer orders or to work according to short-run production plans.

Knowledge management: The process of assessment of the knowledge an organization needs to gain competitive advantage and make an inventory of the available knowledge, and – on the basis of the gap between the needed and available knowledge – develop knowledge, share knowledge, employ knowledge and evaluate knowledge for organizational learning.

Lapping: Accounting early for expenditures or accounting late for receipts aimed at temporarily withdrawing money from the organization.

Local area network (LAN): A computer network that does not go beyond a certain geographical location.

Maintainability (of information systems): The degree to which information systems can be tested, renewed and changed at reasonable cost.

Management (institution): The individuals or groups of individuals who engage in business administration (management as an institution). The process of the integration of resources and tasks aimed at the accomplishment of an organization's goals (management as an activity).

Management accounting: The discipline that is concerned with the use of information for the purpose of making decisions and ultimately controlling organizations.

Management control: All those activities management employs to have its people think and act in accordance with the organization's goals.

Managerial information provision: The systematic gathering, recording and processing of data aimed at the provision of information for management decision-making, for operating the entity and controlling it, including accountability.

Manufacturing resource planning (MRP II): An integrated, computerized planning and control system for production operations. It is an enhancement of MRP and the predecessor of ERP.

Market control: The idea that control can be realized by relying on the price mechanism and norms of reciprocity.

Master file: A file containing data that do not change frequently or that may only change as a result of transactions recorded in a transaction file that has a reference to the primary key in the master file.

Materials requirements planning (MRP): A computerized inventory management system aimed at reducing inventories, starting from sales forecasts rather than from expected requests by internal departments.

Megabyte (Mb): A measure for storage capacity on electronic media. One Mb contains 2^{20} bytes. Cf. Kb (2^{10} bytes) and Gb (2^{30} bytes).

Message authentication code (MAC): An extra data element attached to a message as a check on the correct transferral of that message.

Microprocessor: An integrated circuit that consists of millions of electronic switches that can be switched on or off.

Monitoring: A process that assesses the quality of a system over time.

Moral hazard: The risk that any person will behave unethically if the opportunity is there.

Move ticket: The document that identifies the location to which components and raw materials are transferred, and the time of transfer.

Near money: Goods, typically of low intrinsic but high nominal value, that serve as proof of cash receipts in payment of services.

Neural network: A computerized system aimed at partially or entirely replacing human decision-making, and that contains learning mechanisms for fine-tuning the embedded knowledge just as humans do when encountering new cases.

On-line analytical processing (OLAP): The concept of enabling users of information systems to easily and selectively extract and view data from different points of view.

Ontology: A coherent set of core constructs that underlie a phenomenon in the real world. An ontology provides a directory and dictionary. Such phenomena include disciplines or systems to be modelled. In essence, an ontology is the starting point of a theory.

Operational control: Operational control is the process of assuring that specific tasks are carried out effectively and economically.

Operational excellence: The concept that competitive advantage can be reached by aligning operations, information and communication, and IT at the level of strategy implementation.

Operations list: The document that identifies the components and raw materials used for a certain order, the man and machine hours spent on the order and other order details needed for billing and checking purposes.

Packing slip: See Packing ticket.

Packing ticket: The document containing the items to ship to each customer. The packing ticket is usually attached to the shipment to indicate its contents.

Periodic inventory accounting system: Accounting for the value of inventory in such a way that results can only be determined after having made an inventory count.

Period-to-date figures: Cumulative figures for a specific period, to be compared to the same cumulative figures in a previous period.

Perpetual inventory accounting system (Permanence de l'inventaire et des profits et des pertes): Accounting for the value of inventory in such a way that results can be determined at any moment in time, without making an inventory count.

Personnel controls: Controls on the hiring and functioning of workers within an organization.

Physical security: All those actions aimed at prohibiting access to hardware, data and programs for unauthorized persons by means of physical measures.

Picking ticket: The document containing the items to collect from the warehouse by the warehouse personnel. The picking ticket authorizes the warehouse to release the goods to the shipping department or the carrier.

Planning: The complex of interrelated decisions about the allocation of available resources.

Point-of-sale (POS) systems: Systems that make use of an optical scanner for reading a barcode that contains product data that refers to a certain inventory item, and triggers further processing in the inventory files, and the cash or accounts receivable files.

Post-billing: A billing system where the invoice is prepared on the basis of the packing ticket and the goods are packed on the basis of the customer orders.

Pre-billing: A billing system where the invoice is prepared on the basis of the customer order and the goods are packed on the basis of the invoice.

Preemption (in electronic communication): The deletion of certain messages when the electronic communication network becomes overloaded.

Pretty good privacy (PGP): The software for encrypting and decrypting e-mails, files and digital signatures that are sent over the Internet, making use of a PKI.

Primary key: A unique identifier of a record.

Principles of accounting system design (PASD): The discipline that studies the principles of the systematic recordings of sequential and interrelated actions in a firm which culminate in accounts that reflect the conduct of business.

Priority (in electronic communication): The processing of prioritized messages first when the electronic communication network becomes overloaded.

Process costing: The determination of costs for each cost centre, such as a department or a process.

Prototyping: An approach to systems development in which a simplified working model of an information system or a part of an information system is developed in order to enable user testing.

Public key infrastructure (PKI): The encryption method that enables users to securely and privately exchange data through the use of a public and a private key pair that is obtained and shared through a trusted third party.

Quasi-goods: See Near money.

Radio frequency identification (RFID): Using radio signals as transmitted by a chip that is attached to an object to identity that object.

Receiving report: The statement containing the notification by the warehouse of the receipt of goods.

Record: A collection of data values that describe specific attributes of an entity.

Results controls: Controls on outcomes that are based on confronting the results of activities with preset standards with respect to these activities.

Risk asssessment: The identification and analysis of relevant risks to the achievement of objectives.

Routeing control: Predetermining the path a message must follow to be sent securely.

Routeing sheet: See Operations list.

Secondary key: An identifier of a record that need not be unique because it may refer to a group of records.

Secure electronic transaction (SET): A system for ensuring the security of payment information on the Internet by means of a PKI.

Shared service centre: A single organizational unit that provides a designated service that has previously been provided by more than one part of the organization.

Shop time: The time a worker is present at the site where he is supposed to perform his duties.

Smartcard: A plastic card that contains a chip, which is a microprocessor combined with a memory chip.

Software piracy: The illegal copying of software and files without the publisher's permission.

Source data automation: The use of automated input devices to represent data in a machine readable form.

Spamming: The transmission of electronic messages to users who engage in electronic communication without having their permission to do so.

Strategic control: The processes aimed at formulating the right strategy, given the specific circumstances of an organization.

Strategic enterprise management (SEM): The category of applications that are aimed at information provision for strategic decision-making, thus enabling managers to link strategy formulation to strategy implementation, drive product and customer profitability and increase shareholder value.

Strategic planning: The process of deciding on objectives of the organization, on changes in these objectives, on the resources used to attain these objectives and on the policies for governing the acquisition, use and disposition of these resources.

Subsidiary ledger: A ledger used to record all the financial facts pertaining to one specific sub-account of the general ledger.

Substantive tests: Controls, generally performed by the financial auditor, aimed at directly establishing the reliability of the financial statements.

System: An organized way of undertaking actions in order to attain certain goals.

Systems development life cycle (SDLC): A strictly linear process for the development of information systems consisting of a number of stages that must be gone through in a prescribed sequence.

Systems thinking: An approach that looks for the effects of system components on any of the other system components, hence an integral or holistic approach.

Task control: See Operational control.

Teleprocessing monitor (TPM): A piece of software aimed at controlling access to specific portions of the data base.

Timeliness: The quality aspect of information referring to information being on time to affect the decision-making process.

Tone at the top: The consistency between managers' behaviour and their statements.

Total quality management (TQM): A philosophy focused on the employees in an organization aimed at making them think and collaborate in such a way that products (including services) are produced that meet the customers' demands.

Transaction file: A file containing data that changes on the basis of transactions.

Transferability: The degree to which information systems can be transferred from one environment to another.

Trial balance: A trial balance is the copying of all general ledger account balances into one list.

Understandability: The quality aspect of information referring to information being presented in a format that is useful for and intelligible to the user of the data.

Validity: The quality aspect of information referring to information being in accordance with the represented part of reality, in the sense that what is reported is not too high.

Value-added network (VAN): A public network that tries to enhance the functioning of data processing and information provision by interfacing the different hardware and software components used by participants in the network.

Value chain: A model that represents business processes as value-adding activities toward a specific intended result.

Value cycle: A schematic representation of events in businesses that lead to changes in inventory, accounts receivable, accounts payable and cash.

Virtual private network (VPN): A relatively secure communication infrastructure within an extranet.

Virus: A piece of executable code that attaches itself to files or software, replicates itself and spreads itself to other files or software on the same system or on another system.

Voucher: An internal document that contains data on a purchase transaction for checking purposes, recording purposes and authorization purposes.

Voucher package: The set of documents related to a purchase transaction, consisting of the purchase order, the vendor invoice and the receiving report.

Wide area network (WAN): A computer network that goes beyond a certain geographical location.

Worm: A worm is an independent piece of software that uses a computer's operating system to replicate itself.

Zero balance check: A check on a general ledger clearing account that assesses if its balance equals zero.

Index